LETTERS IN CANADA
1980

Fiction
1 / HELEN HOY 2   2 / R.P. BILAN 9

Romans PAUL-ANDRÉ BOURQUE 20

Poetry SANDRA DJWA 27

Poésie CAROLINE BAYARD 41

Drama RONALD HUEBERT 55

Théâtre GILLES GIRARD 67

Translations JOHN J. O'CONNOR 75

Humanities 95

Les Etudes sociales CÉLINE SAINT-PIERRE 216

Religion EMERO STIEGMAN 222

Contributors 239

Index to Books Reviewed 242

UNIVERSITY OF TORONTO PRESS
Toronto Buffalo London

© University of Toronto Press 1981
Toronto Buffalo London
Printed in Canada

ISBN 0-8020-6456-6

LETTERS IN CANADA 1980
constitutes volume 50, number 4 (Summer 1981)
of the *University of Toronto Quarterly*.

CN ISSN 0042-0247

Letters in Canada 1980

'Letters in Canada' has been appearing as a regular annual feature of the *University of Toronto Quarterly* since 1936. It provides a critical round-up of the more important books produced in Canada in the humanities during the previous year, offering review articles on the various verbal arts (fiction, poetry, drama) in both the official languages and on translations, les études sociales, and religion, as well as individual reviews of relevant scholarly books.

This year, in order to make 'Letters in Canada' available to a wider audience, it is being published as a paperback book as well as in its customary form as the summer issue of the *Quarterly*. This decision has led to two changes in presentation that will be noticed by regular readers. First, the issue is paginated as a separate entity, though it remains the fourth issue of the fiftieth volume of the journal. Secondly, the two articles that normally appear in the summer issue will now be published in an enlarged fall issue; we wish to assure subscribers that this change makes no difference to the overall size of the *Quarterly* on a yearly basis.

Once again there are changes in personnel among our regular columnists for 'Letters in Canada.' We say *au revoir* and thank you to Lise Gauvin, who has written penetratingly on French-language fiction for the past three years, and to Richard Giguère, who discussed with enthusiasm poetry in French for the same period. They have been succeeded, respectively, by Paul-André Bourque of Laval University, host of the popular Radio-Canada program *Book-Club*, and Caroline Bayard of McMaster University, co-author of *Outposts/Avant-postes*, a book of interviews with leading experimental Canadian poets from our two major language groups. Sam Solecki, who wrote on fiction in English together with R.P. Bilan, has had to give up this task to devote himself more fully to his arduous job as editor of the *Canadian Forum*. To him, too, we say thanks for a keen, critical contribution. We welcome, in his place, Helen Hoy, of the University of Lethbridge, a specialist in English-Canadian writing.

WJK and BZS

Fiction

1 / HELEN HOY

For the literary angler the 1980 catch of Canadian fiction by new authors is reassuring if not on the whole exciting: plenty of perch, a few young of the year, not a single arctic char, but several exotic, satisfying trout. The Canadian tradition of strength in the short story continues although no single work excels, and in the area of the novel the most impressive and substantial achievement appears in the experimental fiction, especially in work by Derk Wynand and Robert Allen.

Among seven collections of short stories Seán Virgo's *White Lies and Other Fictions* has the greatest resonance and power while most of the others are solid and workmanlike. I shall deal briefly first with the less satisfying. Stanley Freiberg's *Nightmare Tales* (Borealis, 93, $15.95, $9.95 paper) presents Nova Scotia scenes and people through a distorting lens in brooding and portentous stories of loss, fear, bafflement, and cruelty. While suggestive in evoking the primitive, the stories with their lurid scenes and lush, extravagant, self-indulgent prose ('darksome,' 'vermillion,' 'titans,' 'phosphorescent,' 'lambent') make excessive demands on the reader's forbearance. Similarly flawed is Ed Kleiman's *The Immortals* (NeWest, 154, $12.95), a tribute to Winnipeg's North End. In this uneven collection a poignant sense of change (delicately conveyed in the image of Greenspan's Photo Studio) and some emotional perceptiveness war with clumsiness in tone, stock figures of juvenile and Jewish lower-class life, and, at times, pointed conclusions.

On the whole, though, the 1980 short stories show competence and promise. Varied though it is in its characters and situations, Donn Kushner's *The Witnesses and Other Stories* (Borealis, 77, $14.95, $7.95 paper) is unified by its focus on occasions of emotional unease and uncertainty, often on the part of characters detached from the tangle of life around them – a minister grappling with the death of a drinker, a student disturbed by a beggar, a self-conscious Jew attempting assimilation, a married woman intrigued by her unmarried maid's pregnancy, a scientist's wife caught between academic chilliness and the warmth of simplicity and ignorance. Irony enriches these stories of emotional reaction and many turn skilfully on a final ironic reversal. Both Veronica Ross in *Goodbye Summer* (Oberon, 143, $15.00, $6.95 paper) and Terence Byrnes in *Wintering Over* (Quadrant, 120, $6.95), on different levels of sophistication, examine methods of coping and individuals fighting for a place. Ross's stories about Nova Scotia create unimportant people with modest dreams – of beginning or maintaining a love affair, of finding dignity within an institution for the old, or of resisting eviction. With restraint the author implies the hard necessity of simply persisting, of keeping up one's spirits in the face of disappointment or the absence of remedies. The simplicity of style suggests that she is concerned not with the complexity but with the existence of the emotions she depicts. In *Wintering Over* the attempt to prove oneself, to fit into a particular place or job or social group, is undertaken, for the most part, by more sophisticated characters, often middle-class intellectuals or academics. It is the imperfect alignment of the protagonist and his or her world – the Canadian boy out of place in the hustle of Florida, the academic intimidated by his own provincialism, the businessman condescending to street-wise freeloaders, the town girl and former faculty wife belatedly applying to university, the artist irked by his gourmet acquaintances – which Byrnes explores with precision and wry awareness.

Along with these contributions by relative newcomers, we have the fiction of the poet Ralph Gustafson, written over a number of decades and previously collected only in part in the limited edition *The Brazen Tower*. Gustafson's *The Vivid Air* (Sono Nis, 115, $6.95) includes basically three sorts of stories: stories of children (as intelligent, independent, and vulnerable beings), short reflective pieces in which interest derives from the direct, conversational, and personable voice of the speaker, and, in the predominance, stories of sexual tension, particularly of male frustration over disturbed or frigid women. Despite awkward, abstract, and elliptical sentences (with misleadingly placed modifiers and words given strange new syntactical functions), and despite occasional indirection reminding one of Henry James at his worst, the stories are thoughtful, sensitive, and astute. Although many portray disillusionment or pain, they also convey the beauty and delicacy, the potential, of the world, as the title *The Vivid Air* suggests.

Finally, among the short-story collections, Seán Virgo's *White Lies* (Exile, 150, $8.95) stands out for its powerful evocation of the mystery, the chaos, the archetypal forces underlying everyday existence. The stories are set in Malaya, Britain, France, and northern British Columbia and, apart from two stories of love (one the lyrical 'Interact'), they emphasize the violent, the shocking, and the exotic. 'Ipoh,' the most disturbing and enigmatic, details the nightmarish experience of a soldier wounded and nursed back to health in the Malayan jungle. Provided as we are with all the fine details and no overview, we share Malcolm's fevered descent into dream and discovery of animal spirits. The same kind of revelation occurs in 'Vagabond,' in which a lad on his way to the security of a monastery falls in temporarily with a bizarre band of travelling players and encounters a grotesque night-time world. Closer to home, we have the title story 'White Lies' with its tragic conflict between the rich heritage of an Indian boy and the expectations of his British Columbia mainland school. Summary oversimplifies these stories. Throughout the collection Virgo reveals the power of the irrational in prose and imagery that is vigorous and original.

Among the *novels* written in 1980 by new writers, the more traditonal works are the less substantial. *Odd's End* (McClelland and Stewart, 228, $14.95), written by Tim Wynne-Jones and winner of the $50,000 Seal First Novel Award, is simply a well-written psychological thriller making good use of sensory detail. *Laughing War* (Doubleday, 295, $12.95) by the journalist and filmmaker Martyn Burke, the story of a comedian in Saigon during the Vietnam war, follows *Catch-22* in playing with the absurdities of war, particularly of the Canadian peacekeeping force there. While attempting some insights into the relations of war and comedy, it subordinates profundity to drama. In Elizabeth Brochmann's *What's the Matter Girl?* (Harper & Row, 121, $11.75) thirteen-year-old Anna traces the last days of her vigil for favourite young Uncle Arion, returning home as a psychological casualty of war. Although the novel is, I presume, directed at an audience of young people, it merits reading for its uncondescending skill in creating the voice of a young girl and its indirect revelation of the casual, daily intimacy of a large family group, captured even in the title itself. Carolee Brady in *Winter Lily* (Sono Nis, 109, $5.95) records with gentle and sympathetic humour, with suspense and ultimately pathos, the innocent responses of a sheltered, middle-aged farmer to the intrusion into his life of a young neighbour woman suspected of murder.

Ironically, the most memorable of these traditional novels is also the most heavy-handed. Oscar Ryan's *Soon to be Born* (New Star, 329, $13.95, $6.50 paper), a novel of social protest documenting the social and economic collapse of the 1920s and 1930s, is open to all the charges of didacticism, ponderousness of characterization and action, and oversimplification levelled against hortatory, political fiction. Nevertheless, with its panoramic sweep across Canadian society, its unexpected lyricism, its documentary detail, its sincerity and insistence, the novel finally does succeed in communicating its urgency.

It is the avant-garde or experimental fiction, however, generally a less-developed branch of Canadian fiction, which this year yields the new novels most worth rereading. Bernard Epps, Susan Musgrave, Brian Charlton, Derk Wynand, and Robert Allen employ humour and imagination in creating new but internally consistent worlds. The least inventive of these five writers is Bernard Epps, whose *Pilgarlic the Death* (Quadrant, 166, $7.95) was originally published by Macmillan and has now been reissued. Epps creates a simple valley community somewhere in the Eastern townships of Quebec and, to a large extent, allows the curious events and characters to reveal themselves directly, through overheard thoughts and conversations, auctioneering spiels, classroom teaching, songs, tavern chatter, advertisements, and journal entries. The humour and idiomatic precision of the dialogue give some originality to what would otherwise be stock characters: philosophic Dougal the School; good-natured, slow-witted, sexually generous Milly-from-the-Hill; feisty, incorrigible Old McHugh; the illiterate Hermit attuned to the natural world. In the variety and eccentricity of this isolated rural world and, particularly, in Long George's belated and flamboyant wedding to the mother of his eight children, we may be reminded of Jack Hodgins's Port Annie, lacking to be sure a little of Hodgins's exuberance. John the Law poaches, the lisping Preacher doggedly carves misshapen epitaphs on gravestones, a runaway horse knocks Hell Fire the evangelist into the river in his stage-prop coffin, Dougal the School in his cups produces a fine rendition of a bulldozer, and Alan the Pigman's devoted wife blackmails Long George into fathering her child.

This is not an innocent world – it contains marital discord, frustration, even suicide – and yet we stand above the pain and cruelty like adults watching intense children. It is of course a comic novel. In additon, though, while Epps avoids easy simplification in handling, for instance, Alan the Pigman's attempted change of heart after his wife's death, sentimentality does creep in. This sponginess at the core of the novel, despite marvellous comic moments, is created partly by the authorial weight given the unexceptional but also unoriginal philosophizing of Dougal the School, as he ponders man's place in the cosmos, confronts death (irreverently dubbed Pilgarlic), rails against mindlessness and conformity, and marvels at the miraculous diversity within nature. Epps's rhythmic, musical prose and comic liveliness are counterbalanced, finally, by a lack of real profundity.

Like *Pilgarlic the Death*, Susan Musgrave's *The Charcoal Burners* (McClelland and Stewart, 234, $14.95) hovers on the borderline between mimesis and invention and, like *Pilgarlic the Death*, it is finally unsatisfying despite its imaginativeness. One more Canadian poet – and a well-established one – venturing into the area of fiction, Musgrave focuses first on eccentrics and dead-beats on the periphery of respectable society, portraying them with revelatory detail and none of the endearing but diminishing quaintness of Epps's characters. As we move with the protagonist Mattie from the world of remote West Coast villages, trailer camps, an Indian funeral feast, poaching, shoplifting, and binges, the novel becomes more impressionistic. Mattie, adventuring into the interior, stumbles across a dogmatic Vegetarian Feminist Collective and its even more sinister male counterpart, the Charcoal Burners' Camp, and the rest of the novel deals in the old standbys of nightmare: captivity, primitive rituals, hallucination, sexual assault, and physical violence. In depicting descents into the heart of darkness some of Seán Virgo's stories are less sensational, with more originality and staying power. The extreme distastefulness of the second half of *The Charcoal Burners* comes to seem excessive and pointless, although even here Musgrave maintains the plausibility, the keen eye for character, and the persuasive judiciousness of outlook which have served her well in earlier scenes.

More technically adventuresome is Brian Charlton's *Angel & the Bear (the cosmic york hotel affair)* (Brick/Nairn, 48, $3.95), actually dated 1979. It provides a series of glimpses of an urban world, Anywhere City, composed of pinball, the all-night restaurant, the juke box, beer, and jazz, and presided over by Mother City. An epilogue begins the work, followed in typical fashion by a 'dedication,' 'the night before,' and 'pinball interlude,' and a prologue ends it. Key words like 'shuffle,' 'rain,' and 'neon' are repeated, juggled, and reordered lovingly. Within the narrative the man with the black notebook, who carries messages for Mother City and sometimes becomes the *you* of the story, persistently and unsuccessfully attempts to record the city, while he is uneasily aware of someone apparently looking over his shoulder. The brooding TBM (The Biggest Man in the World) also known as The Bear, who 'knows the secret' and has a nightly neon experience of transcendence, somehow liberates the city by making it rain. Angel Gloria, who waits on tables and bears TBM's child, becomes the new Mother City and the child is seen writing in a notebook. All this is presented in a poetic prose with the syncopated rhythms of jazz and pinball, capturing and celebrating the vitality of the city. Although the energy and the resonance of the rhythms are Charlton's most important accomplishment, the work is strengthened also by its wit. Among the questions in 'from the black notebook: twenty questions,' for instance, are these eight: 'Who is that looking over your shoulder? What if it's me and you're dreaming this? Who's kissing her now? Does your chewing gum lose its flavour on the bedpost over night? Will somebody please move the truck? ... What happens if you see most in the dark and the light blinds your eyes? Eh? What happens?'

In Derk Wynand's *One Cook, Once Dreaming* (Sono Nis, 109, $6.95) the fragments composing a world are even more disorienting than in *Angel & the Bear*. The series of vignettes, of one or several pages, related in the present tense, reveals a cook and his wife and elements from the world around them – the cooking school with its insatiable apprentices, the closed, cruel village with its mysterious fires and truant husbands, the barmaid, the travelling soldiers, the passive and unsightly hermits. Clear connections and a narrative line are absent. This is rather a novel of dream, of analogy, of metamorphosis. The cook and his wife knead each other during sex into the shapes of animals; in a dream the cook becomes floating angelfood; an ice sculpture of a bear attacking a man takes on sexual qualities; instructions on butchering turn into descriptions of blood sacrifice; everything at one point takes on the texture of grey gelatin; and the cook, delivering food to an old man, himself suddenly becomes old, weak, and filthy. Analogies are implied, by verbal play as well as by the action, between dreaming and writing, writing and cooking, cooking and sex. The cook, trying painfully in his drawings to give a hermit the weightlessness of an angel, is said to be 'waiting ... for his subjects to reveal their proper shape'; this is what the novel is doing also. The protean slipperiness of experience and of our means of recording it is reflected as much in Wynand's playful use of language as in his subject matter: 'boiled in their red skins best method for the best potato salad, the red skin of his tongue testing and tasting his own words, a lesson about potato salad and potato skins, the skin peeled off the potato not his tongue, best method for salad not lessons, the lesson itself peeling like a skin from his tongue to make a good word salad.'

Although this is a strange dream world and one seen only in unconnected snatches, it makes direct contact with familiar realities and moves our emotions as well as tantalizing our minds. The touching reliance, for example, of the cook and his wife on each other, the mutual understanding which is implied more than it is described, coupled at the same time with their continued uneasy searching and waiting, are recognizable and suggestive. Wynand's comment about the cook applies also to the reader: 'the mere impossibility of the recipes he dreams of does not prevent him from tasting possible sauces.' With the cryptic concreteness of fable Wynand explores universal human needs and the elusiveness of reality.

Of all these experimental works Robert Allen's *Hawryliw Process* (Porcupine's Quill, 285, $8.95) is the largest in scope, a 'strange waltz through time and space' as it is called in the acknowledgments. Its starting-point is modern physics: '"the pure mathematician may create universes just by writing down an equation, and indeed if he is an individualist he can have a universe of his own" J.J. Thomson.' Acting freely on this principle and on the equally disorienting one that the universe can be seen as the track of a single particle in time, Allen proceeds to challenge our sense of reality. The novel is structured, loosely, around the flight of the narrator, Minden Sills, and two companions, Father Robert and Father Arthur, from a private mental institution where the director, Hawryliw, is perfecting his psychotechnochretical process to reduce unpredictable, complex, non-linear reality, in logical-positivist fashion, to an absolute, objective, and mechanical system. In the course of the narrative four-and-a-half-foot Aunt Moodies proliferate; Asa McRat (the narrator's cousin) is transported in space through mirrors; Oblong Cassidy and a posse of Aunt Moodies rescue Christ (or J. as he is more familiarly known) from crucifixion somewhere northeast of Toronto; Marxist rats conspire to end the oppression of the laboratory; an enigmatic Him, exiled from Eternity since 1550 BC and suffering from total knowledge and total impotence, appears occasionally to brood and send out for more beer; Hawryliw's crew, disguised in elkheads, plot to wrest the narrative away from Sills; and, in the end, J., Oblong, Sills, and company, who have been adventuring together, prepare to harrow hell, as part of J.'s Marxist ministry, through an entrance in Centerberg, Ohio. The novel is toying with notions of relativity in physics, morals, and literature, with moments when 'the linear mind, in a state of pure fun, takes all paths at once, and then things begin to make sense.' It is defending the chaos and variability of life against the values of order, neutrality, and predictability.

Very clearly in the post-modernist tradition, this is a wittily self-reflective novel, playing with all the fictional conventions. It contains instructions on how to read it ('what you really need to do is dip in slowly like a petite four-and-a-half foot aunt into a steaming tub of water') and literary digressions on the twentieth-century novel ('what those hacks give you is life itself in all its thumb-twiddling interminability, its fatuity, and its barns full of learned lumber'). Father Robert uses 'c/o this chapter' as his mailing address and interrupts with complaints about his physical characterization, Oblong blames Sills for the accidental intrusion of Xerxes and the Persian army into the crucifixion rescue, and Hawryliw demands 'strict linear, chronological, and readily demonstrable structures.' The most serious criticism that can be levelled against the novel is already included in parody in its own self-review: 'The antagonist, Dr. Sandor Hawryliw, a rather pathetic behavioral scientist, is made to stand for all such men ... We are given a dismaying black and white world and asked to come down on one side or the other.' (In fact, even in Hawryliw's final transformation – the unpredictable 2 per cent in his process, caused here by memories of his lost Katja – his characterization and significance do remain simplistic, an exception in the novel.)

The absurdities and humour of *The Hawryliw Process* are its main sources of delight, and many of these grow out of Christ's presence as J., the anachronistic, sometimes self-pitying or cowardly, disillusioned, filthy rebel. Among the fine touches are Phil Pharisee's Ski Ship and Norwegian Sweater Centre as one of the businesses carried on in the Temple, J.'s near-crucifixion between a Protestant and a Catholic, the discussion of what to wear to a crucifixion, and the formal introductions after J.'s rescue ('Lord, this is our old compadre, Oblong Cassidy, Rider of the Range. Oblong, this is the Lord'). God the Father turns out to be a philistine, negotiating J.'s story with Houghton Mifflin, protesting about the sheep imagery, and objecting to the banality of martyrdom: 'The place is getting to be full of done-in saints ... There are even some coloreds – well, no matter. I'm old-fashioned, I guess, and you'll just have to put up with your Old Dad.' He is also, significantly, a traditionalist in prose, rejecting surrealism, subjectivism, and stream of consciousness: 'Who is this woman, Joyce, incidentally?'

The humour and imaginative energy documented here are supplemented by a breadth of information in many fields and an impressive command of idiom, whether the jargon of the scientist or literary critic, a medievalist's treatise on worms, Renaissance prose, the clichés of the marketplace, or the cowboy's drawl. *The Hawryliw Process* is an intelligent, witty, solid, satiric novel. Although the slowness of its opening and the intellectual demands it places on its readers will deter some, it is a novel which deserves a wide reading. With the forays into experimental fiction, with the large number of competent if not always exciting new writers, and with such a talented novice as Robert Allen, 1980's fiction by newcomers presents a heartening picture.

2 / R.P. BILAN

In the past year two of Canada's foremost novelists, Mordecai Richler and Hugh MacLennan, ended rather lengthy silences: *Joshua Then and Now* is Richler's first novel in nine years, *Voices in Time* MacLennan's first in thirteen years. The appearance of these two works is the major event in Canadian fiction in 1980. Otherwise, in what on the whole was not a banner year, there were several short novels that should be noted, including one by Rudy Wiebe, and, as always, a number of collections of short stories, the most interesting from Hugh Hood.

One of the books of short stories comes from Sheila Watson, but *Four Stories* (Coach House Press, 80, $6.50) does not represent new work; all these stories appeared some time ago, three in the 1950s before the publication of her only novel, *The Double Hook* (1959). I am not one of the many people who admire *The Double Hook*; the book seems to me excessively symbolic and mythic, a work of archetypes denuded. My view of these stories is very similar. Again Watson is exploring myth in modern form, or seeing modern experience in mythic terms; her characters are named Oedipus, Daedalus, Antigone. There is an unquestionable seriousness lying behind these stories – a concern with the loss of religious belief in the modern world, with the loss of 'eternal verities' – but I don't think it is translated into successful fiction. At times the condemnation of the secular rational modern age is made too explicitly, but the main problem is the uneasy mixture of myth and realism. (I think, in part, that Watson is simply putting a strain on what prose fiction can do; her particular kind of examination of myth might seem more acceptable in poetic form.) As the stories stand we are faced with too many conversations where the realistic and mythic languages pull in different directions; as a result, the conversations are often simply puzzling, the stories mainly things to be deciphered.

Leon Rooke's *Cry Evil* (Oberon, 157, $6.95) opens with one of the most amusing stories I have read in some time. Supposedly concerned with the narrator's injured foot, it is in fact a story about writing a story. The narrator is a writer and he never gets very far in the story about his foot for his wife keeps interrupting him and criticizing the kind of stories he writes. The humour comes from the sharp exchanges between the narrator and his wife and from his partial attempt to comply with her criticisms by, for instance, including a little sex (of sorts) in his story. Her objections, delivered in a wonderfully shrewish way, punctuate the story: 'According to her, the people in my stories are never polite and nice the way people really are. In my stories it is always hocus-pocus, slam bang, and someone has a knife at your throat. Turns people off, she claims.' More specifically, his wife objects that his work has 'no redeeming quality'; that it is too negative: 'gloom, gloom, gloom, that's all you preach'; finally that his stories are not about average, ordinary people, but about abnormal ones. By the time he's finished fending off her objections, his story is amusingly and deftly told. As we read on in *Cry Evil*, however, we suddenly realize that we have been set up by this opening story and that the title of the volume is perfectly appropriate; it is the confrontation with evil that dominates the rest of the book, and the narrator's wife, I suspect, is actually voicing the kinds of objections that have been made to Rooke's own work. And, I must say, much as I enjoyed the opening story, my feelings about the rest are not too far from the wife's. There is a vein of cynicism running through these stories; they are populated by several unpleasant, rather nasty characters, and we see a world dominated by evil. The debate or discussion in the opening story simplifies matters, however, for the problem is not just (if at all) Rooke's subject-matter and views, but his handling of his material. His vision gets exaggerated to the point of caricature. One of the stories deals with a character who makes pornographic films, and who is accused of raping a child-adolescent. The girl in fact is malicious and Rooke gives a convincing portrayal of her mindless, conscienceless evil, but the story ends with a vision of savagery that distorts and simplifies; it is really a kind of inverse sentimentality. And read one after another the stories begin to seem slightly mechanical; there are no surprises for eventually we know what to expect – the appearance of evil. Finally, Rooke fails in a very basic way, for some of his characters are unpleasant without being interesting; Iago and Richard III fascinate us, Rooke's characters do not.

Fat Woman (Oberon, 174, $6.95), Rooke's first novel, is a different matter, however. Here we encounter a character quite unlike those who predominate in his short stories. In its odd way *Fat Woman* is a love story and most of the love comes from Ella Mae, the fat woman of the title. She is a simple, poor woman who comes from what she calls 'dirt people': 'Dirt people, they came up out of dirt and it clung to them along with all other of the soil's rot, to the point that she had come to believe herself that her ancestors, her Family, hardly walked upright like good human beings but instead *slid* where they went.' But the main problem in her life is her obesity and her longing for food, and she struggles (not too hard) to control them. Rooke successfully captures a kind of innocence she has, particularly in her wide-eyed love for her husband, and in her unending, literal-minded, often comical dialogue with God. The novel is not finally comical, though, and there's just enough of an edge to it to keep it from being sentimental in the ordinary sense. There is an aspect of southern grotesque to the novel but it also reveals a distinctive, offbeat imagination – and, in comparison with his stories, a more appealing side of Leon Rooke.

Short stories generally have a difficult time competing with novels, and if a particular author writes in both forms, his stories almost always receive less attention. In the case of Hugh Hood this is perhaps unfortunate for his stories may well be his best work. Compared to his novels – certainly the series The New Age – his stories are marvellously compact and realized; they are, inevitably, much less ambitious, but they are also more obviously successful. In his new collection, *None Genuine Without This Signature* (ECW, 189, $10.95, $5.95 paper), the stories are taut, unified, and admirably concrete; written in Hood's engaging, lucid style, they are all a pleasure to read.

Hood's art is in the service of a conservative moral vision and he is at his best when he 'uses' his conservatism and portrays characters who themselves have conservative feelings. 'Ghosts at Jarry,' for instance, centring on a baseball fan who doesn't like the new Olympic stadium in Montreal and prefers to listen to (and imagine) the Expo baseball games in decaying, deserted Jarry Park, captures superbly a sense of longing for the past (as well as the mentality of a baseball fan). Another story, 'Crosby,' centres on a former part-time singer who idolizes Bing Crosby and detests the new, particularly the new sounds that appear through the 1950s and 1960s – Presley, Dylan, etc. The story works partly because of the sheer energy the character throws into his resistance to the new – to Dylan, for instance: 'Drugging. Overalls. *Overalls*! I don't suppose that boy has ever done a stroke of work in his life. Dresses like a ditchdigger. Like hell, the times they are a-changin. The times are staying right where they are. You hear me, Nancy? Right where they are.' Hood clearly shows considerable sympathy with the character, but he also distances himself; as a result we get a fairly complex (often comic) presentation of a conservative response.

Where, on the other hand, Hood simply allows his conservative views to dominate, his work suffers. The subsequent weaknesses are apparent in such pieces as his satire on commercial society, 'God Has Manifested Himself Unto Us As Canadian Tire.' The story satirizes those ultra consumers Dreamy and A. O., and as their names (and the title) suggest, the treatment is light-hearted. The story is fairly amusing (Dreamy incessantly refers to herself as 'your Moto Mama, A. O.'), but consumer society is a pretty easy target, and with the characters only caricatures, this is extremely brittle satire. Hood's negative attitude to the 'new' also affects 'Breaking Off'; here, even when he shifts to a much more realistic world, all we get are fairly facile caricatures. Hood's conservative views about the modern world – no one thinks about marriage any more, impermanent relationships are the rule, models come from Charley's Angels – dominate the story and in effect deny the characters any individuality.

The remaining stories are free of this kind of problem and a number are impressively adventurous in form. A couple have a strikingly surreal effect, particularly 'New Country' where the ending takes on an eerie resonance. There are also some interesting experiments with point of view. In 'The Good Listener,' for instance, the main character never speaks; his whole being is tied up with listening to other people unburden themselves, and the story revolves around this silent centre. 'Gone Three Days' throws us directly into the consciousness of a retarded boy, and the presentation of his disordered mind is an impressive virtuoso performance. More importantly, these stories reveal a new depth in Hood's work. In comparision with most of his contemporaries Hood is an optimistic writer. This optimism, grounded in his Christian faith, has led in the past to resolutions in his work that are too easy; problems are avoided, not confronted. Hood's basic optimism is apparent again in this book – in the light, amusing title story; in the concluding story which presents Hood's affirmation of the joys of marriage and fidelity. But in the book as a whole Hood skirts nothing. The brief vignettes in 'The Good Listener' of the people overheard are extremely effective in revealing the ordinary, inevitable tragedies of life. And in 'Gone Three Days,' with its focus on a retarded boy who repeatedly has been beaten by his foster mother, Hood confronts directly the brutal kind of experience that tests one's optimism and faith. Nothing is evaded and *None Genuine Without This Signature* touches all the bases.

Richard Wright's compact new novel, *Final Things* (Macmillan, 147, $9.95), deals with the response of a father to the murder of his son. Charlie Farris, divorced, lives in a seedy part of Toronto, and his son comes to visit him on weekends. On one of the visits his son goes out for a walk and doesn't return; he is eventually found murdered and raped. Charlie's initial response is to escape by drinking, and Wright provides a convincing sense of the drinker's mentality. Wright is not primarily interested, however, in presenting subtle character analysis; we get only a glimpse of Charlie's ex-wife, and while our sense of the boy is somewhat complicated – we find out he had been involved in drug dealing – he remains a fairly indistinct figure. Elaborate psychological analysis would simply get in the way of Wright's purpose, for the novel is mainly a fast-paced narrative, extremely readable and suspenseful but, until the very end, little more than that. The ending stands apart from the rest: it is a concentrated explosion of violence as Charlie attacks his son's killers. The description is vivid, gruesome, and powerful. To his credit, Wright does not, like, say, Sam Peckinpah in *Straw Dogs*, unnecessarily draw out or linger on the violence; the ending is as taut as the rest of the novel. This conciseness in fact makes the ending particularly shocking and effective. But this does not make a serious, important work of art. Violence effectively portrayed always has a powerful impact, but unless there is considerable exploration of the feelings that lead up to the violence (not just an explanation of its cause) or of the psychological consequences, we are left with a fairly elementary presentation of outward events. *Final Things* does not go beyond the surface of violence.

If you like Alan Resnais's *Last Year at Marienbad* (I don't; Pauline Kael's description of it as 'the snow-job in the ice palace' seems perfect to me), you'll probably like Helen Weinzweig's *Basic Black with Pearls* (Anansi, 135, $7.95). Like Resnais's film, Weinzweig's novel is full of puzzles: what's going on? anything? To my taste, in both works the puzzles predominate unduly (and in Resnais's film life slips out the window). This desire to be enigmatic is unfortunate in Weinzweig's case, for she is clearly a good writer with an interesting imagination, and some of the vignettes in the novel are quite moving.

The novel centres on a middle-aged woman, dressed in basic black with pearls, and her affair with her supposed lover, Coenraad, a spy for the 'Agency.' He sends her cryptic messages that she has to decipher in order to meet him – and even then he appears in disguise. It is never clear, however, if we are to take the novel literally, or regard it as the story of a woman who has suffered, or is suffering, a breakdown. It we do take it literally, it strains our credibility. A derelict, a wino, approaches her in Eaton's – is it Coenraad? In scenes like this the novel is on the edge of tottering over into absurdity. And I find something absurd about the entire plot of the novel as this woman goes to all the Elm streets in Toronto (her clue) hoping to locate her lover. But the possibility is raised that none of this is happening; that the woman has had a breakdown and is imagining it all. This might resolve my objections to the story's implausibility, but the novel doesn't really give us any way of determining whether the action *is* real or imagined. It leaves us with the puzzle. The tone and attitude are also often elusive. At the end, for example, the woman briefly returns home to see her own husband and children, only to discover that her husband has replaced her with another woman and hardly seems to have noticed that she has left. As a black farce this would be effective, but it's not clear that it's intended that way. And the theme that dominates the ending – empty virtue given up for the needs of passion – is almost trite.

What does come through in the book, and nearly saves it, is the sense of the woman's loneliness, her constant fear of being alone, her anxiety about being abandoned by her lover. Also some of the vignettes of her past and of the people she encounters in her wandering have a real power – in particular her confrontation with a man who abandoned his family to the Nazis and lives constantly tortured by his guilt. We are never allowed to respond for very long, however, to the felt life in the novel but are constantly forced back to the unsatisfying and ultimately unimportant task of trying to unravel the puzzle.

Albert Johnson, the 'object of the largest manhunt in RCMP history,' has always been an enigma. Who was he? Was his real name actually 'Albert Johnson'? But these questions are less intriguing than the general questions his life raises: why did this man withdraw totally from the human community, refuse finally to speak even one word or to acknowledge his name? The manhunt for Johnson in the Arctic arose after he first wounded an RCMP Officer and later killed another; the incredible endurance he showed won him considerable public sympathy and something in this isolate, renegade figure has attracted Rudy Wiebe. Wiebe's interest in Johnson was first shown in his story 'The Naming of Albert Johnson' (1974). This experimental story works backwards from Johnson's death to his arrival in Rat River, and his 'naming'; sticking to the historical facts, the story presents the action from Johnson's point of view, and the result is a very powerful story but a difficult one, for Wiebe assumes that the reader has the necessary historical information. In his new novel, *The Mad Trapper* (McClelland and Stewart, 189, $14.95), Wiebe tells Johnson's story in a much more conventional narrative manner, but he alters certain facts in order to shift the focus of his story. The RCMP corporal, Spike Millen, whom Johnson eventually kills, becomes as important as Johnson. In fact, for large sections Johnson is absent and we are concerned primarily with Millen's efforts not just to track, but to understand Johnson. This concentration on Millen actually works to create sympathy for Johnson; it makes very effective the sudden shifts back to Johnson's point of view and sets up the highly dramatic meeting of Millen and Johnson at the end. Wiebe's novel does involve a violation of historical fact, for Millen was actually killed near the middle of the manhunt, not at its end. Wiebe has always been somewhat free in his handling of historical material, and how one reacts to this freedom here will depend on whether one feels he is being true to the 'spirit' if not the letter of what happened. On these grounds I think it's possible to accept the historical changes in *The Mad Trapper*.

The novel does not really advance our understanding of Johnson. This in itself is not a weakness, for Johnson is an enigma: his total withdrawal, his rage, seems almost beyond explanation. On the whole Wiebe accepts this, but he can't resist making a gesture towards explaining Johnson – he frequently has him singing the phrase of a song: 'Never smile at a woman ... Call no man your friend. If you trust anybody, you'll be sorry ... you'll be sorry, in the end.' This approaches banality and explains nothing.

Simply as a skilfully told narrative with the power totally to engross and engage the reader (at least this reader) the book is superb. The ability to render action (particularly violent action) that Wiebe demonstrated in *The Scorched-Wood People* is developed even further here. Granting this, *The Mad Trapper* is still obviously a minor work: it is finally not much more than a compelling narrative and it represents an interlude in Wiebe's career, a pause, and perhaps a setting to rest of Wiebe's concern with historical figures – or at least with the strange figure of Albert Johnson.

Jane Rule's *Contract with the World* (Harcourt Brace Jovanovich, 339, $16.95) is, as Margaret Atwood claims (on the dustjacket), Rule's 'most sensitively handled book to date.' It is certainly an advance over her last novel, *The Young in One Another's Arms*, and in her examination of the lives of a group of friends living in Vancouver she achieves a new level of seriousness. Rule is perhaps best known as a feminist, and while a concern with lesbian experience is central to the book, it does not seem to me in any sense a feminist tract; Rule's art is in control throughout.

The issue of lesbianism is explored most fully in the portrayal of Alma; her unhappy marriage finally ends and she takes a woman, Roxanne, as a lover. The novel examines convincingly the sensual joy Alma discovers, but also her feelings of guilt, her need for punishment, her ambivalence about her relationship, and even her desire to go back to her husband. Her new relationship doesn't lead to any easy happiness and it is in this presentation of the difficulties of Alma's situation that the complexity of Rule's book is most evident.

Despite the sensitivity and complexity in Rule's handling of the lesbian theme, this novel has some serious limitations. Many of the characters simply aren't all that interesting – for example, Joseph Allen the photographer, even Carlotta the painter. And while Roxanne is presented as being somehow 'special,' she often seems merely shallow. Nearly all of the characters are artists, but I find it hard to believe in Roxanne's music, or in the sense in which Allen, the photographer, is an artist; rather, these two characters seem examples of what D.H. Lawrence called 'being an artist.' Finally, I find Rule's prose fairly ordinary. She has at best a serviceable style, and, say what we will about the relative unimportance of style in fiction (in comparison with poetry), a serviceable style is not enough for a satisfying fictional achievement.

Ian McLachlan's *Helen in Exile* (McClelland and Stewart, 369, $14.95) is an obviously ambitious novel. It deals with the lives of three women – Helen, her mother Hélène, and her grandmother Helena – and examines both their relationships with each other and their involvement in the personal and political struggles of their time. The present of the novel (Helen's story) concentrates on three months in 1970 at the time of the FLQ crisis; Hélène's life takes us back to the time of the French resistance against the Nazis; Helena's life was caught up in the conflict of the Greeks and Turks near the beginning of the century. The social and historical canvas of the novel, then, is vast, and, as with his earlier novel *The Seventh Hexagram*, I find McLachlan most engaging in his presentation of his historical material – in evoking a sense of the conflict between the Greeks and Turks in Smyrna (now Izmir) in the early 1900s, in providing interesting historical information. Moreover, given the almost total absence of political fiction in Canada, McLachlan deserves credit for making a serious attempt to write a 'political' novel.

This novel is of interest, however, more for what it attempts than for what it achieves. Although McLachlan is good at describing historical action, this book does not carry us very far in terms of historical explanation and understanding. Nor does McLachlan offer us particularly subtle portrayals of character. The presentation of Helena (the grandmother) in the nursing home seems less an original creation than an imitation of Margaret Laurence's Hagar Shipley. Helen becomes too obviously a victim (almost, it seems, of her own stupidity). And while I can admire McLachlan's nerve in writing about the struggle of contemporary women, his analysis sometimes doesn't get beyond this: 'This has got to be the hardest time of all, eh? To be a woman?' Helen's own struggle, her 'revolution' to free herself, concerns her being an artist, but Helen as an avant-garde painter is the least believable part of the book. The novel is also heavily burdened with repeated efforts at trendy dialogue that too often suggest only the shallowness of the characters. Finally, there is the political perspective of the book to consider. McLachlan seems to be implying that the behaviour of the police and the government in Quebec in 1970 can legitimately be compared with the behaviour of the Nazis, but nothing I know of the events, and nothing he shows in this book, suggests that we should take the comparison seriously.

At the opening of Mordecai Richler's *Joshua Then and Now* (McClelland and Stewart, 435, $16.95) Joshua Shapiro, well-known journalist, sometime television personality, is recovering from a car accident, caused by his efforts to flee the police, and hiding out from reporters who want to interview him about his alleged homosexual relationship with a now deceased friend. His wife, a beautiful upper-class 'WASP' named Pauline, has suffered a breakdown and withdrawn from him completely. In short, his life is in complete disarray, and most of the novel is devoted to showing us how he got into this mess. Sounds vaguely familiar? It should, for much of *Joshua Then and Now* is a variation on the plot and themes of *Saint Urbain's Horseman* and Joshua Shapiro is a close cousin to Jake Hersh, the protagonist of Richler's last novel of nearly a decade ago.

Richler's new novel is generally entertaining, often very amusing, but it is weakened by the way it repeats the earlier work. Joshua's wooing of

Pauline, for instance, loses some of its force simply because it is so similar to Jake's wooing of Nancy. And where this novel echoes the earlier one it suffers in the comparison. The theme of the anxieties of middle age is repeated here but now, ten years on, some of Joshua's friends are dying – of leukemia, of heart attacks – and much of the humour and energy involved in Jake's absurd attempts to cope with middle age are given up (necessarily, perhaps, but without sufficient gain) in the presentation of the pathos and grief of life. The theme of the desire for revenge on the Nazis (or at least on Dr Dr Mueller) is again taken up, but is handled in a muted way; Joshua is not as obsessed as Jake, and his concern with revenge seems narrower, more personal, a matter of less significance.

For all the similarities, however, Richler is not simply or wholly repeating himself. The depiction of Pauline's anxieties, of her sense of inferiority, of the rage and self-destruction leading to her breakdown, represents a new step in Richler's handling of women. Through Pauline's friends Jane and Jack Trimble and her father, Senator Hornby, Richler gives his fullest portrayal of Westmount society. And there is nothing in Richler's previous fiction quite like Joshua's parents: his father, Reuben, formerly an enforcer, arsonist, bootlegger, etc; his mother, former stripper and operator of a massage parlour. Richler is, then, breaking some new ground here, but with limited success. Pauline – 'Pure joy, his Pauline' – is finally not much more realized than was Nancy in *St. Urbain's Horseman*. Richler's presentation of Westmount society – especially of Jack Trimble the interloper and of Pauline's brother Kevin, the Westmount rich boy who doesn't make good – seems to derive less from life than from a Fitzgerald novel. And some of the scenes with Joshua's mother – in one, for instance, she strips at Joshua's bar mitzvah – are a bit too unlikely; they seem an intrusion into a basically realistic novel.

This is a long novel and parts of it seem thin, stretched out – largely a consequence of the set-pieces that Richler has a tendency to write; once written, whether they work or not he is reluctant to give them up. So here we have such things as the reunion of the William Lyon Mackenzie King Society; a reunion of Joshua and his old schoolmates at the 1967 Grey Cup game; and a fairly extraneous episode where Reuben, Senator Hornby, and Joshua dig up some bootlegged liquor. None of these scenes or set-pieces is particularly funny, nor do they really advance the plot or themes of the novel; they are just there, filling up space.

Finally, there is the matter of Joshua's character and role in the novel. Joshua appears to be offered as the moral centre of the book – certainly Pauline and her father see him as 'moral,' at the very least more moral than they and their rich world are. Joshua's own sense of himself is more complex than this and he is, by the end, aware of his illusions and failures – aware especially of the way he has failed Pauline. None the less, Richler apparently wants us to accept Joshua – fallible as he is – as the novel's moral centre. And this I have some trouble doing. Many of Joshua's activities take the form of a petty, spiteful revenge, such as baiting 'St. Urbain's urchins who had struck it rich. Especially Pinsky.' I find most of Joshua's revenge plots – he removes, for instance, all the labels from Pinsky's expensive wine collection – fairly amusing, but Joshua tends to be self-righteous about his actions and this is harder to swallow. He accredits himself with a moral justification that seems unwarranted. Certainly the Joshua Shapiro who had an affair with his best friend's wife is no more 'moral' than any of the other characters in the book. Richler seems to recognize this – and then again he doesn't: he judges Joshua – whose life after all is in disarray – but he also grants him a moral authority that is unearned.

At first glance *Voices in Time* (Macmillan, 313, $14.95) seems a surprising departure for Hugh MacLennan: a futuristic novel set in the time after the destruction of our civilization. But MacLennan is, in fact, only minimally interested in this new world and *Voices in Time* is really a historical novel as MacLennan looks back on the twentieth century and some of the events leading to the cataclysm. This concern with large public, social issues has characterized MacLennan's work since his first novel, *Barometer Rising*, and in *Voices in Time* he takes his broadest view as he examines the past of our civilization – and what he fears will be its ultimate fate.

The novel opens in the future after the destruction has occurred and introduces us to John Wellfleet, a survivor of our world. He is approached by a young man of the new civilization who has discovered records of the past (the 'voices in time') that relate to Wellfleet's family. Wellfleet agrees to put the records in order and thus tells the stories of his cousin Timothy Wellfleet and of his stepfather Conrad Dehmel. John Wellfleet himself, then, is essentially a minor character, and this is just as well, for he is too passive and ineffectual (too much a George Stewart type) to carry the novel.

The main and best part of the novel deals with Conrad Dehmel and his experiences, not in Canada, but in Nazi Germany in the first half of the century. There is fairly general agreement that MacLennan is at his best in the descriptive and narrative parts of his work – his account of the Halifax explosion in *Barometer Rising*, of Jerome's escape down the river in *The Watch That Ends the Night* – and simply as a compelling narrative the account in *Voices in Time* of people caught up in Nazi Germany is equal to his finest work. The story of Conrad's attempt to save the Jewish woman he loves and her father by joining the gestapo is perhaps slightly improbable, but it makes a moving drama that has a powerful narrative thrust. And in tracing Conrad's life, from his childhood at the turn of the century, through the First World War, to the rise of the Nazis, MacLennan offers a suggestive portrait of German society and of the kind of often decent person who could neither foresee nor prevent Hitler's atrocities. MacLennan's portrayal lacks the intellectual depth of a work like Hermann Broch's *The Sleepwalkers*, but it is a convincing and concrete depiction of a society stumbling into disaster.

The briefer section on Timothy Wellfleet is much weaker; here MacLennan's conservative attitudes affect his portrayal of character and distort his presentation of the 1960s and 1970s. Timothy becomes a famous television journalist in the late 1960s and most of his story concentrates on his behaviour during the FLQ crisis. He seems to embody all that MacLennan feels was wrong with the 1960s, but his credibility as a character and any claim that he can be seen as a representative figure of the 1960s are undercut by the clichéd nature of his thought and language: 'I had no ambition because I honestly did not know where I was so I accepted a place in the plastic paradise-penitentiary our upper middle class had imported from south of the border and paid for by selling out all these billions of dollars worth of national resources.'

John Wellfleet, even with his relatively minor role, is one of the other problems in the novel, for the sections where he speaks of the world before the destruction (our world) are excessively discursive, unrealized. The modern world is talked about, not presented, and it is condemned in too easy a manner: 'He [Conrad] might have given me some mental armor for what lay ahead, perhaps even some moral armor. Not many of us had either.' MacLennan uses Wellfleet to harangue the modern age, although fortunately Wellfleet's intrusions into the novel are infrequent and brief.

There are aspects of this novel that I find questionable, at the very least, on ideological grounds. The comparison MacLennan makes between the FLQ and the rise of the Nazis makes no sense to me and is virtually incomprehensible in light of the last ten years. Further, I do not share MacLennan's feeling that the 'screaming for freedom' is part of our present danger; his analysis seems primarily a reflection of his own conservative attitudes. Neither of these issues, however, bulks large in the experience of reading the novel; they are, rather, problems we are left with as afterthoughts and do not seriously affect the novel's aesthetic quality.

Voices in Time has had, in the reviews I have seen, a very negative reception. The novel has been dismissed as being over-earnest, preachy, more of an essay than a novel. These judgments seem to me unfair and ultimately mistaken. I am not questioning that the novel has a didactic purpose: clearly it is written as a warning and Conrad Dehmel seems to be a spokesman for MacLennan when he claims that, as in Nazi Germany, 'the storm signals are flying again.' MacLennan's fairly explicit didactic intent is not, however, particularly damaging since for most of the novel it is held in check, and the main part, where he simply gets on with the job of narrating his story, is as good as anything he has written.

Romans

PAUL-ANDRÉ BOURQUE

Un regard, même furtif, jeté sur la bibliographie du roman de l'année 1980 révèle immédiatement quelques faits qui étonnent. Première constatation, une certaine maigreur de la création, compte tenu de la production, de la quantité de romans mis en circulation sur le marché par les éditeurs québécois. Des quelque cent quatre-vingts titres mis en marché cette année, plus d'une soixantaine sont des rééditions, soit une proportion de plus de 33 pour cent. On peut s'interroger sur les mobiles profonds des éditeurs quand on considère les masses monétaires servant à rééditer des ouvrages dont souvent on pourrait se passer, sommes d'argent qui n'ont pas été investies dans l'édition d'œuvres nouvelles. Si certains éditeurs y voient des marges de profit plus sécuritaires, d'autres éditeurs ont vraiment comme intention première de remettre en circulation des œuvres importantes devenues introuvables. C'est à ce genre de travail que se livre la maison Fides en nous donnant cette année deux Léo-Paul Desrosiers, *Les Engagés du Grand-Portage* et *Nord-Sud*, ou encore le *Marie-Didace* de Germaine Guèvremont. On pourra encore également se réjouir de trouver en rééditions format poche des titres majeurs de Marie-Claire Blais ou Gabrielle Roy ou quelque autre 'classique' de la littérature québécoise, mais bon nombre des rééditions imprimées cette année ne me sont souvent apparues que comme de purs effets de commerce.

D'autre part, un second regard porté à la bibliographie me rappelle un trop grand nombre d'heures consacrées, par métier, à lire une somme considérable de romans insipides qui, souvent, refusés lorsque présentés à de grandes et bonnes maisons d'édition, ont quand même trouvé le chemin de la librairie ou de l'étalage du marchand de journaux par le biais de la publication à compte d'auteur ou encore par celui de petites maisons d'édition dont les politiques éditoriales n'assureront pas longtemps la survie (pas plus celle du livre que celle de la maison). Quarante titres à rejeter sans regrets. Sur une production totale de cent quatre-vingts, ça ne fait que 20 pour cent. On ne me dira donc pas trop sévère. Mais, si l'on soustrait de ce nombre total les soixante titres qui sont des rééditions, la proportion des rejets-sans-regrets s'élève à $33\frac{1}{3}$ pour cent. Alors, là, je commence à me considérer moi-même comme étant très sévère avec mes quarante rejets-sans-regrets. Un livre sur trois. Quand je chercherai tout à l'heure à établir la liste de la douzaine de livres qui m'ont captivé au cours de cette année, je constaterai toutefois que je n'aurai pas été aussi sévère que les pourcentages pourraient me le laisser croire puisque mon enthousiasme pour chacun de ces douze titres n'aura pas été aussi entier que je l'aurais à priori souhaité. Serait-ce cela la maigreur d'une année de production romanesque?

Autre constatation tirée d'une évaluation quantitative de la bibliographie du roman: seulement 30 pour cent de la production totale est signée au féminin, et si l'on décompte encore une fois les rééditions, cette proportion s'abaisse à vingt-cinq pour cent, diminuant l'apport des auteures à près de la moitié de la production des meilleures années de la dernière décennie. Comment expliquer cette baisse de la production romanesque chez les femmes? Essoufflement des romancières? Indifférence du marché à une littérature de femmes qui, pour paraphraser un titre de roman de Michel Beaulieu, aurait commencer à trop tourner en rond autour de soi? L'avenir nous répondra sans doute, et nous dira, je l'espère, de quels recommencements les auteures du Québec sont capables!

En attendant ces recommencements, mes meilleurs moments de lecture de romans au cours de l'année 1980 ne l'auront pas moins pour autant été sous le sceau de l'écriture au féminin avec en tête de liste l'angoissant *Le Sourd dans la ville* de Marie-Claire Blais, Prix du Gouverneur général du Canada 1980 pour le roman, puis en compagnie du controversé *Héloïse* d'Anne Hébert et du *Double suspect* de Madeleine Monette, Prix Robert Cliche 1980, et encore avec l'époustouflant *La Vie en prose* de Yolande Villemaire ou le tout récent *Bernadette Dupuis ou la mort apprivoisée* de Huguette Le Blanc.

Si mon penchant naturel pour les écritures de femmes a trouvé son compte avec les titres ci-haut mentionnés, la productione de plusieurs romanciers du Québec a également contribué au plaisir du lecteur. On se souviendra pendant longtemps de l'année 1980 comme étant celle où Noël Audet a donné son premier récit(s) (sic), *Quand la voile faseille*, Jean-Paul Filion son *Cap Tourmente*, François Hébert, *Le Rendez-Vous*, Fernand Ouellette, *La Mort vive*, Jean-Marie Poupart, *Le Champion de cinq heures moins dix*, et Michel Tremblay, *Thérèse et Pierrette à l'école des Saints-Anges*. Mais quand la production romanesque d'une année peut être ramenée, réduite à une douzaine de titres, on peut parler de maigreur. Ces douze romans-là méritent quand même lecture et relecture. Méritent qu'on en parle.

Avec *Le Sourd dans la ville* (Stanké, 214), Maire-Claire Blais donne l'un de ses meilleurs romans, sinon le plus achevé, le mieux écrit. Renouant avec une thématique abordée déjà dans ses toutes premières œuvres (*Le Jour est noir*, *Les Voyageurs sacrés*), renouant également avec des procédés de narration utilisés dans ses meilleurs écrits (le *stream of consciousness* poursuivi par le soliloque et le monologue intérieur – souvenons-nous à cet égard des *Voyageurs sacrés* et du plus récent *Les Nuits de l'Underground*),

Blais trace ici encore un univers de contrastes où le bien et le mal, comme la vie et la mort, 'entrelacent leurs tiges.' Propriétaire de l'Hôtel des Voyageurs dans un quartier 'défavorisé' d'une grande ville, Gloria, pour faire vivre une famille orpheline de père, exhibe dans des bars 'louches' un corps sans gloire. L'un des fils, Mike, rappel de Jean-Le Maigre et de combien d'autres adolescents blaisiens, attend sa mort prochaine, sa mort absurde. Florence, qui a depuis peu pris pension à l'Hôtel des Voyageurs après avoir quitté mari, enfants, maison et mode de vie bourgeois, chemine, parallèlement à Mike vers sa propre mort, celle qu'elle se donnera. Contre ces morts, contre la misère, contre l'absurde: la révolte. Celle rêvée de la fuite en Californie de Gloria et Mike en moto. La pitié aussi, celle de Judith Lange. Celle aussi de l'artiste, de son œuvre:

> ... tous les hommes sont seuls ... même si la plupart évitent la voie du suicide (Florence pensait encore qu'elle n'était pas comme ces buveurs d'absinthe, cette chair lamentable se prostituant chaque jour, elle ne ressemblait pas à Gloria, mais elle avait su que tout cela existait, oui, dans les tableaux, Degas et Lautrec n'avaient fait que peindre la vie, ils avaient honoré cette chair menacée de périr, ces visages, elle les avait vus, hier, et elle comprenait pourquoi Lautrec avait accepté de se faire désintoxiquer en clinique, c'est qu'il s'était épris de ces visages qu'il peignait, de cette meute à la dérive ... je les rencontre tous dans la vie maintenant (pensait Florence) je ne pouvais imaginer cela, on oublie que l'artiste peint avec ce que nous sommes aussi et que l'Imaginaire ou tout ce qu'on pourrait qualifier d'invisible, parce que nos yeux sont aveugles à ce que nous voyons tous les jours, est là, partout, dans le malheur, dans la sécheresse, la froideur ou l'aridité, cet imaginaire est une vérité toute évidente que l'on ne peut plus fuir ... (Pp 106–7)

Sur deux cent dix pages serrées, Blais étale avec un rare brio, d'un seul souffle, la misère humaine, l'absurde de la condition humaine, le refus de ses personnages en un long monologue intérieur sans ponctuation autre que celle des virgules qui permettent au lecteur de maintenir le rythme, le *tempo* de ce marathon intérieur des personnages du *Sourd dans la ville*. Aucun essoufflement, aucun halètement de la part du lecteur ... Seul le revissement provoqué par chaque enjambée, par la distance parcourue, par chaque inspiration, par chaque expiration. Parvenu au terme de la course, le lecteur-marathonien se sent prêt à refaire le parcours même si en courant-lisant il a beaucoup souffert, davantage de la souffrance des personnages que de la sienne propre.

Anne Hébert publie relativement peu, mais chacun de ses livres marque le lecteur, *Héloïse* (Seuil, 123) peut-être un peu moins que ne l'avaient fait *Kamouraska* et/ou *Les Enfants du sabbat*. C'est à se demander pourquoi. Une histoire simple, très simple, trop simple peut-être. Bernard est fiancé à Christine. Ils vont bientôt se marier. Ils s'installent à Paris dans un appartement tout blanc, sépulcral, presque. (Sorte de rappel en blanc des chambres de bois où Michel voulait enfermer Catherine.) Même si Christine refuse cet enfermement, refuse d'éprouver la fascination de la mort blanche qu'éprouve Bernard, celui-ci l'y contraindra jusqu'à ce qu'il rencontre, dans le métro de Paris, la femme fatale, toute en rouge et en noir, Héloïse. Il la suivra dans Paris jusqu'à ce qu'elle le conduise auprès de l'énigmatique Xavier Bottereau qui louera à Christine et Bernard un appartement plus sombre, plus chargé de vie, de couleurs. Si Christine est ravie du nouveau mode de vie que leur procure ce nouvel logis, elle sentira rapidement que Bernard lui échappe, que Bernard est fasciné par une nouvelle image de la mort, plus fantastique celle-là, celle 'vampirique' qu'incarne Héloïse. Progressivement le récit quitte les voies du réalisme pour entrer dans les sphères du fantastique jusqu'à l'hallucination de la scène finale, là où, m'est-il apparu, plusieurs lecteurs ont 'décroché.' Si on compare ce récit d'une grande sobriété, d'une grande économie de moyens à Kamouraska et à son ample mouvement où se déchaînent de grandes passions, ou encore au démonisme des Enfants du Sabbat et à toutes ses zones grises, la trame de Héloïse pourra paraître maigre voire même forcée, mais cela étant constaté, la puissance évocatrice du langage poétique apparaîtra d'autant plus efficace.

La Vie en prose de Yolande Villemaire (Les Herbes rouges, 262) a frappé le monde des lettres québécoises comme un coup de fouet. Il faut dire que ce type d'écriture détonne et détone dans le contexte traditionnel de nos lettres. Ce récit porte bien son titre. La vie fuse de toutes parts en rose comme en prose. 'Il y a toujours une femme en rose dans le paysage de ce roman comme il y a toujours du rose depuis que j'en ai entendu la chanson ...' (p 138). 'La vie en prose ... c'est l'univers du rose: entre le rouge de la révolution et le blanc de la fête. Une sorte de tremblement entre le noir et le blanc, un lien dialectique entre la membrane curieuse qui accomplit la mission de son ADN et s'obstine à écrire son nom, se saisit de l'hémisphère du silence pour dissoudre' (p 98)

Récit polymorphe qui court dans toutes les directions: embryon de roman policier plus ou moins érotique qui se situerait dans un Mexique rêvé où la narratrice n'a jamais mis les pieds, pages de journal bourrées d'allusions aux films, aux chansons, aux livres qui l'ont marquée, multiples intrusions de la vie quotidienne dans le récit. Poèmes. Lettres que la narratrice s'adresse à elle-même parce que la poste ne livre pas une lettre à un personnage. Tout cela pour dire 'je je je. je je je,' qui écrit la vie pour mieux la vivre. Automatismes. Flot de la conscience.

> je je je dans la spirale du temps perdu dans la nuit des temps et pourtant ce n'est pas moi qui parle, c'est je je je un autre et je pourtant est *une* autre qui vole une phrase au continuum des calligraphies palimpsestes de ce qu'on appelle les choses de la vie par une sorte d'obscurcissement qui nous fait oublier le décor

de carton-pâte et toute la profondeur des sphères subatomiques qui roulent
sous nos peaux d'iguanes galapagos dans un instant de genèse   (P 171)

Le *je* est ici androgyne et multiple. Le *je* écrivant est à la fois masculin et féminin. Masculin(?) peut-être(?) probablement(?) certainement(!) dans l'aspect traditionnel du vouloir-écrire, dans l'identification de la narratrice-écrivante aux grands archétypes de l'écriture. Sujétion et iconoclastie face aux modèles. Féminin(?) (!) quand *je je je* vit en rose et en prose. Rêve, délire, gueule, braille, rit, connaît l'orgasme, chante. *Je* est à la fois un et *une* autre. Cela ne fait pourtant qu'un et ce *je* est encore pluriel(le). Il-elle est Nanne Yelle. Vava. Elisabeth Swann. Noé Vladimira Yelle. Blanche. Et combien d'autres. Le *je* de Villemaire est américain, européen, mexicain. Punk. Rouge. Blanc. Et puis rose. Et puis vous. Et puis moi. *La Vie en prose*: un livre déroutant-envoûtant. Neuf. Moderne. Authentique. A lire-écrire absolument.

Il m'apparaît important aussi de souligner l'entrée en littérature d'une nouvelle voix, celle de Huguette Le Blanc qui, avec son *Bernadette Dupuis ou la mort apprivoisée* (Biocreux, 137) fait montre, à l'occasion d'une trame trop peu originale (deux vieillards, reclus sur leur ferme lointaine, refusent l'ordre gouvernemental de l'évacuer pour fins de reboisement, et entrent dans l'hospice pour s'enfermer dans la solitude, l'hiver et la mort) d'une qualité d'écriture remarquable. La puissance évocatrice du style, l'économie de la phrase, la structuration sobre de l'anecdote laissent présager pour l'avenir d'œuvres de fort calibre.

On ne saurait passer sous silence non plus le remarquable roman de Madeleine Monette *Le Double suspect* (Quinze, 241). Histoire d'écriture que celle-ci ou Anne, se culpabilisant du suicide de son ex-mari, tente de trouver l'oubli dans des vacances italiennes. Elle y retrouve une amie, Mona, qui quelques jours plus tard trouvera la mort dans des circonstances qui laissent penser qu'il pourrait encore s'agir d'un suicide. Anne entrera en possession des cahiers intimes de Mona. Elle tentera de les récrire au *je*. Nous assistons ici au 'travail de sape qui fait d'une personne un personnage,' à la découverte de l'écriture narcissique révélatrice du moi, par le décryptage d'un double (Mona) devenu suspect, donc interrogé. Aventure intérieure fascinante dans un style alerte. La vie italienne est ici toute chaude et palpitante.

Le poète Fernand Ouellette a lui aussi choisi l'Italie comme cadre principal de son roman *La Mort vive* (Quinze, 208). Les rapports dialectiques en présence ici ne sont plus ceux qu'établissait une Madeleine Monette, mais ceux de la vie et de la mort, déjà suggérés par le titre, de la matière et de la lumière, de la chair et de l'esprit.

Jean, le principal protagoniste, ce 'saint de la peinture,' est un de ces 'anges de sang' que nous propose depuis longtemps Fernand Ouellette. Artiste épris d'absolu, de spiritualité, il cherche à dire la lumière, à 'dire le monde dans sa dimension spirituelle' quand tout contribue à le pétrifier.

Partage entre la vie des corps (celle vécue avec Diane, la jeune comédienne qui survalorise le sien au détriment de la vie de son esprit, celle vécue avec Carmelle la nymphomane), et la vie de l'esprit (celle vécue avec ses amis artistes comme lui: Aimée la musicienne, Roger le peintre, Gilles le poète, Pierre le romancier et critique littéraire), Jean cherche la voie vers une mystique, accessible prétend-il, par l'expression de la lumière pure sur une toile. Ce n'est toutefois qu'un pis aller ... l'idéal aurait été de vivre l'amour fou jusqu'au bout avec Viviane, seul personnage chez qui charnel et spirituel se soient équilibrés.

Proche à certains égards du *Tunnel* d'Ernesto Sabato, ce roman qui traduit de façon prenante certaines angoisses, certains enthousiasmes du créateur, offre une vision trop romantique de l'art et de l'artiste et donne parfois dans le maniérisme et le didactisme de l'historien d'art.

Noël Audet, quant à lui, avec son récit(s) *Quand la voile faseille* (HMH, 312, $11.95) donne dans la veine humoristique comme quelques-uns de ses collègues romanciers dont Jean-Marie Poupart (*Le Champion de cinq heures moins dix*), François Hébert (*Le Rendez-vous*) et Bertrand B. Leblanc, dont on rééditait cette année *Horace ou l'art de porter la redingote*.

Quand la voile faseille, l'un des très beaux livres de l'année par son originalité, son authenticité tant dans les 'beaux sentiments' que dans la grivoiserie, raconte en quatre parties l'histoire d'une famille gaspésienne sur trois générations, l'attention étant centrée sur les aventures amoureuses et cocasses de Graziella Laure et Arsène, principaix tenants de la troisième. Le chapitre intitulé 'L'Arche de Noé' permettra au narrateur une touchante et remarquable apologie du père, type de discours – sujet beaucoup trop rare dans nos lettres. Le livre se fermera sur 'Une simple histoire d'amour' où le narrateur nous entraîne dans un passé très récent où il parle de lui comme 'd'un autre qui dit je.' Aventure amoureuse en quatre temps, c'est l'amour fou vécu dans sa fulgurance et son impossibilité, le narrateur se voyant déchiré entre Alexandra, l'amante, la maîtresse de rêve, et Hélène, l'épouse fidèle, bonne, compréhensive et désespérée. 'Une simple histoire d'amour' eût pu constituer un livre à elle seule tant le sujet (même banal) est complet et complexe et est traité par Audet avec une vigueur peu commune, avec un enthousiasme délirant et sur un ton lyrique qui confine au poétique. *Quand la voile faseille* n'est donc pas un roman mais un récit(s), comme l'écrit l'auteur, hésitant entre le singulier et le pluriel, récit où se mêlent, s'harmonisent les styles et les tonalités propres au mémorialiste, au diariste, au conteur de même que le ton parfois cynique de l'essayiste qui se regarde écrire. Un livre prenant, palpitant, drôle. Tout simplement merveilleux.

Merveilleux aussi, d'une autre manière, que le livre de Jean-Paul Filion, *Cap Tourmente* (Leméac, 163). Troisième volet d'une trilogie amorcée par *Le Premier Côté du monde*, poursuivie par *Les Murs de Montréal*, *Cap Tourmente* nous livre la vision du monde et de l'amour d'un homme parvenu à la maturité, alors que les deux premiers volets nous livraient les souvenirs d'enfance et d'adolescence, puis la vie du travail, de la compétition entre hommes. *Cap Tourmente* est une longue lettre d'amour que le narrateur écrit à sa femme où il s'explique sur les valeurs fondamentales: la spiritualité, les enfants, la maison construite à deux, le vieillissement, la sérénité, la foi en l'avenir. Un livre ouvert, débordant d'optimisme, d'un optimisme dont l'auteur sent le besoin de se défendre:

... essayer de parler de l'envers du vice et du malheur sans faire sourire n'est presque plus dans l'ordre des choses ... (P 115)

Un livre entier, authentique que l'on voudrait pouvoir écrire soi-même.

Le Champion de cinq heures moins dix (Leméac, 302) de Jean-Marie Poupart est lui aussi un récit non-conventionnel, tenant du journal, non pas du journal personnel dans lequel le romancier aurait pu noter des idées à retenir pour la construction d'une intrigue ou l'élaboration d'un personnage, pas plus que du journal intime où il aurait consigné ses états d'âme, ses sentiments, ses frustrations. Non. Le journal que Poupart nous propose est plutôt une suite de faits divers, de réflexions périphériques au champ de l'écriture, réflexions narquoises lorsqu'elles ne sont pas tout simplement cyniques. Poupart utilise à bon escient ce que l'on classe trop souvent comme des 'déchets du quotidien'; il fait en quelque sorte du recyclage de papiers qu'il a froissés et jetés à la corbeille. Exemple, ce brouillon pour son épitaphe: 'Dans sa façon de vouloir être drôle à tout prix, il faisait penser à ces mononcles ivres qui incarnent le père Noël dans les parties de famille.' Cette feuille, ce brouillon aurait-il dû demeurer à la poubelle? Quand 'on traduit du goguenard,' comme le dit l'auteur à propos de son livre, il faut s'attendre à tout, aux perles, comme aux grains de sable. Ce livre a retenu mon attention parce qu'il m'aura fait rire à plusieurs pages, sourire à plusieurs autres et laissé froid à très peu de moments.

Le Rendez-vous (Quinze, 240) de François Hébert m'aura intéressé quant à lui justement par ce ton goguenard qu'il maintient presque tout au long du récit, par ses jeux de mots, son ironie, son cynisme, son pastichage du formalisme littéraire que d'aucuns auront considéré, à tort, comme le *nec plus ultra* de la création littéraire ces années-ci. Hébert s'en moque ouvertement, prétextant écrire une histoire à intrigue policière qui sombrera vite dans l'histoire d'amour un peu à l'eau de rose. Deux histoires banales et cousues de fils blancs qui à la fin se retrouveront, comme par magie reliées, renouées. Le lecteur se rend vite compte que ce qui importe ici ce n'est plus la trame romanesque, mais le traitement, le regard que l'auteur porte sur un milieu, celui des professeurs de littérature dans les collèges, sur la gent étudiante et sur les rapports 'intimes' que les deux parties peuvent entretenir ... Tout est dans la manière ... Dites-le avec des épines. Côté épines, Hébert est garni comme une pelote d'épingles. Tant pis pour ceux qu'il pique, le lecteur, sadique, sourit à s'en ankyloser les muscles des joues.

On ne peut négliger, en dernier lieu, le deuxième volet d'un cycle romanesque de Michel Tremblay amorcé de façon fulgurante par *La Grosse Femme d'à-côté est enceinte*, et poursuivi cette année par *Thérèse et Pierrette à l'école des Saints-Anges* (Leméac, 366). Même observation précise de la vie quotidienne du Plateau Mont-Royal où réalisme et fantastique s'entremêlent. Contrepoids à son univers dramatique. Même capacité d'émotion que dans le premier volet. Même qualité d'écriture. Mais le chroniqueur vaut-il le dramaturge? Si son roman séduit, il ne le fait pas autant que ses meilleurs pièces.

Voilà un aperçu de quelques romans qui ont parsemé une année plutôt maigre. Ce n'est qu'une perception, la mienne, celle de quelqu'un qui pour avoir connu les années de vaches grasses attend impatiemment leur retour. En attendant, les romans retenus m'auront permis de tromper mon attente.

Poetry

SANDRA DJWA

This year's poetry has a regional shape: small piles of books from Breakwater of Newfoundland and little presses in Quebec and Ontario, large bundles from Fiddlehead of New Brunswick, Turnstone of Manitoba, and Talonbooks of British Columbia. It may be the regional distribution of the little presses and the importance of landscape as symbol in some modern poetry which account for the fact that the celebration of region and of place, always significant in the Canadian tradition, is the most important category of poetry written in 1980. Both men and women poets write the landscape sequence, but where men tend to link the landscape with art and the process of creation, often finding in it a means of identifying themselves with a continuing tradition, women poets are more likely to write the landscape or settlement poem in relationship to a more personal discovery of identity, sometimes sexual and often feminist. Another major category is the mythological poem sequence, sometimes overlapping with the landscape poem. Such poems draw from classical myth, from more recondite Indian or Eskimo sources, and from the received myths of contemporary literature, notably T.S. Eliot's *The Waste Land* and *Four Quartets*.

The celebration of place is, in some ways, the most interesting category of poetry written this year. Douglas Lochhead's *High Marsh Road: Lines for a Diary* (Anson-Cartwright Editions, 136, $8.95) is structured as a cycle of poems covering the last quarter of the year. At first this seems like a commonplace book, jottings for poems: simplified statements ('what behind eye'), minimal capitalization, and prose-like rhythms, all contribute to this impression. Curiously, these poems have a strong cumulative effect, expanding in the reader's consciousness. This is partly because of Lochhead's allusive technique but also because of his controlling poetic which, to rephrase Bachelard, might be called 'the poetics of small.' The poet's task is to see, the 'looking out' to find significant detail and to record the process of making: 'this is the place. the marsh. to / keep beginning from such horizons, / it is the fact, the main one.' In the minimal quality of this verse we sense that Lochhead has had enough of poetizing, the poet as 'bull in a word-shop,' but that he still believes in poetry: there is a strong sense of the poet waiting for the voice to come, of the process of art: 'the real round of the saying never forms, / but the poet is constantly working, moulding / it closer and closer to the truth.'

In exploring the processes 'behind' seeing Lochhead writes of the relation between life and art and the poet's struggle to order detail in such a way as to mediate between the two: 'the mind envelops. on the surface / everything moves to its / own level. now I see.' But seeing through Lochhead's poetic eye involves a change in our usual perspective. His art, like that of the Maritimers Colville and Pratt, is grounded in a kind of magic realism which involves shifts in focus. To see how this works in practice we might turn from Lochhead's first poem, the minimal diary entry of September 1st –

Colville's crow mounts higher higher.
the silver spoon is fast in the beak.
what behind eye prompts bird to seize
such objects and hide them away?

– to Colville's painting, 'Crow with Silver Spoon' (1972), where the crow, rising above dappled clouds, fills a brilliantly blue circle of sky – in effect the small becomes the great expanding to fill our vision. Lochhead's direct but minimal statement has much the same effect on the reader: his details, absorbed, expand to fill a world.

The poet's reflections move between memories of past love ('dear x') and the present scene of sea-grasses, cobwebs, and barns. 'The barns on the marsh,' seen from the high road, become 'small blocks fallen as toys' which the mind investigates from a distance: 'they are weathered, / hung with hay, places for owls.' As the rhythm of these allusions suggests, and as the later reference to Charles G.D. Roberts confirms, Lochhead is also making a poet's pilgrimage. What he seeks, initially, is the larger vision:

'the total glimpse of it as Roberts / took to Tantramar. using his telescope / his eye revisited ... it is / good to have such footsteps.' Roberts (in 'pince-nez and tails') is the presiding, if sometimes comic, genius of place. Like his predecessor, Lochhead has come back to Tantramar for renewal; and the diary entries suggest that he has returned for the reasons summarized in 'The Tantramar Revisited' as 'hands of chance and of change' – melancholy, the loss of love, the recognition of time passing. But where Roberts cannot find joy in nature and, indeed, maintains his equilibrium only by distancing it, 'Lest on too close sight I miss the darling illusion,' Lochhead forges his own poetic by taking just the opposite view. By focusing on immediate detail, by limiting his expectations and merging with the landscape, he achieves a minimal solution.

> the snow turns in the wind.
> into a shell's whorl. what
> breaks here to make it so?
> the immensity of small. in
> all this is refuge

What he accepts, ultimately, is a whittled-down world: one characterized by the determination to 'simplify,' and to accept 'joy' when it comes. In the last entry of December 31st, the beloved is seen against the sky emerging from a 'bank of breakers. / sea-swells of night-beginning cloud.' The implied image is that of Venus rising from the sea, but 'the music' the poet conveys is mock-heroic, with 'Charlie Chaplin' for a conductor, the little man headed for a pratfall. Life is often absurd, Lochhead seems to say, but it can be endured and – who knows? – even en-joyed.

Fred Cogswell's *A Long Apprenticeship: Collected Poems* (Fiddlehead, 225, $6.50) begins as the poetry of place; later poems have a wider application. Cogswell's New Brunswick, shaped by the United Empire Loyalist immigration of the late 1780s, still retains many nineteenth-century qualities: as such it is the historical, as well as geographical, extension of Robinson's New England. When Cogswell comes to write of the fruitful Ellen Waring whose 'trunk and limbs grow gnarled and stout to prove / The tree that bears must pay the price of bearing,' he does so not only because Hardy and Robinson had written similar satires of circumstance but also because such examples derive from his own experience. The early Cogswell is a strict formalist; he prefers the Miltonic sonnet, which allows presentation of character and situation in the octave and a turnabout in the sestet.

> She is not so unto her husband's sight.
> The light through which he sees is filtered by
> The colours of one warm September sky

>   When she, on their first morning of delight,
>   Stood bare in limbs' and body's symmetry,
>   As lissom-lovely as a poplar tree.

'Valley Folk,' like many of the early poems in this collection, appeared in Cogswell's first book, *The Stunted Strong* (1954): 'O narrow is the house where we are born, / And narrow are the fields in which we labour.' Cogswell is writing an anatomy of a particular region of the Maritime spirit. His 'Rose,' scarlet in blossom, is transformed, at her father's death, into 'A thin, tall scare-crow dressed in faded black.' 'Art,' once the 'hellion with the grin' who traded rides for sexual favours, becomes in later years a balding clerk whose 'gold tooth spoils his style.' The girls, now prosperous matrons, 'grope with memories, grown vague and dim, / To wonder what they ever saw in him.' That this St John River valley is a constricted area of human experience is underscored by Cogswell's reference to the river, flowing freely by to 'wider regions.' He knows well the rigidities of small-town morality but he also understands the virtues of human community. It is this 'reciprocal wine of shared communion' that we find in Cogswell's 'Statement of Position.' 'So sustained / Who feeds upon the fruit of lives he feeds / Need never look behind to fear of salt / Nor forward to terror.' The journeying need of such a man, Cogswell tells us, is 'justified / Not in new road nor record-breaking climb / But by a humbler kind of pilgrimage.' Cogswell's own long pilgrimage as poet, publisher, and translator is reflected in the *Collected Poems*. He enjoys a plain truth plainly told: 'Oh, for an honest child to cry halloo / For naked truths that Burke and Johnson knew'; he has an unexpected and delightful gift for parody, as in 'Spiv's Innisfree.' His later poetry, freer in form, has a conversational and reflective strain. Cogswell joined the Fiddlehead poetry group in 1945, was long associated with their magazine, *The Fiddlehead*, and, as publisher of Fiddlehead Poetry Books for over twenty years, took on the task initiated by Lorne Pierce, the publishing of promising younger poets such as Gail Fox, Robert Gibbs, Don Gutteridge, Leona Gom, Alden Nowlan, Al Purdy, Kay Smith, and David Solway. His translations are collected in *The Poetry of Modern Quebec*.

Stuart MacKinnon in *Mazinaw* (McClelland and Stewart, 75, $7.95), Gordon Turner in *No Country for White Men* (Turnstone, 57, $5.00), and Dale Zieroth in *Mid-River* (Anansi, 71, $6.95), all write of landscape in relation to the primitive. 'Mazinaw' is Algonquin for 'picture writing book' and MacKinnon uses some of the legends associated with the pictographs as a framework for his tale of Flora Denison, suffragette, socialist, and mystic of sorts, the founder of the Whitman Club at Bon Echo Inn, near Belleville. There is no great distance between Indian earth spirits, Whitman's sense of the 'kosmos,' and Maurice Bucke's 'Cosmic Consciousness,' and MacKinnon is able to get them all in because the great rock at Bon Echo incised with the pictographs of Skunk, Rabbitman, Heron, and Turtle also contained lines by Whitman. Horace Traubel, Whitman's biographer, visited there in 1919 where he supervised the engraving ceremony – 'My foothold is tenoned and morticed in granite / I laugh at what you call dissolution' – before unluckily expiring two days later. The Flora Denison story has many such pithy ironies and home truths and MacKinnon makes good use of them: 'In a one-horse town / you'd best be friendly / with the man / who owns the horse.' *Mazinaw* traces the history of place from primitive beginnings to Flora's impetuous life: her retreat to Bon Echo, the teachings of Sunset, an Indian shaman, and her subsequent career torn between 'social issues and Cosmic Consciousness.' As chronicle, this is fascinating material; as poetry it is sometimes a little too prosy to be effective.

Gordon Turner in *No Country for White Men* writes of a variety of environments, including the Eskimo village of Igloolik, NWT, and the Indian village of Mount Currie, British Columbia. For Turner subject and locale are also ways into a Canadian tradition; he invokes Al Purdy when he remarks 'This is no country for white men / Tourists for a year, a month, a day.'

> Morning, waking to the gnaw in his gut
> surveys the raw chunk of caribou
> plunked in the middle of the gravel-floor
> black meat, aromatic with sweet rot

Turner's descriptive conversational poetry, like Purdy's, keeps the reader wondering what will come next: 'Picking late black raspberries on a / mountain slope / I stepped on a rancid / dark tumble of bear-shit.' He is usually sure-footedly raunchy; he has a good sense of narrative ('The Story'); and he stands as a keen observer of Indian and Eskimo life ('Old Rosie in the Indian Senior Grades' Class').

Dale Zieroth's *Mid-River* is a poetry of description and celebration which verges on primitive myth-making. His is an ecological imagination faced with the perennial problem: 'how to live on the earth / and belong to the world of men'; his locale is the Columbia River valley and Kootenay and Banff National Parks. The first poem, 'Baptism,' sets out his poetic stance:

> In mid-river, it is
> still possible to imagine Thompson's world,
> without roads or bridges, rivers that
> go back beyond white lives into the rocks
> that push and fold, fault and break
> as the new world rises from
> the old.

In one sense a canoe trip along the river is the old story of man meeting the water from which he emerged; but when the canoe capsizes and the poet goes under: 'a scream / goes dead in my throat, we do not / belong here, it bubbles and swallows / silt, the taste of ice' – his first easy truth is also reversed. Desperately regaining land, he reflects: 'I sit and watch the water with the oldest eyes of men: / if I trust the river, I will be / caught in it, rolled backwards into the / simplest race of all, the first.' Zieroth has a technique of giving a poetic dimension to his observations by similes which suggest the larger-than-life context; here it is the first great race, 'the ancient force / of mud and leaves moving in their journey / down the face of the continent.' In the poem 'Out Walking' this larger dimension is introduced casually: 'Sometimes I go out for walks / walks along the edge of the earth'; elsewhere in the poem 'the thunder breaks its back across our roofs / and the rain turns all its dark eyes on us.' This technique is particularly appropriate for the poetry of place because it animates and personifies, rather like native Indian language. Zieroth's command of the line and stanza is often fluent, sometimes excellent; if there is any caveat to be made, it is simply that the book has a sameness of tone.

David Arnason in *Marsh Burning* (Turnstone, 88, $7.00) and Leona Gom in *Land of the Peace* (Thistledown, 87, $14.00, $6.95 paper) juxtapose photograph and text in their settlement poems. Arnason writes of the Icelandic colonies in Manitoba, making very effective use of diary excerpts, Gom of family life in the Peace River country of Alberta. *Marsh Burning* unites personal and tribal experience within an Icelandic mythic framework. Gom approaches her subject from a more personal view, beginning with an attempt to reconstruct a prairie homestead from a pile of chimney bricks and ending with 'Geological Time': 'You need the beginnings, / the first excavation, / the root cellar / down the crumbling steps, / into the primal dark.' The importance of the journey backward into time is the discovery of 'why you changed, / what you have become.' Gom's subjects are the family ('My Mother / My Self') and the *mores* of prairie life. She is interested in identity, the process described in 'Metamorphosis' by which girl becomes woman. The young girl playing hopscotch in the schoolyard adjusts 'to a new centre of gravity,' and 'the beginnings of breasts / push at her sweater.' As the boys in the playground 'move toward her, / something sure and sinister / in their languid circling,' she suddenly straightens: 'her face gathers / the bewildered awareness / of the body's betrayal, / the unfamiliar feel / of the child's toy / in her woman's hand.'

Women poets writing the landscape poem rarely make direct claims on the tradition; none the less some do so implicitly by writing what might be called the Atwood poem. This poem is identified by a wilderness setting, a body of water, a descending or drowning poet, and a kind of evolutionary or geological structure in which drowned bodies (often lovers) merge into the landscape; there are sometimes presences from the past and, frequently, references to art as photograph or language. Barbara Sapergia's *Dirt Hills Mirage* (Thistledown, 97, $14.00, $6.95 paper), Kathleen McCracken's *Into Celebration* (Coach House, 80, $4.50), Gail Fox's *In Search of Living Things* (Oberon, 83, $12.95, $5.95 paper), and Marilyn Bowering's *Sleeping with Lambs* (Press Porcépic, 107, $5.95), all contain the Atwood poem. Sapergia's 'New Place,' 'in the picture I'm hovering over your left shoulder / waiting for a new place / to be born,' suggests 'This Is a Photograph of Me.' McCracken's 'Heritage Song' is a variation on Atwood's 'Death of a Young Son by Drowning.' 'This is / ... the cold ground / where they buried you. / ... I plant flags / ... I dig / this cold land / with my / green hands.' Fox's 'Poem for Nick' is characteristic of the Atwood amalgam of two lovers, the descent into water and the creation of language: 'The rocks are sinking the / island drops inches into water ... The forest of your body falls / beneath the surface ... The language we try to speak / and drowning, cannot articulate.'

Similarly Marilyn Bowering refers to the familiar concepts of survival, animals, and drowning in 'I Will Remember a Beautiful Lake,' but this poem also owes something to Cohen's 'You Have the Lovers.'

> I push the water away and discover dry land.
> I pull the unessential parts of my body apart.
> I make a raft of my cast off limbs
> and wait to see what creature remains
> to climb out of the water.
> I chant to the pieces of flesh growing together:

The culmination of the poem in which the two lovers 'blend into a heap of earth and stones,' the references to animals and the creation of language, all employ counters developed by Atwood. There is a kind of fertility-myth structure implicit in these poems; in some ways, it is a view of landscape as female generative process.

To judge from this year's collection, the mythological poem is both the easiest and the most difficult poem to write: easy because any given myth provides an organizing structure for the poet's experience; difficult because the poet who embroiders the Psyche or Inanna story is likely to believe that he or she has written a poem when all that has been accomplished is to render Bulfinch or Kerenyi in verse. Myth, if it is to be poetry, must be transformed. If we do not hear, running within or as a counterpart to the received story, the poet's own voice, the poet's own psyche, we cannot believe the poem. If on the one hand, myth poetry can be over-simple, it can also be over-obscure. Richard Outram's *The Promise of Light* (Anson-Cartwright Editions, 117, $50.00), falls near this category with the important distinction that his poetry has sufficient verbal punch for us to recognize that his solipsism is integral to his stance as a religious poet. His affinities are with the metaphysicals, especially with the later and more baroque line of Carey, Cleveland, and Crashaw but as approached through the moderns, expecially Auden. Outram's style is the gnomic, his characteristic mode a riddle; consequently, as in the first poem 'Riddler' ('I am the long life found / out underground'), reading his poetry can become a test of one's agility. In *The Promise of Light* he takes an inventory of the universe under two headings, 'The Presentment of Death' and 'Birthward.' I find myself liking the free-flowing way that some Outram poems begin, like 'Scarlatti at Improvisation,' but dissatisfied with their metaphysical moral.

> Felicities like butterflies,
>   brilliance everywhere given
>   over to broken flight;
>
> We, cumbersome, attend,
>   impatient for them to settle,
>   to pulse with light;
>
> Truths are moths. That blossom
>   to seek out, feed on
>   corruption by night.

The combination of the didactic and the arcane (disregarding Vaughan) is particularly Audenesque, and indeed it is to W.H.A. that Outram dedicates 'Elm,' the excellent penultimate poem of the book: 'great root, feeding a rare / Elm from the living air, / Underground, everywhere.'

Robert Finch's *Variations and Theme* (Porcupine's Quill, 79, $16.00, $5.95 paper), itself a variation on a musical phrase, indicates this poet's interests. Some of his poems, like 'Moments Musicaux,' are poems about music; some of his poems, like 'Stay, Lovely Rose,' are variations on old themes. But Finch's most persistent theme is one which echoes Eliot's *Four Quartets*, especially the meditation on time and memory from 'Burnt Norton': 'Footfalls echo in the memory / ... Towards the door we never opened / Into the rose garden.' The 'Theme' of Finch's title poem is the convergence of past and future in the moment:

> Points of arrival and departure are
> Identical and yet dissimilar
> As, for a moment, future, present, past
> Seem in a timeless unity held fast.

His mode of exploration is like Eliot's: 'Staircase and window-sill and balcony / Are passports to the poles of revery; / A picture-frame holds open wide a door / To far excursions never dared before.' The last and best section of the book, beginning with the poem 'Variations,' is a series of linked poems on the return to childhood summers. Finch is deft, formal, witty. His characteristic mode, the sonnet, is sometimes excessively rigid but sometimes, as in 'Merger,' extraordinarily effective for its confined subjects; on other occasions, as in 'Grey: grey morning, grey rocks, grey water, grey sky,' his slight variations transform the mode.

Tom Marshall's *The Elements* (Oberon, 183, $17.50, $7.95 paper) offers a mythology of subatomic particles, an updating of Heraclitus beyond Eliot's Bergsonian flux. We recognize the prophetic voice: 'Let us go forward / then, let us now set sail'; we are assured of the mystic experience: 'I was pierced by the white, corrosive eye of God'; we understand by the careful pruning of four earlier books – *The Silences of Fire* (1969), *Magic Water* (1971), *The Earth-Book* (1974), *The White City* (1976), into *The Elements* – that a careful poetic ordering is indicated. None the less, despite some good poems, notably 'Macdonald Park' and much of 'Islands' and 'Indian Summer,' the book is amorphous: partly because Marshall's poetic, like his mythology, makes 'a virtue / of shifting perspectives, a thing / finally complete, and whole, and moving'; partly because his poems do not usually stand alone but take their meaning from their place in a complex structural myth. The poem's coherence rests largely with image and, to some degree, with the mythic structure generated by image and allusion. Marshall is a highly allusive poet whose references to the 'waste place,' the 'waste lake,' the 'bird voices [that] haunt us,' and the 'multifoliate rose' are conjoined with oracular statement: 'Let us go forward / then,' and 'Return to your beginning.' As these images and concepts demonstrate, his mythic structure owes most to the central matter of twentieth-century poetry, Eliot's *The Waste Land* and *Four Quartets*.

But there is also a sense in which Marshall is attempting to update and broaden Eliot in a Canadian context. Negation and mystic illumination, to some degree sorted out in *The Waste Land* and *Four Quartets* respectively, tend to collocate in *The Elements*. 'There is a single / wave, a single flame / moving into white light, / ... the body burning, / Dresden and Hiroshima burning, / Sodom and Auschwitz burning / all unspeakable / parodies of true / burning.' The sequence proceeds from illumination to the fires of holocaust and lust, the latter parodies of spiritual burning. Marshall can make these leaps because his cosmology extends from outer space (and possible atomic holocaust) to subatomic particles. Moreover, the wasted land is given a local habitation and a name in 'Macdonald Park.' Canada is a 'waste place' because it is 'a winter land / no spring has entered': 'The explorers, those who walk / in a waste place / unceasingly / These we celebrate.' The 'explorers,' a term which in Eliot's use referred to the aged but questing poet, now applies to figures from the Canadian past: to Prime Ministers Macdonald and Laurier and to poets like Pratt and Klein. For

Klein such exploration is a quest that fails, ending in death by water: 'the poet / in his shuttered room / lives alone, becomes his own garrison (a garrison / is a sunken island ...' I begin to feel at this point that neither Klein nor the verse is sufficiently robust to withstand the application of both Eliot and Frye and to question the nature of the whole enterprise.

Any poet who sprinkles his title poem with 'uvular,' 'persiflage,' 'elenchus,' 'tocsin,' 'blik,' 'sniter,' 'canzicrans,' and 'sark' expects a sense of humour from his readers. David Solway in *Mephistopheles and the Astronaut* (Mosaic Press/Valley Editions, 63, $4.95) is principally interested in redefining the archetypal in poems like 'The Promised Land,' 'Penelope,' and 'Love's Particulars.' In the latter poem especially he displays a nice sense of argument, and in 'Elegy of Cassio' Shakespearean diction and density. Solway is a mercurial poet, alternately idealistic and sardonic about things like love and the eternal verities. His closest links are with the dandies; his description of Noah, 'sea-buffeted, salt-encrusted, blind,' echoes A.J.M. Smith's mythmaking and 'Old saltencrusted Proteus'; his delightful 'Apologia' suggests Wallace Stevens.

It is characteristic of Daryl Hine's poetic imagination that in the *Selected Poems* (Oxford University Press, 128, $5.95) he presents the myth of the expulsion from Eden within the context of the Sun King's levée ('Noon'). His is a baroque imagination which becomes progressively more affected in style from the embroideries of 'Psyche' and 'Bluebeard's Wife' in *The Wooden Horse* (1965) to his out-Audening of Auden in 'Vowel Movements' in *Resident Alien* (1975): 'Proper noun or pronoun, indubitably human, / ... Doomed to the brutal unsufructu of the future, / Consumed by the illusions of jejune amours.' It is fitting that he ends the volume with 'Memo to Gongora': I 'pilgrim' towards you [Gongora] with 'your conceits unequalled in my head.' Hine was one of the most exciting poetic voices of the early sixties; rereading early poems from *The Carnal and the Crane* (1957) and *The Devil's Picture Book* (1961) one understands why. 'The Wound' is a genuinely moving love poem. 'Under the Hill' displays absolute control of form; with *doubles entendres* in the Beardsley manner, it echoes with an appropriately evanescent refrain.

> The gates fly open with a pretty sound,
> Nor offer opposition to the knight.
> A sensual world, remote, extinct, is found.

'The Double-Goer' is impressive in structure and concept: 'Source of a comfortable terror now and then, / And romantic: What good is a fiend unless / I can think and he, my double, act?' These last lines, reminiscent of Sartre on sadism, are memorable. But after the excellent early poetry one finds few comparable lines with the exception of the Wordsworthian 'But I have learned to appreciate the faint / Deliquescence of the atmosphere, / As of the world dissolving in a tear' in 'A B.C. Diary.'

The documentary continues to thrive in Tom Wayman's *A Planet Mostly Sea* (Turnstone, 62, $5.00) and Stephen Scobie's *McAlmon's Chinese Opera* (Quadrant Editions, 93, $5.95). The latter might have been discussed under the category of literary myth as the book takes its title from an incident in the late John Glassco's *Memoirs of Montparnasse* where the young Canadian, 'Buffy' to his friends, described the drunken McAlmon at a bar: he would customarily shout, 'This is an aria from my Chinese opera,' and then begin a hideous, toneless screaming. McAlmon's scream was a demand for recognition: overshadowed by his more gifted contemporaries, Hemingway, Joyce, and Stein, he went to his death an embittered man who insisted 'What I never wanted was pity.' Scobie uses this phrase to begin and end the life; but his tone, faithful to McAlmon's character, combines surface spareness with a deeper sense of the pathos of that lost generation.

McAlmon's relationship to his contemporaries is implied in a poem beginning 'Glow, glaux, glaucoma'; here Scobie is working within a recognizable tradition, that of Pound's lament for the nineties generation in 'Yeux Glauques,' and he employs the punning extensions of Joyce's *Ulysses*.

> Glow, glaux, glaucoma,
> grey-eyed Athena, goddess of wisdom,
> blind
>   – the pain increasing, he
> would turn to me: 'Bob, for
> pity's sake, get me home!' –
>   Astarte,
> Esther, estarr, dark star. Ineluctable.
>
> The left eye sinister, bound in black

This poem is mostly about Joyce, the closest of McAlmon's drinking buddies (the book's cover is appropriately illustrated with bar bottles), but expands from Joyce to the Paris literary coterie. Joyce's blindness is emphasized, not just his glaucoma but the hardening and impairment of vision which led him to dismiss McAlmon's biography, *Being Geniuses Together*, as merely 'the office boy's revenge': 'Black wine, glaucoma. Pressure on the nerve: / in pain of sight / in a world, in a word, in a work / in progress.' Scobie has Poundian tricks of style which rely on allusion, rhythm, and language. There is a similar deftness in his versification and his manipulation of language for comic effect: the first three lines of one poem set up a linguistic structure – 'Quote: / From an h'English printer / to an English publisher' – which encourages the reader to continue to misapply the *h* throughout the poem.

An important theme in this book is McAlmon's concept of art, which in its 'abundance' implicitly criticizes views held by William Carlos Williams, by Gertrude Stein, and by Hemingway. McAlmon eventually takes his stand with Pound: 'This was the true abundance / the century aimed for: not the concise / particular image, shining / caged within limits – but Contact / wide as the eagle's eye, uniting / continents and centuries.' Scobie's art, as he tells us in the afterword, is a dialectic between objective fact and subjective interpretation. From those snippets of fact at hand, I would judge this to be the case. Leon Edel in his introduction to Glassco's *Memoirs of Montparnasse* recalls Glassco's 1929 racoon coat, his assumed air of indifference; he quotes McAlmon's remark that Buffy at 18 was 'ironic and disillusioned.' All these references come together in Scobie's portrait of Glassco:

> For Buffy, to be cynical was one
> of the social graces: I envied the ease
> of disillusion worn like a coat
> with impeccable taste.

But they are transformed, just as Edel's recollections of 'the parties of d'antan' found their way into Scobie's own nostalgic conjurings of this world of the last romantics: 'Where are they now, the legendary / drinkers of years gone by?' Their songs are nothing more than 'echoes ... from the dark oak walls.'

> The hell with it. Time passes,
> that's all that happens;
> the body rots a little, and the mind
> fills up with sand. One last
> romantic chorus for you all:
>
> où sont les neiges d'antan, old friends,
> where are the years downtown?

This book is an auspicious introduction to the first publications from Quadrant Editions, a new subscription little press established by Gary Geddes at Concordia University.

This year's poetry brings with it the usual complement of books from established poets: a reissue of Irving Layton's *Love Poems* (McClelland and Stewart, 139, $8.95) and Ralph Gustafson's impressive *Landscape with Rain* (McClelland and Stewart, 109, $8.95). The more experimental poetry, especially the linking of the aural and the pictoral, is to be found in Wayne Clifford's *An Ache in the Ear 1966–1976* (Coach House, 144, $6.80) and Steve McCaffery's *Intimate Distortions: A Displacement of Sappho* (Porcupine's Quill, 96, $40.00, $5.95 paper). Finally, the poetry of 1980 contains a sizable group of collected and selected poems; in addition to those already cited there is the *Collected Poems of Raymond Souster*, vol 1, 1940–55 (Oberon, 323, $21.50, $9.95 paper), and Louis Dudek's selected poems, *Cross-Section: Poems 1940–1980* (Coach House, 93, $7.50). Largely because of the successful Vancouver Poetry Conference in 1979, Talonbooks has published six attractive volumes, all approximately 150 pages and all but one priced at $5.95: George Bowering's *Particular Accidents: Selected Poems*; bill bissett's *Beyond Even Faithful Legends: Selected Poems*, Frank Davey's *The Arches: Selected Poems*; Daphne Marlatt's *Net Work: Selected Writing*; bp Nicol's *As Elected: Selected Writing*; and Fred Wah's *Loki Is Buried at Smoky Creek: Selected Poems*.

The *Collected Poems of Raymond Souster* covers the period from 1940 to 1955. The early Souster has a lyric voice; the self is an instrument played upon by loneliness, the horror of war (especially the horror of broken bodies), and the need for consolation. A typical poem develops an antithesis between pain and consolation, as in the early poem 'The Fond Desire,' which begins with darkness, loneliness, and pain and ends with a cry for consolation: 'let love, let peace, / though unearned, though foreign in these gates, / wing back, surge over this sky with a roar of gladness.' These are clearly the concerns of the British war poets, MacNeice, Spender, and Day Lewis; like these poets, Souster writes documentary, but initially with far less lyric. His poems are honest, often moving, although sometimes over sentimentalized. It is not until after *Cerberus* (1952), published in tandem with Irving Layton and Louis Dudek, that Souster begins to write his more impressive poems: 'The Man Who Found His Son Has Become a Thief' – where the evidence mounts inescapably; 'Study: The Bath' (1954), with its precise, imagistic details; and 'Girl at the Corner of Elizabeth and Dundas' (1955), with its supple colloquial language: 'I'm twenty-one / I ain't / got any time / to waste / You want it / or you don't / Mister / make up your mind.' Contact with the *Origin* group at the beginning of the fifties helped Souster's poetry immensely; he and Dudek in turn were to influence the poets associated with the Vancouver *Tish* movement.

Louis Dudek's view of poetry as expressed in *Cross-Section* is one that strikes a balance between views identified with William Carlos Williams and Wallace Stevens. The first poem, 'Tree Noises,' refers to 'a laughter inaudible / gurgling always under the bark of trees': we are advised – 'Listen sometimes.' What Dudek is often writing about is the 'sounds' we half-perceive and half-perceiving make; that is, poetry that is spontaneously generated, a view associated with the Pound-Williams line, but with the proviso that the poet is always a maker, a view suggestive of Stevens's 'The Idea of Order at Key West.'

Dudek's affinity with Williams, Pound, and the Black Mountain tradition is that his poetry is always poetry prompted by the concrete: 'Artist Life' is an example of the spontaneous as a poetry of enactment:

> How do I live? I live
> now drinking tea
>   (drinking tea!)
>   listening to the finale
>   of the last Quartet,
> that comes to joy, 'the difficult decision'
>   and then suddenly
>   stops.

With many so-called free verse poets the line breaks are chaotic or they employ simple syntactic breaks, but Dudek uses his poetic line in a manner faithful both to the particularities of his own experience and his own nature. In 'The Secret' he emphasizes that such skill is learned: 'Every poet at the beginning / has a lot to learn / of what is all his own / a uniqueness gradually revealed.'

In 'A Torn Record' he remarks that all is flux: 'Nothing that man makes, or believes, is permanent ... What matters always is energy, how you can laugh, / your mouth wide and wonderful against the wind.' In 'Tao,' dedicated to F.R. Scott, he speaks again of the living moment that he perceives in nature and desires in poetry. In the last poem in the volume, 'Fragment of Continuum,' many of these observations are brought together. Poetry, he says, 'is neither feeling, nor thought, / nor the unconscious process ... / Arranging the poem.' Rather it is 'An arrangement / of poetical pieces / (not very poetical) / An order.' If poetry were just experience, then 'better the real thing' –

> But the poem is not the real thing
>   is not made of the real
> It is another thing
>
> 'Variations and inflections of the naked self'
>
> Like nature's doughnut machine
>   making the atoms
>
> The key to identity and order

Dudek is establishing a relatively sophisticated poetic stance. It is not, he seems to say, that the poem merely reflects the poet, but that there is to be found in it a continuum, something in which the fundamental common character of the internal and external worlds can be discerned.

All of the collections of poetry published by Talonbooks are supplied with critical introductions explicating the poetics of the Black Mountain school: fundamental is Charles Olson's concept of 'composition by field,' or the 'proprioceptive.' Warren Tallman, the most VIGOROUS spokesman for the Tish movement, observes that the 'proprioceptive writer sees the surrounding world in the midst of himself as subject – "sensibility within the organism".' George Bowering, introducing Fred Wah's *Loki Is Buried at Smoky Creek: Selected Poems*, suggests that Wah comes closer than other writers of the group in enacting a holistic image of the world. This can be glimpsed in 'Forest,' a poem identified by Bowering as typifying Wah's use of language.

> And we just stood there
> in the Forest
> look at
> everything around us
> looking
> surrounding

The beginning 'And' suggests a process that is continuing. Pauses, between the lines, as distinct responses to the occasion, are registered. First, they 'just stood there,' then a fuller recognition of where they were, 'in the Forest,' with a capital F – appreciation of where they were. Thus, the imperative, 'look,' followed by the particularity which impresses them, of being in the midst of a host – 'around' them, rhyming with 'surrounding' just as 'look' rhymes with 'looking.' There is a Gestalt in those active verbs, in the rhyme and syntactical sequence of 'looking' and 'surrounding.' It is they who are surrounding the Forest, assimilating it, just as, or so it seems to them, the Forest is looking back and surrounding them. There is a certain charm in this close-to-the-ground poetic which aims to recapture primitive wonder; at the same time it is disconcerting to recognize that without the proprioceptive lens 'Forest' is not immediately accessible to the common reader.

Poésie

CAROLINE BAYARD

L'année qui boucle une décennie se veut souvent le lieu d'une rétrospective. C'est la simple logique mathématique qui lui confère ce rôle: besoin de synthèse, exigence analytique globale, on observe le champ, pour mieux le dominer, on traverse du regard l'épaisseur d'une durée pour en extraire les significations et les cassures. C'est moins la chronologie qui importe alors que le sens de l'ensemble. Le tout pour le tout. 1980 confirme la règle. Le point clé-stratégique de la décade c'est le fameux colloque de la Nouvelle Ecriture, tenu à Montréal en février 1980, dont les travaux ont été publiés par *La Nouvelle Barre du jour* le mai suivant. Pourquoi accorder tant d'importance à ce colloque dans ce qui ne devrait être que le survol de la production poétique de l'année? Parce que le colloque a évalué la particulière écriture d'une certaine décennie. Il a regardé en arrière et en avant, se faisant ainsi le pivot d'une pluridimensionalité d'écritures et de lectures. En tant que regard sur une époque, ces réflexions valent d'être examinées en détail.

Certains s'accordent pour situer les débuts de la nouvelle écriture au Québec en 1970 avec la parution dans la presse des 'Dix Propositions du Groupe d'études théoriques.' D'aucuns affirment qu'il ne s'agit que de la théorie qui a suivi la pratique, ou les pratiques déjà courantes ici depuis deux ans. Les théoriciens et les historiens en décideront. Ce qui compte ici et aujourd'hui c'est de voir les rôles que s'est tracée la nouvelle écriture, quelles différenciations elle s'est choisies dans ses fonctions et surtout, quel sens la distance lui confère à présent. En se voulant de la modernité il est indubitable qu'elle a cassé les ponts avec la terre, la femme et la patrie et tourné résolument le dos aux préoccupations des générations précédentes, de l'Hexagone à Parti pris. Mais est-ce à dire qu'en s'éloignant d'une thématique fermement nationaliste et enracinée dans une idéologie sinon marxiste (souvenons-nous du Paul Chamberland de *L'Afficheur hurle*) tout au moins en appelant à des idéaux de justice sociale (Gaston Miron et Michèle Lalonde) la nouvelle écriture s'est voulue a-politique? Non, certes, et tandis que ruissellent de toutes parts les écarts à la norme, le discontinu, l'inintelligible, le non-figuratif ré-introduisent le sujet psychanalytique, le 'ça,' les pulsions. La théorie, comme les textes, valorisent le ludisme, le plaisir, la sensualité. Claude Beausoleil disait qu'ils forcent à se déplacer, à quitter l'établi d'un point de vue, pour se perdre dans la relativité du désir de comprendre ce qui et comment 'ça' arrive: 'je est *un* je. Il est un jeu, tu est un autre.' Du sujet au savant réseau des intertextes qu'il aime poser, collager et confondre, ce nouveau texte tourne vite et fonctionne sur un présupposé de dire plus qu'il ne dit (dixit France Théoret). Il appartient à l'urbanité, à la métropole contemporaine, son enjeu est dans la facticité, la productivité. Il est marrainé par les gratte-ciel en verre, les performances, les films, inscrit aux rainures de la pollution et du bruit. Il ne s'agit pas seulement de dévier, se démarquer, parodier et reproduire mais parfois aussi de manier l'art d'utiliser les restes, les ordures, de recycler, de collager. Ce n'est pas pour rien que Francine Saillant parlera au cours de ce colloque de la ré-organisation des déchets pratiquée par la nouvelle écriture, à l'instar du courant d'art italien, *arte povera* ... Finalement il ne surprendra personne que le discours féministe de la décennie se soit trouvé d'exactes conjonctions théoriques et pratiques avec cette écriture. On pourrait même dire qu'il a investi et débordé son ouverture à la diff-errance, au déploiement, au tabou, à la marginalité – Brossard, Théoret, Yolande Villemaire – autant de noms qui vont et viennent au cours de ces dix années et finalement reviennent en cette année qui nous intéresse.

La première à s'exporter, à publier hors Québec, hors Amérique aura été Nicole Brossard qui, par l'intermédiaire de Flammarion nous apporte *Le Sens apparent* (76). Il y a là des métaphores, des centres nerveux qui méritent d'être retenus. Des récurrences que l'œil saisit au hasard: spirale, cycles, coquillages, ondes, arcs et hélices. Toutes liées au mouvement, certaines à la pellicule, à l'objectif, d'autres au sens fabriqué. L'espace du *Sens apparent* synthétise jusqu'à la perfection cette fameuse modernité de la décade. Les mécanismes langagiers y sont déboutés, deux villes effleurées (New York, Montréal), le texte est un corps exploré, certainement désiré, mais en définitive toujours échappatoire, à jamais, à regret exutoire. Un des mots de passe chers à cet espace temporel fut l'adjectif pluridimensionnel. Il ne nous venait pas de si loin après tout, il avait vu le jour en France avec Julia Kristeva, précisément à l'aube de ces dix ans-là et il nous avait révélé le texte poétique comme un corps résonnant à registres multiples dont chacun des éléments renvoyait à des langues, à des discours absents ou présents. Rien n'est jamais saisissable, uniforme, ni simple. Vertu et talon d'Achille du *Sens apparent* qui précisément joue tant de ces apparences, de ces reflets de surface et de fond qu'oreille et mémoire déchaînent, et dans sa finalité nous laisse grisés par les tentations, les appétits de toutes ces significations. Urbanité, certes, mais fébrilité aussi et épuisement pour le lecteur-lectrice qui veut trop suivre toutes les pistes. Un texte qui ne devrait pas dépayser les Français, auxquels il est offert en primeur, ni bien sûr les Québécois mais qui risque de dérouter le Canada anglais et même – c'est à parier – l'Américaine dont il nous parle: Adrienne Rich qui apparaît et disparaît constamment dans ce livre. Choc de voir un poète surgir dans le corps textuel d'un autre poète. Cela tranche sur la fiction, dédouble l'illusion, et peut-être même détourne encore plus le sens. Mais l'auteur de *Of Woman Born* (1976) démarque une fiction bien différente de celle de la nouvelle écriture, elle ne décolle pas systématiquement du réel: le mimétique, le clair, l'évident sont des pôles de valeur autrement significatifs pour elle. A preuve du contraire l'accueil tiède réservé à son texte par les Québécoises lors de sa récente représentation au Théâtre des femmes. Il est de profondes solidarités idéologiques qui ne passent pas forcément par la même politique textuelle. Avec *Amantes* (109), publié cette fois chez Quinze, Brossard développe encore les rapports entre la fiction et le réel. A la difference qu'ici c'est peut-être moins d'écriture et de production de texte dont il est question que de lecture. Délice de lire l'autre et d'errer au fil des décodages:

> je te dis ma passion de la lecture de toi,
> cachée derrière tes citations.

La nouvelle écriture et/ou le féminisme ne vont pas seulement éclore chez Flammarion ou aux Quinze, car Les Herbes rouges nous apportent cette année une moisson qui vaut un examen attentif. Yolande Villemaire semble avoir suscité l'intérêt d'un large public avec *La Vie en prose* (262, $14.95). Il faut dire tout de suite la vertu quintessentielle de l'auteur, rare de notre temps et encore plus rare dans les cercles féministes: l'humour. Villemaire a une manière imperturbable de déclencher l'hilarité: on hésite, on pouffe, on s'étouffe, on se déchaîne. Jeux de mots et mots pour jouer, mise en boîte de ce moi cocasse et des autres. Il est difficile de résister à cet à-bout-de-souffle railleur qui frôle le pathétique pour plonger à pieds joints dans l'irrésistible ridicule. Si Villemaire nous fait réfléchir, c'est par le biais du rire. Thérapeutique inhabituelle autant que merveilleuse. Madeleine Ouellette-Michalska dit un jour de Yolande qu'elle était la cousine de Jack Kérouac, la sœur de Réjean Ducharme et Michel Tremblay. Logiques parentés.

Il est peut-être un peu injuste de passer de Villemaire à France Théoret. *Nécessairement putain* (l'Herbe rouge, 66) ne détourne pas les sens par le déclénchement de l'hilarité, mais bien plutôt par le caractère évasif de son *je* narratif. C'est une trame qui n'a pas la densité, l'épaisseur de celles de Brossard, ni ce génie à fuser le rire propre à Villemaire. Elle joue tant sur les demi-tons, les fines nuances, les déplacements de focalisation qu'elle exige beaucoup de son lecteur pour finalement ne lui laisser arracher que des bribes, des éclats: elle se prête ludiquement à notre désir d'avoir une histoire, une histoire qui n'arrive jamais, qui est toujours remise à plus tard. C'est son droit mais cette stratégie du fuyant lui fait perdre l'impact que s'arrogent Brossard et Villemaire.

L'on sent cette ré-introduction du narratif, du narratif qui colle plus nettement au réel chez deux autres auteurs des Herbes rouges, Pierre Monette et André Roy. Le premier, avec *Ajustements qu'il faut* (66), son troisième volume chez cette maison d'édition, a une immédiateté surprenante, inattendue, presque choquante après les textes mentionnés ci-dessus. *Ajustements qu'il faut* sont des poèmes pour journées de travail, de routine, d'usure. Des mots qui nous parlent de travail et de corps, de sommeil et de fatigue. De courses à faire, d'épicerie, de métro, d'ancrage dans la ville mais aussi de chaises tirées et de feu de bois. La voix de Monette est à la fois courageuse et attachante. Critiquement consciente aussi. (Voir pour preuve l'avertissement qui clôt le volume, une citation de Brecht sur la situation du poète qui se veut compagnon de lutte du prolétariat mais qui, de par les limites et les faiblesses propres à sa classe, doit toujours être un compagnon à considérer d'un œil critique.) *Le Petit Supplément aux passions* (52) d'André Roy partage l'urbanité des précédents – nous passons de New York à Montréal – mais cette fois c'est le nocturne et ses labyrinthes émotifs qui nous sont contés. Comme Monette, Roy cède aux tentations narratives, au sens de l'histoire à raconter, à l'envie de la suivre surtout à travers les pièges de la nouvelle écriture. Sa poésie est un défi à la pudeur, à la bienséance la plus étroitement traditionnelle:

Je m'attendais aussi à ta queue/un atlas de l'érection.

Et au-delà de ceci, un abandon aux mythes qui ont tenté la culture homosexuelle nord-américaine (John Travolta / le blanc / la nuit / New York / les discothèques). Mais c'est un abandon intense établi dans un dispositif serré, à la trame impétueuse. La métonymie établie entre la passion et les mythes à la mode, entre le désir et le périssable, entre l'amour et le rétro de demain, emporte notre adhésion, notre attention.

Plus jeune ou sans doute et encore douée de moins de métier nous apparaît Suzanne Meloche, auteur des *Aurores fulminantes* (Les Herbes rouges, 42). (Quel titre indicateur de ce tissu d'images à implosion!) Il y a là plus que des promesses mais pas tout à fait encore des certitudes. La mise en page surtout en est médiocre, le texte s'inscrit en colonnes monotonement régulières, sans écarts, espaces blancs ni ruptures. Ce qui manque ici ce ne sont ni le souffle, ni le rythme qui sont attirants et cernent souvent ces curieuses métaphores, mais la stratégie de la page, l'économie des étapes, cette subtile logistique du sens qui fait qu'un auteur établisse son dispositif en fonction des significations à produire. Meloche nous offre d'intéressants croquis mais pas encore de constructions.

Avec Normand de Bellefeuille et *Dans la conversation et la diction des monstres* (Les Herbes rouges, 27) – titre point indicateur de ce qui suivra – les vertus et les vices sont inversés. Il y a là trop de métier, trop de conscience des réflexes, des mécanismes. Les sens sont morts depuis longtemps. C'est décevant car de Bellefeuille triomphe souvent dans l'essai, dans la théorie qui ne cesse d'attaquer le théologique ou, comme il le dit, le sémantique au crayon gras, le sens Dieu-le-Père. (Voir son brillant essai du colloque sur la nouvelle écriture, 'le caca et le lisible,' dans *La Nouvelle Barre du Jour* de mai 1980.) Ce qu'il y a d'attirant chez de Bellefeuille c'est cette obsession de faire la toilette du poétique, cette volonté de décaper, de récurer le langage. Malheureusement *Dans la conversation* est une toilette décevante qui parle de nettoyage sans vraiment le faire, qui bavarde en refusant de nous offrir les fruits de cet insolent mais si désiré travail. Un texte qui promet plus qu'il n'offre.

Peut-on en dire autant de la moisson poétique du Noroît? Pas vraiment. *Un train bulgare* (83) de Francine Déry passe mais laisse beaucoup de traces. Il y a là une riche écriture qui a volé au surréalisme et à l'automatisme le meilleur d'eux-mêmes. Cette traversée d'un pays laissé hors de l'histoire et qui n'a sur des atlas que l'image d'un insignifiant satellite bénéficie évidemment des privilèges de l'insolite, du bizarre, du différent. Mais c'est l'écriture de Déry qui accroche surtout: elle fuse et délie, elle plagie les couleurs et sème les morceaux d'un univers. Un nom à retenir, un nom qu'on ne pourrait se permettre d'oublier.

Le *je* et le lyrisme ne sont pas morts au Québec. A preuve de défi, quoiqu'en écritures dissemblables, *Plaine lune et corps fou* (Noroît, n.p.) de Jean Charlebois et *La Promeneuse et l'oiseau* (Noroît, 86) de Denise Desautels. Le verbe de *Plaine lune* est une parole de mesure qui n'entraîne pas, comme le texte de Déry, mais incite plutôt à une lente réflexion. On pourrait dire que c'est un verbe pour songer, dont les intertextes sont plus méditatifs qu'explosifs, plus pensifs que déclencheurs d'automatisme:

> le commencement du monde approche
> approche approche regarde
> le temps qu'il fait quand il s'allonge
> quand il s'embrume d'explications
>
> (*se reconstruire* hubert je sais
>   soit dit, soit-il)

Les italiques ici se réfèrent à un fragment de la dernière lettre d'Hubert Aquin à sa femme. Troublant et parfait intertexte dans cette longue réflexion sur l'amour et la mort qu'est le volume de Charlebois. Le tracé thématique de *La Promeneuse et l'oiseau* est semblable mais l'écriture en est totalement différente. Prose poétique qui suit le flux de la mémoire, ses va-et-vient, ses associations, ses cassures, ses liés et ses blancs. La promeneuse tâtonne dans le labyrinthe de la mémoire et esquisse le schéma d'un passé, ou de plusieurs. L'oiseau est à la fois aigle et enfant. Oiseau de proie, donc signe de deuil, et enfant pris au piège.

> L'enfant oiseau. Une naissance. Je veux un
> oiseau comme on dit ... une place pour la
> folie le délire ... J'ai un oiseau. Mal
> tombé au mauvais moment. Il aurait fallu une
> île chaude.

Chez Desautels, comme nous le verrons plus tard chez Lili Côté, l'intertexte féministe sous-tend le donné immédiat; les balises familières (Hélène Cixous, Madeleine Gagnon, dans d'autres cas Monique Wittig et Françoise d'Eaubonne) sont présentes et nous aident non pas vraiment à décoder mais plutôt à repérer les isotopies et à nous orienter. L'intertexte est une boussole.

Le Noroît a aussi publié cette année un livre qui a fait couler pas mal d'encre, ainsi que valu à Claude Beausoleil le prix Emile-Nelligan – *Au milieu du corps l'attraction s'insinue* (234). C'est certainement un des sommets de l'écriture de l'auteur, qui travaille les reliefs arides de la modernité depuis bientôt dix ans et joint dans ce dernier volume les tracés – érotisme textuel, subversions lexicales, infractions syntaxiques, urbanité et fiction du rétro (Judy Garland, Marilyn Monroe surtout) – de prédilection de cette écriture-là. Regardons plutôt des bribes de textes:

   06.   une érotique d'avant-garde
          devenir une vie
          (profuser) intentions en probables
          la fiction du collage – forme
   0.10 écriture – nuit – infusion
          nier – moderne – délicatement
          surface ———
          excessif – noir irrationnel

La stylisation poussée à l'extrême de ce qui est devenu le ou les codes de l'avant-garde devient ici inquiétante. Le raffinement en est si quintessentiel qu'il se fait narcissiquement parodique. Texte qui tourne en rond, qui fait le fou, comme dirait Nicole Brossard, mais qui pose aussi – de biais – la vraie question: lorsque la subversion est à l'ordre du jour, combien de temps lui reste-t-il pour prétendre à ce titre?

Telles ne sont pas les préoccupations de l'Hexagone dont une partie de la production semble nostalgiquement tournée vers les années soixante. *Femme souveraine* (52) de Jean Royer en particulier est magnifiquement à la proue de cette époque où la femme était terre et s'écrivait avec une majuscule. Il est troublant de lire Royer en 1981. C'est un poète qui s'est soudainement arrêté dans le grand manège des textes ou peut-être qui tourne avec celui, désuet, des grands chevaux de bois. Après les fusées et satellites chrome et plastique de Beausoleil et compagnie le contraste ne manque pas d'étrangeté. Mais pourquoi pas? Avec Georges Dor et ses *Poèmes et chansons* (67), c'est le retour dans un café-terrasse d'été: il aurait mieux valu les appeler chansons tout court ou ballades, peut-être. Mais l'Hexagone ne nourrit pas forcément la pure nostalgie: *Le Fou solidaire* (66) de Gilbert Langevin n'est ni ballades ni chansons, plutôt une série de courtes pièces dédiées à des couples amis. En nos temps qui ont mis l'épistolaire au rancart, l'art de la dédicace devient troublant, tant c'est la voix de leur destinataire que ces pièces nous renvoient. Echo, jeu de miroir qui fait trembler parfois, tant l'intuition semble juste, voyons à cet effet les quelques vers envoyés à Yolande Villemaire:

Elle ressac à cœur fou
Elle remue l'air et l'onde
Elle en donne d'elle
plus que jamais l'on vit

On décèle la même aptitude à la condensation peut-être même à l'âpre abstraction cette fois-ci, dans *Couleur chair* (L'Hexagone, 92) de Pierre Nepveu. L'écriture de Nepveu est un cas intéressant. Bien sûr elle est issue de la modernité et la ville est son terrain, elle sait jouer les doubles tours de la nouvelle écriture; et pourtant elle n'en *est* pas vraiment. Elle a un autre intertexte, anglo-américain celui-là. T.S. Eliot et Wallace Stevens surtout et d'un tout autre temps. Elle pratique subtilement l'art de la réduction, elle condense le concret en une abstraction, le dépouille, le dénude lentement. Refuges de l'inaptitude à vivre, les mots deviennent des cristaux parfaits mais irréellement schématiques:

> Blessé à vie il se dépense
> dans l'éclat congelé
> d'un présent comestible
> son démon de midi s'alimente
> où restent du voyage les traces mêlées
> de paroles égarées dans les veines

C'est un texte qui nous force à tourner et retourner les mots dans l'espoir d'y guetter une sensation mais qui finalement nous échappe et emporte le vécu, le senti, le sensuel avec lui. Geste à la fois protecteur et jaloux, antithèse de l'imagisme et intellectualisation de l'expérience. En ce sens l'écriture de Nepveu occupe une place unique au Québec.

Unique aussi est le retour de Gatien Lapointe après treize ans de silence. Quête de 'l'originaire alphabet,' par delà le grand intertexte rimbaldien et surréaliste, *Arbre-Radar* (L'Hexagone, 139) célèbre plus que sons ou syntagmes, l'épaisseur des espaces, les odeurs, les touchers:

> dans la corne du fleuve s'entrechoquent
> écalures de braise, vignes qui éclatent
> fauves   outre du tain
> du lointain quoi se fait dévoreux je?
> plaquant l'ocre écorce (bras hanches ventres)
> sens ou courant de sueur, alphabet qui rapatrie
> ...   ô la-bàs la
> puissante matière qui me redonne l'élan
> chair sans tristesse
> machouillant du rêche de friches ou
> des chiques de lichens, roué/troué

C'est un très beau retour à l'écriture et qui, espérons-le, ne sera pas suivi d'une aussi longue absence.

L'Hexagone nous aura aussi donné cette année *De l'œil et de l'écoute*, où vingt années de la vie de Michel van Schendel (1956–76), prix du

Gouverneur général. La voix qui traverse une si longue durée s'impose de par sa force, sa situation au monde, sa continuité aussi. Il y a une certaine étrangeté à l'écouter en terre québécoise car elle *y* est sans *en* être malgré le 'Poème au vent Indien,' malgré le recueil de 'l'Amérique étrangère,' malgré la violente intuition avec laquelle elle déchiffre ce continent:

> Amérique amérique de soufre
> Amérique d'écorce hoquet des hurleries et saxo
>   noir des fous
> Amérique tendue aux quatre clous du vent
> ...
> Amérique concave enfant vieillot manne vaine
> ...
> Amérique abattue abattoir de tes rouilles
> Ivrogne du matin léchant des horizons de pluie
> Terre de futur vague et de rencontre Amérique

Mais l'écriture de van Schendel n'a pas de stricte appartenance, pas plus à une nation qu'à une théorie de l'écriture. Elle évolue, elle se déplace dans l'architecture de ces vingt années et des géographies. Et pourtant elle se cisèle dans l'épaisseur du politique, du ou des sens de l'histoire, des solidarités, des combats. Elle s'en fait l'inscription, elle développe des complicités et plonge dans la grande mêlée de l'histoire majuscule et plurielle: celle des Juifs, des immigrants et des Québécois:

> à la phrase épelant la grammaire des mains
> au peuple silencieux qui guette sa mêlée
> à la grande sidérurgie de la patience
> à la terre noire au moment d'y tendre le brandon
> j'écris le mot québec pour une rose étrange
> alphabet poudreux aux premiers temps du monde
> langage d'os et de pétale morceau d'âme d'agonie

Nulle abstraction détachée des sens ici. Un corps à corps plutôt. C'est un texte qui agrippe et ne laisse pas en paix. Ni émotivement, ni analytiquement.

Quant à la parole de Gaston Miron (si rare et qu'il nous a tant mesurée dans ses livres) c'est dans la revue *Possibles*, au printemps 1980 qu'elle nous arrive. Pour avoir publié les autres avec beaucoup plus de conviction qu'il ne s'est publié lui-même, il nous a trop souvent privé de ses mots. 'Femme sans fin' répare cet état de choses en nous offrant une suite de textes dédiés à Sandrine B. et d'où la voix de cette dernière se juxtapose à celle de Miron, en exergue, citations, conclusion. Le montage est troublant tant l'absence de l'autre se fait présence, palpable dans le texte même, dans les lettres qui s'y pressent. Il y a là aussi évidemment la voix de Miron, qui reste longtemps avec nous, qui est si forte qu'elle se fait inoubliable.

> Je ne sais pas qui tu es, mais *tes pas sont parfois*
> *dans mon âme*, comme un sonar parfois tu me trouves
> et parfois tu me perds

Pour clore la production de l'Hexagone, il convient de jeter un coup d'œil sur l'important volume de Paul Chamberland, *Terre souveraine* (79), paru peu avant le référendum du 20 mai 1980, et qui s'ouvre sur les paroles suivantes:

> J'ai pour matrie la terre et Kebek est mon
> point d'attache à la matrie terrestre.

C'est le travail sur le langage religieux et sur l'idiome politique qui compte ici: définir le cœur de la souveraineté dans ce que Chamberland perçoit comme la dérive apocalyptique de ce monde. Cette définition vaut d'être citée:

> se dire oui à nous-mêmes, nous absoudre et nous exaucer.

Le courage de Chamberland est d'accepter un certain langage politique, celui des partis traditionnels, des pamphlets, des annonces, et de le travailler au corps, de lui faire dire ce qu'il ne savait pas, d'en extraire une analyse, de réfléchir, dans le flux de l'histoire, à la trame qu'il faut en tirer, en sauver. Il est intéressant de voir à quel point il vise à la transcendance de l'exclusif du nationalisme et en même temps croit en sa capacité d'exaucer le meilleur. C'est un livre-pierre d'angle, philosophique et poétique, dont on se souviendra d'ici la fin du siècle.

Leméac, lui, suit des sentiers battus avec *Demain d'hier l'antan* (145) de Gilles des Marchais et *Ellipse en mémoire* (66) de Lili Côté. Surrané et à rebours sont les épithètes que le premier déclenche immédiatement. Compter les pieds et faire sonner les rimes, joindre jasmin et parchemin, glaçons et frimassons, cela a aujourd'hui la bizarre délicatesse de l'anachronique. Gilles des Marchais semble sorti d'un après-midi de Jeux floraux circa 1913. S'il n'est pas dépourvu de charme et encore moins de douceur, il nous communique la vertigineuse certitude d'avoir saisi un horaire des trains de province (Trois-Rivières–Québec) d'avant la Première Guerre mondiale et d'être dûment monté dans le wagon de tête entre un notaire bedonnant et une beauté au chapeau jardin fleuri. A conseiller aux amateurs de sensations étranges. Nationalistes/nouvelle écriture/féministes/amateurs de science fiction, s'abstenir. Lili Côté, elle, est clairement des années 80. Ce qui n'est pas un critère systématique de talent, non plus que son obtention d'un prix au titre suranné, le prix Octave-Crémazie. Autre contraste amusant quand on ouvre le livre puisqu'on y trouve une écriture ancrée à la contemporanéité:

> révoltes aphones
> je traverse d'un trait l'histoire masculine
>
> rompre au terme le propre du mot
>
> et recommencer au corps le langage au vol
>
> la femme tient de l'oiseau

Ellipse en mémoire a la certitude d'une déjà puissante et sûre écriture. Il y a là une vision, une perception qui n'a pas trompé le jury du prix. C'est un nom que nous reverrons sûrement.

Naaman aussi nous amène quelques voix qui resteront dans nos mémoires. A retenir surtout *Les Voix closes* de Maurice Jacques, poète d'origine haïtienne qui a déjà publié trois pièces de théâtre et un autre volume de poésie et qui ne se laisse pas oublier. Un verbe simple, parfois percutant, toujours sobre, qui donne envie d'en lire et d'en savoir davantage.

> danser pour enterrer nos morts
> chanter en pleurant
> parce que
> vivre près du soleil
> loin de nous autres
> très loin du pain et du miel
> parce que
> glaner le tiers
> la planète tourne lointaine et nuageuse
> glaner le tiers

D'autres volumes aussi: *La Saison des papillons* (Naaman, 71) de Jocelyne Villeneuve, tentative d'adaptation du *haïkaï* à notre langue, une tentative pas entièrement convaincante qui laisse percevoir la traduction, l'effort, l'écart qui sépare deux univers linguistiques et n'arrive pas vraiment à se faire pont. Et aussi *Mon pays éventré* (Naaman, 59) d'Alexandre Namian, poésie d'un apatride qui écrit dans 'l'Amérique du doute' d'immigrants, d'anarchistes, d'exilés et de Juifs avec des accents qui émeuvent, dans une langue qui demanderait à se travailler davantage, à nettoyer des angles. Mais il ne faut pas en oublier l'émotion.

Un autre niveau émotif, un autre registre de sensations puissantes nous arrive de chez VLB éditeur, en collaboration avec les Editions Parti pris, en le personne des *Œuvres poétiques complètes* (336) de Denis Vanier (1965-79), une autre rétrospective de 1980, et qui s'imposait du reste après quinze années de travail. Vanier dérange, dans tous les sens du terme. Si l'on veut se rassurer on peut le qualifier – comme le fait André Bourassa – de surréaliste. On peut essayer de trouver toutes les épithètes logiques de l'ordre et de la raison pour calmer cette déraison qui se veut si systématique qu'elle enrage autant qu'épuise. Il y aurait beaucoup à dire sur ce voyou et voyant (Bourassa encore) qui voulait pratiquer l'intrusion forcée des abattoirs de l'ordre pour l'illumination et la suprême conjonction avec l'au-delà! On peut se demander – et d'autres l'ont fait – si ces textes représentent vraiment une transgression et non l'exact envers des produits du système qu'il affirme débouter. Le temps et la place manquent ici pour faire leur juste part à ces questions; qu'il suffise de dire que Vanier n'a pas fini de nous départager et qu'il s'agit là d'une importante et nécessaire rétrospective.

Maternative (158) de Louky Bersianik est l'autre volume produit cette année par VLB. Nous y retrouvons Ancyl, sœur-compagne-chercheuse de *L'Euguélionne* et du *Pique-Nique sur l'Acropole*: Poésie ou prose ... les parois différentielles sont minimes, c'est toujours la même voix, celle qui tente l'immense pari d'écrire la symbolique des femmes, territoire dont elle les voit dépourvues, ou plutôt dépossédées par l'histoire et le pouvoir masculins. L'écriture de Bersianik est une coupe à travers l'utopique des mythes (il n'étonne personne que son prochain volume soit intitulé 'l'archéologie du futur'), discours qui joue de l'impossible, du contradictoire, du non-dit, du tabou et tente, magistralement, d'esquisser le début de la symbolique féminine. A noter ici une vertu rare sous tous les cieux, l'humour. Très différent de celui de Villemaire, plus nettement accroché au signifié, à l'ordre sémantique qu'au fonctionnement du signifiant, mais présent dans les courtes scènes du 'Jazz des nébuleuses.'

Il serait impossible d'omettre de ce survol critique les deux tomes d'un des météores de la poésie québécoise, Paul-Marie Lapointe. *Ecritures* (L'Obsidienne, 836) – décade oblige – nous place dans une perspective rétrospectiste et nous fait nous souvenir du point d'origine de la trajectoire: *Le Vierge incendié*. Les points de référence sont les mêmes, folles associations, jointures illogiques: les choix surréalistes et les déterminations automatistes, la désinvolture brutale, hasards phonétiques, phonologiques, lexicaux.

La lecture psychanalytique aurait là un terrain de prédilection. Les deux volumes d'*Ecritures* avaient été précédés d'un texte théorique, 'Histoire d'écrire,' publié dans *La Nouvelle Barre du jour*, trois ans auparavant. Il est clair à présent que ces réflexions annonçaient un texte à venir, en préparaient le balisage:

les mots ne sont plus les messages soumis qui désirent, le message livré, reprendre leur place propre dans l'ordre des choses ... les mots ne traduisent pas le monde extérieur ... écrire dans l'écriture, sans autre référent au monde que les mots. Le poème dé- parle, parle seul.

On peut être de la nouvelle écriture sans signer des manifestes ou prêter sa présence à ses colloques. L'appartenance de Lapointe à cette recherche, à ce travail en corps à corps avec les mots est explicite dans ses écrits. Nouveaux pour lui sont ces explorations du concrétisme, ces échafaudages et épaisseurs de mots, qui s'entrecroisent, s'agglomèrent et se détachent dans la joie spatiale de la page. Ils démontrent une ouverture, chez cet auteur qui a dépassé la cinquantaine, à tous les possibles verbaux, l'acquisition d'une jubilation typographique et visuelle absente du *Vierge incendié* ou du *Réel absolu*. *Ecritures* est un monument d'hiéroglyphes, de mythes qui ont éclaté en idiomes pluriels et sèment les murs de l'histoire. C'est un livre que les rescapés d'une Apocalypse aimeraient récupérer parmi les décombres, pour le déchiffrer et se souvenir des fragments de leur civilisation disparue.

Si l'on cherche des écrits théoriques autant que de la pratique poétique, c'est du coté des Forges qu'il faut regarder cette année. Pour commencer par la pratique, il faut se pencher sur *Ici la parole jusqu'à mes yeux* (65, $3.50) de Pierre Desruisseaux, un volume qui échappe à l'actualité, aux modes, à la vogue de ce qui se fait – ou ne se fait plus. Economes, laconiques jusqu'à la simplicité schématique du minimal, ses mots se détachent petits dans l'immensité de toute une blanche:

Pourtant la pierre
cette maison
qui porte ton nom comme
avant la parole

Desruisseaux condense, synthétise les sensations sans effort apparent. Son verbe est l'envers du bavardage, du défoulement, du recyclage. Le ciseleur et le tailleur de pierre y sont à l'œuvre:

Je pense à toi tu es un lac

plus rien désormais
ne viendra déranger la quiétude
que le chant des oiseaux
ou le bruit d'une pierre qui dévale la montagne.

Une voix très différente nous parvient avec *Les Feuillets embryonnaires* (Editions des Forges, 65, $3.50) de Jocelyne Felx, lignes qui retracent une gestation et une naissance – sujet qui a jusqu'à présent moins inspiré les féministes que Dieu, le mythologique ou la subversion. Indubitablement c'est un verbe qui est exigeant, souvent difficile, lové à tel point sur lui-même qu'il fait regretter les distances entre le texte et le soi que certaines écrivaines réussissent à démarquer. Pourtant le territoire qu'il découpe n'a été que peu sémantiquement exploré jusqu'alors, surtout en poésie où *L'Amer* (1978) de Brossard est un premier jalon, mais plus idéologique que perceptuel, plus théorique que sensuel. C'est cette seconde qualité qui appartient à Jocelyne Felx et qui prête à ses mots un poids et un relief particuliers:

> Là-bas l'enfant du ventre rit encore avec les
> Muppets de jolie bure amniotique. Leurs
> imperméables burent la pluie de l'intérieur
> et du lointain contrepoids de l'astre qui l'a
> provoquée détentrice déjà de son capital
> d'érotisme. Il rit et son cœur bat quand
> un grand Tarzan poursuit quelque crocodile
> dans les indispositions de mon sensible estomac
> qui le surplombe et ses rencontres concertées
> comme des figures de danse.

Du point de vue théorique, deux volumes, toujours aux Forges, appellent notre attention sur les processus de lecture et d'écriture. *Simulacre dictatoriel* (70, $3.50) d'Yves Boisvert et *Tête de lecture* (76, $3.50) de Bernard Pozier. Le premier reprend les arguments de la lecture-performance, de la lecture-participatoire, rien de terriblement nouveau depuis *L'Œuvre ouverte* d'Eco. *Tête de lecture* est plus provocante et – corollaire attendu – plus hermétique. Pourtant il y a là des intuitions sur trente ans d'écriture qui nous font respecter le jugement de leur auteur. En commentant les textes de l'amour et du pays (récupéré ce dernier par les politiciens) et sur le formalisme, qui 'bâillerait ses derniers points de suspension,' en cette année où la boussole marque le 80, Pozier conclut qu'il n'y a plus ou qu'il n'y a pas de nouvelle écriture mais seulement un mur de briques, échafaudé lentement, qui nous empêche de voir la grande tour de Babel de tous les textes. Intuition décapante.

Qu'est-ce que le pan de la tour révèle à nos yeux en 1980? Au-delà de la mort du pays et de l'amour, par dessus les convulsions de la nouvelle écriture et les audaces d'une sexualité qui aime les mots, une poésie qui vit, survit aux vogues et se vrille vivace dans ce pays qui ne s'est pas encore – en cette année-là – voulu nation.

Drama

RONALD HUEBERT

As everybody knows, though nobody says it publicly nowadays, there has never been a female playwright of the first rank. Try to imagine the English novel without Jane Austen, the Brontës, George Eliot, and Virginia Woolf. Ridiculous indeed. And poetry too would be impoverished, though not as drastically, without Christina Rossetti, Emily Dickinson, Denise Levertov, or Marianne Moore. Now try to imagine English drama without ... Susanna Centlivre? The exercise is worthwhile, if only as a way of understanding what it means when two of the more promising new playwrights in this country turn out to be women.

Circus Gothic by Jan Kudelka (Playwrights Canada, $3.50) is a one-woman show. An experienced performer in productions ranging from *Hair* to *18 Wheels*, the playwright herself created the 22 roles of her script in productions at Theatre Passe Muraille and the Manitoba Theatre Centre in 1979. Beginning as the Narrator/Ringmaster, the performer paints and mimes her way through six comic masks, until at last she is ready to attach her nose. Now she has become Corky, the Clown. She has also introduced us to a set of simple conventions which we shall need to honour if we are to absorb the rest of the play.

Having given us the clues to her theatrical shorthand, the performer is now in a position to create more complicated scenes by using similar techniques. Whenever she puts on a cowboy hat, she becomes Johnny Frazier, the circus manager:

When you juggle with him ...
you always end up holding
the blade end of the knife.

Or, when she puts on a yellow satin shirt and cape, she is Eddie Rawls, the 28-year-old tightrope walker and Vietnam veteran who believes he is the jinx of the circus. With the help of a grey overcoat she becomes Elly the Elephant:

Hmmmm Hot
Hmmmm Humans
Humans milling about my kneecaps,
their frail bones
sounding boards
for shrill voices.
Their sounds bruise me.

Inside my hide is a cavern of silence.
Between my bones one sound reverberates
for a century.
In the space between my footsteps
empires rise and fall.

By frankly adopting an unrealistic technique the performer convinces us that a talking elephant is the most natural thing in the world. These are genuinely imaginative lines, in both a poetic and a theatrical sense. Simultaneously, they look inward to reveal a 'cavern' that we would not have sensed without them, and they reach outward as well to define the special 'empire' in which the clown is king.

The undisputed emotional climax of *Circus Gothic* is the story of Big Bob, 'Bosscanvasman of the Loyal Brothers Circus,' identified whenever he appears by a red baseball cap. Big Bob left his wife, his kids, and his job as a steelworker in Kentucky for the heroism of pitching and unpitching canvas. 'I remember,' says the Narrator, 'what an art Big Bob made of it.' Steve Raeburn, Big Bob's eldest son by a previous marriage, works alongside his dad as a roustabout. Miss Virginia, the English actress turned trapeze artist, falls in love with Big Bob and becomes his lady. For one night only, this whole extravagant family is on display in Minto, New Brunswick. It rains. The electric generator fails. There is a riot. In the crackdown after the disaster Steve Raeburn 'reaches up to grab / the last lightning bar' and '1500 volts wraps itself about his fist / and grows up his arm.' Enter Big Bob to the rescue.

Big Bob moves, clumsy for once
now across the sandlot he runs
beergut bouncing
under a T-shirt
dark green work pants sagging in the ass.

While trying to knock Steve free, Big Bob touches him, 'falls on top of his son,' and dies instantly.

Circus Gothic is a splendid script for an actor with enough daring, skill, stamina, and creativity to perform it well. I suspect that Kudelka is such an actor herself, but I am also convinced that few other players will be able to revive her play. This is true in part because of her biographical advantages: the play is quite openly 'based on her experiences as a student clown with a traditional American circus which toured the Maritimes in 1974.' But the script is also unusually demanding because of its style. One performer has to be, by turns, a car salesman, an unemployed miner, a trapeze artist, an elephant, Bosscanvasman, circus manager, clown. The techniques Kudelka uses for accomplishing these transformations are loosely the same as those James Reaney used in *The Donnellys*: music, mime, costume fragments, and above all poetry. Not poetry in any weak-kneed sense of that word, but the imagery of living language supercharged with the vital electricity of theatre. I take it as a positive sign indeed that Kudelka has learned from Reaney's example without for a moment being a mere imitator. That is what can happen when the playwright sees his or her work as part of a culture far too healthy to be mummified as tradition.

With her fourth play, *Automatic Pilot* (Playwrights Canada, $3.50), Erika Ritter won the Chalmers Award for 1980. In a sense this too is a one-woman show, though the cast includes three supporting male actors; and this play too is based on the author's personal experience, this time 'as a stand-up comic.'

The one woman is named, with a touch of ambiguity, Charlie. A touch did I say? No, Charlie's name is virtually an announcement that this is a play about sexual roles. Turned out in her Annie Hall costume and grasping the mike at her local nightclub (The Canada Goose), Charlie is every inch a professional. She is funny, and she is in control. But in her private world, unprotected by clothing or custom, she becomes slavishly vulnerable to her need for men. And she chooses her men with a flawless instinct for frustration. Now thirty years old, she is separated from her husband, Alan. Alan Merritt the actor, that is, pathologically dishonest, chronically out of work, socially devious, and gay. She is seduced, bedazzled, and betrayed by Nick Bolton, the ambitious motion-picture executive who sleeps with all the girls but gives himself to none. And at last she is passed on to Nick's younger brother, Gene, age 23, law-school dropout, Hudson's Bay salesclerk, and aspiring novelist.

This trio of male stereotypes allows Ritter to dish out an amusing meal of feminist revenge. Nick is by far the stupidest and most cruel of the three men, so nobody minds when Charlie deflates him. On the morning after their first night together Nick tries to compliment her on the success of her comic routine:

NICK How do you think that stuff up?
CHARLIE Well ... I just lie there, and it comes to me ...

Charlie's 'late husband,' Alan, is just as roundly punished; he is the butt of a series of anti-homosexual jokes that no male writer today could dream of putting into print. And poor Gene is just a babe in arms compared with his jaded patrona. He falls in love with her, moves into her apartment, wears her aprons, cooks her soufflés, tolerates her infidelities, and leaves when she no longer needs him.

If the hollowness of her male manikins is Ritter's gravest artistic fault, her biggest technical error is the starring role she gives to Bell Canada.

Imagine all the wonderful things an alienated single woman in apartment city can accomplish through the impersonal medium of the telephone. She can place a long-distance call to her estranged homosexual husband in Stratford. She can unplug the jack when she's depressed and wants to get drunk by herself. She can forget to plug it back in when she's still depressed but wants her lover to call. She can overhear her estranged husband making a rendezvous with his gay boyfriend. And there are further combinations, limited only by the number of extensions which the theatre can supply. Still, a playwright who relies so heavily on the telephone for conducting the social life and revealing the emotional self of her protagonist must be suffering from poverty of theatrical inventiveness.

Somehow, I should emphatically add, the character of Charlie surmounts her environment. Hers is a magnificently actable part: witty, tender, flamboyant, defensive, always the centre of attention, yet always alone. Well acted, this part should guarantee not only a very funny performance but a moving one as well. None the less, I think Ritter is at her best, not when she's providing Charlie with polished one-liners (as she frequently does), but when she has Gene sit down at his desk to write his novel. Gene composes by reading into a tape recorder:

> It came as a surprise to him that this was what being in love felt like. He'd imagined the feeling many times, of course, and it had been different. Better circumstances, more exotic locations, a different kind of woman. For he wasn't so caught up in emotion that he couldn't admit that to himself. He'd simply never expected to fall, when he fell, for a woman like her. She was taller than what he'd had in mind, she smoked too much, and she was absolutely nothing like Jane Fonda. And she was older than he was. Most of all, she was older. And while it was nice to be around someone imbued with the kind of wisdom that only comes with age – like knowing all the lyrics to old Everly Brothers songs, and understanding more than he would ever know about how to fold a fitted sheet – while it was nice to have a shortcut to that kind of knowledge, it was also true that she'd had more time to accumulate bad memories.

This passage is enough to convince me that Erika Ritter is already a very fine writer. Furthermore, there is evidence here of a deeply dramatic imagination at work: the kind of imagination which can see the world through *someone else's* eyes, and find the words which allow that otherness to express itself. I am not saying that Ritter should abandon the theatre to complete Eugene Bolton's novel for him. But I am saying that she is a better writer with a richer imagination than one might guess from her achievements as a playwright thus far.

Against a social backdrop which includes the Québec referendum, the constitution debate, and the issue of language rights, two recent plays read like experiments in biculturalism. Both plays are set in Montréal, and both are winners of major awards. David Fennario's *Balconville* (Talonbooks, $4.95), commissioned by and premiered at Centaur Theatre, won the Chalmers Award for 1979. *Aléola* (Talonbooks, $4.95), the first play by Québec playwright Gaëtan Charlebois, opened at McGill University in 1977, won the Clifford E. Lee Award in 1978, was revived in Edmonton and Minneapolis in 1979, and was at last brought back to Montréal in a French production at the Théâtre du Rideau vert in 1980.

As the work of a beginning playwright *Aléola* does have its merits. But it is a sentimental play, as indeed one might expect from a very young dramatist who begins his career in the genre known as geriatric melodrama. This is a play about an old couple (Barné, aged 72; Kitoune, aged 68) who share a crumbling apartment in the '*McGill student ghetto*,' a marriage which has lasted for fifty-three years, eight children who have left for the anglophone world of Toronto, and above all a nostalgic reverence for the past.

At the outset Charlebois is rather too eager to establish that Barné and Kitoune have reached the enduring splendour of a perfect relationship: a mixture of warmth, understanding, acceptance, trust, humour, and untarnished love. They spend a day celebrating their wedding anniversary; the mood is marred only by the neglect of their selfish children. That evening, Kitoune awakes and reports a savage nightmare in garish detail. After comforting his wife and putting her back to bed, Barné adds a strong dash of poison to the decanter of wine. The next morning the two of them embrace for the last time; they drink the wine as a prelude to the *Liebestod* which concludes the play.

This harsh summary does not do justice to the gentleness of the emotional effects which Charlebois can often achieve. Among the best of these moments is the one in which Kitoune reports her dream:

> Please, laugh when you can. Your stomach rumbling makes me warm. Makes me feel protected. *She pauses.* I got dressed quickly. Oh yes, very quickly. I slept ten minutes more after the clock. I go out to the chicken house. Time to feed the chickens ... Feed them all. And there's the dog. The one we love. A handsome bitch with brown fur. Buséphale! The beauty. The one who listened. The one who always jumped at us with devotion. *She remembers the dog lovingly.* Buséphale! And every morning Buséphale would run for the cats who were in the field across the road.

Here, and indeed in much of their dialogue, this couple is quite believable, especially when they feel drawn back to the rich rural past which fails to compensate for the constricted urban present. At its best the mood of the play resembles the pathos created by Gabrielle Roy in *The Road Past Altamont*.

What Charlebois lacks, however, is Roy's restraint, finesse, and infinitely patient understatement when dealing with subjects so dangerously close to the sentimental. And, as a dramatist, he has not yet learned to distinguish between what his characters feel and what they can be allowed to say about their feelings. For example, he has Barné explain to his wife why he forbids her to converse in her mother tongue:

> French is the language of the earth. Of the good soil in my hand. Of the farm. When we moved out of the farm and into the city, this big English city with the French name, we lost the right to speak French. We must never dirty the French we speak with asphalt and concrete.

I have no doubt that this is exactly what a sensitive man in Barné's position would feel. But I am equally certain that he would never express his feelings in this way. Before long Charlebois may well be skilful enough to permit his characters to reveal themselves without making explanations. If he accepts the discipline which the playwright's craft imposes, he should be able to progress beyond the sentimentality of *Aléola*.

Barné's linguistic instincts are of course a clever theatrical technique: they give the playwright the freedom he needs to write an English play about a French-Canadian couple using only miscellaneous fragments of French. David Fennario invokes no such prohibition, and I suspect he would not want to. The often amusing amalgam of languages in *Balconville* is one of Fennario's devices for defining the social context of his play: namely, the working-class wilderness of Pointe Saint-Charles.

The setting for *Balconville* is the upper and lower balconies of a tenement house, not far, one assumes, from the tavern which enclosed *Nothing to Lose* or the dress factory which served as the habitat for *On the Job*. The people who converse, complain, drink, and quarrel on this double balcony are ordinary in the attractive sense of the word. Claude Paquette – fat, forty-ish, and French – has lost his ideals, his faith in the future, and the respect of his teenage daughter. Cécile, his wife, emerges from every domestic crisis with the firm conviction that the best thing she can do is to water her plants. Muriel Williams, still hoping vaguely that her husband will return to her section of the balcony, spends most of her energies trying to supervise the life of her teenage son. Johnny and Irene Regan, in their mid-thirties, are mournfully aware that life is no longer what it used to be. In his youth Johnny played lead guitar for 'J.R. and the Falling Stars'; now he is resentfully dependent on what Irene can earn as a waitress and what he can get from the UIC. Irene explains her predicament to Muriel with a shrug: 'Oh, well, ya know how it is? Ya marry a prince and he turns into a frog.' This pattern of disappointment is the one experience which makes Fennario's collection of characters more than an assortment: which defines them, in fact, as a community.

Balconville is by far the best of Fennario's plays to date. His ability to create atmosphere by using simple touches of setting or dialogue is rapidly improving. In support of this claim one could cite the broken step on the stairway which connects the two balconies, or Thibault's position on bilingualism: 'Oui, and me too. I don't speak the English since last week. Maybe a few times, but that's all.'

Still, *Balconville* is a static play because the characters do nothing beyond creating the atmosphere. The only events are imposed by external forces. Paquette, after grumbling for years about his mechanical job, is crestfallen when he loses it because the company is moving its plant to Taiwan. Everyone shares Paquette's dejection, except his daughter Diane. 'Je vais m'en trouver une job, moi,' she announces. 'C'est facile. Ils ont toujours besoin de waitress cute.' The final event is a fire which rages out of control, offstage, while the *Balconville* community unites in order to salvage the goods and chattels which have arranged themselves in the few private corners of their disappointed lives. Even the title of the play signifies the embittered passivity of its characters. Ask any of them where they are going this summer and the reply will be, 'Moi? Balconville.' In any language this is the fatalism of people who no longer believe that their world will change.

Both of George F. Walker's new plays are concerned with the brutality of what normally passes for civilized language. *Gossip* (Playwrights Canada, $3.50) is ostensibly a murder mystery: we witness a crime in the opening scene, and the rest of the play consists of a pleasantly bizarre parade of suspicions and evasions. Our private eye is Tyrone Power, nihilist and investigative reporter. During the dinner-party scene which concludes the action, virtually every character is exposed as a hypocrite, a psychopath, and a criminal. If the official language of *Gossip* is a destructive social ritual, in *Rumours of Our Death* (CTR, 25, $3.50) it is the belligerent anaesthetic of propaganda. The most eloquent character in *Rumours* is the King, who appears frequently '*on the terrace*' to address the docile inhabitants of his nation. 'You see,' says the King, 'the national disease of talking to yourself has passed ... This is bound to have a positive effect in the long run. However, in the meantime, because things are worse than ever in the areas of finance and political stability, I have been forced to sell our country to foreign interests, with an option to re-buy when things get better.' Among the policies which the King announces are the suspension of all civil liberties, a taxation programme to generate a ransom fund for his kidnapped daughter, and the conversion of the ransom fund into 'a national endowment for the arts.' Is the King a machine, or is he human after all? Will he follow his father's example and turn himself into a tree? Is there really a new bomb which kills nobody but evaporates the entire water supply? Or are all of the above merely rumours? As usual, Walker has the last laugh in the final speech of the play: 'No one wants to know.'

Walker seems not to have progressed beyond the level he achieved in

Three Plays and *Zastrozzi*, reviewed here two years ago (48:4 [1979], 366–70). His new plays again have plenty of clever lines, like the description which Margaret (in *Gossip*) gives of a party at the Danish embassy: 'An odd evening. All these healthy-looking Scandinavians walking around looking so chipper then disappearing into the bathroom to slit their wrists.' But clever lines are a talent, not a virtue; by themselves they are not enough. What remains disappointing is Walker's indifference to the management of plot. In *Gossip* there are far too many events, especially offstage events, and the connections between them are not only complicated but adventitious. The spectator may feel cheated when he discovers, long after it matters, that the real motive is revenge. And in *Rumours* there is only the episodic plot which depends on the whims of the King and the counter-whims of the foreign terrorists. *Zastrozzi* must still be regarded as Walker's best play, because in this instance he discovered a story which could be readily turned into a plot. There's nothing dishonest about such a procedure, or if there is, Shakespeare didn't let it bother him. Walker could be a better playwright if he paid less attention to the modern obsession with theme, which in any case is none of the playwright's business, and worried more about the disposition of plot, which is.

A self-conscious absorption in the craft of theatre is the direction which David French has taken in *Jitters* (Talonbooks, $4.95). This is by now a well-travelled road, and not one which every playwright should choose. *Jitters* is a 'rehearsal' play: that is, the characters in the cast of French's play are all engaged in rehearsing a play-within-the-play, *The Care and Treatment of Roses* by Robert Ross. The actors keep up a tolerably amusing patter of theatrical small-talk, most of it quite stereotypical. The make-believe author is a meddlesome figure whose literal-minded integrity seems oddly out of place among the fopperies and vanities of the greenroom. Even worse, the director of *The Care and Treatment of Roses* is an unimaginative wimp whose notion of an opening-night ultimatum is to shout, 'We're not cancelling the show unless the actors want to. Is that understood?' *Jitters* contains a series of what I take to be satiric references to national stagefright in the theatrical community at large: we're afraid of testing ourselves in New York, but at the same time we don't believe in homegrown success. Unfortunately, this play is simply not good enough to inspire the confidence which its author claims we lack.

A year ago in these pages I outlined the dimensions of the dramatic world – a world of crime, violence, heroin, pimps and prostitutes – created by Tom Walmsley in *The Jones Boy* (49:4 [1980], 375–6). Walmsley's first full-length play, *Something Red* (Virgo Press, $4.95), again exploits his favourite obsessions, but in ways that require further critical treatment. Indeed, *Something Red* is a play which will shock its readers by challenging many of their assumptions, not only about Canadian drama, but about the dramatic experience itself, and especially about the relationship between the playwright and his audience.

Walmsley is more ambitious in *Something Red* than in his previous work: he has expanded his dramatic scope beyond a single act, and he has correspondingly enlarged the social context of the action. Only one of the four characters – Bobby – is an outlaw. Fully committed to the values of the street, and rigorously contemptuous of any compromise with straight society, Bobby seems to be what remains of *The Jones Boy* after five years. But in his thirties Bobby can no longer be the youthful rebel. And because he has a criminal record, because he has unpaid debts in the underworld, Bobby is afraid to leave the sanctuary of his apartment. He is a prisoner now, trapped by his past and his paranoia, supported entirely by the indulgence of his girlfriend (Christine) and the loyalty of his best friend (Alex).

Both Christine and Alex are in the process of making the transition from the distorted idealism of Bobby's world to the diluted pragmatism of ordinary life. Significantly, Bobby first met Christine when she was working in a massage parlour ('Eve's'); now she has a more mundane job which pays just enough to support both of them. Alex, Bobby's old partner in his period as a biker and hit-man, now spends his days at a regular job in a textile factory and his evenings working on an autobiographical novel. Though entirely dependent on them, Bobby feels betrayed by both Christine and Alex. He mentions their 'normal' activities, their connections with the straight world, only with derisive irony or dismissive hostility.

The fourth character, Elizabeth, is the most radical innovation. A university graduate, in fact an MA student, Elizabeth lives with Alex in the apartment directly above Bobby's domestic prison. In Act I, while Alex and Elizabeth pay a Friday evening visit to Bobby and Christine, we observe in Elizabeth's behaviour the indelible marks of her cultural superiority. Even her casual remarks are witty, precise, and articulate. When the two couples sit down to play Scrabble, Elizabeth at once outshines her opponents. Her very first word is the source of controversy:

ELIZABETH Brace yourselves, everyone. (*Puts down letters*)
BOBBY What kind of fucking word is that?
ELIZABETH Dotage, darling. It means senility.
BOBBY Well I never heard of it.

Elizabeth is not trying to establish her superiority. But, by the standards of literate culture, she simply *is* superior, and the difference will always show.

If anything, Elizabeth is uneasy about the privileges conferred upon her by training and talent. After Bobby and Alex have exchanged anecdotes about their dope-dealing past, Elizabeth feels socially deficient: 'I'm afraid my adventures would sound somewhat pale by comparison.' Elizabeth wants desperately to belong; she is fascinated by the violence from which she has been sheltered. And she uses her verbal inventiveness to upstage the men even at their own game of swapping vulgarities.

Alex is deeply in love with Elizabeth. He approves of her superiority, not only because she carries it gracefully, but because it endorses his own aspirations. (Why write a novel anyway unless you have a girlfriend capable of reading it?) But for Bobby Elizabeth's alien values are intolerable; instinctively he hates her for what she represents. 'I'm glad all that education's good for something,' he remarks when she confesses that she's a winner at Scrabble. Thus, the central conflict of the play is in part the result of a clash between two social worlds. Elizabeth, like Strindberg's Miss Julie, is a superbly confident woman within her own system of values, but an innocent when she steps into an unfamiliar world. Bobby, like Strindberg's Jean, recognizes vulnerability as surely as if it were the taste of blood. He seduces her, initiates her into a fantasy world of sado-masochistic sexual violence, and finally kills her.

I have already said enough to imply that I admire the perverse vitality of *Something Red*. But I must add at once that this is a deeply flawed play: Walmsley can be a clumsy craftsman and an emotional extortionist. The carpentry is especially bad near the end of Act I, after Elizabeth has told Alex of her affair with Bobby. Alex returns to Bobby's apartment, attacks him physically, explains the reason for this assault, and then exits threatening to kill Bobby. This episode is awkward in itself, and it is even less palatable once we discover that most of Act II will be concerned with the protracted rivalry between the two men.

Indeed, it is in this admittedly powerful antagonism that Walmsley exploits our emotions unfairly. Most of the second act is an extended game of Russian roulette. Bobby loads his gun with '*a single bullet*' and, after spinning the cylinder, hands the gun to Alex with a challenge: 'I'll make a deal with you. You pull the trigger, and if that's where the bullet is, I'm dead.' But instead of obeying instructions, Alex points the barrel at his own temple and pulls the trigger. Click. The game is on, and with each subsequent click the probabilities escalate. Finally, when Bobby fires the sixth shot, there is another click. The rules of the game have changed, and we realize that Bobby (like Joey in *St. Urbain's Horseman*) is only a tin soldier after all. 'Maybe the bullets are duds. Maybe the firing pin's broken. I don't know enough about guns.'

Walmsley cannot be faulted simply for using the same technique that most of us were willing to accept in *The Deerhunter* (1979), and he certainly can't be accused of borrowing it, since *Something Red* was initially staged at Vancouver's New Play Centre in October of 1978. But a device which works in a movie, however grotesquely, does not necessarily work on stage. There are a number of reasons for this. First, the spectators in a theatre know in advance that the bullet will not be discharged. In this case, no scene in live theatre could simulate either what the imagination requires or what the movie industry can easily supply. So, armed with disbelief, the spectators can't really participate in the game of chance. What they fear is not the sight of either man losing the game, but the deafening roar which turns any small theatre into an echo chamber when a fake bullet is discharged. This doesn't happen in *Something Red*, though the irrelevant expectation that it might is enough to confuse our already complicated responses to the play.

And the spectators' emotional responses, no matter how elusive or subjective they may be, are without question the key to the special merits of *Something Red*. I don't think anyone will express indifference after reading this play or seeing it performed. Hostility, curiosity, repugnance, fascination, yes. But not indifference. Both the potency and the ambivalence of these responses are the direct result of Walmsley's unquestionable skill in creating the character of Bobby. Here is a man who is vulgar, dishonest, belligerent, cruel, perverse, tyrannical, and self-indulgent. And, like Mr Dedalus in *A Portrait of the Artist*, he is 'at present a praiser of his own past.' Still, Bobby dominates the play just as surely as Jimmy Porter dominates *Look Back in Anger*. Bobby gains his hold over us in the same way that he gains control over the other characters: that is, largely through his insane commitment to an emotional absolute so intense that we must either censor it or be destroyed by it. In Bobby's own language this is called going the whole hog. He explains his notion of commitment to Elizabeth in terms that make it not only acceptable but appealing. 'You got to have one thing that makes everything else look like shit. That's how I used to feel about armed robbery, before it started scaring me ... Hendrix on guitar. You know what blows me away? That he even existed. Everything's so square, you wouldn't even think he'd be allowed. Like coming. It's so good, you don't think they'd allow it. Yeah, that's about it, I guess. Robbery, Hendrix, and you.'

When Bobby satisfies his erotic hunger for Elizabeth and his need for violence at the same time, he can achieve the absolute condition which he describes as 'standing on the edge of something red.' At the end of the play, after he has shattered the loyalty of Alex and Christine, Bobby rushes once more towards that ecstatic edge, gets carried away, and plunges overboard. Walmsley has done the virtually impossible: he has given us a plausibly sympathetic portrait of a sexual killer.

The emotions of the spectators are necessarily ambivalent because, though the play demands that we succumb to the magic of 'something red,' we realize that we are being threatened. Playgoers at the Tarragon Theatre are, by definition, not members of Bobby's world, but of Elizabeth's. That, in the last analysis, is the reason for the exceptional power of *Something Red*: the moment we allow ourselves to respond at all sympathetically, we find ourselves and our values at the point of extinction. And that is not a comfortable place to be.

Since this is my last contribution to 'Letters in Canada,' I shall take the risk of disclosing what I take to be true, in general, of English drama in this country. First, let's face facts. Even when due allowance is made for the achievements of the last decade or so, the quality of dramatic writing has not yet reached a level of excellence comparable to that of our best fiction or poetry. No English-Canadian playwright can justly lay claim to the critical esteem or the popular acclaim which endorse such writers as Margaret Laurence, Alice Munro, or Mordecai Richler. Our best poets may not outrank our playwrights quite as decisively, but they still outrank them. I am not blaming anyone for this state of affairs, though I am curious enough to look for explanations.

Traditionally, dramatic writing has been able to thrive only when there is a metropolitan centre, an audience, and a cultural consensus. The presence of all three requirements in Québec is no doubt connected to the emergence of a playwright as magnificent as Michel Tremblay. In English Canada circumstances are less congenial. While three or more cities may offer to accommodate potential playwrights, our heritage is still solidly rural, and therefore more amenable to treatment in fiction or poetry. Even if our cities were to become genuine metropolitan centres, our playwrights would still be faced with the task of luring their audience away from the blandishments of imported Broadway hits, cable TV, and Hollywood. Geographical and sociological considerations prevent the emergence of a cultural consensus among members or potential members of the theatre audience. This is by no means a fluffy or abstruse idea. Every Elizabethan spectator, regardless of class or personal taste, must have felt that Falstaff and Prince Hal were competing for his very soul. And I would be willing to make a similar claim for the French-speaking spectators of *Les Belles-Sœurs*. But it cannot be obvious to an audience in Edmonton or Vancouver that *Balconville* is in any meaningful sense a play about them. I don't think there is a solution to this problem, but I believe there is at least some value in recognizing it.

Without a cultural consensus it is difficult for playwrights to develop a secure feeling for dramatic language. Again, this problem is less acute for poets (who can be as innovative as they like without losing their clientele) or for novelists (who are allowed to explain innovations by virtue of their medium). But dramatic language, necessarily the language of implication, rests on a series of assumptions about what can be and what cannot be implied. Our failure to develop a widely shared set of theatrical conventions helps to account for the notorious amount of explanation in our drama. Some playwrights, like Jan Kudelka, are bravely supplying the deficiency. Others, like Tom Walmsley, make minimal assumptions about language and therefore remain verbally underdeveloped. Still others, like George F. Walker, are unable to find the perfect relationship between language and theatre: namely, the point at which a brilliant metaphor loses its independence and becomes indispensable to the dramatic experience.

If politeness is indeed the great Canadian virtue, then perhaps it is also our besetting theatrical sin. Imagine the Canadian Coriolanus just after he's been issued his marching papers by the people's representatives. What will he do? I doubt that he will bristle with contempt as he returns the indictment: 'I banish you!' Rather, I suspect that he will offer an apology, do his best to understand the validity of his opponents' position, and then give a full explanation of the motives for his own conduct. Such a defensive posture may be wise diplomatic procedure, but it is disastrous in drama.

Genuine drama is impossible without conflict, because conflict is the material from which a plot can be made. Too many of our playwrights see conflict in abstract terms: the proletariat versus the establishment, the French versus the English, male versus female, or illusion versus reality. As a result, many of our plays are deficient in plot; what conflict there is has been superimposed and hence remains lifeless. Perhaps our habit of evading conflict is not based on simple cowardice, but rather on the conviction that the real battles are being fought elsewhere. At any rate, I shall continue to prefer those dramatists who are daring enough to exploit and provoke conflict, creatively, and who are ingenious enough to expose conflict where it really hurts and matters: somewhere, that is, within ourselves.

Théâtre

GILLES GIRARD

En 1980, l'écart est plus marqué encore que lors des années précédentes, entre les pièces publiées et le théâtre représenté. Ce dernier éclate dans toutes les directions, se diversifie, piétine dans certains thèmes mais se renouvelle formellement, constitue au total le mouvement culturel le plus actif et mobilisateur, le plus en prise sur l'identité nationale au début des années quatre-vingts, rôle déjà assumé précédemment par la chanson. Mais le monde de l'édition ne rend pas compte, loin de là, de toute cette activité théâtrale. (Ceci s'explique, entre bien d'autres facteurs, par la fermeture pour des raisons financières, d'un des éditeurs les plus audacieux: les éditions VLB. Heureusement que la maison de Victor-Lévy Beaulieu a refait surface en toute fin d'année). Les caprices de l'édition nous valent cette année des études sur le théâtre, évidemment des pièces de la production courante mais aussi d'heureuses plongées dans le passé avec une anthologie remontant à 1890 et des textes des années quarante, contributions importantes dans la remise à jour du corpus théâtral québécois.

Gratien Gélinas, ou est-ce encore une espièglerie de Fridolin, nous aura fait patienter trente-cinq ans avant de livrer ses Fridolinades au monde de l'édition. Voulant souligner la filiation entre Fridolin et Tit-Coq, Gélinas et les Quinze publient les deux dernières revues de la ribambelle des 'Fridolinons': *Les Fridolinades, 1945 et 1946* (272). Tit-Coq pointe déjà le nez dans 'Le départ du conscrit' (1945) et surtout 'Le retour du conscrit' (1946). Trois autres volumes devraient compléter sous peu cette parution à rebours: 1943 et 1944, 1941 et 1942, 1938-1939-1940. (Semblent exclus pour l'instant 'Les Fridolinades '56.')

Fridolin, ce gavroche autochtone, émouvant et hilarant, aux culottes courtes mais à l'œil frondeur, fait revivre les beaux jours du Monument national et d'un public qui apprend à se reconnaître dans ces personnages d'ici, complices dans l'utilisation des mêmes expressions et campés dans le décor familier de la ruelle, des hangars et cordes à linge. Les thèmes changent aussi; de ces héros classiques avides de gloire qui ne mangent ni ne dorment on passe à un fond de cours où un gamin arborant fièrement un chandail délavé du club de hockey 'Canadien' gouaille malicieusement sur les faits et gestes familiers et sur l'actualité politique. Cette thématique emprunte la forme très souple de la revue où alternent ou s'entrecroisent sketches, monologues, fables, parodies, chansons, pantomimes, et où se juxtaposent ou se marient satire et émotion.

Puisant dans ses archives riches en manuscrits, films, enregistrements, photographies, affiches et coupures de journaux, Gélinas nous procure une édition définitive de ses œuvres. Il enrobe les répliques de didascalies nombreuses et détaillées; certaines indications scéniques, pour les pantomimes par exemple, semblent de par leur caractère 'littéraire' évident, avoir été retouchées ou complétées pour les fins de l'édition. Le volume présente aussi une iconographie fort précieuse, même sur le public, contribuant à reconstituer rétrospectivement, de façon pittoresque et dans ses principales composantes, cette étape marquante aux origines du théâtre populaire 'canadien-français.'

Les Quinze avaient précédemment cette même année offert une édition de *Tit-Coq* (235). La précédente, aux Editions de l'Homme, datait de 1968. Celle-ci s'additionne surtout d'une présentation critique et d'une bibliographie de Laurent Mailhot qui a également assuré la présentation des *Fridolinades*.

Le corpus littéraire québécois s'est aussi enrichi cette année de la parution chez Leméac d'un recueil de 420 pages de monologues sélectionnés et présentés par Laurent Mailhot et Doris-Michel Montpetit:

Monologues québécois 1890-1980. Une centaine de textes de cinquante-sept auteurs populaires constitue un échantillonnage représentatif d'une production s'étendant sur près d'un siècle.

Une part d'arbitraire est inévitable devant un éventail aussi large et l'on peut discuter, en fonction de ses intérêts et de ses goûts, du choix de tel texte apparaissant mineur ou de l'absence de tel autre perçu comme essentiel. On peut regretter ici que les critères de sélection soient restés plutôt flous. Dans ses remarques critiques il ne faut cependant pas perdre de vue que l'anthologie s'est transformée en panorama suite à des facteurs indépendants de la volonté des auteurs comme des questions d'exclusivité de droits ou de redevances ou, plus discutables, des 'impératifs de temps.'

L'introduction, version remaniée et complétée d'un article de Mailhot dans *Canadian Literature* (Vancouver, no 58, 1973) disserte sur la notion de 'monologue' et sur sa place dans le théâtre québécois dont il représente 'la forme la plus ancienne et la plus moderne,' le point d'ancrage formel privilégié, de la tradition orale jusqu'au théâtre contemporain, celui de Tremblay par exemple, dont il constitue l'élément structural le plus spécifique. Sans tenter d'homogénéiser dans une même perspective méthodologique les diverses acceptions du terme, les auteurs parcourent ses différents sens et, par enchâssements et juxtapositions, tissent progressivement leur définition du monologue et le situent par rapport à des formes parentes comme le soliloque, le chœur, l'aparté, etc.

Le monologue (de 'money' et 'logos,' disait plaisamment Paul Coutlée) se définit comme 'une quête d'identité et d'unité, un arrêt devant ou avant l'action ... interrogation, suspension, affirmation (de soi), assertion (d'une vérité), intimidation ... une forme de communication *intrapersonnelle* ... *un langage vu*, objectivé, spectaculaire ... une stratégie du refus et du remplacement ... Le monologue est un ressourcement du langage aussi bien que du théâtre ... Le monologue est ici, maintenant.' La définition très englobante chapeaute des fables, déclamations, sketches, etc., et nous vaut un fourmillement de thèmes et de titres hétéroclites: 'Les promesses électorales,' 'Le Torticolis,' 'Le Skidoo,' 'La Microbiologie,' 'Soulographie,' 'Le Jeu de golf,' 'Le Pendu,' 'Le Football américain,' 'Le Fœtus,' 'Monologue du oui,' 'Ma grand-mère sous le pic du démolisseur,' 'Maudit Cul,' 'Les Bancs d'église' ...

Des glissements formels et thématiques traduisent à leur manière l'évolution du Québec au cours de quatre-vingt-dix ans d'histoire socio-politique. Un principe de segmentation temporelle découpe les cinq premières parties du corpus: I (1890-1920) Choses à dire: fables, déclamations, gazettes rimées. II (1920-1945) Revues, sketches, variétés. III (1945-1960) Du cabaret à la radio (et vice versa). IV (1960-1970) Entre la politique et la poésie. V (1970-1980) Nouvelles voix, nouvelles voies. Enfin, la sixième partie est réservée au monologue au théâtre.

Rehaussé de photographies, de croquis et caricatures ainsi que de notes biographiques (trop brèves et incomplètes), ce volume vaut par la réflexion théorique et par le choix de textes qu'il propose. Ce premier déblayage moderne du vaste corpus des monologues constitue une encyclopédie sonore des avatars de la personnalité culturelle québécoise perçue dans sa forme d'expression 'théâtrale' la plus vigoureuse et souvent la plus savoureuse.

Avec *L'Impromptu d'Outremont* (Leméac, 118) Michel Tremblay franchit le Rubicon de la 'Main' avec ses personnages qui passent à l'ouest. A l'occasion d'un goûter d'anniversaire, quatre sœurs se rencontrent pour 's'entre-tuer selon la tradition.' Les masques tombent et dans un salon cossu commence le rituel bourgeois sado-masochiste du jeu de la vérité où l'on flirte avec la lucidité et gratte les 'gales.' Dans ces duels de cape et d'épée, de fiel et d'insinuations, Fernande Beaugrand-Drapeau, déjà programmée par son nom (en plus, son fils s'appelle Nelligan), se découvre 'maniérée, hypocrite, inhumaine, entremetteuse et calculatrice,' sans oublier sa paranoïa, son alcoolisme, son avarice et pire, son élitisme, 'jusque dans les gâteaux.' Du 'Upper Outremont' c'est la désescalade à Saint-Léonard avec un double antinomique, Lorraine Ferzetti, 'la brebis galeuse qui s'est sauvée avec le jardinier pour aller élever de petits enfants noirs et frisés dans le fin fond du ghetto italien.' Plus vraie ou moins 'pognée' que les autres, elle se libère partiellement en changeant de nom, de quartier, de langage. Yvette dorlote, cultive ou endort sa névrose et son ennui sur un air de Purcell. Elle vit par procuration et meurt tous les jours avec Didon en chantant avec elle 'Remember Me.' Lucille y voit une proie facile pour exercer son ironie et défouler son agressivité. Dans ce joli portrait de famille, ces sœurs dont la plus jeune a quarante ans, se dépècent à qui mieux mieux et rendent, sauf pour Fernande, leur mère et leur classe responsables de leur aliénation.

Cette séance de thérapie de groupe se double d'un débat tout aussi houleux mais moins original et plus lourd, sur la culture: (l' 'impromptu' – Molière, Cocteau, Giraudoux – commande ce type de recul critique d'un auteur sur son art) idéologie du *statu quo* et valeurs culturelles de surface des dilettantes d'Outremont *versus* l'esprit critique et les forces créatrices; culture élitiste ou populaire. Le *Robert versus* le 'joual,' la litote contre l'hyperbole; débat ainsi résumé par Lorraine: 'J'aime mieux être bruyante et en santé que discrète et constipée!' Plus spécifiquement, débat sur le théâtre entre l'esthétique du 'salon' et 'l'ère du lavabo et du fond de cour.' Le point de vue de Lucille (Tremblay?) est le plus pondéré: 'Qu'il y ait de la place pour les deux, ... Pour la bouteille de bière comme pour le martini.'

Les sœurs Beaugrand ont reçu une éducation 'de ronds de jambe, de salamalecs, de baise-main, d'oui-dire et de m'as-tu-vu!' Mais le langage les trahit; derrière les figures de style et le vernis du beau langage se dissimulent et fusent dans les moments de vérité, les 'Chus t'en forme,' les 'j'y écrapoutirais dans 'face!' et les 'tu me fais chier, Fernande! c-h-i-e-r, chier!' Même quand bien astiqué et fleuri, le langage se veut oppression et non élément de libération et de création; l'écriture aussi, celle de Fernande, se fossilise dans des manuscrits jamais publiés. Comme les personnages de l'est, les sœurettes Beaugrand charrient leurs déceptions, leurs frustrations, leur incapacité de s'assumer, leur peur de vivre. 'Tu peux sortir la fille de l'est mais pas l'est de la fille'; c'est vrai de *Demain matin Montréal m'attend* et tout autant, quoique sur un air de Purcell, des quatre (belles-) sœurs d'Outremont.

Coordonnées spatio-temporelles habituelles du théâtre de Jean Daigle: le passé et Sainte-Croix de Lotbinière. *Le Mal à l'âme*, paru dans une belle édition du Noroît (95), ne fait pas exception: en 1880, dans le huis-clos d'une 'maison aisée' du village, quatre femmes, un peu 'le Quatuor des dissonances de Mozart' selon Daigle, se situent, évoquent leur résignation ou leurs aspirations, proposent différentes conceptions de la vie de femme.

Trois générations de femmes. Louisa, 52 ans, sereine mais surtout résignée. Après le remariage de son père, elle s'est sacrifiée à l'éducation de ses deux demi-sœurs. Angèle, 38 ans, de la race des forts, gourmande devant la vie, 'accepte de vivre les bras ouverts comme une écluse,' ne s'embarrasserait ni de marmots ni surtout d'un mari. Vit une relation cachée avec David sans y 'accorde[r] aucune importance sentimentale et lui non plus.' Virginie, 36 ans, schizophrène, souffre d'un mal de vivre, du 'mal à l'âme.' Le cœur en écharpe, éprise de beauté et d'idéal, elle se réfugie dans un monde de rêves et d'illusions. Le beau David, présume-t-elle, étancherait sa douloureuse soif d'amour. Empêchée de le rejoindre, elle trouvera un dernier refuge, ou selon Daigle une 'affirmation de soi et une délivrance,' dans le suicide. Rose-Aimée, la cousine de 19 ans, apeurée par l'amour trop insistant de Maurice, cherchait dans son séjour 'chez les vieilles filles du notaire' un peu de recul et une occasion de réflexion. Le leitmotiv, 'J'ai mal à l'âme,' qui, dans la bouche de Virginie, fermait les trois premières scènes, appartient désormais à Rose-Aimée qui le reprend pour clore la pièce.

Dans cet univers de femmes, les personnages masculins ne sont qu'évoqués: un père 'bourru,' un David 'casse-cœur,' un Maurice amoureux impatient. Ils brillent par leur absence et leur insignifiance. Sauf pour l'aînée Louisa que le destin a obligée à assumer un rôle de mère pour ses demi-sœurs, la maternité est crainte ou rejetée par les femmes de cette supposée société conservatrice des valeurs traditionnelles.

L'action est lente à démarrer et les discussions s'enlisent mais cette forme bien particulière de théâtre à la parlure surannée et au charme d'antan, n'en continue pas moins à s'affirmer progressivement, en passant par *Coup de sang*, *La Débâcle* et *Le Jugement dernier*. Daigle, qui par ailleurs signera un feuilleton humoristique à la télévision de Radio-Canada en 1981, fait cavalier seul dans 'son genre' usuel mais il est aussi désormais membre à part entière de la 'confrérie' des dramaturges québécois.

La Guerre, yes sir et *Il n'y a pas de pays sans grand-père*, entre autres, ont déjà donné lieu à des représentations, après adaptation des romans pour la scène. *La Céleste Bicyclette* (Stanké, 82) est le premier texte de Roch Carrier écrit directement pour le théâtre. L'auteur a arrêté temporairement la rédaction d'un roman apparareneé par la thématique, pour produire ce monologue 'écrit pour [le comédien et metteur en scène] Albert Millaire.'

L'anecdote présente peu d'intérêt: 'l'Acteur,' 'idiot officiel, compétent, qui souffre d'un courant d'air entre les deux trompes d'Eustache,' est enfermé dans sa chambre cellulaire d'un hôpital psychiatrique et raconte quelques épisodes de sa vie professionnelle et conjugale, et surtout une escapade céleste sur sa bicyclette qui nous vaudra le fruit de ses cogitations philosophico-lyriques. Du contenu émergent le motif pascalien de la petitesse de l'homme devant les espaces infinis et le thème du refus par la société des valeurs débordant de ses cadres et qu'elle ne peut étiqueter avec ses rassurants codes philosophiques, scientifiques ou psychanalytiques. Mais surtout, la pièce propose une méditation poétique sur les pôles réalité et rêve (faut-il choisir Courbet ou Chagall?), sur la dichotomie qui les oppose ou les paradoxes les faisant se télescoper: 'l'homme est un rêve mal adapté à la réalité ... Il y a là-haut une place pour l'homme qui refuse une différence entre le rêve et la réalité.' C'est le même éloge de la folie ou la même réconciliation de la terre et de l'utopie que propose le roman écrit en parallèle, *Les Fleurs vivent-elles ailleurs que sur la terre*? La leçon de la courte pièce est séduisante mais trop insistante, tourne au cours magistral. Ce monologue qui s'ouvre à la fonction conative de par ses interpellations aux autres personnages de l'univers évoqué et surtout à l'égard du public, les convie 'à sauter d'étoile en étoile,' à 'crever le plafond de la nuit.'

Chez Leméac, une pièce de jeunesse de Claude Jasmin, écrite en 1955: *Le Veau dort* (121). Effets spectaculaires et foisonnement thématique. Trop. Intérêt historique mais aussi recherche, originale à l'époque, de nouvelles structures.

Une amie d'enfance (Leméac, 127) de Louise Roy et Louis Saia met brillamment en relief le caractère conventionnel et factice d'un langage de poncifs. Communication rendue impossible par l'utilisation d'un vocabulaire non senti, non vécu; transposition ou décalque des annonces publicitaires télévisées; parole truffée de clichés bien commodes derrière lesquelles se dissimulent les interlocuteurs et le vide.

Les Editions de la pleine lune se mettent au service de l'écriture des femmes. Objectif: 'cerner le non-dit de notre identité singulière et collective.' Dans ce non-dit figure le drame de l'inceste père-fille abordé dans *Un reel ben beau, ben triste* (179) de Jeanne-Mance Delisle. L'émotion est servie par un langage cru, trop systématiquement provocant mais déchirant comme un cri de rage et de douleur.

Il s'agit d'une première pour la troupe du Théâtre de la Marmaille: la publication chez VLB d'une création collective, *La Vie à trois étages* (150). Un thème et un objectif précis: 'valorisation de la vie d'un quartier' et 'insuffler vie à la collectivité afin qu'elle se prenne et re-prenne en main.' L'intérêt tient moins au texte de la pièce qu'à la démarche concrète proposée en préface et postface: 'grille-questionnaire,' 'ateliers d'écriture,' consignes, 'exemples d'improvisation,' 'préparation du local,' 'rôle de l'animateur,' 'le jeu d'improvisation verbale,' etc. Le tout abondamment illustré. Forme de théâtre ancré dans le tissu social et qui redonne même la parole aux 'spectateurs.'

Québec/Amérique inaugure une nouvelle collection, 'Jeunes publics,' qui propose trois textes destinés aux enfants: *Cé tellement 'cute' des enfants* de Marie-Francine Hébert, *Une lune entre deux maisons* de Suzanne Lebeau et Georgette Rondeau, *Un jeu d'enfants* par le Théâtre du Quartier. Matériellement, la présentation est agréable et le texte s'accompagne d'un utile cahier explorant la démarche et les objectifs. Ce théâtre n'est pas 'innocent'; *Un jeu d'enfants* a même encouru les foudres et la censure de la Commission des écoles catholiques de Montréal. La pièce présentait le tort de ne pas s'inscrire dans le registre douceureux et idyllique habituel; le père doit entrer en grève, la mère éprouve des difficultés à boucler le budget et les enfants contestent leur aire de jeu: des balcons bien étroits ou des rues inquiétantes. Dans ces pièces, c'est du moins leur objectif, l'enfant y apprend ses droits et ses responsabilités dans ses relations à autrui. Un théâtre qui divertit aussi mais tout en se voulant un outil pédagogique.

Jeu, publication trimestrielle paraissant depuis 1976, s'affirme de plus en plus comme un instrument de travail indispensable pour tous ceux qu'intéressent la pratique et la théorie théâtrales au Québec. Transcendant l'éternelle dichotomie si souvent puérile entre les 'vrais,' les 'authentiques,' les artisans de la scène et les 'frustrés' ou 'eunuques' de la réflexion spéculative, *Jeu* tente de réconcilier les deux approches, qu'ont toujours assumées de façon concomitante les plus intéressants (Stanislavski, Brecht, Grotowski). Les troupes sont amenées à réfléchir sur leur pratique et à définir leur problématique et leur esthétique, à effectuer un bilan de leur production et à procéder à une autocritique. La revue demeure pluraliste même si elle ne cache pas son 'préjugé favorable' à l'égard du 'Jeune Théâtre' et de la recherche.

Deux numéros retiennent particulièrement l'attention. Le numéro 15, 1980, détermine l'impact de plus de vingt ans d'existence du théâtre 'intervenant' de l'ACTA (Association canadienne du théâtre d'amateurs)/AQJT (Association québécoise du jeune théâtre), 'en position, selon Gilbert David, de précurseur, sinon de catalyseur de l'expression culturelle la plus signifiante et novatrice de notre collectivité.' Dans 'théâtre-femmes' (no 16, 1980), les femmes de théâtre prennent la parole et témoignent poétiquement, rationnellement, viscéralement, de leur oppression et exploitation et dressent un tableau décapant et stimulant de leurs revendications: 'Québécoises deboutte!' *Jeu* affirme rapidement son discours critique et répond de mieux en mieux à son objectif de cerner et contester les rapports instaurés entre le théâtre et la collectivité tout en contribuant au décryptage des 'codes' intervenant dans toute représentation théâtrale.

Dans sa livraison de décembre 1980 (13:3, 379–575) *Etudes littéraires* publie enfin, après treize ans de parution, un numéro exclusivement consacré à l'art dramatique: '*Théâtre et théâtralité.*' Préparé sous la tutelle éclairée de Jeannette Laillou Savona, ce numéro regroupe une série d'essais articulés, sans exclusive, sur des bases essentiellement sémiotiques, linguistiques et structuralistes.

La plus importante partie de cette publication hautement internationale propose des textes théoriques de Régis Durand, Ross Chambers, Ivo Osolsobě, Ilie Balea, André Helbo et Jeannette Laillou Savona. La seconde partie illustre la pratique des textes selon les perspectives de Wladimir Krysinski, Patrice Pavis et Dina Sherzer. Enfin, quatre comptes rendus de volumes de sémiologie théâtrale complètent heureusement ce numéro questionnant avec rigueur des aspects fondamentaux de la théâtralité et contribuant à cerner, au-delà des particularités de tel ou tel corpus, le caractère spécifique du discours théâtral.

Dans *le Théâtre québécois (1)*, Jean-Cléo Godin et Laurent Mailhot avaient fourni en 1970 une introduction remarquable à dix auteurs dramatiques jugés les plus marquants. *Théâtre québécois II* (HMH, 248) dresse un bilan critique des spectacles et des dramaturges de la dernière décade. Dans une première partie, l'étude porte sur des 'fonctions, formes, spectacles': théâtre éclaté et polymorphe avec des exemples aussi divers que *Un pays dont la devise est je m'oublie, Wouf wouf, Hamlet, prince du Québec*, le Grand Cirque ordinaire, etc. Une deuxième partie regroupe des analyses des 'univers dramatiques' de Jean Barbeau, Robert Gurik, Jean-Claude Germain, Antonine Maillet, Michel Tremblay, Michel Garneau. L'approche méthodologique oscille 'de l'axe Duvignaud à l'axe Ubersfeld' sans s'inféoder à l'une ou l'autre méthode. La démarche retenue se réserve plus de latitude et s'inscrit 'dans un aller-retour constant, sinon toujours explicite, du pôle société (ou situation historique) au pôle texte (ou signification littérale, littéraire, scénique).'

Les auteurs sont conscients d'avoir écarté des noms importants: Claude Gauvreau, Roch Carrier, André Ricard et d'autres. L'ambition de Godin et Mailhot se limite peut-être à ne fournir que des 'éléments d'interprétation, de mise en place et en perspective'; mais, leur étude n'en constitue pas moins actuellement la vision d'ensemble la plus exhaustive et l'apport critique le plus important sur le théâtre québécois contemporain.

Cette année donc, des études intéressantes sur le théâtre, mais statistiquement une baisse à un plancher de quelque vingt pièces publiées alors qu'inversement le nombre de troupes et théâtres professionnels et amateurs au Québec grimpe à quelque deux cents soixante-dix. De l'activité protéiforme du théâtre professionnel, du théâtre-laboratoire, du théâtre pour la jeunesse, du 'jeune théâtre' pour adultes et du théâtre d'été, l'échantillonnage des publications est peu représentatif, surtout en ce qui concerne les secteurs clefs du 'jeune théâtre' et des créations collectives. Tout ne mérite pas d'être publié non plus, mais l'éventail pourrait s'élargir. En somme, un bon cru au niveau des représentations et une année un peu décevante sur le plan des publications des pièces, qualitativement et quantitativement.

Translations

JOHN J. O'CONNOR

While T.S. Eliot's reflections in *Four Quartets* are widely relevant to twentieth-century experience in general, certain of his observations in 'The Dry Salvages' might be used as a particular description of both the function and the effect of translations for unilingual readers: 'We had the experience but missed the meaning, / And approach to the meaning restores the experience / In a different form.' Every literary translation is just such an approach to the meaning of the original text; if it succeeds, it not only provides a clear and reliable echo of the initial voice, but also illuminates some aspects of the original work, and may prompt the reader to examine the source itself. However, if the translator is to restore the experience generated by a reading of the original text, he must be willing to exercise some restraint on his own creativity, always remembering his exacting responsibility as the medium between the language of the writer and that of the reader. Given the peculiarities of every language, it is clear that even the best translation must be inadequate in some respects. Of necessity there will always be significant differences between the 'experience' and the 'restoration'; but the ideal of every translation remains the same: to produce a single work in two languages rather than two similar works. For the most part this ideal has been realized by Canada's literary translators in the past year.

Literary translation in Canada continues to be as prominent an activity as in the past. Recently translated works of Quebec literature were originally published as early as 1945 and as late as 1979. Of the sixteen books considered here, however, only three (and parts of a fourth) appeared before 1972. Thus, Canadian translators continue to focus on recent and contemporary Quebec literature, with the usually predominant interest in prose fiction still evident and, this year, a substantial offering of poetry. Although seven of these sixteen translations bear pre-1980 imprints, none of these was received from the publishers until recently. In the interest of chronology, therefore, these seven works will be examined first.

Tales of Solitude (Intermedia Press, 120, $13.95 cloth, $8.95 paper), Margaret Rose's translation of Yvette Naubert's *Contes de la solitude*, vol II (1972), is a collection of twelve short stories dealing with a variety of characters whose lives have reached a point of crisis. These stories examine, for example, violence stemming from overwork or monomania and feelings of puzzlement and alienation caused by marriage break-up, suicide, political terrorism, ill health, or a guilty conscience. Naubert's original and engaging talent is repeatedly demonstrated, and deserves the wider familiarity it will receive through Rose's translation. When *Contes de la solitude* and *Tales of Solitude* are juxtaposed for a concurrent reading, we discover that the latter is a generally reliable English version of the French stories, reflecting great care and sensitivity on the part of the translator. Of particular merit are Rose's translations of 'Obedience,' 'The Cat,' 'The Muffins,' and 'The Pigeons in St. Louis Square.' Where necessary, Rose corrects errors in the original text and usually finds equivalent English idioms for difficult French expressions. Certainly anglophone readers will often hear the clear echo of Naubert's voice in Rose's work.

However, *Tales of Solitude* is not without its shortcomings, all the more regrettable since they stem from the translator's inattention rather than from the limitations of her language. There are intermittent instances of grammatical and spelling errors, as well as distorting imprecision – for example, *curé* (in this context pastor) is translated as 'parish priest' (p 98) – and inconsistency in the handling of French names (some translated, some not). Repeated references to St Joseph's Orator*io* suggest a similar unfamiliarity with Naubert's setting. A few numbers have been inaccurately translated, and *gauche* is once rendered as 'right.' Rose reverses the names of the two sisters in 'The Muffins' (p 62) and overlooks an important sentence about the protagonist's loss of faith in 'The Thief on the Bridge' (p 81). Occasionally we encounter phrases like 'the perfect love' as a translation of *le parfait amour* (true love), which misses the exact idiomatic English equivalent. In 'The Butterfly' a similar concern to present a literal English version of Musset's poetry prevents Rose from trying to find a *poetic* English equivalent. She also ignores comic overtones when she translates *Esquimaudes* (Eskimo women) as 'Eskimos' in the conversation of two homosexuals. Throughout the text there are occasional omissions of adverbs, adjectives, and phrases, as well as four full sentences and all of the second-to-last paragraph of the first story. In two instances the mistranslation is more substantial: *C'est un boeuf de labour à l'antique* (He's an old-fashioned work-horse) is literally, and improperly, rendered as 'That's a type of ox used to till the fields in the old-fashioned way' (p 52); and in 'Adaption to High Living: A Difficult Business' Rose misses the point about Bruce's anxiety *à descendre en soi* (to look into himself) when she translates the expression as 'to come down to earth' (p 94). Another major problem throughout *Tales of Solitude* is the translator's mishandling of Naubert's direct references to the use of English and French. Thus, although the protagonist, in the translation, has been speaking English to the cat from the beginning, Rose makes no adjustment in translating *Au cas où elle comprendrait mieux l'anglais, il traduisit* as 'In case she understood English better he translated from the French' (p 29). Similarly, in 'The Murderer' the translator specifies that the distraught policeman reads a prayer 'aloud in French' but proceeds to give the prayer in English. My final reservations about *Tales of Solitude* concern the translator's failure to identify exactly which text she is translating (she does not indicate that *Tales of Solitude* deals only with vol II of Naubert's stories) and her gratuitous insertion of an epigraph by Naubert.

To turn from *Tales of Solitude* to the bilingual anthology edited by Nicole Brossard, *Les Stratégies du réel / The Story So Far 6* (La Nouvelle Barre du jour / Coach House Press, 344, $7.50 paper), is to move suddenly from the traditional to the avant-garde. If the two works share the theme of solitude, they are, nevertheless, manifestly different in technique and range. Solitude for Brossard and the fourteen other young Quebec poets and fiction writers included in the anthology is not often a state of anxiety and doubt, but rather a desirable condition that permits self-possession, personal strength, and vital re-affirmation. The fifteen selections of previously unpublished material broadly represent the vanguard of new Quebec writers (centred in Brossard's *Nouvelle Barre du jour*) at the start of this decade; and, as such, their work can clearly lay just claim to our attention and respect. The excellence of this book is undoubtedly a result of the careful collaboration of Brossard with Coach House editors Frank Davey and Barbara Godard, and their intelligent choice of the nine different translators who meet the daunting challenges of such eclectic, experimental work. Beginning in each case with a photograph of the author and a brief biography and bibliography, the selections demonstrate the variety of visions held by this diverse group of writers, ranging as they do over problems of language, freedom, all forms of love, death, radical feminism, identity, etc. All nine translators (several of whom have translated complete texts, discussed below) should be commended for their diligent efforts in creating skilful English versions of these very demanding texts. Certainly there is, as François Charron suggests, 'dans ces harmoniques un côté intraduisible,' which is an important *caveat* for both francophone and anglophone readers of this book. On the whole the nine translators of *Les Stratégies du réel* display their skills very impressively. Their close attention to minute shades of meaning, sound, and even typeface is remarkable. Especially noteworthy are their ingenious solutions to the problems of translating word-plays and puns. Ray Chamberlain, who has translated six of the fifteen pieces (including some of the most difficult), often excels in finding English equivalents for linguistic games; but the considerable merits of the translations by Plourde, Brown, Godard, and Ellenwood should not be forgotten. Nor, indeed, should any of the others, for there is much to praise in each selection.

This is not to say that the translations are without fault of any kind, though none is too seriously flawed. The book contains a few dozen typographical errors. In addition, there are many discrepancies between information offered in the headnotes in French and in English; often the English version is truncated, but occasionally it supplements the original in a way that is particularly useful to an English reader. Along with intermittent instances of unnecessary imprecision in translating certain words, there are two more substantial omissions: the large stamp containing the words *300 Enfants Eblouis Par Les Frankenstein* (p 271) is not translated; and the failure to translate the words *le diable n'était jamais mort, qu'il visitait certaines* (p 335) in the final selection produces a fractured, unintelligible sentence. A final difficulty for English readers results from the editorial decision to depart from the useful practice of placing French and English texts on facing pages in the case of Roger des Roches and Normand de Bellefeuille. For no apparent reason their texts face each other, and Alan Brown's translation trails twenty pages behind – hardly a convenience for a reader already facing many other obstacles in his approach to the meaning of these selections. In general, however, the nine translators of *The Story So Far 6* offer reliable echoes of the original voices. If the language of the original texts is rich, evocative, and very demanding – and it is – the language of the translations is no less so, but no more so. The translators have done all they can, perhaps even all that the English language can, to mediate between francophone writers and anglophone readers. The remaining verbal struggles are our own particular task. (Some assistance can, however, be found in *Ellipse*, 23/4 [Université de Sherbrooke, 176, $5.00 paper], which offers informed analyses of *La Barre du jour* and its English counterpart, *Open Letter.*)

The challenges faced and met repeatedly by Ray Chamberlain in the Brossard text are akin to those he had earlier faced in *A Québécois Dream* (Exile Editions, 102, $7.95 paper), his 1978 translation of Victor-Lévy Beaulieu's *Un rêve québécois* (1972). Beaulieu's title is manifestly ironic, for in this dark night of the mind and heart Joseph-David-Barthélémy Dupuis faces a hallucinatory nightmare of violent rages and physical injury, waging war against his estranged wife and the demon-memories that haunt their residence during the War Measures occupation of Montreal. Within the frustrations of his madness Barthélémy finds liberation only in illusion; unable to distinguish between memory, reality, and desire, he passionately seeks deliverance from his unhappy past and jealous rages. To reflect this acute mental torment Beaulieu's style is a fluid, Faulknerian continuum of convoluted syntax, complex and evocative imagery, and deliberate confusion and distortion. Any translator's mettle would be tested by it, and Chamberlain fares very well indeed. Exercising over the novel the kind of control Barthélémy so desperately seeks, Chamberlain skilfully hides this command so that the translation has the wild madness appropriate to it. In the first six 'cuts' of the novel Chamberlain does his work very diligently, particularly in handling the protagonist's raging curses and Beaulieu's puns, and in finding exact English equivalents for the idioms of the original.

Of course, not all the features of Barthélémy's derangement have exact English equivalents, so the translator does have some latitude. Chamberlain seldom gives too literal a translation of meaning and rarely strays unnecessarily from the original, though he does embellish a little, occasionally. At times, words and phrases are overlooked, along with four full sentences, and a few words are mistranslated: *avoine* (oats) as 'wheat' (p 93) and *cuisinière* (kitchen stove) as 'kitchen' (p 51). The major weaknesses of the translation can be found in 'Cut Seven,' the final section. A repeated 'in' (p 85) has been overlooked by the proofreader. Then, *Tu vois ben que t'es toute seul* (you can see you're all alone) is incorrectly rendered as 'you can see that for yourself' (p 85). On the two following pages, *on* and *soi* are twice translated as 'they' and 'them' (the police), when the context directly refutes this possibility and makes it clear that the terms refer to the protagonist. These oversights give way to the elaboration of *leur espace* into 'the very foundations of the structure they had built around themselves' (p 87), and *boulets* (bullets) is subsequently mistranslated as 'gas' (p 90). These lapses in the final section are all the more surprising after the careful and accomplished work that precedes it, for Chamberlain is not merely an energetic and courageous translator, but also a talented one. Still, a final *caveat* must be made: the copy I received of this translation stopped at the bottom of p 96 instead of p 102 – the final gathering had not been bound in. These final pages are, however, well translated and provide a fitting conclusion to a good piece of work.

In addition to these works by Naubert, Brossard, and Beaulieu, translations of three books of poetry by Robert Marteau, all published in 1979, have now been made available for examination. The first of these is *Salamander: Selected Poems of Robert Marteau* (Princeton University Press, 114, $12.00 cloth, $4.95 paper), a bilingual selection translated by Anne

Winters from four collections of Marteau's poetry published between 1962 and 1978. His rich, metaphorical vision, imbued with medieval imagery and the language of art, alchemy, and myth, celebrates an ordered and unified existence greatly at odds with the surreal, chaotic world of a Barthélémy Dupuis. Marteau's imaginative investigations, grounded in vivid, concrete detail, are highly allusive, and thus make considerable demands on his translators. But Winters has met the challenge with great expertise, and produced a remarkably reliable English version of his vision. Her translations of 'Lozère,' 'Ode Number 8,' 'Circe,' and 'The Lovers' Metamorphosis' are particularly good. In full command of Marteau's material and its sources, as demonstrated in her intelligent and informative introduction, she repeatedly finds a language and tone to reflect the poet's insights and meditations. No doubt her collaboration with Marteau on these translations accounts for some of their accuracy and excellence. Moreover, the bilingual presentation conveniently invites anglophone readers to explore the original material in order to hear those nuances of sound that cannot be caught in a translation. For these reasons my criticisms of this translation are minor: a few terms have been overlooked; the English version misses the pun in *aubes* (vestments/dawns); and *de fer* (iron metal) is translated as 'meat' (p 83). But lapses of this kind are very rare, and readers of *Salamander* can be confident that they are dealing with a very competent translation.

Winters's text does not constitute the sole English approach to Marteau's meaning. While her anthology contains only an excerpt from *Traité du blanc et des teintures* (1978), Barry Callaghan's translation, *Treatise on White and Tincture* (Exile Editions, 63, $6.95 paper), is complete. Its other virtues include sensitivity, intelligence, and reliability. Furthermore, the visual and tactile quality of its white-on-white cover (by Gérald Tremblay) make this one of the most beautiful Canadian translations ever produced. This fine example of first-rate bookmaking marries stunning design to the profound meanings of the poetry in a compelling union of medium and message. Produced in bilingual format on facing pages, the words by Marteau and Callaghan tint these white pages in memorable mirror images of Adamic man's perceptions and prospects outside the walled garden. While not every detail of such poetry can be accommodated in an English version, Callaghan nevertheless works very diligently, rarely straying from Marteau's lines (though he does alter their disposition in keeping with the shape of his own version) and often finding intelligent solutions to Marteau's word-plays. Sensitive to the demands of Marteau's craft, Callaghan's language corresponds in tone and richness, often evoking the sounds as well as the sense of the French verse. The translator never takes undue liberties with *Traité*, and consistently reveals his concern to offer a graceful, respectful transformation of it. (The English version could, however, be somewhat improved by a more careful proofreading to eliminate spelling and typographical errors.) In *Treatise on White and Tincture*, then, Marteau's voice has found a worthy echo, an authentic English counterpart. No translation can be definitive, and comparisons with Anne Winters's excerpt demonstrate how separate visions can merge at times, then run parallel, offering an alternate but equally acceptable route to follow. For the truly adventuresome and carefree, of course, Steve McCaffery, in *Ellipse*, 19 (1976), has offered an entirely different road, based on principles of 'acoustic ... equivalence' and a 'kinship of sound'; but his version has no kinship of *sense* with Marteau's work, and thus cannot lead us intact to the original. McCaffery's is an approach to the sound rather than the meaning of *Traité du blanc et des teintures* as he attempts exclusively to make us *hear* the experience. Of the three versions, Callaghan's offers the best equivalent of evocative and reliable phrasing, finely etched diction, and an appropriately succinct style.

Given Callaghan's skill in translating *Traité*, it is not surprising to find comparable excellence in *Atlante* (Exile Editions, 79, $6.95 paper), his 1979 translation of Marteau's *Atlante* (1976). This English version also adopts the useful bilingual format of *Treatise*, and is equally sensitive to Marteau's imagery, diction, and poetic rhyme. When Callaghan does depart from Marteau's text, it is usually to find an equivalent English idiom or pun. Nevertheless, the English *Atlante* is less satisfactory than *Treatise* because the former contains more spelling and typographical errors in both French and English versions, and because the French varies from the 1976 text on a half-dozen occasions. There are also a few mistranslations in *Atlante*: *Princes du Sang* (Princes of the Blood) is given as 'Princes of the Line' (p 29), apparently a misreading of 'Sang' as 'Rang'; *servantes* (maids) is translated as 'butler' (p 77); and *sans luxure* (no lust) is mistakenly rendered as 'no luxuries' (p 55). These oversights are all the more surprising in the light of Callaghan's excellent work in *Treatise*, and qualify somewhat his generally reliable work in this translation. If there has not been collaboration by Marteau and Callaghan on these translations, they nevertheless do clearly share a reciprocal interest in each other's work (Marteau translated *The Hogg Poems* in 1978). Shared interests of this kind help to explain Callaghan's able and sympathetic response to Marteau's work.

A final pre-1980 work, also by Robert Marteau, is his novel *Pentecôte* (1973), translated in 1979 by David Ellis as *Pentecost* (Exile Editions, 118, $8.95 paper). The novel's originality in conception and characterization and its thematic concerns are very reminiscent of Leclerc's vision in *Le Fou de l'île* and Watson's in *The Double Hook*. Like them, Marteau's work deals with interrelationships in a poor but closely knit community; these are revealed primarily through its response to an aging painter (nicknamed Pentecost) who deliberately disappears into the marshes surrounding the district's old abbey and chateau. Aspects of this setting, popularly associated with past legends and medieval exploits, figure prominently in the obsessive speculations of the large cast of supporting characters who set out to find the old man. Before the violent climax they have instead found themselves and learned important lessons about their own interdependence. This gift of wisdom and light is, in fact, the old painter's legacy to them and partly explains the symbolism of his name. Although the richness of Marteau's language and the complexities of his plot pose great challenges for a translator, Ellis is often equal to them. *Pentecost* is particularly good in its handling of dialogue, especially Dorbreuse's conversation with Vence (Canto xxv), and in Ellis's skill at finding authentic equivalents for the colloquial peculiarities of *Pentecôte*. His attentiveness to detail and nuance can produce very fine work, indeed – notably, the flawless translation of Cantos x, xvi, and xviii.

However, there is much in *Pentecost* that might be improved by greater care and effort on Ellis's part. In addition to occasional omissions of single words and full sentences (cf the end of Canto xxvi), we also find confusing comma splices, clumsy phrasing ('death-agonized lungs'), and awkward syntax at times; usually this is the result of too literal a rendering of the original text. Thus *Elle raccrocha* (She hung up) becomes 'She replaced the receiver' (p 66); *horizon indécis* (Blurred horizon) is translated as 'undecided horizon' (p 52); and *répéta le geste* (did the same) is given as 'repeated the move' (p 91). There is, too, some inexactness here – *foin* (hay) as 'straw,' *gendre* (son-in-law) as 'son' – as well as direct contradiction (*gauche* as 'right,' *quelques* as 'several,' *antérieure* as 'rear'). Unaccountably, Ellis twice translates *le Menteur* as 'the Poet,' and alters the reference to the Psalms in Canto II. His gratuitous alteration of a sentence in the middle of Canto xv also misrepresents Marteau's text; it reads 'taken aback it seemed, suddenly fallen silent' (p 55) whereas the original clearly means 'taken aback, it seemed, at suddenly finding themselves silent.' More substantial mistranslations are also evident: for example, *Ils ne se voyaient pas l'un l'autre. C'était la nuit* is translated as 'they were unable to see the night' (p 62); when Marie-Rose says to Dorbreuse, '*ce n'est pas Prestance qui va le contredire,*' Ellis translates it as 'you won't find Prestance telling you otherwise' (p 36), though *le* clearly refers to her husband, Piedlevé; and *il ne nuisait pas* (he never hurt anyone) is given as 'there wasn't a bad thing in him' (p 92). The French text is directly contradicted when Ellis describes the dangerous Captain Casse-cou as the one who was 'long ago put out of harm's way' (p 30); and the translator introduces confusion when he specifies that Orphée knocks on the wooden *door*, when the original clearly indicates *shutters*. Still greater confusion results when the translation drops *Dieu ait son âme, fit encore Antoinette* in the middle of her conversation with Dorbreuse after Didi's funeral. Thus, when Dorbreuse replies, 'There's nothing more to wish for him' (p 114), his remark has no reference point, and appears to be an expression of despair rather than support for Antoinette's prayer. Finally, a major weakness in the translation is the inadvertent omission of six sentences (p 68) that fall between the repeated phrase *grande maison de verre* in Didi's conversation with Orphée. As a result, the latter's consolation, 'Don't worry, Didi, your horse's already got into the big house,' is quite puzzling in *Pentecost*, since Didi's expression of concern for his horse occurs in the omitted section. This kind of oversight is unfortunate in a translation that shows much talent and promise.

The general search that follows an old man's disappearance in *Pentecost* is a feature that Marteau's novel shares with *The Draft Dodger* (Anansi, 150, $8.95 paper), David Toby Homel's translation of Louis Caron's *L'Emmitouflé* (1977), which won the 1977 Prix Hermès and Prix France-Canada. Within the framework of a Vietnam draft dodger's flight from a violent demonstration to refuge at his family's homestead in New England, Caron's novel moves back in time to various periods in his uncle's life, particularly the time he spent as a deserter during World War I. For the translator the challenge of this novel lies in reflecting the narrator's reverent attitude to Uncle Nazaire, and the unadorned style in which the old man is evoked and praised. At the same time, it is important to maintain control over the various levels of discourse and structure to be found in *L'Emmitouflé*. On both counts, *The Draft Dodger* is a first-rate translation carefully and competently presented, with only an occasional inaccuracy in verb tense. The translation is often flawless for pages at a time, and is especially reliable and competent in Part III. Usually the extravagant curses of Caron's characters are translated into equivalent English expressions, though it is unclear why Homel is not completely consistent in this regard.

These inconsistencies do suggest some inattentiveness, which manifests itself in other ways in *The Draft Dodger*. But the reviewer of Homel's translation must also bear in mind the 'Translator's Note' that precedes the novel: 'During the preparation of the translation of *L'Emmitouflé*, the author took the opportunity to make certain changes in his novel. These have been incorporated in this version.' It is, therefore, probable that, in the majority of cases, Homel has merely copied Caron's revisions in dropping single words and phrases, and some sentences. However, *The Draft Dodger* must still be faulted for not always indicating where *L'Emmitouflé* uses English, and for failing to translate the expression *ceinture fléchée* (which has no meaning for an anglophone reader) or the French Christmas carols (for which well-known English versions do exist). While Homel's text often improves the English dialogue found in the original, it is not always clear why the words are changed; and the substitution of 'What's My Line?' for 'Guess Who' as the name of an American television game show does not resolve the original problem, since the correct name of the game Caron describes is 'To Tell the Truth.'

Whatever the revisions made by Caron, four substantive problems remain, for which responsibility must be laid at Homel's feet. The first is the contradictory translation of *nous autres les enfants derrière, pêle-mêle mais en silence et respectueusement* as 'the children behind, every which way but quiet and respectful' (p 33) because the necessary comma after 'way' is omitted. Secondly, the translation often adheres too slavishly to a literal rendering of the original French, and consequently fails to provide an idiomatic English version; phrases like 'explain the business,' 'I was too far back in childhood,' 'rendering homage to,' and 'pronounced a sermon' too readily echo Caron's French diction, which should not cast such shadows over an English translation. Thirdly, Caron's title means, literally, 'the one bundled up' – figuratively, perhaps, 'the introspective one' (in a footnote to his novel Caron translates 'draft dodgers' as 'les insoumis'). It is clear from Caron's title that Nazaire is a draft dodger only from the public's viewpoint, but that in his private life he is much more. This distinction is not reflected in Homel's title. Finally, the translation offers mistaken page references on its contents page, and radically shifts the order of several paragraphs in Part II: the sentence at the bottom of p 113 is continued at the top of p 117; the first three and a half paragraphs on this page should directly follow p 113. Moreover, the sentence begun at the bottom of p 116 is left dangling, and is completed nowhere in the translation; it should, in fact, read: 'What could we ever have done to the Good Lord to make Him send us trials like this?' But unless the reader is prepared to juggle the pages in this way, he will be completely baffled by this section of *The Draft Dodger*. Such confusing oversights are surprising in a book from the House of Anansi, particularly one in which so much is so carefully done.

For excellence in book-making as well as translation all publishers and translators would do well to emulate the quality of *Inspector Therrien* (Press Porcépic, 191, $9.95 paper), Mark Czarnecki's recent translation of André Major's *L'Epidémie* (1975), volume II of his 'Histoires de déserteurs' trilogy. (The first volume was translated by Sheila Fischman in 1977 as *The Scarecrows of Saint-Emmanuel*.) Like the first volume *Inspector Therrien* returns us to the small town of Saint-Emmanuel, where the protagonist has just retired in order to be close to his beloved Emérence, the hotelkeeper's wife. Gradually, Therrien is drawn into the lives of her husband and sister, and of other inhabitants of the region, including Momo, the accused killer of *The Scarecrows*. As Therrien's sympathy shifts to this 'criminal' element, his retirement is greatly disturbed, and the open-ended, violent conclusion makes it clear that his life will remain unsettled. The descriptive and narrative excellence of Major's novel requires careful work by the translator in order to capture all the nuances and subtleties of the original. *Inspector Therrien* offers a remarkably clear echo of Major's voice, and a largely undistorted reflection of the original image. Czarnecki's approach to Major's meaning is confident, straightforward, and very reliable. Not only does he usually find authentic English phrasing for difficult passages of dialogue and prose description, but he also skilfully handles comments on the use of *tu* and *vous*, deletes duplicate lines in chapter 1 and inserts the two missing lines in their place (p 7), and finds an inspired solution to Therrien's *boucher/bouché* pun (p 137). With great sensitivity and intelligence Czarnecki has produced here a translation of very considerable beauty and accuracy.

Nevertheless, some errors do creep in. These shortcomings range from typographical and careless errors – 'fumbling' for 'rumbling' (p 155) and 'prospective' for 'respective' (p 56) – and the omission of occasional words and phrases, through some awkwardness and inexactness in phrasing ('complicity after the fact'), to mistranslations of single words and whole sentences. Some of these stem from too literal a translation of the French: *spectacle* would at times be better rendered as 'sight' or 'view' and *masse* as 'size.' When Jérôme tells Emérence, *'ça faisait ton affaire ... J'étais sûr qu'on s'entendrait mieux que ça,'* he means 'you wanted to ... I was sure we'd get along better than this,' but Czarnecki has him say, 'it was your business ... I was sure we understood each other better than that' (p 57). Similarly, 'if everything were to start all over again' (p 69) could better reflect Major's meaning if changed to 'if she had it to do all over again,' and *Rien qu'à l'voir marcher* (Just by watchin' him walk) is improperly rendered as 'We couldn't do nothin' 'cept watch him walk on' (p 173). More serious than these examples of approximations are the instances of misinterpretation: *quelques* (a few) as 'several' throughout; *jailli* (spurted) as 'jelled' (p 49); *oreiller* (pillow) as 'ear' (p 49); *me débrouiller* (to manage) as 'go out' (p 37). Two major mistranslations occur in the first chapter: the idiom *J'ai pas mal de bagages* is directly contradicted by 'I don't have much luggage' (p 4), and *les diverses boîtes de cigares devant lesquelles il affectait de ne pas se retrouver* (the various brands of cigars about which he pretended to know nothing) is completely misrepresented as 'various boxes of cigars in front of which he ended up, pretending not to be there' (p 8). Despite these oversights and errors, however, *Inspector Therrien* remains a translation of impressive skill and precision. The real measure of Czarnecki's success is the sense we have that the novel was originally written in English.

By contrast, David Lobdell's translations in recent years of fiction by Marie-Claire Blais, Jacques Benoit, and Wilfrid Lemoine have been largely unsatisfactory and unreliable, generally offering so carefree and casual an approach to their meaning that his readers receive, at best, only an approximation of the originals, indistinct echoes of the French voices. Lobdell simply puts too much into the work gratuitously, and leaves out a great deal that belongs. However, he has recently published three translations of fiction, two of which are good, and lead me to hope they represent a permanent turn to more reliable and careful work from so prolific a practitioner of the art of translation.

Let us move, then, from weakness to strength. *The Mole Men* (Oberon, 95, $15.00 cloth, $6.95 paper) is Lobdell's translation of Négovan Rajic's novel *Les Hommes-taupes* (1978), the journal of a psychiatric patient about the effects of authoritarian censorship of thought, art, and literature. There are also suggestions of political allegory here, as the unnamed narrator, who has observed a race of entranced mole men inhabiting a vast underground network of tunnels beneath his city, is persecuted as a subversive dissident for publicizing this information. Rajic's handling of this theme, similar at several points to aspects of Hugh MacLennan's *Voices in Time*, explores the effects of ubiquitous state control on the life of a sensitive individual, and thus recalls the anxieties of Barthélémy Dupuis in *A Québécois Dream* (though the novels by Beaulieu and especially MacLennan are greatly superior to Rajic's).

Lobdell's translation of Rajic's novel reflects the translator's heretofore typical disrespect for the sanctity of the original text and his disregard for the responsibility to provide a faithful English version. We find, on every page, substantial evidence of omission, distortion, gratuitous embellishment, or misinterpretation. The important qualification in the verb 'to seem' and in other words that express impressions or opinions is routinely ignored. Continued here, too, is Lobdell's usual practice of dropping single words, phrases, and sentences, and adding his own at will (especially 'suddenly'). For example, a sentence like 'I couldn't keep my eyes off the clock' (p 57) has no basis whatever in the French text. Related to this shortcoming is the practice of amplifying the original thought unnecessarily; one example must stand for dozens: *Dès le mois d'octobre de l'année dernière, j'aurais dû me douter de quelque chose* is translated as 'In all my deliberations on the subject, there was one thing I had overlooked and that ought to have aroused my suspicions' (p 70). Such distortion graduates to mistranslation when, for instance, Lobdell gives *Il n'est pas nécessaire que je revienne là-dessus* (I don't have to mention it again) as 'The more I think of it, the more convinced I become of this fact' (p 73). There are dozens of examples of such distortion in *The Mole Men*. Added to these errors are numerous mistranslations of single words and phrases: *quelques* as 'several'; *dérisoire* as 'small'; *poursuivi* (prosecuted) as 'followed'; *mois* as 'weeks'; *une noyée* as 'drowned men'; *cinquantaine* as 'about a hundred'; etc. In three cases the misinterpretation is more substantial: *les avantages l'emportent sur les inconvénients* (the advantages outweigh the disadvantages) is given as 'there are definite advantages to be derived from these inconveniences' (p 74); secondly, Lobdell is repeatedly deceived into translating 'arche' (ark) as 'arch' (pp 51, 53) although he is dealing with a description of Noah's ark in Bosch's *The Flood*; and finally, the deceptive similarity to English again traps him when he renders the description of the doctor (*empâté dans une chair jaunâtre et flasque*) as 'ensconced in a big yellow armchair' (p 88); *chair*, of course, means 'flesh.' Readers should also be warned that the translation omits two pages at the beginning (one a photocopy about moles from Buffon's *L'Histoire naturelle*, the other an illustration of a mole man), drops the title 'Postface' from the final pages, and overlooks entirely the third paragraph of chapter 6. For all these reasons Lobdell's translation of *Les Hommes-taupes* is most uneven and unreliable.

Lobdell is, however, capable of much better work, as demonstrated in *The Ceremony* (Oberon, 105, $12.95 cloth, $5.95 paper), his English version of Marie-José Thériault's collection of stories *La Cérémonie* (1978). A number of the twenty-three stories recall the themes and characters of Naubert, Beaulieu, and Rajic, for Thériault's vision repeatedly encompasses the macabre, the grotesque, and the violent. Prominent here are predatory, failed relationships, vengeful lovers, and metamorphoses of humans to animals and insects, though Thériault also provides evidence of a witty side to her talent in the imaginary conversations she constructs out of situations and figures presented in four classical paintings. Because her vision ranges from the comic to the bizarre, with as many tones as tales, the translation of *La Cérémonie* is a demanding task. Lobdell's achievement in *The Ceremony* is superior to his work in *The Mole Men* for the simple reason that he has restrained his own voice more often, thereby allowing us to hear what Thériault has to say. This approach guarantees that a good deal of *her* meaning emerges, and the anglophone reader can therfore be confident that nearly everything he reads in *The Ceremony* has a basis in the original text. The merits of the translation include Lobdell's skill at finding English equivalents for word-play in the original, especially in his adept transformation of points about grammar from French to English in the final story. Related to this strength is his wisdom in transposing details of French culture: thus, Madame Sévigné becomes Emily Post, while Maurice Grevisse turns into Noah Webster and the *Petit Robert* is changed to the *Oxford English Dictionary*. The translation of Boileau's *Satire* VIII is skilfully handled, and the entire English version of 'Elsa's Joachim' is superb – welcome evidence of Lobdell's ability.

Why, then, is he not more consistent and careful as a translator? The above assets are shadowed by a number of the weaknesses we have come to expect: a large number of adjectives and adverbs overlooked and many gratuitous additions; loose translations that embellish the original unnecessarily and thereby mislead the reader; approximations of the original vocabulary (a kind of inelegant variation for its own sake); the misuse of 'presently' (a problem in *The Mole Men* also); stilted English prose caused by too literal a translation ('inspire him with remorse,' 'tired my eyes'); and a number of mistranslations of single terms: *quelques* as 'several,' *luxurieux* (lustful) as 'exquisite,' etc. While Lobdell handles the problem of grammar lessons well, he does not always indicate where English is found in the original text. Furthermore, he eliminates a great deal: all Thériault's footnotes, all her information about the four reproductions, the two footnotes that accompany Giorgione's *The Concert*, the reference to Victor Hugo that should follow the title 'She Crossed Over Toledo Bridge in a Black Corset,' and Thériault's dedication at the beginning of the collection 'A eux, et aux autres ...' But the most serious shortcoming in *The Ceremony* is the omission of one of the stories in Part I, 'La Commodité,' which should follow 'Goat Road.' Clearly, then, while *The Ceremony* is demonstrably a better translation than *The Mole Men*, Thériault's work deserves better treatment from its translator.

All the virtues of *The Ceremony* are present to a greater degree in the third of Lobdell's 1980 translations, *The Umbrella Pines* (Oberon, 137, $12.95 cloth, $5.95 paper), his English version of Gilles Archambault's *Les Pins parasols* (1976). In its examination of one year in Serge Gaucher's troubled life as son, husband, father, and grandfather, the novel's reflective and introspective mood focuses on his failed aspirations and current circumstances as he struggles to regain the affection and respect of his estranged daughter, Emmanuelle. As in so many works of fiction translated this year, the conclusion to *Les Pins parasols* is shocking and violent, though Serge is sustained by the love of his wife, Danielle, and his determination to devote his life to his grandson's wellbeing. Lobdell's *The Umbrella Pines* respects the tone and substance of the work in a generally reliable and careful translation. There is less gratuitous addition and deletion of detail here, and very few examples where full sentences are overlooked. In this English version the descriptive and reflective passages are fluid and articulate, and Lobdell's handling of dialogue, always his particular strength as a translator, is especially good. *The Umbrella Pines* is the best he has yet done.

For all its strengths, however, the translation is flawed by inexactness, carelessness, and misinterpretation at a number of points. Some of this imprecision is caused by details deleted or added at will, others by translation so loose as to constitute a précis. Unclear antecedents often create confusion about characters in the novel, whereas Lobdell's concern to be accurate leads, at other times, to a stilted prose style: 'do his father a service,' 'lived on social welfare,' 'paying me little attentions,' and 'receive no guests' all echo closely Archambault's phrasing but clearly fail as examples of idiomatic English. Here, too, we find a number of terms and phrases mistranslated — for example: *quelques* as 'several'; *déception* (disappointment) as 'deception'; *compagne* (female companion) as 'natural world'; *le soir* (every evening) as 'one night'; *'J't'en veux pas* (I don't hold it against you) as 'I don't want you' (p 52); and *son inquiétude à elle* (her worry) as 'he'd begun to worry about her' (p. 78). In some cases the misrepresentation is still more serious: *ne s'épuisent plus à lutter* is directly contradicted by 'still struggling' (p 72); *secouée par une crise de larmes* (shaken by a fit of crying) is mistakenly rendered as 'his voice broken with sobs' (p 127), which obviously overlooks the feminine agreement in the past participle; and *pleurant trop souvent par pure détresse pour autant qu'il se mette à réfléchir* (too often crying from unrelieved anxiety whenever he began to think deeply) is completely mistranslated as 'often reduced to tears for no reason at all, though he did his best to remain calm' (pp 134-5). In addition to these errors, Lobdell drops both the dedication and the reference for the epigraph, and fails to correct Archambault's misspelling of *Finnegans Wake*. While *The Umbrella Pines* is the best of Lobdell's many translations, much room for improvement still remains.

In addition to the many works of fiction, English translations of three prominent Quebec poets have appeared in the past year, presenting work originally published in the last two decades. The first of these, Anne Hébert's *Poèmes* (1960), has recently been translated into English by A. Poulin, Jr, as *Anne Hébert: Poems* (*Quarterly Review of Literature*, 21: 3-4, Contemporary Poetry Series, 60, $20.00 cloth, $10.00 paper). These poems of vivid imagery, condensed language, and haunting vision continue to draw the attention of translators; we can now add Poulin's approach to earlier expeditions by F.R. Scott, Peter Miller, and Alan Brown. Of the many translations so far published, including several different attempts by Scott, only Brown's offers a complete version of the 1960 text. Miller's work conveniently includes the French text on facing pages, a feature promised in Poulin's translation but not provided. Furthermore, Poulin's work omits eight poems from the 'Tombeau des rois' section, two from 'Mystère de la parole,' and the intervening prose text, 'Poésie, solitude rompue.' By using the concluding words of 'Eve,' in French, as his epigraph, Poulin gives a balance and symmetry to his translation and thus in his end is his beginning. Many of the translations are ably handled, always sensitive to the sound and meaning of the original – in particular, 'Old Picture,' 'The Birth of Bread,' 'Annunciation,' and 'Eve.' No doubt some of Poulin's achievement can be explained by his work with the author on his translations, but this collaboration still does not equal the success of F.R. Scott's co-operative venture with Hébert. It is true, of course, that all translations, particularly those of poetry, are necessarily only approximations, so that alternate readings are always possible. Anglophone readers of Hébert are thus well served, for they can read as many as a half-dozen English versions of some of her poems. Poulin's is yet another echo of her voice, often skilful and generally trustworthy. His translation is more monosyllabic and poetic than Brown's, but less reliable in content. He overlooks 'Et vos feuillages' in 'A Wall' and 'Goutte à goutte' in 'Inventory,' for example, alters verb tenses from conditional to future in 'The Alchemy of Day,' and reverses the order of the first and last pair of poems in 'The Mystery of the Word.' In Poulin's translation a typesetting error in 'Eve' is overlooked, and the fact that Hébert's speaker is often identifiably female is rarely reflected in this English version. Nevertheless, although some of Hébert's ambiguity is lost and a few terms are mistranslated, all respectful and diligent voices are welcome in the chorus of translators singing her score, and Poulin's makes a worthwhile contribution.

Another distinguished Quebec poet whose work has recently been translated into English is Gaston Miron. It is entirely fitting that Miron, as one of several prominent Quebec poets who lured Robert Marteau to Canada, should at last have his own work made available to English Canadians. Although translations of brief selections from his work have appeared in anthologies and in *Ellipse*, 1 and 5, Miron's work has yet to achieve the full exposure it deserves among anglophone readers. However, this situation has been partly redressed by the recent publication of *The Agonized Life* (Torchy Wharf Press, 79, $4.00 paper), Marc Plourde's translation of the dozen poems in the 'Vie agonique' sequence as well as eleven other poems and an essay from *L'Homme rapaillé* (1970). Plourde's representative selection includes work from all but one section of the 1970 volume, and adds his translation of Jacques Picotte's 1972 interview with Miron. The prose works are illuminating supplements to the poems, for both demonstrate aspects of Miron's vision and commitment as a modern Quebec poet struggling for an authentic identity, defined through his demanding vocabulary and syntax and complex metaphors of arresting originality. Most of the time Plourde meets the challenges of Miron's language with great skill, often finding impressive and intelligent English equivalents to interpret Miron's 'strange rhetoric, difficult enough to translate, especially in any literal way' (*Ellipse*, 5). The bilingual presentation of all but one of the poems will encourage readers to return to the source; comparison of the originals and the translations will reveal the particular merits of 'Afterwards and Later,' 'Monologues on Raving Alienation,' and 'The Age of Winter' (though 'age' inadequately renders 'siècles' in the original). However, Plourde has overlooked some of Miron's word-play and his use of internal rhyme, omitted some important ellipses, and at times adhered too strenuously to the French text – for example: 'The poets of our age mount guard' (p 37). Furthermore, inexact or awkward phrasing ('ferny underbrush,' 'ear of wheat,' 'unhappiness is what I've got,' and 'your ruined smile smiles back at a ruined future') mars somewhat the quality of *The Agonized Life*. In 'Goddam Canuck' Plourde fails to deal with the mixture of English and French found in the original poem, and deletes '(extrait de *la Batèche*)' from two poems. As a result, his reference in the prose essay is lost. Furthermore, the translation provides no information on the original publication of 'A Long Road' (*Parti pris*, janvier 1965), and eliminates the concluding date and the eight important footnotes that represent Miron's elaborations or afterthoughts. Finally, there are occasional errors in reproducing the French text, most notably in 'Pour mon rapatriement,' where the second line is omitted and the fourth repeated. Let us hope Plourde's efforts here will lead eventually to a complete and reliable English version of L'Homme rapaillé.

Certainly completeness and reliability are two of the virtues found in *Daydream Mechanics* (Coach House Press, 92, $4.50 paper), Larry Shouldice's translation of Nicole Brossard's *Mécanique jongleuse / Masculin grammaticale* (1974), winner of the Governor General's Award for poetry. Shouldice, who has previously demonstrated his skill as a translator of both Brossard's fiction (*A Book*, Coach House Press, 1976) and her poetry (in *Les Stratégies du réel / The Story So Far 6*), brings his considerable talents to bear on the puzzles and codes of Brossard's 1974 text. Demonstrating the passion of/for words and a predilection for puns and word games, Brossard presents a variety of perspectives on female sexuality, always linked to language. This liaison between the sexual and the textual is pivotal and pervasive because her language has gender (she speaks, for instance, of 'her desire / in the masculine singular'). Thus, Brossard's subject is both body language and the body of language (presumably, also bawdy language), much in the manner of A.M. Klein's explorations in 'Portrait of the Poet as Landscape'; and, like Klein, she investigates the inevitable con-fusion between landscape and language. By the very nature of the two distinct languages, the English version must overlook some nuances and ambiguities, and introduce others, so that the second making will be a separate poem, but one with fundamental links to the French original. Brossard's poetry poses many formidable challenges for her readers, and still more for her translator; but Shouldice consistently reveals his respectful attention to the intricacies of her art and his skill at finding ingenious equivalents for her word games (for example, cøQUILLE is translated as '$HELL'). However, a few specific improvements might be made to *Daydream Mechanics*. The occasional variations in form and punctuation seem accidental rather than deliberate, and several typographical errors have been overlooked: 'hey' for 'key' (p 19); 'liason' (pp 44 and 83); 'CLAPS' for 'CLASP' (p 57); 'treat' for 'threat' and 'on another' for 'one another' (p 78); 'mulitple' and 'subversibe' (p 90); and 'origional' (p 91). The translation of *toute surface l'exhibe* as 'all surfaces reveals her' (p 22) clearly contains an error in agreement. Finally, there are three mistranslations: in 'Articulation' the word 'encre' is overlooked, thereby deleting Brossard's specific link between landscape and language; 'plage' (beach) is confused with and translated as 'page' (p 53); and 'gachette tira' (trigger fired) is more literally, but improbably, interpreted as 'trigger drew out' (p 70). But such oversights are rare in this excellent translation. There is, of course, no guarantee that Brossard's vision will be any more accessible or intelligible in English than in French, but the quality of

Shouldice's translation ensures that it will not be any less so; indeed, it is also, as Frye suggested of all thorough translations, a critical elucidation of the original text.

The final work to be reviewed for 1980 is, paradoxically, the best known by anglophones and the most widely read in English of all Quebec novels. Until now, however, readers of Gabrielle Roy's *Bonheur d'occasion* (1945) have encountered her work through the medium of Hannah Josephson's 1947 translation, *The Tin Flute*. Indeed, this novel was the only work of Quebec literature to appear on the 'Top Ten' survey list compiled a few years ago at the Calgary conference on the Canadian novel. The popular acclaim won by this translation is all the more ironic when we recall its manifest inadequacies, of which the best known is, perhaps, the preposterous transformation of a blizzard (*poudrerie*) into a munitions-factory explosion (chapter 12). The Josephson translation suffers from the translator's gratuitous insertions and deletions, from loose and inexact interpretations, and from her unfamiliarity with the language and locale of *Bonheur d'occasion*. Thus, after thirty-five years, a fresh and competent translation of *Bonheur d'occasion* is long overdue. The publishers have finally moved to rectify the harm caused by the promotion and sale of a poor translation by publishing a new one, by Alan Brown, which is also called *The Tin Flute* (McClelland and Stewart, 384, $35.00 cloth), a deluxe, slip-cased, limited edition of the novel that includes two handsome drawings of the author by Harold Town. Readers of Quebec fiction in English will be familiar with Brown's recent translations of Roy (*Garden in the Wind, Children of My Heart*), and will be eager to compare these earlier achievements with his most recent endeavour.

How closely has Brown approached Roy's meaning? Has he restored it after the damage *Bonheur d'occasion* sustained during Josephson's expedition? To answer these questions a brief history of the French text is essential. The first edition, in two volumes, published in Montreal by the Société des Editions Pascal, is the text upon which the Josephson translation of 1947 is based. That same year *The Tin Flute* was almost immediately made obsolete by the publication of the second (and substantially revised) edition of *Bonheur d'occasion* in Paris by Flammarion. Roy's changes involved major cuts to superfluous descriptive and analytical passages, particularly at the end of paragraphs. Ironically, the elimination of redundant material greatly improved her novel at the same time that anglophone readers were celebrating Josephson's unreliable English version of the inferior first edition. Nevertheless, *The Tin Flute* was republished in the New Canadian Library series in 1958 and widely disseminated; it is probably true to say that the translation has found more readers than the original. In the mid-sixties Beauchemin in Montreal published a 'nouvelle édition' in French, which substantially reproduced the 1947 text, adding a few further cuts of unnecessary exposition and making certain stylistic changes. Finally, in 1978 Editions internationales Alain Stanké published another edition, which notes on the verso of the title-page: 'Texte revu par l'auteur.' This edition does make some minor revisions to the 1965 Beauchemin edition, but in fact reproduces the novel in a form very similar to the 1947 edition. Nevertheless, the Stanké edition is now indisputably the most authoritative, and ought to serve as the basic text for any contemporary translation of *Bonheur d'occasion*.

Which edition has Alan Brown used for his *Tin Flute*? He does not say precisely; indeed, the only text to which he refers is the first edition. The question can only be answered by comparing his translation to the editions of 1945, 1947, 1965, and 1978. Brown's text is certainly not a translation of the first edition, for there are hundreds and hundreds of major discrepancies between the two. Similarly, *The Tin Flute* is not, apparently, based on the editions of 1947 and 1965, although the English text more closely approximates the material found in them, especially the latter. It seems, then, that Brown has very properly used the 1978 edition in preparing his translation. And yet, there are so many variations between the two that this particular connection, too, seems unlikely. Clearly we are dealing here with a translation that is not a diligent echo of the original novel. The problem of major omissions, so often a distraction and distortion in Brown's earlier translations of Roy, recurs here still more extensively. In the course of the translation more than a hundred sentences are dropped, including several full paragraphs (among them the final paragraph of chapters 7, 14, 26, 27, and 31). While Brown very rarely makes gratuitous additions to the text, he regularly omits descriptive adjectives, adverbs, phrases, and clauses. Consequently, the substance of Roy's novel is contained in *The Tin Flute*, but much of the colour and style of *Bonheur d'occasion* is lost. Such shortcomings are somewhat counterbalanced by instances of very competent work (see, for example, the beginning of chapters 6 and 7, and the final pages of chapters 2, 12, and 30). Brown also reveals some skill in transcribing colloquialisms into equivalent English speech, although a greater and more consistent use of slang is required.

While the positive elements in its translation are manifest, much more in evidence are its limitations, in particular three major weaknesses: imprecision and inexactness in the translation, resulting in approximations that distort Roy's meaning; repeated examples of awkward phrasing that produces a cumbersome, unidiomatic English prose; and finally, a large number of mistranslations. In the first category, for example, Brown interprets *désormais* (from now on) as 'now,' *moins que de coutume* (less than usual) as 'no longer,' and *Peut-être trop précoce pour son âge* (Maybe too precocious for his age) as 'Precocious.' In addition, he regularly fails to give precise terminology for figures and rituals of the Roman Catholic faith, and distorts the order of the 'Our Father' (p 355). At the same time, the translation often adheres so rigorously to the original French diction and syntax that the result is a very stilted and clumsy English style. Examples abound, of which the following is a representative selection: 'enhanced the preciousness'; 'her nose grew pinched'; 'Her cheekbones were shining'; 'heard them their catechism'; 'The avenging arm of society outraged'; 'with his naive and miserable air'; 'He couldn't refuse this mark of politeness'; 'a place where her regrets might withdraw their pursuit'; 'risked a glance'; 'at a vertiginous speed'; 'seized by a fever of intrepidity'; and 'the easy tapping of her toe beneath the table presaged the facility with which her new sacrifices would be borne.' While these examples scarcely disguise the French that gave rise to them, none of them has the precision and clarity of good English prose, particularly if it is to reflect the power and grace of Roy's style. Brown's readers and Roy herself deserve better. Thirdly, there is a great deal of mistranslation of numbers, single words, phrases, and complete thoughts. Thus, *est* is translated as 'west' (p 245), *petite* as 'large' (p 219), *sucres* (sugaring-off) as 'sugar shack' (p 218), *joue* (cheek) as 'chin' (p 145), *Salut* (So long) as 'I salute you' (p 298), and *poudrerie* (blizzard) as 'powdery snow' (p 144). The meanings of *quelques* and *plusieurs* are often reversed; and the translation includes a number of contradictions: for example, *comme pas beaucoup de monde* is completely misinterpreted as 'just like a lot of other people' (p 57); *Il n'y avait plus que de petits métiers* means just the opposite of 'there were no more little jobs' (p 157); and, as other conversations in the novel indicate, *On pourra plus se remettre sur le secours* does not mean 'We can always go back on relief' (p 85), but rather the reverse. At times Brown also deals unsatisfactorily with the use of English in *Bonheur d'occasion*, and mishandles the point of Daniel's attempt to spell his mother's name (p 227).

There are other shortcomings. Granted, there seems to be no entirely satisfactory or adequate English equivalent for Roy's title, but the decision to copy Josephson's title will not only create unnecessary confusion for readers of Quebec literature in translation, but also perpetuate the poor choice she made in 1947. The strong emphasis on happiness in Roy's title and novel demands some acknowledgment in the English title. Moreover, the 'tin flute' is but one symbol of happiness, and then only for a secondary character. Such a title therefore deflects attention both from Roy's central theme and from her two main characters, Rose-Anna and Florentine. At the same time, it must be observed that the publishers of this new translation, presented in a limited and expensive edition, could hardly expect to attract the wide popular notice among anglophone readers that Roy's novel needs and deserves. The book *is* well made, and the Town drawings *are* very fine. But we must look beyond the cover and bindings; and when we do, we could wish the publishers had used their energy and funds in order to offer a reliable English counterpart to *Bonheur d'occasion* at a reasonable price. Translations can be beautiful *and* affordable (witness Barry Callaghan's *Treatise on White and Tincture*) but they must first of all be competently written and carefully edited. All this means that, having waited over thirty years for this second approach to Roy's meaning, we must already begin to hope for a third. *Caveat emptor!*

Humanities

Northrop Frye. *Creation and Recreation*
The Larkin-Stuart Lectures. University of Toronto Press. vi, 76. $3.95

As the author tells us in his preface, these lectures, given under the auspices of Trinity College and St Thomas Anglican Church, Toronto, 'draw on earlier material ... some of it now out of print ... they are also connected with an ongoing project of greater length, a study of the narrative and imagery of the Bible and its influence on secular literature.'

Frye reads the Bible as William Blake read it, in its 'infernal or diabolical sense,' and he uses a typological strategy to arrive at configurations which would have dismayed the Fathers of the church. At the centre of his thesis is the contention that human creativity is quite at odds with what is 'supposed' to be 'the original divine act of making the world.' More explicitly, 'the humanly creative is whatever divinely disturbs our sense of "the" creation, a reversing or neutralizing of it ... What seems one of the few admirable forms of human achievement, the creation of the arts, turns out to be a kind of decreation.'

The biblical myth of the 'sky-father,' of the artificer god 'who starts everything off by making all things in more or less their present form, is not very encouraging for the human artist.' Consequently, in much traditional Christian art, man 'has no real initiative; liberty, for example, in Milton is nothing that man naturally wants but is something God is determined he shall have.' And orthodox Christian dogma, we are told, has served to inhibit human creativity:

> Everything that raises man from his fallen level to his originally designed one involves some degree of returning to his original creation. It is recreation only in the sense that man is included in it: the actual process is God's redemption of man, man doing very little for himself that is of any real use. The whole process of human response, in Christian doctrine, is contained within the Holy Spirit, so that man's redemption is a drama within the persons of the Trinity in which man has a very limited actor's role. As the Holy Spirit guides the church, the doctrine of the Trinity, which is so central to Christian dogma in both Catholic and Protestant contexts, seems to have been, in its historical setting, a doctrine designed primarily to prevent man from slipping out of the grip of the church.

The Fathers of the church (and many of her children) would seem to stand accused here of a cunning conspiracy. Nevertheless, the crude secularism of our own time has done nothing to deliver us from the inhibitions contrived and imposed by the church. 'The older construct wore out because it repressed the sense of human autonomy ... But a purely secular construct whether it be humanist or communist may be expressing complementary things.'

It is in opposition to all repressive ideologies or myths, whether they be sacred or secular, that Frye proposes his own visionary theorem. His approach to the mystery of creation 'starts with the vision that man has a nature recreated in humanized form, the vision recorded in various forms of the arts ... It culminates in a vision of recreation in which man himself participates, and which appears to be in fact the total goal and aim of human effort.'

In this new vision God 'the sky-father,' the artificer, the designer, is dead. God, 'the noun' (the God 'who belongs to the category of things and objects'), is replaced in this higher vision by God as 'verb,' and as 'verb' expresses 'a process fulfilling itself.' One supposes that Person is a noun, too, and not an 'object' or a 'thing.' But this noun is avoided. Similarly the nouns 'Word' and 'Spirit,' once thought of as divine Persons, are, we are told, better understood as 'qualities of self-transcendence.' These two nouns, if not 'extended into areas beyond the human,' can signify and proclaim 'the power that has created all our works of culture and imagination,' the power 'that is still ready to recreate both our society and ourselves.'

It is therefore not without some bewilderment that we read a few pages later on that Word and Spirit, in a kind of dialectical identity with their new-found significance as 'qualities of self-transcendence,' may still be known as 'divine persons ready and willing to redeem mankind.' After Frye's reservations about all forms of 'professed belief' and his pejorative comment on trinitarianism and on the divinity of nouns, it is not altogether clear what he means by the divine personalities of the Word and the Spirit, extended as they here seem to be 'into areas beyond the human.'

But at the very end of these lectures he assures us that 'the goal of human recreation ... bears a curious resemblance to the traditional versions of divine creation at the source.' Is he not saying that man, in transcendence of himself and of all 'professed belief,' may yet sail on to Byzantium where, freed from all dogmatic repression and outmoded myth, he will see that creation has 'finally become one with recreation and the revelation at the end of human effort [will also] be a recognition of something at the beginning'? In our end, perhaps, is our beginning? Does he not mean that in the full and final release of our own creativity we shall at the last know creativity 'at the source'?

But when the 'process' fulfils itself – in our art, in our action – shall we see IT face to face? And what are we to understand by this 'something' which happened 'at the beginning'? Was the Word in the beginning? And was this the Word made flesh – the divine Person? Is it that we do not need to be told? Or could it be, as Richard Webster said recently of the structuralists, that Frye is providing 'a church for those too pure to entertain the idea of a god'? Such a church, I must suppose, could not be called St Thomas – or Trinity. Certainly Frye does less than justice to the main line of Christian theology, to the doctrine of Christian liberty, and to the often vivifying influence of the church on all the arts. But Frye's church is not the church which Richard Webster locates in structuralism. Frye's church is The Church of the Holy Verb. And it is indeed a church! For throughout this intriguing and provocative essay in mythologizing and de-mythologizing, done in the hope of searching out the dark mystery of creation in the visible act of human creativity, we cannot be unaware of an authentic kind of religious impulse. Frye's quest seems to be a quest for *pure act*, nameless, beyond personality, beyond and before the tentative transience of myth – *pure act* to be made present to us ultimately in the untrammelled freedom of our own creativity. This *is* the religious quest – or, rather, an aspect of the religious quest. But one wonders if Northrop Frye has not needlessly hampered this great enterprise and narrowed and shortened his own bright vision by the repression, or dismissal, or avoidance of the pertinent insights of Christian theology and the rapt knowledge of the mystics.   (MALCOLM ROSS)

Kenneth Quinn. *Texts and Contexts: The Roman Writers and Their Audience*
Routledge & Kegan Paul 1979. ix, 266. $36.75

Professor Quinn's latest book is a new departure for him, an introductory overview of Latin literature in the classical period. The task calls, it might be supposed, for impassive factuality first, convincing summary second, and controversial exploration last of all. Not so, it appears. When the 'blurb' promises 'a history of Roman literature in which the emphasis is laid on the quality of the texts discussed rather than on comprehensiveness of treatment, and on organic relationships rather than on chronology,' those who know Quinn's earlier *Latin Explorations* will rightly expect a display of provocative judgments, unorthodox perspectives, and saltatory connections. I am not convinced that it becomes the professional *enfant terrible* to shift his aim from unsettling the stuffy academics to assuring novices a safe entry into classical writings. I *am* sure that the book will not become an accepted handbook.

Texts and Contexts offers its text for a range of contexts, among them 1/ use as a textbook, 2 / interest in literature from the proverbial General

Reader, 3 / not least, I think, though least proclaimed, the public image presented by Latin studies.

1 / Most of the information is, of course, correct (odd to find Seneca and Lucan cousins, p 213). But the coverage is wilfully erratic (e.g., five slighting pages for Propertius, three for Juvenal – most of the space taken up with translated extracts). The evaluations are idiosyncratic and at times bizarre (in particular post-Augustan literature is stigmatized with a moral fervour – 'morbid symptoms of the time in which Lucan lived,' and so forth – unrepresentative of responsible post-Victorian criticism; at times Quinn seems to be writing series of 'examination questions': e.g., 'Persius may be described as a Horace who has turned Stoic and lost his sense of humour' [p 196] – discuss!). Most seriously of all, however, the review is vertiginously disengaged from chronology – on principle. The strategy no doubt keeps Quinn's interest going, but I think it betrays a lack of pedagogic realism. 'Students taking classical literature in translation courses and ... students of English literature,' to quote the blurb again, will *not* be able to use *Texts and Contexts* as a reference book without losing the contexts of the texts they are set to read. For instance, the relationships between writers under Augustus singled out as 'organic' by Quinn destroy any possibility of observing the developments in literary production through the 20s BC as a close-knit, indeed incestuous, phenomenon. Constant flipping back to the pair of tables, pp 27–8, wouldn't happen and would hardly help. At a more pedantic level I can't see students being lured out of the 'conservatism' that 'has always been the mark of the reading public' (the first sentence of the book) by the sporadic references to eighteenth-century string quartets, Eliot, Bach, Empson. (The first remark I would delete would be the patronizing reference to 'the good student essay which substitutes empathy and enthusiasm for understanding. He misses things that are there, and sees things that aren't there,' p 39. Don't we all?)

2 / The General Reader may well find *Texts and Contexts* more entertaining. But this will depend a lot on his age, innocence, ideology. The opening chapter, which sets up a range of 'morals,' from critical methodology to the lessons of history, gives 47 generous pages to whet the appetite: McLuhanesque eschatology on the likely disappearance of literature from culture – 'There are signs that our generation (I speak of myself and some of those who will read this book) is the last in which literature occupied a natural and central place in cultural life' (p 33); robust dismissal of glibly deterministic theorizing – Bateson from thirty years ago is the only named victim (pp 40–6); and an introduction to the sublime rhetoric of the grand vision, the truly original genius, the timeless masterpiece, in which the book will operate – my own favourite mysticism here is on p 47: 'The work which is not somehow fresh in its form remains an inadequate embodiment of fresh insight.' My feeling is that there are quite

a number of General Readers who will find the recipe appealing – but they must not be too young, too well-acquainted with the last half-century of critical theory, or (obviously) too concerned with the ins-and-outs of Roman cultural history.

3 / Housman's edition of Lucan was 'for the use of editors': much of Quinn's prolific writing has, ex- or im-plicitly, been designed for the use of professional Latinists who propose to write *their* books on each subject. *Texts and Contexts* may count as a useful irritant, perhaps even a thorn in the flesh, when the next introductory survey is to be written: on the one hand an easy conventional 'what? when? 'approach must come to terms with Quinn's arguments in favour of 'why? and how?'; and on the other hand a traditional ratification of inherited judgments based on inscrutable appeals to taste and experience will be harder to write after the involuntary discrediting of the procedure available for inspection in *Texts and Contexts*. I am not, however, persuaded that either lesson will, in fact, be learned. (JOHN HENDERSON)

W.K. Thomas. *The Fizz Inside: Critical Essays of a Lighter Kind*
University of Waterloo Press. x, 389. $9.95

The reader need not beware: despite the title, one may open Professor W.K. Thomas's *The Fizz Inside*, even after agitation, without the danger of being drenched by a Niagara of sweet champagne: pop do not go the essays. What is contained is much more palatable: light, yes, but with body and bite.

The genre is becoming rare: who except the superstars can get collected essays published now – and when was the last one at only $9.95 in hard cover? More's the pity (less is more?), for Thomas, in a belles-lettristic spirit, offers us a generous share in his wide reading and perceptive analysis. There is no pressure to use the material in one's courses, though it is evident enough that some of the questioning and research that lie behind the essays was prompted by his teaching. One benefits simply from the reading and the reflection and rereading the book prompts.

The collection is, then, non-professional, which is not of course to say unprofessional. Thomas must command a retentive memory, a capacious filing cabinet, and the leisure to browse: of these only the filing cabinet (until the word-processor with bottomless capacity is installed) is mandatory for the professional, and my filing cabinet even now lacks a folder tabbed 'Relax and Enjoy.' As to the browsing: the essays (twenty-one in all, reprinted from many journals), while revealing Thomas's central concern with the eighteenth century, and particularly with its poetry, include discussions of *Catch-22*, A.P. Herbert (here and elsewhere too much summary), Milton, nineteenth-century Canadian oratory (a particularly valuable account, there being so little study of our tradition), Rupert Brooke, Sidney, translation, satire, and a good deal more. Throughout there is a demonstrated skill in exposition, a nice turn of scholarly inquisitiveness, a happy attention to detail, and an admirable willingness to grant great authors their askings. Thomas can run a stiff line: 'the paraphrastic kind of translation that seeks to create responses equivalent to those created in the original audience comes the closest to fulfilling the desires of those readers who wish to experience as much as possible of the literary excellence of the original works' (p 160). And occasionally the rough side of his tongue rasps away at silliness, but no brutal critical wars are waged. It might be admitted, in fact, that theory is not a strength of the individual essays, *a fortiori* of the collection as a whole – but that is a purely professional remark.

On the negative side, one might also say (and without contradicting the judgment about theory) that some of the fun is diminished by Thomas's too-pressing analytic spirit, which sometimes lets the air out: he is enjoying his authors, but he's not laughing. This spirit shows to disadvantage in the index, which unbelievably in a book of this kind runs from page 343 to page 389, and includes entries for 'Africa' and 'agriculture,' 'Zeus' and 'Zollverein': knowing the industry and proclivities of Waterloo (where Thomas teaches and where the book was published), I suspect a computer at work (and some of the typos smell of the terminal); knowing the industry and proclivities of our colleagues, I suspect that no one will ever consult the index, so perhaps as little is lost as is gained by it. The exordial striving in 'To the Reader, especially the *Potential* Reader' is also misjudged, for the attempts to tie the essays together made here (and repeated at the section divisions throughout the book) are a trifle arch and, I think, unsuccessful.

They are also unnecessary, for the pleasures and benefits are in the individual pieces; unity comes from the authorial voice which, even when one wants to dissent from assertion, implication, or tone, is a welcome one, inviting contemplation, admiration, and a humane balance. (JOHN M. ROBSON)

William Blissett, editor. *Editing Illustrated Books: Papers Given at the Fifteenth Annual Conference on Editorial Problems, University of Toronto, 2–3 November 1979*
Garland Publishing. 133, illus. $17.00

For fifteen volumes the Toronto Conference on Editorial Problems has sustained high interest and standards in directing attention to major issues in scholarly publishing. The current volume, continuing those standards, follows the fourteenth volume's lead (*Editing Correspondence*) in moving away from a single historical period to 'the specific editorial problems that arise in connection with illustration,' as William Blissett says in his introduction. He defines illustration, noting that originally the term referred to what shed light, made lustrous, beautified, exemplified, elucidated, or, in these less illumined days, what renders clear by means of drawings or pictures. The entire etymology concerns, variously, the five editors whose papers are gathered here along with some illustrations. They treat medieval illumination, eighteenth-century master-drawings (Tiepolo), late eighteenth-century illustrated folio publishers and Blake, nineteenth-century illustration on microfiche, and contemporary illustration from the private presses. Differing and usefully complementary meanings for 'editing' these illustrated books appears in these papers.

Luba Eleen, giving a tempting glimpse of her forthcoming *Illustration of the Pauline Epistles*, discusses the role of models for the medieval illuminator in copying, with significant changes, cycles of biblical pictures, traditional in subject-matter (whether narrative or doctrinal) as well as in design motifs. By studying various manuscripts of the Acts of the Apostles (made at Verona, first half of the thirteenth century) and the Pauline Epistles (Paris, 1220s) Eleen can determine priorities and lines of descent of these manuscripts. Hence 'editing' appears in two important senses in her paper: the illuminator was himself an editor in using picture cycles available to him as models; and the modern scholar is an editor in studying these family trees of illuminations.

In preparing Tiepolo's drawings for his edition George Knox has come upon the conundrum of widely scattered drawings and paintings on the Anthony and Cleopatra theme. To bring order to the facts (surprisingly rich as Knox assembles them), Knox's hypothesis is that Tiepolo was commissioned by the Czarina Elizabeth Petrovna in the 1740s for an Anthony and Cleopatra cycle for the New Summer Palace. Using editorial method (comparing versions of drawings and paintings, supporting documents, and historical data) he even gives a conjectural reconstruction of the room in which the paintings were hung. So to Knox 'editing' these drawings means determining their subject-matter, their purpose and place in the whole cycle, and their entire context in the Russian court. The argument is fascinatingly complex, and has all of the plausible conviction of conjecture artfully displayed.

To G.E. Bentley, Jr, writing on the great illustrated book publishers of the 1790s and William Blake, 'editing' means publishing (following Dr Johnson), the task of these impresarios of the book. He shows that Blake's illuminated books 'were fostered if not begotten by the surge of interest in illustrated books in the 1790's.' After justifying engraving as a fine art, more time-consuming and profitable by far than painting, Bentley leads us through the publication of such massive illustrated works as Martyn's *Universal Conchologist* (1784-7, 160 plates coloured by hand by children specially trained), Boydell's Shakespeare (9 and 2 supplementary volumes of plates, 1791-1803) for which 185 paintings were commissioned from leading artists, Macklin's Bible (6 volumes, 1791-1800, 71 plates), and Bowyer's editon of Hume's *History of England* (6 volumes, 1793-1806) involving 195 commissioned paintings. Each publisher established a gallery in Pall Mall to show the paintings, but it was not surprising, in the light of the Napoleonic blockade and the collapse of the continental book and print market, that several of these editors went bankrupt. Such lush volumes provide the context for Richard Edwards's edition of Young's *Night Thoughts* (1797) for which Blake was asked to provide a design for each of the 537 pages. As it turned out, only the first volume appeared, with 43 plates, but *Night Thoughts* has an artistic unity found in none of the other illustrated books, in that one artist's vision had inspired it, and had completed the designs and engravings, making it 'one of the supreme achievements in illustrated books' of the age, and preparing for the even greater achievement of Blake's *Milton* and *Jerusalem* when the artist wrote the large volumes he illustrated, and edited and published them himself.

The remaining two papers recount the practical editors' adventures in the book trade. Thomas V. Lange, who supplied the bibliographical entries to *The Illustrator and the Book in England, 1790-1940* (the catalogue of the Pierpont Morgan Library's 1976 exhibition of Gordon Ray's collection of 100 illustrated books), has become the adviser (another meaning for 'editor') to a microfiche edition of all the illustrated pages from the Ray 100 on some 229 fiches. His problems involved what pages to include, with how much text, and, worst of all, where to find acceptable copies to film. Since the catalogue is included with the microfiche cards, Lange worries that the user might be misled into thinking that the fiches reproduce pages from the Ray copies ('Each entry describes the specific copy examined, which is from Mr. Ray's collection unless otherwise stated' says Lange's catalogue note) although the copies photographed are all in England. Lange chronicles the editor's difficulties in translating Ray's delight in specific copies of his magnificent collection into a bibliographical reference tool on nineteenth-century English illustration. It attempts to be a definitive record of the published state of books which, because of the vagaries of illustrated book publishing, tend to exist in a variety of states.

Charlene Garry, the founder of the Basilisk Press, writing on the modern illustrated book as a work of art, skilfully contrasts the era of the English private press (1890-1939) with the modern efflorescence of private press publishing. She illustrates her argument that the modern private press is operated by an artist-writer-craftsman with examples from English and American presses, finally giving an account of problems involved in editing (the traditional meaning) and printing books at her own press.

The volume outlines a broad range of current scholarly and practical problems in editing illustrated books; it also extends the meaning of editing beyond other volumes in the series. It is a pity that no record of the discussion which the papers doubtless engendered could be included. And what *did* John Leyerle say 'on the workings of the bicameral mind in medieval illuminated pages' to which the volume's editor makes only that reference? (WILLIAM WHITLA)

Martin Puhvel. *Beowulf and Celtic Tradition*
Wilfrid Laurier University Press 1979. x, 142. $8.00

The theory that the Beowulf poet may have been influenced by Celtic culture and tradition has been with us now for close to a century, and yet for most of this time, rather than being tossed about vigorously as a critical football should be, it has mostly lain on the ground with only the occasional scholar venturing to pick it up. Early proponents of the theory, such as Deutschbein, von Sydow, and Dehmer, often overstated their cases and mixed thoroughly reasonable hypotheses with flights of fancy so unlikely that their entire work fell into disrepute. Such an attitude must also explain the relatively little attention which has been paid to James Carney's essay 'The Irish Affinities of *Beowulf.*' Carney, like many of his predecessors, linked a central thesis which was so weak as to be basically untenable (that the Irish tale *Táin Bó Fraích* provides 'a small-scale model for *Beowulf,*' p 121) with other arguments of lesser import but far greater probability. Chief among these was the suggestion that the list of the progeny of Cain (or Ham, since the manuscript is confused on the point) which forms Grendel's genealogy derives from Irish ecclesiastical lore – more specifically, from Isidore of Seville's *Etymologiae*, filtered through an Irish source, the *Sex aetates mundi*. Whenever precisely we may date the poem, the chance of its author's coming into contact with Irish clerics, whether in Mercia, Anglia, or Northumbria, is high.

Martin Puhvel has now taken up the subject and has examined nine elements of the poem in the light of possible Celtic (usually Irish) influence. He has selected these examples with the intention of 'referring to what appear to me the truly significant and cogent ones' (p 13, n 43). Among his useful chapters is the discussion of the light which illuminates Grendel's cave as Beowulf decapitates the monster's corpse. Puhvel associates this light, whose source is left very unclear in the Old English poem, with various light-emitting swords of Celtic tradition. Though much of the chapter (which previously appeared in *Folklore*, 83) is convincing, Puhvel is misleading when he claims that in the Welsh tale *Culwch and Olwen* the giant Wrnach is decapitated 'with a lightning stroke' (p 32). The Welsh text simply states that the giant's head is struck off 'y ergyt' 'at a blow.'

Puhvel's best argument deals with the origin of Grendel's cave. The so-called 'waterfall theory' has been popular now for over half a century, but it fails to explain why the cave appears more like an inhabited hall than a natural cave, nor does it explain why Beowulf swims *down* to it. Carney suggested that the cave and its approach resemble more closely the common Irish tales of visits to the otherworld beneath a body of water, the Tír fó Thuinn. Puhvel adds little to Carney's argument, but it has not been widely accepted and is well worth repeating.

Many of Puhvel's arguments remain unconvincing. His chapter on Beowulf's prowess as a swimmer dismissees too casually both the extensive Icelandic parallels, whose relevance to the Breca episode is that they are often competitions, and the arguments of Karl Wentersdorf and F.C. Robinson that Beowulf, in his escape from Frisia, may not be swimming at all. It is simply not true that 'palpable parallels to the swimming feats of Beowulf are lacking in Scandinavian tradition' (pp 59–60). Similarly, while the description of Beowulf's state of mind before Grendel's attack might conceivably owe something to stories of Irish battle-rage, this does little to explain his passive observation of the death of Hondscio.

Far too frequently Puhvel writes as if the time and place of *Beowulf*'s composition were established facts. In his critique of the 'waterfall theory' he finds it highly unlikely that 'a poet from the northern part of England' (p 107) would be unfamiliar with waterfalls. (Puhvel also, rather perversely, cites *Sir Gawain and the Green Knight* as 'another poem from the northern part of England,' p 108). Similarly, he rejects the influence of Scandinavian folklore on the water monsters 'on account of the early date of the epic' (p 65). Puhvel does make a useful case for the reconsideration of the place of the Hand and the Child type of folktale in the genesis of *Beowulf*, but it is both overstated and premature to say that 'the basic, central ingredients of the plot of the story of the fight with Grendel and his mother can thus, it would seem, be identified' (p 130).

Finally, it should be said that the book is one of the worst examples of the publisher's art I have ever seen. Generally sloppy production, including the presence of pasted-in pages, suggests that the book has not passed through the hands of an editor. A competent editor would also have been able to correct Puhvel's stylistic shortcomings; every page has examples of solecisms which should never have appeared in a work of scholarship. This is especially unfortunate in that the 'Celtic question' in *Beowulf* has received far less attention than it deserves, and Puhvel's book is unlikely either to stimulate or focus that attention. (DAVID N. KLAUSNER)

JoAnna Dutka. *Music in the English Mystery Plays*
Medieval Institute Publications, Western Michigan University.
viii, 171, illus. $18.80 cloth, $11.80 paper

This book is the first full-length study of a subject for which adequate treatment was long overdue: and although the work has limitations, Professor Dutka deserves our gratitude. The book studies the English cycle plays in order to determine where music is required in them – in itself no easy task, for several reasons – and sets out the information in the following sections: 1 / an index of songs (both Latin and English), with commentary; 2 / an index of instruments, with commentary; 3 / a glossary of musical terms, with commentary; 4 / a list of sources for the musical settings; and 5 / a summary table listing the musical items in the six cycles (Chester, Coventry, N-Town, Norwich, Towneley, and York) side by side. The index of songs includes transcriptions of all the extant music – the Chester *Gloria* fragment, the two Coventry 'carols,' and the six York pieces (two settings of each of three texts).

To this work Dutka has added a second arm by making use of guild accounts and civic records. Two factors have always suggested that this was at least highly desirable: first, the evidence offered by the plays themselves (in text references and stage directions) and such related texts as the Chester banns is clearly incomplete; secondly, the extracts from guild accounts, etc, cited by scholars such as Sharp and Salter show that these records were a rich potential source of information on the music. Dutka's PHD thesis (on which this book is based), completed a year before the REED project started in 1973, included an impressive set of transcriptions from manuscript account-books, material fully utilized in *Music in the English Mystery Plays*. (The transcriptions are not presented in the book: no doubt it was considered that the publication of REED volumes from 1979 onwards made this unnecessary.)

From all this material Dutka constructs a fascinating and comprehensive discussion (partly in the introduction and partly in the commentaries) of the uses of music in the plays. In doing so she considerably modifies John Stevens's view of the music as primarily representational, emphasizing instead the music's functions in articulating the dramatic form (at entrances, exits, changes of focus from one location to another, the passage of time, and so on). Although this explanation follows hints thrown out by Nan Cooke Carpenter and by Stevens, it is the first discussion of these functions and constitutes an important addition to our understanding of the subject.

A work of such thoroughness as this must be taken seriously, and Dutka lifts the subject at last away from the sidelines of literary study. But the approach is still basically a literary one, and the book's limitations stem from this. In the first place, the work cannot easily be used in the preparation of a performance, a matter that has become of importance following the productions of complete cycles from 1975 onwards. A producer needs a cue-list giving him all the necessary information, but the information is here scattered in several places – principally in sections 1 and 4 of my first paragraph. Moreover, while the index of songs (section 1) gives the sources of texts, the sources of the music are relegated to an appendix (section 4): again, this hides away vital information, and is especially strange in view of the book's title. Secondly, this and other matters suggest that more expertise on music and liturgy must eventually be brought to bear on the subject. For example, is the Gloria of the Mass really a possibility when we look for a musical setting of the angels' *Gloria*? Musical and liturgical considerations suggest not, but the opposite is implied by Dutka's listing of three possible sources for the text – the Mass Gloria first – without any critical assessment of their relative merits (p 29).

In one sense these are quibbles, however, for the book does not pretend to approach the difficult practical questions concerning the use of polyphony, etc, that it will eventually be our aim to answer. Dutka's purpose has clearly been to present the results of literary and musical archaeology, and future researchers in the subject will be grateful to her for accomplishing a much-needed task so successfully. (RICHARD RASTALL)

John Ripley. *Julius Caesar on Stage in England and America, 1599–1973*
Cambridge University Press. xiii, 370, illus. $37.50

For one reason or another *Julius Caesar* has not been at the centre of modern critical readings of the Shakespeare canon, though it has long been a favourite school play, because of its 'sensational action, straightforward characters, and absence of sex,' and actors from Betterton to Gielgud have delighted in it, as have literary actors from Polonius to James Tyrone. Its popularity on the stage was perhaps at its peak in the nineteenth century, in England and America, but it was also surprisingly successful in the Restoration, when the subject of political assassination might have seemed too touchy; it remained one of the Shakespeare plays that Restoration audiences saw unaltered and largely uncut. Its political 'relevance' has always been emphasized in one way or another by directors or audiences: early American audiences were drawn to the virtuous republicanism of the play, lending less attention to the success of the ruthless demagogues, one assumes, while a more recent American production, that of Orson Welles in 1937, provided the political colouring that has largely prevailed in staging for the last forty-odd years.

John Ripley's book is at its best as a fascinating chronicle of the taste through which the play has been filtered over the four hundred years of its stage career. The myth of Rome, exotic and noble, has always been most tellingly reflected in the second-rate art of any period, and in the theatre we can locate certain stylistic touchstones which have had their effect on the reading and playing of *Julius Caesar*: in 1713 Addison's *Cato*, a hundred years later the *Virginius* of Sheridan Knowles, one of Macready's great vehicles, and a hundred years after that the 1926 film of *Ben Hur*. The aesthetics of staging have changed as the presence of the *populus Romanus* has been more or less insisted on. Shakespeare's own Roman mob was probably quite small, as stage mobs continued to be in the seventeenth and eighteenth centuries; their schoolboyish misbehaviour on the 'lend me your ears' speech is frostily recorded by Francis Gentleman. The careful rehearsal and grouping of many actors to form a massive spectacle is perhaps best known as the hallmark of the Meininger troupe at the end of the nineteenth century, but this fashion of staging the play began with Kemble's production in 1812 and reached its absurd peak in a production in Los Angeles in 1916, with five thousand performers as gladiators, slave girls, and soldiers. Ripley is less interesting as a critic of the play itself; he feels that it has not been well served by modern productions and calls it 'a heroic play adrift in an anti-heroic age.' He is more sanguine than Granville-Barker about its construction, and he does not really compare it, as modern critics and theatregoers have done, with Shakespeare's other plays on classical themes.

One cavil and one cheer. The 'Chronological Handlist of Performances, 1599–1973,' which should be a very useful tool, is not rigorous in its principles. Either it should list only stage performances, or it should include a complete broadcast record and a record of all film versions, which are in any case briefly mentioned in the text. Since both major films include Gielgud, who has been acting in the play from the age of twelve, they should be in any list of 'performances.' The cheer is for the jacket design, an elegant, energetic Roman group by Eric Fraser. (JOHN H. ASTINGTON)

Anne Lancashire, editor. *The Second Maiden's Tragedy*
Revels Plays. Manchester University Press / Johns Hopkins University Press 1978.
xix, 317. $20.00

George Hibbard, editor. *Bartholmew Fair*
New Mermaid Edition. Benn 1977. xxxvi, 180. £1.95 paper

These two distinguished examples of the editing of seventeenth-century drama address editorial challenges as different as the texts themselves. *The Second Maiden's Tragedy* exists in a unique manuscript in the British Library and has had few modern editions; Professor Lancashire's can justly claim to be the first authoritative text. *Bartholmew Fair* (Professor

Hibbard restores Jonson's spelling of the title throughout), badly printed in the Folio of 1631, has already been scrupulously edited in Herford and Simpson's authoritative complete *Ben Jonson* and has made numerous other modern appearances. Lancashire thus has the task of introducing an obscure and neglected work to a modern audience, while Hibbard seeks to shed new light on a classic. It is appropriate to the widely divergent challenges involved that Lancashire chooses a conservative, Hibbard a somewhat more radical, editorial approach.

Lancashire's conservatism manifests itself first of all in her treatment of the disputed question of the play's authorship. Her introduction argues persuasively for Middleton as the author, a view which necessitates ascribing *The Revenger's Tragedy* to Middleton instead of to Cyril Tourneur. She presents her evidence completely and convincingly, but refrains from making the ascription definite and so makes no more claims than the evidence will bear. The edition itself, with the many parallels to other Middleton plays which she adduces, must become part of the continuing debate.

Conservatism is evident as well in the minute detail she lavishes on every aspect of the edition, from the lengthy introduction with its exhaustive treatment of manuscript problems through the copious annotations of the text itself to the detailed appendices, one of the most useful of which deals with the question of dramatic censorship under Elizabeth I and James I. The obvious benefit of such detail is thoroughness; there are few questions about the text which are not considered somewhere in the critical material. Its only drawback is a tendency towards excessive annotation. The General Editor's Preface reminds the reader (p ix) that 'one of the hallmarks of the Revels Plays is the thoroughness of their annotations.' Even so, is it necessary, in a serious scholarly edition, to gloss 'expound' (I.i.94), 'Mass' (I.i.229), 'maid' (IV.iv.37), or 'love' (V.i.17.1), all adequately defined for textual purposes in the *Concise Oxford Dictionary*? Or to inform the reader that 'pirates were a constant menace to sea travellers in the early seventeenth century' (III.71)? This kind of annotation simply impedes the reader's progress through the text without eludicating genuinely difficult material and calls too much attention to the editor's presence. Yet where elucidation is genuinely required, Lancashire is always ready with a helpful note, and zealousness is doubtless preferable to indifference. By contrast, her notes on the probable staging of a given scene are always pertinent and far too infrequent. More notes on staging at the expense of some of the most obvious lexical glosses would have been welcome and might have intensified the sense of the play's theatrical potential.

For *The Second Maiden's Tragedy* seems so stilted and artificial on the page that I question whether it fulfils Clifford Leech's criterion for inclusion in the Revels series (p vii), that it 'should be such as to deserve and indeed demand performance.' The scholar will value this text for its place in the history of drama. Lancashire attempts to rescue it from theatrical obscurity by applying a heavily allegorical reading to its main plot and by praising the subplot for its 'psychological depth' (p 33). But I doubt that these qualities are enough to make it live onstage again (if, indeed, it ever achieved such life). To locate a work within a complex and unfamiliar literary tradition, in this case the saint's life, does not necessarily prove its quality or theatrical appeal. Lancashire admits that the effect of *The Second Maiden's Tragedy* 'has been lost for modern readers because of our unfamiliarity with the conventions and motifs ... upon which it depends' (p 33). Her edition serves to bring those conventions into focus but does not convince me that the literary complexity thus revealed has strong dramatic potential today.

Hibbard has no such battles to fight. The modern theatrical effectiveness of *Bartholmew Fair* has been argued critically and demonstrated in production. His challenge is to present an accurate, readable modern text and to elucidate it with appropriate annotation and commentary. He approaches this task with a grateful acknowledgment of the herculean labours of Herford and Simpson before him and achieves an enviable balance of recapitulation of their work and radical departure from it.

His introduction briefly considers a moral and didactic reading of the play that emphasizes the conversions of Wasp, Busy, and Overdo, then rejects it as inadequate to the play's complexity. In its place he suggests an interpretation that plays upon puppetry and the puppetlike 'ruling passions or ... idées fixes' (p xxv) of most of the play's characters. This reading is valuable for its truth to Jonson's overall development. Jonson soon outgrew the explicit conversions and rigid humours of the early plays (*Cynthia's Revels* and *Everyman Out*, for example). Yet he never forsook completely a conception of human nature and of dramatic construction that relied heavily on the recurring idiosyncracies of human behaviour as revealed and tested by experience.

Hibbard's annotations are exemplary. His general principle, a wise one, is to gloss more frequently but in less scholarly detail than do Herford and Simpson. Consequently, his annotations are less cumbersome and more immediately accessible to the layman than are his predecessors'. Furthermore, his keen eye for social context as it illuminates the text leads him to some genuine improvements over their precedent. See, for example, his notes on 'Jack' (I.i.17), 'tokenworth' (I.ii.33), 'Meal-tide' (I.ii.59), 'sweet singers' (I.ii.60–1), 'fleaing' (II.ii.66), 'hole in the nose' (II.vi.44–5), 'because Destiny' (IV.iii.48–9), and 'Bridget' (V.vi.67).

The radical nature of his editorial stance becomes clear in the textual emendations. The Folio of 1631 is faulty, Jonson himself having despaired at the carelessness of 'the Lewd Printer,' and the conservative policies of Herford and Simpson have transmitted many of these textual difficulties.

But Hibbard is concerned to present a readable text, not simply an accurately reported one, and he regularly identifies these cruxes and fearlessly suggests solutions. His emendations are bold and often convincing. Thus in his text Adam Overdo will 'wind [not winne] out wonders of enormity at the fair' (II.ii.110). This emendation bolsters the introduction's assertion (p xx) that 'the play is shot through and through with references to hunting and falconry, because the world it depicts is very decidedly a predatory one,' although it is not there identified as an emendation. Mistress Overdo 'does so law [not love] 'em all over' (IV.iii.111) in Edgeworth's report of the vapours scene, a sensible enough description of her subsequent threat to commit Quarlous and Cutting upon her 'justice-hood.' And in the most radical emendation of all Quarlous advises Overdo at the play's conclusion to 'save your estimation in pardoning him [Nightingale]' (V.vi.78-9), where the Folio reads simply 'save your estimation in him.' The accompanying note argues plausibly for the conjectural insertion of 'pardoning' by analogy with the conclusions of several other Jonson plays.

Such emendations are substantive, strong, and intellectually stimulating. Future editors of the play will have to consider them in their own commentaries; students of the play will be grateful for their clarity and innate good sense. For Hibbard is at all times bent on illuminating a masterwork which he clearly loves, by a playwright whom he deeply admires. He serves Ben Jonson well. (JAMES E. NEUFELD)

Robert James Merrett. *Daniel Defoe's Moral and Rhetorical Ideas*
English Literary Studies, no. 19. University of Victoria. 112. $4.25 paper

As a writer and thinker Defoe appeared so various that he seemed to be not one but all mankind's epitome. He knew it, of course, cultivating his 87 *personae* (Moore's count) and proudly imitating the apostle by being all things to all men. With the longest canon (much of it still, and probably forever, uncertain) of any major writer in English, Defoe both provokes and mocks attempts to grasp his essential ideas. Not until the early sixties, when Maximillian Novak began the serious modern study of Defoe's vast output, did anyone attempt to set Defoe's house of fiction in order. Novak identified the existence in Defoe's work of 'two valid but separate moral systems,' namely divine and natural law. While acknowledging that Defoe's fictional narrators often determine the morality of their actions by religious law, Novak argued that 'the answer to the problem of morality in Defoe's fiction may be found in his allegiance to the laws of nature.' Whenever the positive law, or even Christianity, came into conflict with the natural law, man was not required to heed or obey. In understanding the primacy of natural law for Defoe we are in effect one jump ahead of the narrators and so 'we can evaluate the morality of a given action far better than the narrators themselves' (*Defoe and the Nature of Man*, pp 2-3).

Robert Merrett challenges Novak's thesis by arguing that Defoe's social, political, and moral ideas follow from his religious ones, and that his use of natural law is, for the most part, 'rhetorical exploitation' (p 8). Merrett wishes to 'make it clear that Defoe did not conceive of natural and divine law as two equally valid but separate moral systems and that he treated them neither separately nor systematically. Far from believing that divine law confused natural law, he judged the latter of value only as it was related to or justified by the former' (p 47). Renewed emphasis upon the importance of Defoe's religious beliefs is valuable, and offers insights into the way the interconnection of social and religious ideas in Defoe's thought is worked out in his novels. Like other recent scholars, Merrett concludes that Defoe's novels, despite their 'escapist' mood, are didactic and moral.

Merrett's knowledge of Defoe's works is admirable, but his study is ultimately disappointing because it is not supported by the comprehensive scholarship that Novak was able to bring to his books. There is neither a bibliography nor an index (the latter is a serious omission) but a glance through the notes will reveal only occasional references to the main religious and moral thinkers of the seventeenth and eighteenth centuries. One cannot help feeling that over-immersion in Defoe may have reduced scholarly detachment. The case for the centrality of religious belief in Defoe's thought is frequently overstated. When, to take but one example, Defoe argues that '*a Standing Army, With Consent of Parliament, Is not Inconsistent with a Free Government,*' he asserts that he is '*as positively assur'd of the Safety of our Liberties ... as I am of the Salvation of Believers by the Passion of our Saviour*' (p 52). For Merrett, Defoe's 'support of a standing army is a statement of a political faith which contains an analogy to religious testimony.' Is it? Defoe, and it is typical of him, was trying to enforce an assertion by making his comparison as strong as possible. And so he swears by the passion of Christ.

The study suffers, too, from a number of stylistic infelicities (beginning with the title) and slips in the proofreading, both of which suggest the absence of a firm editorial hand. What *are* 'rhetorical ideas'? Surely 'rhetoric' is meant? In the first few pages I noticed a word missing (p 13, line 2) and the following phrases: 'methodic doubt' (p 13), 'harmonical nature' (p 16), and 'communicate essentially to himself' (p 21). On p 85 we are told that Moll 'uses language to perform meaning.' And on p 103 that, 'Since he is a very fallible individual, the Cavalier is not presented as a paradigm.' Moll's recollection of the '*Gypsies* or *Egyptians*' is not an instance of her 'appreciation of the variability of names' (p 83); she is simply following a common but mistaken idea about the supposed origin of the word *gypsy*. And something is askew in the numbers of the notes on pp 107 and 108. (DAVID BLEWETT)

Richard Bevis. *The Laughing Tradition: Stage Comedy in Garrick's Day*
University of Georgia Press. x, 282. $18.00

One of the happier results of the appearance of *The London Stage, 1660–1800* has been the correction over the past generation of a number of fundamental errors of fact about the history of the drama. The results have been most impressive for the earlier period, but the Garrick era has also received noteworthy attention. As his title indicates, Professor Bevis's concern is the state of traditional comedy during the third quarter of the eighteenth century. It has been a critical commonplace of our century that traditional or 'laughing' comedy was replaced in this period by 'sentimental' comedy, a commonplace that only recently has received serious challenge. One of the most important discoveries to emerge from the examination of the material made available in *The London Stage*, and to a lesser extent by systematic study of the plays in the Larpent Collection (manuscripts submitted for licensing from 1737 to 1824, now housed in the Huntington Library), was that most of the stage comedy of the eighteenth century was not sentimental, regardless of definition. Instead, as Bevis points out, the line of English comedy survives unbroken until the likes of Inchbald, Cowley, Holcroft, Cumberland, Reynolds, Burgoyne, and Colman the Younger – the post-1780 generation of playwrights – devote themselves to 'farce, spectacle, "benevolist" comedy, and melodrama to a degree that almost excluded traditional comedy' (p 11).

Bevis's study is divided into four parts. First, he provides an account of the almost arbitrary nature of success and failure in the Georgian theatre, and of the important differences between printed and acted texts of the period. Failure to take these factors into account results in distorted views of mid-eighteenth-century comedy. Having provided this contextual corrective, he then turns to 'the rivals of laughing comedy,' sentimental comedy and the '*illegitimi*,' principally farce. Though sentiment struggled with laughter for dominance in traditional comedy, both ultimately were 'annexed into the melodrama, the musical farce, and the extravaganza.' For Bevis this is the beginning of the modern entertainment world, one brought about by the dynamics of the free marketplace; it was 'the most significant development on the eighteenth-century stage' (p 65). Next, he considers the forms of laughing comedy: the full-length play (essentially the comedy of the Restoration transformed in the image of its middle-class audience) and the afterpiece (increasingly the form in which traditional comedy was realized). Finally, Bevis surveys the major comic writers of the period, all of whom devoted most of their energy to laughing comedy: Macklin, Garrick, Foote, Colman, Murphy, Goldsmith, and Sheridan.

Bevis is not the first critic to take exception to the received notion that sentiment dominated the stage between Fielding and Sheridan, but his challenge is more wide-sweeping and detailed than any other to date. (In his appendix, a discussion of the history of criticism of eighteenth-century comedy, he nicely places this notion as the product of a late nineteenth- and early twentieth-century revaluation of Georgian comedy.) By examining the performance records for the period, the acting texts in the Larpent Collection, the works of the major writers, and, especially, the afterpiece tradition, he should lay to rest once and for all the myth of a sentiment-dominated comedy in the mid-eighteenth century. Bevis's most original contribution is his survey and extensive analysis of the afterpiece. He considers the afterpiece the mainstay of traditional comedy in the period, arguing that neglect or contempt (following Goldsmith's prominent example) of it has been a central factor in our distorted view of stage history.

An ongoing problem in *The Laughing Tradition* arises from the need to define some of the most difficult and perhaps hopelessly muddled of critical terms, such as 'sentimental,' 'laughing comedy,' and 'farce.' Bevis recognizes the problem, and the inadequacy of Georgian critical theory to offer solutions, but a successful alternative none the less evades his grasp. His contention that sentimental drama was largely a closet drama of reading texts, which were often quite different from acting versions, builds expectations for a challenging new overview. But when he turns to the comedies themselves, he resorts to Arthur Sherbo's subjective 'definition' in *English Sentimental Drama*, that 'a sentimental comedy is one that affects us now as disproportionately emotional, mawkish, inappropriately tender, pathetic, and excessively refined' (Bevis's paraphrase, pp 48–9), a position he recognizes as one which 'virtually defined the genre out of existence' (p 49), so he attempts to strengthen it with the theoretical precision of Elder Olson's *The Theory of Comedy*, particularly Olson's insistence that generic forms be defined as wholes rather than through constituent parts. The resulting hybrid is a quantitative definition: if the majority of the parts are sentimental, the whole is sentimental – a definition that, at least in Olson's terms, entirely begs the question by refusing to *define* the whole. (For a more successful attempt see the chapter on 'Georgian Comedy' in Mark S. Auburn's recent *Sheridan's Comedies: Their Contexts and Achievements*.) Moreover, the weakness of theory has practical consequences. Bevis's concept of sentimental comedy leads him to include Garrick's *The Lying Valet* in the camp as an example of 'that rare bird, a sentimental afterpiece' (p 140), principally because of the 'sentimental clichés' that occur at the end of the play. Although he acknowledges the presence of elements that are nearly parodic (the heroine's maid punctures the climactic outburst of sentiment as the heroine raises the contrite hero from his knees with 'A reprieve! A reprieve! A reprieve!'), he is especially severe on the play because he considers it sentimental.

Critical theory, then, is not Bevis's strength. No useful, new critical vocabulary or concept emerges from his study. Nor are there many fresh insights into individual plays or playwrights. One noteworthy exception is his comparison of *The School for Scandal* and Congreve's comedies; another is his characterization of Georgian comedy as a form which deliberately deflates comic tension. In general, the play-by-play discussion of the major writers is a traditional descriptive survey in support of Bevis's historical argument, though not without considerable evaluative commentary. The result will change few opinions about the value of the plays, but should, one hopes, contribute greatly to an improved understanding of their place in the history of English comedy. (BRIAN CORMAN)

J.R. de J. Jackson. *Poetry of the Romantic Period*
Routledge History of English Poetry, vol 4. Routledge & Kegan Paul.
xvi, 334, $41.95

The Routledge History of English Poetry series is designed, says the general editor, to provide 'a fresh appraisal' and 'new critical history' of English poetry. Professor J.R. de J. Jackson, in designing his contribution to that series as 'a history of literary taste,' neutralizes that larger aim. Far from offering a re-assessment, Jackson accepts established popular estimations and asks his reader to attend too strictly to the results of his cautious and reductive scholarship. The book is a striking example of the helplessness of a literary historian who is not first a literary critic.

Jackson's specific concern is to 'throw fresh light on Romantic poetry as a whole' by placing still famous works against 'works of a similar kind fashionable at the time but now neglected.' He is occasionally enlightening when in the first three chapters he defines some prevailing fashions and conventions (the simple and artless, the gothic and fantastic, and the narrative and dramatic) and traces a few lines of influence. These chapters help to correct the false sense of isolated literary life propagated by modern anthologies. When, however, in the remaining six chapters he settles into often monotonous thematic readings of the 'major' poems, his organizing theses become more facile and opportunistic and the sense of background less dynamic. As we approach the end of the book, the chapters lose cohesion and reach fewer conclusions. It is as if the author were rushed or simply lost interest as the work progressed.

Also his contextual approach, while sometimes constructive, is too strict to prevent the evaluations (unavoidable in any discussion of fashion, taste, influence, and neglect) from being irresponsible. Most of the time Jackson accepts without question what has already been accepted by twentieth-century professional readers of Romantic poetry, for him a conveniently homogeneous body of opinion, referred to in such easy phrases as 'modern approval' and 'modern estimation.' The major exception to this critical dependence is his reluctance to accept even the sanctioned discriminations: for example, one cannot from his account detect any difference in value between *The Prelude* and *The Excursion*, or between *Childe Harold's Pilgrimage* and *Don Juan*. Such tolerance with only some poems places Jackson in the indefensible and stifling position, too common among academics, of asserting that we can distinguish between those poems that are of the canon and those that are not, but that within the canon all judgment is impossible.

When he is not condescending towards currently unfashionable poets (such as George Crabbe, arguably, I think, the most morally intelligent poet of the period, who is by Jackson dismissed as simply 'the best of the provincial poets,' and whose greatest work, the 1812 *Tales*, gets only passing mention in a list of popular descriptive poems), he is overlooking what is inconvenient. This is particularly evident in his treatment of Wordsworth: when praising the free experimentation with metres at the end of the 1790s, he overlooks the flat-footed rhythms in many of the *Lyrical Ballads*; Wordsworth's frequent emphasis on solitude and his own religiously elect status ('My spirit, thus singled out ... For holy services') in the early books of *The Prelude* are not mentioned at all, so that Jackson can argue, trying too hard to place the poet in a popular convention, that Wordsworth presents himself in his autobiographical epic as common and ordinary ('he makes himself one of a crowd as much as possible'); and nowhere does Jackson confront the problem of the unorthodoxy and peculiarities of Wordsworth's pantheism (or panentheism), a glaring neglect in a book purporting to re-establish contexts.

When, on a few occasions, he cannot help acknowledging weaknesses in major poems, he goes out of his way to excuse them. Byron's opinion 'that every woman is at heart a rake,' may not be sound, Jackson concedes, but it is, in *Don Juan*, 'made subversively attractive.' The same poet's 'Vision of Judgment' is unfair in its characterization of Southey, but then Byron, we are told, did not want to be topical; he 'releases satire for a moment from the bondage of current events' – that is, I guess, from the necessity to be accurate and responsible. The most telling excuses are for obscurity. He grants that Blake's work is often obscure, but is at the same time beautiful and exhilarating. Jackson apparently is excited by confusion and irresolution. He would have it no other way with Wordsworth's 'Ode: Intimations of Immortality'; he agrees with Southey that it is 'a dark subject darkly handled,' but adds, 'who would wish it otherwise?'

His intense concern with discernible influences and therefore with readers' expectations and associations allows him to accept too easily the

Romantic notion of creative reading. The failure to give particularity and definition to poetic characters, such as the Ancient Mariner and Manfred, says Jackson, makes them universally sympathetic ('helps us to experience his dream as if it were our own'; 'enlists an imaginative resonance in our mind'). Precise definition and resolution are synonymous, for Jackson, with 'preaching directly'; he commends poets who allow their readers to draw their own conclusions. One wonders how the sympathetic response to something imprecise can itself be other than imprecise. Such poems are instruments of complacency. If the poet has not made the subject-matter his own, the poem can be made by the reader to confirm anything; it becomes a universal pat on the back, rather than a form of discovery or a technique of contemplation, as it has to be if it is to have the kind of value and importance we have always recognized in the best poetry. His constant references to the receptive reader (in an overused 'we'), who is always 'sharing' and 'accepting' the feelings and experiences of the characters and poets, indicate not so much uniformity as an indiscriminate breadth of response. Romantic obscurantism has thus fed our enshrined pluralism, and Jackson indirectly celebrates the process.

Jackson is, after all, like all the critics whose values he cannot challenge, himself a Romantic. For him a poem is primarily the recreation, not the understanding, of an emotional experience (he cannot, therefore, criticize Shelley for wishing 'his readers to respond emotionally rather than intellectually to his ideas'). Poetry must essentially be spontaneous (only then, assumes Jackson, can it be realistic and natural), dramatic (Wordsworth in being 'genuinely dramatic ... wisely refrains from conducting a systematic argument'), and metaphoric ('Wordsworth proceeds by analogies rather than analysis, as a poet should'). The book, however, also displays an almost negligible sense of those stylistic elements (especially metre and rhyme) that define and control the emotional content of a poem, so Jackson has no way of dealing critically with what he considers (wrongly, of course) to be the isolable essence of poetry. His approach and these assumptions then deflect his interest from the precise and individual meanings of poems towards whatever echoed themes he can detect. The result is little more than a series of plot summaries and paraphrases interspersed with comments on the almost always successful manipulation of readers.

There is finally in the book little awareness of the adequate or the appropriate. This passage, commenting on a passage in Book IX of *The Excursion*, is typical:

> Although the dream may seem too good to be true and although it may be difficult even to remember it in any detail, we can remember that for a time we were permitted to share in it. If that recollection plays its part in strengthening

our resolution in the face of adversity, Wordsworth would have felt, I think, that *The Excursion* had had the effect he hoped for.

One wonders how that which is untrue and unmemorable can strengthen anything. There is no real argument in the book. In the place of independently reasoned conclusions we get circular statements, such as 'Blake's new myth is of interest to us because in his longer poems he assumes that we are familiar with it.' It never crosses Jackson's mind that informing ideas in poems may be wrong and therefore damaging. Chapter 8, which deals with poems that promote idiosyncratic and, for many, unacceptable ideas, he titles, 'Unfamiliar Ideas.' It is safer to reduce critical disagreement about some poems' meanings to 'our uncertainties about the conventions they employ' and to praise a poet's 'tact' in revising or even reversing conventional ideas than to defend the truth as he knows it. (RICHARD HOFFPAUIR)

<blockquote>
Tilottama Rajan. *Dark Interpreter: The Discourse of Romanticism*
Cornell University Press. 281. $15.00
</blockquote>

In *Dark Interpreter: The Discourse of Romanticism*, Tilottama Rajan sets out to illuminate 'the Romantic mind's dialogue with its own assumptions' (p 29). For appropriate concepts and vocabulary she turns to nineteenth-century German philosophy and twentieth-century French linguistic criticism and to an abstract and generalizing mode of thought that makes unusual demands on the reader. The book is given for the most part to the examining of works by English Romantic poets, and especially to the later work of Coleridge, Keats, and Shelley. At the end of this ambitious work Rajan concludes:

> Where previous periods saw literature as not permanently subject to temporality, as the unmediated ... or mediated expression of a transcendent language, the Romantic period recognizes that the discourse of innocence is spoken from within experience. The simultaneously liberating and mimetic nature of art, arising from the fact that the unreal is created to free us from the world by a consciousness which stays in the world, makes of art a dialogue between illusion and its own deconstruction. (P 261)

In the critical examination of individual texts Rajan often shows strong powers of judgment, as for example in her comment on Wordsworth's 'The Two April Mornings,' of which she rightly asserts that 'Wordsworth, less naive than he seems, recognizes that images are not simply phantoms of delight, but products of the mind's dusk as well as its dawn' (p 211). A similar liveliness and good sense appear elsewhere in the detailed discussion of texts, and the general ideas produced seem by contrast not only less authoritative and convincing but also much less well expressed. The book moves between concrete and lively perception and a stratosphere of abstractions, of which the most prominent are 'Romanticism,' 'the Romantic mind,' and 'the Romantic period.' 'The Romantic period' is invested not only with common characteristics but also with a common consciousness; Rajan's own language shows that she takes Arnold Hauser seriously when she quotes him as saying that Romanticism 'represented one of the most decisive turning-points in the history of the European mind', and that it 'was perfectly conscious of its historic role' (p 260). So confident a use of high-level abstractions seems all the more surprising when it appears that 'the Romantic mind' is equally involved in 'Tintern Abbey' and *The Mysteries of Udolpho* (pp 260–1), to say nothing of the many and varied continental works which are necessarily subsumed in the grand generalization. A deconstructionist critic might be tempted to say of such expressions as this that the presence of the sign may indicate not merely the absence of the thing signified but its actual non-existence.

The thesis developed is twofold – that pre-Romantic writers had a naive belief in the relationship between literature and reality, and that the later Romantics were beginning to arrive at a more sophisticated, that is to say modernist, view of the nature of their art. On the first view, which is advanced as an assumption rather than argued, we should have to suppose that the authors of *The Canterbury Tales*, *King Lear*, and *Gulliver's Travels*, partaking in the common consciousness attributed to 'previous periods,' 'saw literature as the unmediated expression of a transcendent language,' and failed to realize that 'the discourse of innocence is spoken from within experience.' There is no good reason for supposing that Chaucer, for example, was as naive, in any sense of the word, as this thesis requires us to believe.

It might however be held that the Romantic poets at first attempted an art that was to be *naive*, in Schiller's sense of the word, but were later driven to irony or to self-contradiction and frustration, as the gap between life and art yawned ever wider. Rajan has too lively a critical sense to advance this thesis, and though she suggests that Wordsworth is at times unable to face the contradictory nature of his art, she also comments that at other times 'he seems to accept the stubborn muteness of the objective world, and the ambiguity of these dispossessed figures, who, like Keats' Titans, reveal both the survival and the erosion of vision in such a world' (p 235). 'Romantic poetry,' she writes, ' is certainly not what Schiller calls a naive poetry, a poetry free of doubt and irony' (p 24). Further: 'It becomes a simplification to dismiss Romantic idealism as a wilful blindness to an awareness concealed in the sub-text of poems – the view tacitly taken by proto-deconstructionists like Bostetter' (p 24). It is sad that Rajan should have to call her own attention, as well as ours, to this simple truth; but who – outside the earnest ranks of 'Romanticists' – ever believed that poetry of any value could be written by persons practising a 'wilful blindness'?

In the interpretation of actual works Rajan, perhaps because her thinking is haunted by the ghost of a hypothetical 'naive' poet, sometimes assumes a lack of adequate critical consciousness in the poet. Of Keats she writes, for example:

> 'The Eve of St. Agnes' has its place in the process of reassessment that leads Keats toward a new typology of creative artists: one which recognizes that the gods ... are immune from experience, but that those who attempt to reproduce such innocence in the human sphere are merely fanatics who have refused to risk their dreams in the real world. But the poem seems sentimentally unwilling to commit itself to so radical a revision of its sense of what poetry is.   (P 113)

The dream of joy in 'The Eve of St. Agnes' is set in an iron frame of death, and the ultimate cold; it is gratuitous to suppose that the poem has a 'sense of what poetry is' that forbids us to read it as the expression of an adult consciousness – or that Keats had any such limiting 'sense' of the nature of poetry. Rajan seems to refuse to Keats the kind of critical intelligence she somewhat grudgingly grants to Wordsworth, perhaps because in this instance the thesis about 'Romanticism' is given more weight. General propositions about very various works of literature usually become difficult to sustain when each work is closely looked at, and this book is no exception. It does however show genuine powers of discrimination and of resistance to its own abstractions.   (GEOFFREY DURRANT)

Samuel Taylor Coleridge. *Marginalia 1.* Edited by George Whalley
Collected Works of Samuel Taylor Coleridge, Vol 12
Routledge & Kegan Paul / Princeton University Press. clxxiv, 879, $60.00

This massive volume heralds four more; it contains editorial front matter and the marginalia from authors and books A–B in an alphabetical scheme. A typical presentation gives as headnote: the author and his dates; the title of the book annotated; its present whereabouts, or a statement that it is not located; a general description of the book; a history of its ownership and provenance; dates or conjectured dates of the annotations. The text annotated is presented in appropriate extracts printed in black; Coleridge's annotation follows each extract and is printed in brown. Textual notes explain, where necessary, the layout of the annotations, and provide occasional editorial emendations; a generous commentary completes the presentation. Translations are provided, both for Coleridge and for the author annotated, where the language in use is not English. The Coleridgean matter is, of course, taken usually from Coleridge's manuscript in the books concerned; sometimes it is derived from secondary sources (usually manuscript transcripts from books now missing, or H.N. Coleridge's versions in *Literary Remains*); or again, rarely, the fact that an annotated book was once known to exist has had to be recorded without any Coleridgean matter.

Professor Whalley's interpretation of 'marginalia' is broad: as well as verbal annotation, he records Coleridge's corrections of misprints, marginal markings (some of which may not be Coleridge's), and bowdlerizings (by cancellations with or without translation of the offending words into a learned language) of texts which appeared offensive either to Coleridge or to a reader he had in view. Certainly the third category, even when represented only by a line of cancellation, throws light on Coleridge's mind, or taste, or the taste of his time; whether we are as interested in his acuteness as a proofreader might be more open to doubt. On the whole, however, Whalley's arguments for completeness of presentation (p clv) are sound. There are, of course, trivia, such as Coleridge's objection to the use of 'whose' with an impersonal antecedent (pp 723, 725; in item 6A, p 725, his rewriting is neither correct nor as verbally neat as the original); but these are part of the man and must be endured.

In nearly 900 pages of text in this volume the proportion of matter likely to engage the merely literary taste is rather small. Anderson's *British Poets* (pp 37–87) and Beaumont and Fletcher (pp 362–408) are the main representatives (the comments on Sir Thomas Browne, pp 741–99, are not usually on the works as literature). Here are shrewd comments on Spenser's allegorical method (p 54), Crashaw ('too too apt to weary out a Thought,' p 68), and a good many others; together with several statements of Coleridge's antipathy towards the Scots (pp 57, 74–5), such as appeared in the third volume of the *Notebooks* and not explained there or here. The section on Beaumont and Fletcher is less attractive: it is largely confined to complaints about the thinness of the plays and about editorial shortcomings, and to attempts, often unconvincing, to emend the texts. On a smaller scale there are good observations on Henry Brooke's *The Fool of Quality* (pp 722–37) and on *Pilgrim's Progress* (pp 801–27).

The bulkiest sections in this volume are the marginalia to Richard Baxter (pp 230–361) and to Jakob Böhme (pp 553–696); they are also the most obscure. Those on Baxter are full of the technicalities of religious controversy; those on Böhme, of specimens of Coleridge's extraordinary attempts to unify scientific concepts. Neither group makes for easy reading, and the second, like the comments on Hermann Boerhaave just preceding, frequently appears nonsensical to a twentieth-century reader.

Although Whalley's introduction refers to 'emergent chemical theories that were eventually to join hands with physics in modern molecular and subatomic theory' (p lxiv), he does not, I believe, claim that Coleridge anticipated twentieth-century thinking in this field, nor does he make any sustained effort to translate Coleridge's language into an intelligible modern idiom. (The same problem, I complained in another place, arises in the third volume of the *Notebooks*.) Yet there is the occasional relief of good sense, as in the protests against Böhme's monstrous theories of the representative powers of language (pp 606-8).

Whalley's commentary does not deserve the phrase 'blizzard of footnotes' which he allots to it in his introduction (p clv); it is (like those in the Collected Coleridge generally), learned, full (unless in the matter of Coleridge's science, mentioned above), and thoroughly useful. Inevitably I suggest a few addenda. The comment on Thomas Adam (p 10) – 'As Light alone mixes with Light' – receives an abstract parallel from *Biographia Literaria*; a closer one might be found in Wordsworth's *Prelude* (1805), x. 756-7 – 'losing, in no other way than light / Is lost in light, the weak in the more strong.' Certainly the distinction between People and Public (p 220) deserves a reference to Wordsworth's Essay, Supplementary to the Preface, and to earlier versions of the distinction in Wordsworth. On p 569 'terrific,' in the phrase 'an etherial Metal terrific, or an earth metallific,' looks as if it is intended (perhaps jokingly; there is no such sense in *OED*) to mean 'earth-making'; it is difficult to extract sense from the ordinary meaning. On p 572 '*Atomist*' (= a follower of atomic theory) needs a note, or a cross-reference to p 596, n 46[11]. On p 632 n 95[2] should read 'To learn, and to teach.' On p 872 the phrase 'the Race of Legion,' especially in view of the deleted 'his name is' just preceding, should be referred to Mark 5:9.

Considering the magnitude of the undertaking, this volume is pleasantly free from errors of the press. There are obvious mechanical misprints on pp clii, clvii, 167, 181, 470, 749. On p 44, n 3[1], a duplicated line of type obscures the sense beyond guesswork. Since Richard Baxter was born in 1615, it is unlikely that he 'adopted Presbyterian views c 1600' (p 230), but the remedy is not obvious (? 'c 1640'). On p 462, n 122[1], the concluding phrases are obscured by (apparently) the use of 'sentence' in two senses in two lines, whether by accident or design is uncertain. On p 652 Coleridge's comment should (I guess) read 'but yet it is not "so also" either.' On p 752, n 22[4], I see no relevance in the reference to item 3618 in the *Notebooks*, but again no remedy suggests itself. On p 865 sense requires 'without breach of his Oath,' *vice* 'without breath of his Oath': the source, here a transcript in Victoria College from a book not now located, is correct but the print is not. A very few other errors seem not to be due to the printer: Ernest de Selincourt's edition of Dorothy Wordsworth's *Journals* was issued in London in 1941, not in Oxford in 1939 (p xxxv); Roberta F. Brinkley appears with her Christian names reversed on p cliv; Joseph Cottle, according to *DNB*, died in 1853, not in 1865 (when he would have been 95) (p clxi).

Such a wealth of new material as Whalley offers in this volume seems to demand an index; regrettably, but obviously rightly, there is none. It is to be hoped that we shall not wait too long for it and for the rest of the matter which it will analyse. (W.J.B. OWEN)

Jeffrey Baker. *Time and Mind in Wordsworth's Poetry*
Wayne State University Press. 212. $16.95

When one considers the brevity of his book and the complexity of his subject, Jeffrey Baker's account of time and mind in some of Wordsworth's major poetry seems very ambitious. Baker begins by identifying a qualitative order of time in Wordsworth, from the rigidity of clock time, to nature's time, to inner time, which sometimes obliterates even itself in a vision of an eternal present. This is well illustrated by his later analysis in chapter 5 of the skating episode in *The Prelude*, 1.425-63, where he is particularly concerned to show the importance for Wordsworth of the 'holiday' from an ordinary experience of time. But the emphasis throughout the book is on the relationships among different ways of experiencing time, and finally on the vantage-point of an eternal present from which at particular moments the poet is able to see time from the perspective of eternity. Dealing in his first chapter with other critics who have written on related subjects, especially Lindenberger (*On Wordsworth's 'Prelude'*), Baker admits his indebtedness but emphasizes that his own interest is less in Wordsworth's beliefs or ideas than in their poetic effect and value: his book is concerned with time and mind primarily as images rather than as ideas, and on the basis of this literary emphasis Baker justifies his choice of texts (1850 *Prelude, Excursion* I rather than 'The Ruined Cottage') and his preference for close reading over specific discussion of sources and ideas behind Wordsworth's treatment of time.

His close readings of poems and of passages from poems seem to me to be more interesting and convincing than the larger points they are meant to illustrate. Baker's usual technique in each chapter is to connect a number of these readings in order to illustrate a particular theme or subject. Sometimes the choice of examples seems arbitrary and the splicing of paragraphs becomes obvious: especially in later chapters Baker stops too often to offer explanations of what he is doing or to justify a change of direction. At its best, however, his writing is lucid, unpretentious, and personal, with a pleasant witty allusiveness, qualities which make the reader expect and welcome associations that might otherwise appear arbitrary, like the quotations from William James in chapter 6, where Baker is concerned to distinguish religious experience from particular doctrine.

Baker returns to James in his final chapter, to compare the mystical experience of one of James's contributors with Wordsworth's account of the ascent of Snowdon. The comparison is interesting but excessively long, and the emphasis on James makes one suspect that Baker is more concerned with what Wordsworth believed than his literary approach readily admits. Similarly the appendix, 'The Ruined Shrines,' which Baker includes to emphasize the resonance of certain settings in *The Prelude* and to reveal Wordsworth's historical sense as 'a sense of tradition,' takes on a disproportionate importance by being the single appendix to such a short book and – though interesting in itself – does not illuminate the text sufficiently to be helpful to the reader. Any necessary information about these shrines might have been incorporated in the text or the notes.

Individual readings are always perceptive and often superb: here Baker seems most confident and authoritative. The treatment of Wordsworth's syntactical ambiguities, particularly in the discussion of *Prelude*, II.54–65, in chapter 6, is especially interesting, and the treatment of the 'spots of time' is illuminating in its emphasis not on the static quality of such moments but on the energy within them and its effect on the imagination of the reader. Chapter 4, 'Margaret and Michael,' is my favourite: Baker reads the fate of each character in terms of temporal disturbances, Margaret falling victim to 'the subtly addictive pain of unjustifiable hope,' while Michael, through love for the child of his old age, makes himself equally vulnerable to disappointed hope. The bleak ironies of time that Baker uncovers in this chapter are counterbalanced in chapter 5 by emphasis on idleness and wise passiveness, which lead beyond the prison of time to the visionary state achieved through spots of time, explored most fully in the last two chapters. In this way the argument of the book unfolds lucidly and logically. This is not only a book written by one specialist for others; it is also a book with much to say to students and other interested readers of Wordsworth, especially to those who might approach the poetry either as vague and impressionistic or as versified philosophy. It is an uneven book and one that necessarily limits itself more than its title might suggest, but it defines its limits conscientiously and within them it invites the reader to approach familiar texts freshly. (ANNE MC WHIR)

W.J. Keith. *The Poetry of Nature: Rural Perspectives in Poetry from Wordsworth to the Present*
University of Toronto Press. xi, 219. $20.00

The Poetry of Nature examines the work of nine poets: Wordsworth, Clare, Barnes, Hardy, Frost, Edward Thomas, Edmund Blunden, Andrew Young, and R.S. Thomas. Professor Keith gives particular emphasis to the technical influence of Wordsworth on the other eight and demonstrates how Wordsworth's bold experiments with perspective and viewpoint are an important part of his poetic legacy. There is hardly a poem chosen for discussion which Keith does not illuminate by making one see it from an unusual perspective, and here he has himself learned from Wordsworth. I found myself continually forced back to the original texts with a shock of both recognition and fresh delight. The subtle discussion of a 'simple' poem like 'I Wandered Lonely as a Cloud' underlines Wordsworth's originality and artistry; indeed, Keith's technical analysis of even the slightest 'nature' poem tends to strengthen it rather than demolish it. One thinks of 'Thaw' by Edward Thomas, 'Field-Glasses' by Andrew Young, 'Mouse's Nest' by Clare, and the Iago Prytherch poems of R.S. Thomas. Keith, as critic, keeps a delicate finger on the focus wheel, providing the reader with the sort of binocular vision he so admires in the poets themselves.

Not everyone will agree with Keith's emphases – for my money he overrates Edward Thomas (fine as that poet is) and he dismisses Dylan Thomas rather brutally in one phrase, 'undisciplined romanticism' (p 196). I wish also that Keith had extended his discussion to include Philip Larkin, surely the most distinguished of modern English poets who acknowledge Hardy as a technical progenitor. Larkin is not, of course, a 'rural' poet, but if one substitutes suburbia for the countryside and a railway carriage for Hardy's waggonette, one can see him using the same tricks of perspective to shock us into vision.

Keith quite rightly castigates Geoffrey Grigson for believing that Barnes loses little in translation into standard English, but he leaves himself open to question in his treatment of Clare, holding the curious belief that to leave Clare in the original is more condescending than to tidy him up: 'significant differences between Clare's poetry and that of other nature poets can best be discussed, I believe, without the distractions of an unpunctuated and uncorrected text' (p 201n). But once editorial tampering begins, where does it end? I believe that Keith's procedure is as questionable as Grigson's. J.W. and Anne Tibble, who did so much to restore Clare's reputation, also took liberties with his texts. Anne Tibble, however, in her recent edition of *The Midsummer Cushion* (1979) is at pains to present us with what Clare actually wrote. The effect is to enhance Clare's stature, not undermine it.

This issue aside, Keith has written an excellent book, meticulous in scholarship, elegantly written. It is a worthy successor to his *The Rural Tradition*, which discussed the non-fiction prose writers of the English countryside. Taken together, the two books comprise an impressive achievement and put forward a strong case for the tenacity and centrality of these too long neglected areas of prose and verse. (TIMOTHY BROWNLOW)

J.M. Gray. *Thro' the Vision of the Night: A Study of Source, Evolution and Structure in Tennyson's 'Idylls of the King'*
McGill-Queen's University Press. ix, 179. $25.00

J.M. Gray's book-length study of *Idylls of the King* meets the high standards set by the series of authoritative essays he has already written on the poem. Gray offers useful discussions of the idylls' serial evolution and of Tennyson's adaptation of his Arthurian, classical, and biblical sources. In examining the issue of stylistic and dramatic unity in the poem Gray breaks new and important ground. Whatever one may think of his exalted claims for the *Idylls*, one is grateful for the insight he has given.

The defence of Tennyson's natural descriptions, which Gray himself calls a 'hazardous enterprise' (p 62), seems to me successful. He shows how settings are often presented not through 'detailed description but through the deeds that are enacted or commemorated' in these settings (p 66). As Arthur Hallam anticipates in his 1831 review essay of Tennyson, the landscapes in the *Idylls* often function as internalized geography, as regions of the mind. In many of the apocalyptic and infernal settings Tennyson has allowed primitive forces, far below the level of the conscious mind, and what Hallam calls 'innumerable shades of fine emotion' (far beyond the capacity of concepts to define) to acquire a life a precision of their own.

Naturally few critics can accomplish in a single volume everything a reader hopes for. Sometimes Gray terminates a discussion prematurely. He argues persuasively, for example, that Percivale's quest in 'The Holy Grail' is not to be dismissed as a failure. But in showing how Tennyson 'singles out Percivale's hesitancy' (p 24), Gray fails, I think, to track down the implications of his argument. This hesitancy, far from being a defect, is inseparable from Tennyson's own sceptical distrust of vision, from his restraint, deferment, and reserve. The subtle grandeur of 'The Holy Grail,' its power of self-critical nuance and hesitancy, can never be adequately systematized in a doctrine of personal immortality such as Arthur tries to formulate at the end of that idyll. Indeed, such a doctrine is precisely the form of reductive dogma that Tennyson, in the free intelligence of his visionary poetry, tries to defer till the final moment. The result, at its best, is an extraordinary fusion of the diffidence and visionary authority that a knight like Percivale embodies.

Gray includes in his book an intelligent discussion of Tennyson's Spenserian allusions. I should have welcomed, however, more discussion of those cultural and stylistic differences which divide Tennyson's Arthurian firmament from the allegorical world of *The Faerie Queene*. *Idylls of the King* seems constructed over the lovely ruins of an older allegorical tradition. Except for an icon like the Holy Grail or the Sword Excalibur, the emblems in Tennyson's poem often resemble Merlin's rainbow: they are evanescent as 'Rain, rain, and sun! a rainbow on the lea!,' for 'truth is this to me, and that to thee' ('The Coming of Arthur,' lines 405-6). Such emblems are not true mirrors of analogy like Spenser's icons, but mirrors in which each observer sees reflected an image of himself.

I suspect that the reputation of Tennyson's *Idylls* has never quite recovered from Christopher Ricks's well-documented and damaging charge that the 'failure of style' in the poem 'renders vacant or academic or wishful the larger claims which the *Idylls* precipitate' (*Tennyson* [New York 1972], p 269). Gray often comments perceptively on language: he notes, for example, that 'Tennyson's imaginative use of conjunctions is one of the secrets of his style' (p 25). But any refutation of Ricks is weakened by the fact that Gray cites him on only one passage in the poem (p 90), and that single citation prejudges the case because it chooses those lines from 'Merlin and Vivien' (lines 228-31) which Ricks himself calls 'the finest' in the *Idylls* (*Tennyson*, p 276). A full-scale defence of the language of the poem may have to await the publication of Walter Nash's dissertation, which Gray quotes approvingly throughout his study. Until we possess such a defence, Gray's claim that the *Idylls* is 'one of the most successfully sustained long poems in English' (p 137) is likely to seem a triumph of faith over demonstration, a conviction that is incapable of winning widespread assent. (W. DAVID SHAW)

Patricia Clements and Juliet Grindle, editors. *The Poetry of Thomas Hardy*
Vision Press. ix, 194. £10.95

This volume of critical essays on Hardy's poetry is a companion to the previously issued Vision collection of essays on his novels. Like its predecessor, it exemplifies a variety of approaches, attempting to re-evaluate the poems in the light of Hardy's prosody, imagery, and diction; new aspects of his 'poetry of perception'; his uses of literary tradition; and interrelationships between the fiction and verse. More striking than the diversity of topics, however, is the consistency of basic concerns throughout nearly all the essays. Hardy's 'harshness' and incongruity, fondness for double meanings, use of moral and aesthetic perspectivism, and related interest in the limits of vision are all repeatedly alluded to and treated in the papers. These recurrent themes remind one how long a time has passed since Donald Davie asserted confidently in *Thomas Hardy and British Poetry* that no consensus existed as to what was centrally significant in Hardy's poetry.

The first three papers, considering Hardy's vocabulary, syntax, and verse form, are among the most satisfying in the volume. Isobel Grundy argues convincingly that Hardy's placement of language 'under strain' (p 7) through puns and multiple allusions, tongue-twisting rhymes, elliptical syntax, and related deformations of style reinforces his message of the unexpectedness and dissatisfactions of life. S.C. Neuman provides a detailed, and ultimately persuasive, case for the way in which Hardy frequently undercuts the semantic and imagistic content of a poem's cheerful surface by employing an incongruously gloomy prosody. In a complementary paper Ronald Marken incisively demonstrates the manner in which a number of Hardy poems chime inexorably, through subtly graduated premonitory rhymes and irregular 'cadences of regret' (p 23), to their tragic conclusions.

Almost as rewarding is Cornelia Cook's comparison of the different attempts in the poetry of Hardy and Meredith to 'read' a world despite the lack of received scriptural, scientific, or philosophic text. More properly a monograph compressed into the format of an essay, Cook's paper suffers somewhat from being too extensive in scope and too restricted in space. In a more manageable treatment of inconsistency in *The Dynasts* Glen Wickens argues cogently that the truth of the poem resides neither in the sceptical Spirit of the Years nor in the more optimistic Spirit of the Pities, but in a philosophy of multiple perspectives, an acceptance of several contradictory, incompletely resolved points of view. Employing a similar form of aesthetic perspectivism Jeremy Steel accounts for Hardy's shift from prose to poetry as his way of recording freely the diversity of his moods and memories without the constraints of a larger structure. In a somewhat different, though related vein, Rosemary Eakins examines the poetry and fiction as 'phases of one' Muse (p 52), considering – through a more dogged sequence of prose summaries than some readers will find entirely necessary – poems connected with *Under the Greenwood Tree* and *Tess* as amplifications of, corrections to, or variations on the novelistic portrayals.

The final, and in many ways, most imaginative group of essays traces patterns of imagery and perception in the poems. Both Patricia Ingham and Jon Stallworthy present highly distinctive treatments of Hardy's configurations of imprisonment. In 'Hardy and the "Cell of Time",' Ingham examines Hardy's obsessive patterns of retrospection through interlocking images of entrapment: galleries, caves, winding stairs, and mirrors. Stallworthy provides a complementary perspective on Hardy's images of mirrors, considering them along with images of vision and moonlight as emblems of narcissistic, deluded romanticism. Both Ingham's and Stallworthy's discussions are among the finest I have read on Hardy's imagery: keenly focused yet highly evocative, they clearly escape the cold and sterile circuit which each variously sees as one of Hardy's central images of limitation. By comparison, Simon Gatrell's discussion of Hardy's images of travel often seems unduly tentative, his interpretations undermined in advance by too many disclaimers and uncertainties ('Hardy may have felt ...,' p 164; 'This poem may be Hardy's attempt ...,' p

165; 'It may seem perverse to begin my discussion ...,' p 156). Patricia Clements is as sensitive as Gatrell to the ambiguity and manifold perspectives of Hardy's meanings, but she offers a more convincing and illuminating theoretical pattern to account for the precariously balanced points of view in the verse. Many of Hardy's poems, she suggests, detail a moment in which a quester's perception or expectation of order crumbles in the face of overpowering contradictory experience and must be subsequently reformulated. Within this context Clements places Hardy's poems of repetitive return and his pivoting, antithetical verse structures.

Despite the diversity of topics, then, these essays reflect a substantial coherence that does credit to the editors' stated purpose of contributing significantly to the 'renewed conversation about Hardy's poems' (p vii). Dedicated to the memory of its late co-editor, Juliet Grindle, the volume is a worthy commemoration of her own notable contributions to Hardy studies. (ILA GOODY)

J.L. Wisenthal, editor. *Shaw and Ibsen: Bernard Shaw's Quintessence of Ibsenism and Related Writings*
University of Toronto Press 1979. ix, 268. $20.00

Readers of Shaw's essay on Ibsenism have frequently fallen into one of two errors. One is to suppose Shaw to be arguing that Ibsen was a socialist and his plays sociological tracts. Ibsen himself dealt with the question of his views in a letter correcting a journalist's account of an interview:

> What I really said was that I was surprised that I, who had made it my chief business in life to depict human character and destinies, should, without consciously aiming at it, have arrived at some of the same conclusions as the social-democratic moral philosophers had arrived at by scientific processes.

Shaw was defining the quintessence of Ibsenism only within limits suitable to a Fabian Society lecture.

He was not, moreover, defining the quintessence of Shavianism. The second error is to make that assumption and apply it after this fashion: in pursuit of a thesis Shaw argues that people fall into three readily defined groups and he classifies Ibsen's characters accordingly; *ergo*, he must have created his own characters with that thesis and classification in mind, and they should be studied simply in the light of it. Shaw commented on that approach in 1919, in less restrained language than Ibsen's:

> Would anyone but a buffleheaded idiot of a university professor, half crazy with correcting examination papers, infer that all my plays were written as economic essays, and not as plays of life, character, and human destiny like those of Shakespeare or Euripides?

Professor Wisenthal's book, a timely reissue of what Shaw called a 'major critical essay,' will surely put an end to both errors. Shaw's words of explicit caution at the end of his 1891 preface to *The Quintessence of Ibsenism* did not avert them, perhaps because, while calling his piece an 'exposition,' he did not sufficiently emphasize that he was not so much an 'expositor' as a debater and propagandist, setting up a thesis, selecting the evidence that suited his case while ignoring what did not, and presenting it with the brilliance, energy, and wit of an orator intent on shaking up his audience. Wisenthal's inclusion of much of the typescript of Shaw's original lecture provides a useful basis indeed for reconsidering the *Quintessence*.

The volume includes a valuable introductory essay that provides biographical and other background material. I disagree with some of Wisenthal's views and do not share his appetite for the gratuitous pursuit of analogues. And I regret the absence of any account of an article that Shaw worked on in November 1889 entitled 'Dickens to Ibsen,' the manuscript of which is, I believe, in the British Museum.

I regret also that Wisenthal has virtually ignored, as other writers tend to do, the role that must have been played in Shaw's early Ibsenite years by Philip Wicksteed. Shaw and Wicksteed were members of a small group that met fortnightly in 1885–90 to discuss economic theory. Wicksteed's proper field was literature, and in February 1888 Shaw heard him lecture on Dante and was exhilarated. Wicksteed could read and translate Danish, and later in 1888 gave a series of lectures on Ibsen that included detailed accounts of *Brand* and *Love's Comedy* as well as comment on other plays up to *Hedda Gabler*. Whether Shaw attended those lectures is not known, nor whether Wicksteed was involved in Shaw's beginning to study Danish in September 1888. But I find it inconceivable that Wicksteed would not have had a very significant part in exciting Shaw's interest in Ibsen, or that that interest was so emphatically attributable to William Archer as Wisenthal claims.

Notwithstanding such reservations, I find Wisenthal's book a valuable addition to Shavian scholarship. (J. PERCY SMITH)

>Phyllis Grosskurth. *Havelock Ellis: A Biography*
>McClelland and Stewart. xvi, 492, illus. $22.50

Havelock Ellis's life project was the seven-volume *Studies in the Psychology of Sex* (1897–1928). The aim of the *Studies* was to treat all the phenomena of sexual behaviour in a rational, enlightened way. By so doing, the limits of acceptable practices could be enlarged, prejudice overcome, and a wider tolerance achieved for sexual deviance. Ellis compiled masses of data, undertook extensive interviews, and researched all the available literature in the field to carry out his task. He expended truly Herculean efforts over several decades in devotion of his 'life's work.' His writings had an enormous effect on the prevailing social morality; they helped to change the climate of his age. Yet who reads the *Studies* today? The very revolution which they ushered in has rendered them superfluous. We no longer need their plea for tolerance; if anything, we would welcome some guidelines for discriminating between moral and immoral behaviour. Further, as Phyllis Grosskurth indicates, the project was flawed from the start.

First, though Ellis struggled with Victorian morality, he was a stern partisan of Victorian science. The enormous, exhaustive collection of data which fills up the *Studies* no longer convinces. We have become suspicious of the methodological basis on which the data were compiled, and we long for an interpretation which would illuminate all these facts from within. The kind of objectivity which Ellis demonstrates in the *Studies* wears thin as we come to experience the superficial level of understanding to which all this mass of material leads. As his biographer states: 'while Ellis described, enumerated and recorded the manifestations of the erotic impulse, he lacked the ultimate courage to look into his own soul, to make the kind of discoveries or "decisions" that are only possible to a man who combines deep insight with extraordinary fearlessness.'

In fact, what makes this excellent biography so gripping is the attempt by the author to look into Ellis's soul, to see the person who stands behind the work. And what could be more amazing than to discover that this prophet of sexuality was himself probably impotent as well as perverse and that his primary sexual satisfaction came from observing women urinate, preferably standing up! Ellis does talk about his urolagnia in his biography, and he even provides a 'scientific' account of it in the seventh volume of the *Studies*; but it is always presented as a harmless anomaly of little consequence. For Grosskurth, though, it is perhaps the central fact of Ellis's emotional life: it can be traced back to his childhood experiences, and it affects all his adult relationships.

Though the author strives to avoid being reductive in her explanations, there is a clear sense that Ellis's work is a compensation for his own inadequate sexuality. Perhaps it is this compensatory quality which most robs it of its staying power. Ellis's life has a fascination that is missing from his work.

The best parts of this biography are those that detail Ellis's relationships. In spite of the scientific detachment of his book on sex, he was himself primarily a feeling type; he suffered both the joy and pain of love throughout his life. Though he was incapable of normal sexuality, Ellis had an extraordinary ability to become intimate with women. With women he was father-brother-son in turn; he nurtured and cared for them in a way that made them experience their own self-worth, often for the first time.

Grosskurth is perhaps right to be ambivalent about Ellis's relationship to women. On the one hand, he can be seen as a figure in the history of feminism: his books were influential in the movement towards a fuller sexual life for women; he was a friend and firm supporter of Margaret Sanger in her pioneering work in birth control; and his work was read and responded to by women all over the world. Yet there is something infantilizing in his attitude to women. He wished his tombstone to read:

> Here lie the Remains of
> *Havelock Ellis*
> He had many Faults
> *But his Breast was Useful*
> For Women to come and Weep on
> Now only the Skies Weep there.

Women found him consoling, and he took care of them as he perhaps wished to be taken care of himself. When he was not being parental, he often played at nursery-games. It seems that he never had a mature, adult heterosexual relationship. Yet his friendships with women were deep and lasting. He even devised substitute satisfactions that were for several women their first opportunities of experiencing real sexual pleasure. Even his urolagnia was taken in good spirits by his lovers. Beyond the clinical evidence, what Ellis had was an ability to care for others and to affect them deeply in a healing way. As his biographer concludes: 'The people still living who knew him continue to speak of him as a radiance who touched their lives in a way they will never forget.' (STEPHEN K. LEVINE)

Camille R. La Bossière. *Joseph Conrad and the Science of Unknowing*
York Press 1979. 112. $17.95 cloth; $12.95 paper

Gary Geddes. *Conrad's Later Novels*
McGill-Queen's University Press. xi, 223. $15.95

Camille La Bossière's short book is an examination of what he perceives to be a common feature of the Conradian text: its expression of the fundamentally irresolvable contradictions of existence through 'dream logic' – or 'Eastern,' or 'synthetic,' or 'analogical logic' (he uses the terms interchangeably). Conrad's awareness of the inability of traditional logic and finite reason to reveal or explicate the human predicament and his use instead of a 'circular logic of contraries' constitute, for La Bossière, the 'central theme' as well as the formal principle underlying 'the entire corpus of his work.' Such a sweeping claim requires cogent demonstration, yet assertion is more common here than proof and at crucial points in the argument the reader finds himself adrift among uncharted ambiguities, with an ill-plotted course and faulty navigational aids.

In his chapter on Conrad's 'Ars Poetica,' in which he tries to define his central idea of 'dream-logic,' La Bossière seems, in fact, to be saying little more than that literary artists like Conrad seek 'the essential truth of the universe' through analogy and symbolism rather than through the more formal logical methods of scientists and philosophers. But later 'dream logic' is brought into service to describe the non-rational quality of the visionary world which the Conradian hero, at some stage, inevitably enters. The fundamentally different roles this phrase is forced to play are reflective of larger inconsistencies in the book's overall structure. On the one hand (and this is perhaps the most interesting section of the book, and certainly the most carefully researched), La Bossière wants to place Conrad within a European mystical tradition based on Calderón and Nicholas of Cusa. But he demonstrates no direct influence and admits that Conrad could have picked up similar notions from German and Polish Romantics, French Symbolists, and even from Shakespeare. On the other hand, he is concerned to show how this irrational, visionary impulse functions in the works. The problem is basically that the underlying argument is weak and broken-backed. After the initial chapters Calderón and Nicholas of Cusa are barely mentioned, and the analyses of the individual works are simply too insubstantial to enhance our understanding of Conrad's career.

While La Bossière attempts to reassess Conrad's entire œuvre, Gary Geddes more narrowly, but still ambitiously, tries to re-evaluate Conrad's later novels (*Chance*, *Victory*, *The Shadow Line*, *The Arrow of Gold*, *The Rescue*, and *The Rover*) by challenging the generally held achievement-and-decline thesis. Clearly Geddes wants to make a case for Conrad's 'mature' fiction, yet it is hard to determine exactly what kind of case he has in mind, especially since, in his eagerness to refute established positions, he tends to lose sight of his own central argument. For example, one reason for the 'misinterpretation' of the later texts, Geddes believes, is a critical predisposition towards 'psychological fiction' that is blind to the value of the broader scope and less subjective modes of the final six novels. Yet his own examinations of the novels stress again and again the protagonists' individual destinies and dramatized psychological conflicts: he sees *Victory* as 'cast somewhat in the light of an ironic redemption parable or psychodrama, in which the various types are projections of the hero's subconscious struggles' (p 71), and *The Shadow Line* as a study of a 'manic-depressive' (p 96); he notes in *Chance* the importance Conrad places on 'our understanding of the psychology of Flora's situation' (p 15), and views *The Arrow of Gold* as a means to 'redefine dramatic action in psychological terms' (p 135). Geddes seems in fact to be arguing at cross purposes, insisting both that the later novels are substantially different in kind – and even in genre ('ironic romance') – from the earlier works, and that the corpus reveals continuity. He concludes that in the later works Conrad is still simply Conrad: he 'neither suppressed his awareness of the heart of darkness, nor lost his interest in the craft of fiction' (pp 197–8). But the question that Geddes does not adequately address is whether Conrad successfully translated that 'awareness' and 'interest' into fiction that could match that of his earlier achievements.

New readings of these little discussed texts will contribute to a better understanding of their author's career, and Geddes's comments on *The Shadow Line* are clearly valuable. But, in general, his examinations of specific texts are substantially weakened by his ignoring significant recent studies of narrative and style: his discussion of Conrad's language points out little more than recurring terms and the creation of mood and 'flavour'; his examination of first-person narrative forms relies upon and progresses no further than Scholes and Kellogg's discussion of autobiography; and, over all, his speculations on Conrad's fictional strategies conclude merely in the judgment that he melded form and content. Re-evaluation of Conrad's later novels may indeed be in order, but we need a more rigorous analysis of their informing structures than Geddes has given us. (MARTIN KREISWIRTH)

Elliott B. Gose, Jr. *The Transformation Process in Joyce's Ulysses*
University of Toronto Press. xix, 228. $25.00

This study is in two parts, each consisting of six chapters, and is mostly concerned with two major influences on Joyce's thought and so on *Ulysses*. The first part pursues Joyce's indebtedness to the work of Giordano Bruno, 'the Nolan' as Joyce was pleased to call him; the second part both examines the influence of the father of modern psychoanalysis on Joyce and subjects the writer as well as his work to Freudian scrutiny. An important third source of influence is the philosopher Bergson. Elliott Gose is also, I believe, attempting to go beyond questions of influence and offer a more general account of 'the transformation process' as essential to Joyce's life, thought, and writing, though he has very little to say about the work in which Bruno and Freud figure prominently, *Finnegans Wake*, or any of the fiction apart from *Ulysses*.

Joyce's use of Bruno as a complement and corrective to the Stagyrite has often been observed, and I began to read Gose's book in the enthusiastic expectation that it would be a thorough study of this aspect of *Ulysses*. Gose's apposite quotations from Bruno in the introductory chapters establish the theme well: Joyce's interest in the perpetual transformations by which kings make their progresses through the zoological food chain into the guts of beggars and, more positively, by which we perceive the divinity that doth hedge a dog. Unfortunately the discussion of Bruno, soon spent, gives way to a drifting commentary, overloaded with allusions to other commentators, in which the analytical procedures too wantonly mix up Joyce's biography and his fiction, while the prose often groans for further editing. So, in a passage launched from a reference to Joyce's glaucoma, we are told that 'Proteus and Glaucus may well come together in Joyce's description of the sirens in "cool glaucous eau de Nil"' and that the god Glaucus 'may serve us as a paradigm for the Joyce who had to give himself to the style of each chapter, who by descending to animal state in the writing of "Circe" became the god-like creator who could look back on that episode and say "I think it is the best thing I have written".' This example of critical quilt-making may serve as a paradigm for the overall method of the first part of the book, I am sorry to say. 'May' and 'would have' are the critical needles and the thread is a quantity of propitiatory verbiage which assures us that the author is about to say, or has just said, something significant, in such terms as this: 'I have looked in the last two chapters at the characteristic process to which Joyce committed himself in his efforts to realize and express fully the material he dealt with.' I soon began to feel quite put upon, as if nobody had really taken the trouble to *read* this text before it came to me.

For some reason the second part of the book is much more readable than the first and is characterized by a fine bravado. It contains such challenging remarks as Gose's claim that 'at some level of the psyche, all Western men' see mothers as betrayers, sex as castrating violence, and fathers as threatening and (sexually) tempting. As opposed to the stuff that real (Western) men are made on, Joyce's text seems rather pallid, though not uninteresting. Its role is intimated by Gose's interpretation of Stephen as perceiving 'that textual criticism and masturbation are interchangeable forms of solipsistic exercise for the man who cannot otherwise stand up to the dominant woman in his background.' This, of course, is not the only possible interpretation of 'Unwed, unfancied, ware of wiles, they fingerponder nightly each his variorum edition of *The Taming of the Shrew*.' Another reader might interpret this fingering of the text as inadequate substitute for sexual activity, whether other- or self-directed, Stephen's comic presentation of the emotional and sexual deprivations of bachelor scholars.

Gose's key term in the Freudian part of the book is 'ambivalence.' Ambivalence is slung across the gap between Joyce's awkwardly (for the literary psychoanalyst) conscious use of Freudian psychology and its further use as evidence of Joyce's own complexes. In theory, Gose is quite definite about differentiating art from analysabilia, and he reproves such commentators as Schechner for confusing the two. In practice, however, his insistence on 'Joyce's deep ambivalence' (in such matters as the portrayal of the psychopathology of filial affection) rests on his own very ambivalent use of rhetorical techniques that convert literary into psychoanalysis. This transformation process is neither dull nor, as psychoanalysis, altogether unconvincing. Joyce 'may' have been a 'woman-killer' with repressed emotions for his father and have been attracted to Nora Barnacle for her 'masculine authority' (though his pornographic letters to Nora are not easy to analyse, being so deliberately written to induce physiological and emotional effects) and he certainly (like many artists) admitted to having a feminine element in his nature. But bringing Freudian insights to bear on *Ulysses* can be, and to a large extent here is, a dubious tautology if the evidence is also drawn from the fiction. (Jung, however, towards whom Joyce felt particularly antagonistic, does offer a description of 'ego-inflation' resulting from the acquisition by the conscious mind of its formerly unconscious contents that fits the Joycean bill very neatly.)

Gose's textual fingerpondering often lacks what one might call literary tact, as in such an analysis as this: 'If he [Stephen] could somehow admit his attraction to his father's neurotic anti-feminism (which points to covert homosexuality), he could free himself of the unconscious hold the attraction has on him and be able to love a woman.' All this Stephen himself knows, according to Gose. But where do we see Stephen's perception of Simon Dedalus as a neurotic anti-feminist and closet homosexual and of himself as unable to love a woman? I suspect Gose of confusing the biographical with the fictional data. Moreover, there may even be a covering cherub or two between him and the biographical facts.

Sometimes, in order to make sense of the study on its own terms, the reader is required to see the analyst as analysand – a reversal of roles for which Joyce cunningly laid the bait. I take not a major but an amusing minor instance: shortly after some considerable discourse on the verbal manifestations (including dangling modifiers and such) of *The Psychopathology of Everyday Life*, Gose writes: 'On her deathbed, in the presence of James and Stanislaus, he blurted out "Die and be damned to you!"' The subject of this sentence, John Joyce, emerges from it, psychopathologically speaking, a very sick man. However, Stanislaus Joyce (Gose's source) has Mrs Joyce on the bed and her husband at the foot of it, so we must qualify the analysis accordingly; even, I suggest, considering the possibility that Gose's grammar is something other than what Joyce called a 'Freudful mistake.'

Jokes and ambivalences apart – but not excluded – this part of the study is stimulating, despite its methodological impurity. And when he brings Bruno and Freud together, Gose gives us rather more than a glimpse of the Joyce he wants to bring into full view: the writer and man in whom awareness of the processes of transformation strongly tempers his innate or acquired tendencies towards scholastic categorization. (MICHAEL J. SIDNELL)

Morine Krissdottir. *John Cowper Powys and the Magical Quest*
MacDonald and Jane. xi, 218. $33.95

This ambitious study seeks to explain the mythological content of John Cowper Powys's entire fictional canon from *Wood and Stone* to *All or Nothing*. To provide a guide to the 'philosophy' that is expressed obliquely in the literature some of the non-fictional prose is examined in the introductory chapter. Simultaneously there is a desire to place Powys's own voluminousness within the cultural context of virtually the whole world. In many ways these aspirations are commendable. All Powys's works endeavour to reach what he called in *Owen Glendower* the 'mysterious underworld of beyond-reality whence rise the external archetypes.' His writings are indeed interdependent, and the appreciation of their richness is undoubtedly increased when they are read, in so far as anyone can do so, against the vast background of all that has been thought and said.

However, the working out of these grand objectives causes some demurs. By treating Powys's thoughts as a collective entity Dr Krissdottir makes them appear less susceptible to development and emendation than they actually were. This approach also means that there can be no opportunity to show the illumination that is given to a particular fiction from a collateral reading of the non-fiction of the same period. Further, the assertion of the many points of contact between Powys's ideas and those of 'mystics of all ages and places' (p 15) gives the impression of minimizing his idiosyncrasy. In Krissdottir's discussion no distinction is made between entirely coincidental points of agreement with certain members of the multitude into whose allegiance he is forced and potentially verifiable lines of genuine influence.

To raise these issues may be mere pedantry. For the critical procedure used here could be said to be Krissdottir's free adaptation of her author's own. Whenever Powys wrote or spoke about another author, he allowed his personality to be absorbed into sympathetic union. Without vexing himself unduly about factual details, as an objective appraiser would do, he became instead an inspired interpreter. While there is therefore a sense in which Powys requires a commentator who is as liberated as he from the conventional restraints of literary criticism, his dithyrambic analyses are exceedingly difficult to emulate.

After the critical methodology is set forth in the opening, the rest of the book gives explications of the secret mythological overtones of individual works. All these chapters have the solid virtue of recognizing that Powys's imaginative constructs cannot be judged fairly by criteria appropriate to realistic novels. A welcome challenge is thereby made to the hasty underestimation of Powys's worth that comes from the application of rigid mimetic standards. But the claim that his fictions must be seen exclusively as myths or visionary stories may be the substitution of an equally severe restriction. Except for recurring symbols and structural patterns, Krissdottir refuses to be concerned with 'artistry.' The result is that little consideration can be given to the way in which the mythological references are set forth in specifically fictional terms. Value judgments about the relative merits of the various books as fictions are ventured. *Weymouth Sands* is said to be 'slack and disoriented' (p 107) and *Morwyn* 'disappointing' (p 120), while others are declared completely successful. Without any elaboration of the artistry involved the basis for these discriminations is unclear.

Nevertheless, it is the implication that Powys's literature is fully appreciable only to the *cognoscenti* that is the most troublesome. Habitually Powys used arcane lore and *recherché* myths to create an aura of wonder. Any exegesis of his treatment of esoteric doctrine is valuable for demonstrating that he gave more conscious care to the creation of this mysterious atmosphere than he himself pretended. For establishing this point Krissdottir's analyses of the Grail legends in *A Glastonbury Romance* and of alchemy in *Porius* are particularly admirable. But appreciations of his intricacies must not make Powys appear less approachable or less enjoyable than he unquestionably is for the reader who is not familiar with alchemy or the perennial philosophy.   (MARGARET MORAN)

R.P. Bilan. *The Literary Criticism of F.R. Leavis*
Cambridge University Press 1979. vii, 338. $32.95

Most of what has been written about the criticism of F.R. Leavis can be safely disregarded. Few serious students of literature could produce a compelling justification for sifting the dust-heap of wilful misrepresentation and blank imperception, the gleeful sneering of literary racketeers and the embarrassing effusions of misguided discipleship, that constitutes the greater part of the response to Leavis's work. There are, nevertheless, some commentaries on Leavis that must be read, and Professor Bilan's book (although open to critical objection at some crucial points) properly belongs in this category. He approaches Leavis with the mixture of admiration and respect appropriate to the discussion of a great critic, and yet it can be fairly said that his treatment of Leavis resembles Leavis's own treatment of Dr Johnson – critical 'greatness' is not a quality that, once recognized and demonstrated, absolves other critics of the responsibility for pointing out errors of judgment, limitations of sensibility, and weaknesses of theory and practice. Infallibility cannot be the touchstone we use to identify the great critics; if it were, we would have no great critics. And the picture of Dr Leavis that emerges from Bilan's study is impressive primarily because Bilan is willing to admit the imperfections of his subject, with the result that Leavis never appears to us as less than human, never becomes an *object* to be approached with the deadly professionalism of 'academic detachment.'

Because Bilan's book attempts a comprehensive and detailed assessment of Leavis's achievement, summary or paraphrase would have the effect of transforming complexity into apparent superficiality. It would be fairer to draw attention to those parts of his work that seem persuasive, and then to note aspects of the book that are more likely to provoke dissent than to elicit agreement.

Leavis's criticism was always distinguished by his refusal to separate literature from life, and Bilan argues effectively that Leavis's social and cultural concerns were consistent throughout his career and that his critical practice cannot be properly understood without a recognition of this consistency. Related to this point is Leavis's consistently asserted view that the literary critic's concern with language extends to its use in society, and that usage can be reliably taken as an indication of the state of cultural health. In other areas Leavis is shown to be, if not always less consistent, certainly less clear. Bilan addresses, for example, the problems of definition that cannot be separated from Leavis's use of words such as *culture*, *tradition*, and *standards*, and proceeds from this to a serious consideration of the difficulties that Leavis faced because of his insistence that criticism was *doing*, not theorizing.

Bilan is also effective in distinguishing Leavis's 'evaluative' criticism from the concept of 'judicial' criticism with which it is often (and often deliberately) confused; he provides a valuable sorting out of the complex and developing views that Leavis held of Eliot and Lawrence; and he makes an important distinction between the ways in which Leavis criticized poetry and the essentially different approach he brought to the study of the novel. He is also prepared to state, what for Leavisites will no doubt be unpalatable, the case that Leavis does not always support his judgments with reasons – and that in some places in his criticism he has a 'tendency to offer rhetoric in place of reason' (p 149). His treatment of Leavis as a critic of Lawrence will displease not only the disciples: Bilan's assessment is not always favourable, and yet he does conclude that Leavis, whatever his shortcomings, is to date the best of Lawrence's critics. Finally, Bilan makes a point of major importance when he argues that Leavis's development as a critic reveals him to be essentially 'romantic' rather than 'classical.'

There are other qualities of Bilan's book that could be praised; there are as well questionable aspects. For example, Bilan admits that Leavis's social criticism is open to objection, and that serious objections have been made, by Raymond Williams and others. Yet he leaves the matter hanging, quoting opinions on both sides and then moving on. Something more could have been done, if only to show that Leavis has a fondness for what he considers the single telling example rather than an assembly of detail. Hardy's 'Dorsetshire Labourer' outweighs, for Leavis, the more substantially supported arguments of Williams. This habit of mind limits his effectiveness as a social critic somewhat more than Bilan is willing to admit, and these limitations are reinforced by Leavis's apparently resolute avoidance of writers who might have helped to clarify his thinking in this area. Jacques Ellul is the obvious example. (George Grant, of course, would be another; but here we encounter another problem. Leavis's emphasis on the 'right kind' of provincialism leads not only to a proper distrust of rootless cosmopolitanism but also to a comfortable ignorance of much valuable writing that is neither British nor American. His distrust of the social scientist presents an equivalent problem: had he read with discrimination in this area his unfaltering faith in the power of education to change society might convince more readers if they could see him taking into account what is known about the ability of elite groups within mass societies to pervert education for their own purposes.)

Among other questionable aspects of Bilan's book are his treatment of Leavis's shifting view of Dickens (he confronts the problem, but his explanation comes close to being a case of special pleading) and his failure to comment on Leavis's unwillingness to engage in sustained critical analysis of literature from the post-war period. To take this point one step farther, why did Leavis choose (it must have been a choice) not to discuss Graham Greene? There is one other perplexing omission that must be noted: Bilan shows that he understands very well what Leavis means by 'collaborative' criticism, yet by neglecting the work of Q.D. Leavis he misses an opportunity to show Leavis's finest collaborative achievements.

At the centre of *The Literary Criticism of F.R. Leavis* is the argument that Leavis's criticism increasingly demonstrated, particularly in the last twenty years of his life, the importance for him of 'the religious sense.' The claims made in support of this argument are not altogether convincing, and the short final chapter, in which Bilan turns his attention directly to this argument, seems more the prospectus for a future study than the last word on the issue. Leavis's thinking on religious issues is said to be 'subtle and penetrating,' to stand comparison with the work of Tillich, and to possess in its 'apparent vagueness' a source of strength (p 301). The conclusion that Leavis's thought 'about the religious dimension of life ... represents a considerable achievement' (pp 301–2) may pass as a statement of belief on Bilan's part; it will not convince those whose study of religion begins with writers other than Lawrence and Leavis. How are we to define the term 'religious sense' in such a way that it could be applied both to Leavis and to George Grant? And here we return to the question of Leavis's social criticism, and to a problem that Bilan might have considered: Leavis is praised, finally, for 'pointing us towards Blake,

Dickens and Lawrence as the source of wisdom, health and life that our civilization needs' (p 302), but this 'pointing' excludes from the tradition that which precedes what Grant has defined as 'modernity'; Leavis's admired writers may be critics of modernity, yet they are as well the products of it. Our critical sense, if criticism is to be meaningful, must include a greater awareness than the later Leavis demonstrates of what preceded – and was destroyed by – the modern spirit.

Notwithstanding the objections that can be made to Bilan's arguments, his book deserves our attention. And because he is part of the Canadian academic community, perhaps his work will set some Canadian critics to reading Leavis with attention. Leavis does not require disciples, but his achievement – properly appreciated – could give to those who study our literature the conviction that evaluation, and the relationships between literature and life, are concerns we have, for too long, neglected.   (DAVID JACKEL)

Charles Doyle, editor. *William Carlos Williams: The Critical Heritage*
Routledge & Kegan Paul. xix, 436. $47.25

Williams's reputation remains equivocal nearly twenty years after his death. Dorothy Dudley in 1918 found the poetry of *Al Que Quiere!* 'at its best fibrous, marvelously observant, delicate, haunting; then at moments stilted, confused, obtuse.' As late as 1964 James Dickey, reviewing *The Collected Later Poems*, observed: 'One will find here, also, Williams' most discouraging qualities, monotony and arbitrariness, which proceed from what looks suspiciously like the notion that to *present* were sufficient – were *always* sufficient' (Dickey's emphases). Yet Dickey can also ask in the same notice: 'Has any other poet in American history been so *actually* useful, usable, and influential?'

Usable but arbitrary, observant yet obtuse. A word which recurs in this volume is 'naive' and sometimes the term 'faux naif' to suggest a rhetorical stance of bluntness. That this element of sincere 'posing' in Williams served a conscious strategy from the time he found his own poetic voice seems clear enough. In 1924 Paul Rosenfeld noted: 'He can give himself ... in his crassness ... in absurd melancholy, wild swiftness of temper.' Williams knew better than anyone else the risks he was running in his literary radicalism. He realized the division of opinion he would create and pugnaciously rejoiced at the prospect.

Following the general format of The Critical Heritage series, this volume contains 132 items of varying length and importance covering almost 60 years from 1909 to 1967. One checks for the major items. Here is D.H. Lawrence's review of *In the American Grain* (1926), a work owing something to Lawrence's own *Studies in Classic American Literature* of 1923.

Lawrence praises Williams's attempts to 'bring into his consciousness America itself, the still-unravished bride of silences.' Here also is Wallace Stevens with his review of *Collected Poems 1921-1931*, including the goading repetition of the phrase 'anti-poetic' which so infuriated Williams and which still continues to reverberate in critical discussions of the poet. We find Randall Jarrell's two reviews of books of *Paterson*: enthusiasm for Book 1 and disenchantment with Book 4. Robert Lowell's notice of Book 2 of *Paterson*, praising Williams's 'combination of brilliance, sympathy, and experience,' also appears. So does Leslie Fiedler's review of the same book, attacking Williams because he 'pursues absolutely the seen poem.' Consequently 'there is no song in him.' This, if true, would prove devastating, yet there is generally in Williams criticism a lack of textual analysis. Too often the poems are treated as footnotes in the history of an idea rather than as autonomous entities. It is a relief to find someone such as Alan Stephens engaging seriously with Williams's abiding concern with 'measure.' Such a consideration helps to remove some of the 'arbitrariness' from the poems and renders them more 'usable' to others.

By the end of his career Williams had attained the status of an American classic, at least in the United States. In Britain during the 1950s and 1960s, when his work first became available on any significant scale, the pattern of incomprehension and resistance was repeated. 'The case of William Carlos Williams remains the rock on which Anglo-American literary opinion splits,' Donald Davie starts a review in December 1964, adding that 'Williams' intrinsic achievement is altogether more precarious and perverse' than his admirers will admit. The battle over Williams's position in the canon continues; the jury is still out.

Charles Doyle offers a helpful introduction outlining the general history of critical response to Williams. For supplementary reading there is Paul L. Mariani's *William Carlos Williams: The Poet and His Critics* (1975), which provides an extremely useful commentary on the subject including many of the texts printed here. (ERIC DOMVILLE)

Victor E. Graham and W. McAllister Johnson. *The Royal Tour of France by Charles IX and Catherine de' Medici: Festivals and Entries 1564-6*
University of Toronto Press 1979. Pp x, 472, illus. $50.00

To understand the Renaissance vision of the world, that ideal Platonic universe in which all the arts united to celebrate the triumph of Beauty, Truth, and Goodness, one can do no better than study the magnificent festivals and royal entries of the Valois kings of France. The key concepts governing the political, moral, and aesthetic theories of the period are to be found in the elaborate decorations, festivities, and ceremonies surrounding the monarch and his court during tours of his kingdom and important international conferences, such as the one planned by Catherine de' Medici with Philip II of Spain at Bayonne in 1565. It is within such a context that the importance of this splendid volume, the third to appear at the University of Toronto Press, under the joint authorship of Professors Victor Graham (Department of French) and McAllister Johnson (Department of Fine Art), can best be measured, and its contribution to research into aspects of literary and artistic collaboration be seriously analysed. The scholarship is impeccable, the illustrations magnificently reproduced, and the printed text in its clear and elegant type a joy to read: it is a fitting reminder of the Renaissance humanistic tradition of close collaboration between writer and printer.

As in their previous volumes, *Estienne Jodelle 'Le Recueil des inscriptions 1558': A Literary and Iconographical Exegesis* (1972) and *The Paris Entries of Charles IX and Elisabeth of Austria 1571, With an Analysis of Simon Bouquet's 'Bref et sommaire recueil'* (1974), the authors have assembled an impressive number of original documents, drawn from a wide range of contemporary sources, such as those to be found in municipal and departmental archives along the route of the royal entries. In addition they consulted royal acts and correspondence, notably that of Catherine de' Medici, and the official 'Comptes de bouche' which recorded daily expenditures of the king's household, and the 'Extraordinaire de l'argenterie' for 1565 which reveals the vast sums of money spent on the Bayonne conference, described by the authors as 'an occasion of international stature masquerading as a family reunion elaborated within a provincial context.'

The Royal Tour of France undertaken by the young king, Charles IX, and his remarkable mother, Catherine de' Medici, was clearly a political exercise, designed to glorify the monarch, whose personal motto, 'Pietate et Iustitia,' was a recurring theme in the artistic and literary celebrations. Catherine de' Medici was anxious to establish the power of the throne and to emphasize its mission of pacification and unification of the French provinces at a time when civil and religious dissension was still in the air. All means were employed to this end. So the 'external trappings of the tour' become the legitimate focus of the book.

Taking as their central document the brief detailed itinerary of the tour, recorded by Abel Jouan, 'sommier en nostre cuisine de bouche' at the royal court, in his *Recueil et discours du voyage de Charles IX* (1566), Graham and Johnson have painstakingly reconstructed the magnificent and varied pageantry of the tour in which the talents of major poets and dramatists, such as Ronsard, Baïf, and Garnier, were involved. Given the wealth of the historical, literary, and artistic documentation incorporated into over 400 pages of introduction, appendices, iconographical illustrations, indexes of place names and biographies, as well as an excellent general index, as opposed to 72 pages of the Jouan text, meticulously annotated by the authors, one might well expect to be submerged in a sea of erudition. Not so. Each piece of information is carefully set in place, as in a mosaic, in order to create the atmosphere of 'divertissement et fête' which the official 'recueils' of 'Triumphes et Magnificences' only remotely suggest. One marvels at the ingenuity, erudition, and imagination displayed by the civic organizers of each solemn royal entry. One is delighted by descriptions of tournaments, bull fights, regional dances, citizens in costumes representing ancient civilizations as well as the 'savages' of the New World, and the mechanical crocodile at Nîmes. During the splendid court festivities of Fontainebleau and Bar-le-Duc one moves into an imaginary world of chivalry in which the king was both actor and spectator, as he fought his way to rescue maidens held prisoner in enchanted castles, while other less virtuous knights were dropped into dungeons, or, like the Duke of Orléans, carried off in a cloud. Masquerades, ballets, plays, and fireworks all played an essential part in the festivities. One of the most enchanting events, evoked on the jacket of the book by Antoine Caron's drawing of the excursion to the island in the Adour, is that of the sumptuous 'fête champêtre,' with all its literary and classical reminiscences, offered by Catherine de' Medici to her children at Bayonne. It is wonderfully appropriate that it should figure as one of the scenes depicted in the beautiful Valois tapestries now hanging in the Uffizi Gallery, Florence.

Unlike Bouvard and Pécuchet, Flaubert's comical researchers into the history of France, Graham and Johnson deserve a well-earned 'Chapeau bas' for their rigorous application of logical method, coupled with true perception and interpretation of such a massive array of documents. Their research sheds light upon all aspects of Renaissance thought and art and their book is to be recommended to every serious scholar of the period, as well as to the bibliophile who will covet such a beautifully produced book. (ELAINE LIMBRICK)

Etienne Bonnot de Condillac. *Les Monades*
Edited with an introduction and notes by Laurence L. Bongie
Studies on Voltaire and the Eighteenth Century, vol 187. £24

Professor Bongie's identification of the author of the anonymous *Les Monades* as Condillac is an astonishing event. Was the author of the *Traité des systèmes* a crypto-Leibnizian?

In the Berlin Academy the lines were drawn between the Newtonians and the Leibnizians over the question of monads. A contemporary refers to the 'bruit à Berlin où, à la cour, à la ville, dans les clubs des savans, et dans les sociétés de tout ordre, on ne parloit presque d'autre chose que de monades; et Dieu sait comment l'on en raisonnoit ou déraisonnoit.' The issue was to be decided by the Academy's prize essay on the question whether the doctrine of monads could be either firmly *refuted* and destroyed by unanswerable arguments or *proved*. Among the anonymous submissions was *Les Monades*. In the following year, 1748, it was published, still anonymous, together with six other of the entries.

A peculiar feature of Condillac's dissertation is that it seeks to satisfy both sides of the question. Part I is a critique of the Leibnizians and much of it was to appear verbatim in the *Traité des systèmes* in the following year. In Part II Condillac constructs a 'new system of monads' purged of the errors alleged in Part I, which have mainly to do with the doctrines of force and of perception. At the end he claims: 'J'ai démontré qu'il y a des monades, qu'elles diffèrent nécessairement entre elles, et qu'elles produisent les phénomènes de l'étendue et des corps, qui n'en sont que des aggrégats. J'ai prouvé qu'elles n'agissent point les unes dans les autres, et que, par conséquent, elles ne concourent à former l'univers qu'en vertu de l'harmonie qui a été préétablie.' This is enough to mark down the 'French Locke' as indisputably also the French Leibniz. That the Academy's prize should have gone to Justi, whom he despised, and that he himself should be well down the list could be reason enough for Condillac not to acknowledge authorship. What is mysterious is that in his subsequent writings he never reveals himself to be a monadist.

In his introductory study Bongie has tried to solve the mystery. His thesis is that Condillac yielded to the prevailing anti-metaphysical pressure as a matter of caution (pp 37ff); rejected his own monadism under this pressure (p 90); did not give it up but found a way of expressing the same thing in the epistemological or logical mode rather than in the metaphysical, not, however, realizing that he was doing this until later (pp 91ff). In the case of Leibniz the logical doctrine that true propositions are identical would be the counterpart of the metaphysical doctrine of windowless monads, and in the case of Condillac it was the logical doctrine which would now be developed. Bongie calls it Condillac's 'monadic logic of identity.' It seems to me, however, that the sole and essential link for Leibniz between his theory of the proposition and that of the monad is entirely lacking in Condillac, namely that for every monad there is a concept so complete that everything predicable of it can be deduced from the concept. To account, as Bongie does, for Condillac's mysterious silence as the result of his yielding to pressure is to impugn his intellectual integrity and his moral courage. I find this very difficult to accept.

In his introduction Bongie is also concerned with another mystery, without, however, having much luck in dispelling it, namely the striking similarity between some of Condillac's and Leibniz's logical doctrines, for at the time Leibniz's logical writings were not available. On this I have a simple hypothesis to suggest: it is unlikely that Condillac was unacquainted with the logic of Hobbes. This was the part of Hobbes's thought which most interested Leibniz. In Hobbes are to be found the counterparts of Condillac's most characteristic logical doctrines: that philosophy begins with the analysis of conceptions given in sense experience; that the propositions of science are analytical or reducible to identities, as following from definitions; that deduction consists in linguistic transformations of the same proposition; that to reason is to calculate with names or, as Condillac puts it in the *Langue des calculs*, 'calculer c'est raisonner, et raisonner c'est calculer.' Bongie's editorial treatment of the text is superb and the book production is beautiful. (ROBERT MCRAE)

Kay Bourlier. *Marcel Proust et l'architecture*
Les Presses de l'Université de Montréal. 238. $19.75

L'opposition mémoire volontaire/mémoire involontaire qui fonde l'œuvre proustienne s'exprime au moment de sa formulation en termes d'architecture. Arrivé à l'âge adulte, le Narrateur ne se rappelle plus la maison de sa tante que sous la forme d'un 'édifice ... à la base assez large, le petit salon, la salle à manger, ... l'escalier, si cruel à monter, qui constituait à lui seul le tronc fort étroit de cette pyramide irrégulière; et, au faîte, ma chambre à coucher avec le petit couloir à porte vitrée' (*A la recherche du temps perdu*, éd Pléiade, I, 43). Aussitôt goûtée et reconnue la madeleine trempée dans la tasse de thé, 'la vieille maison grise sur la rue, où était sa chambre, vint comme un décor de théâtre s'appliquer au petit pavillon ... qu'on avait construit pour mes parents sur ses derrières (ce pan tronqué que seul j'avais revu jusque-là)' (I, 47). On s'étonne dès lors de constater qu'il n'est nullement question de ces textes essentiels dans le livre de Kay Bourlier, et qu'on n'y retrouve pas non plus la description détaillée de la maison d'Odette (I, 220) ni celle du sous-sol de l'Hôtel de Guermantes (II, 607). Toutefois, il s'agit là moins d'inadvertances que d'une conception de l'architecture dominée par le monumental: 'églises, cathédrales, palais, châteaux' (p 56). Cette conception restrictive du sujet, qui limite nécessairement l'intérêt du livre, s'accompagne d'autre part d'une définition curieuse de l'architecture, qui dans la pensée de Bourlier se colore de considérations purement sculpturales et décoratives (pp 131, 146–7, 192–3, etc). La réserve la plus grave qu'on puisse formuler à l'égard de ce livre est donc un certain défaut de rigueur conceptuelle. En délimitant de manière plus réfléchie l'extension d' 'architecture,' Bourlier aurait mieux cerné toute la complexité du sujet, tout en éliminant des éléments souvent associés à l'architecture mais qui sont en fin de compte accessoires.

S'ajoutant à ce flou conceptuel, on rencontre ici et là des maladresses de style qui vont jusqu'à friser l'incorrection grammaticale. La phrase suivante servira de témoin, mais d'autres semblables se trouvent aux pp 13, 15, 46, 66, 71, etc:

Parmi les modèles les plus évidents, on reconnaît les petites églises de Criqueboeuf et de Hennequeville qui se trouvent sur la côte normande entre Trouville et Honfleur, que Proust avait visitées avec des camarades de lycée en 1892, puis, plus tard, comme nous l'avons déjà mentionné, avec Madame Straus, et la petite église de Dordrecht en Hollande. (P 101)

Nous nous abstenons de relever toutes les petites fautes de français qui jalonnent le texte par endroits. De toute manière, même si l'on regrette que Philip Kolb soit rebaptisé 'Philippe' et que Bourlier semble confondre 'romain' et 'roman' (p 206), ce genre d'erreurs ne gâte pas la lecture d'un livre qui reste dans le fond intéressant et valable pour le lecteur qui ne s'obstine pas à y rechercher ce que l'auteur n'a pas pensé à y inclure.

Il est indéniable que Proust a étayé certains thèmes de son roman en recourant à des images formées par la description d'édifices réels ou fictifs. Depuis le premier éveil à l'érotisme du jeune Narrateur jusqu'à sa pleine connaissance de la sexualité des autres et de la sienne, des structures au style marqué symbolisent les diverses formes de l'amour, du clocher gothique de Roussainville (la masturbation) à l'architecture orientale de Venise (l'homosexualité). De même, la structure complexe de la cathédrale sous-tend l'ensemble du roman, étant la métaphore à la fois de l'œuvre, de la vie du Narrateur, de l'Histoire et du Temps. Bourlier nous retrace de manière fine et intelligente l'évolution parallèle de ces thèmes et de leurs supports imagés. Ce faisant, elle nous propose une lecture de Proust nouvelle et tout à fait stimulante. Il eût suffi qu'elle eût élargi et raffiné sa conception de l'architecture, qu'elle eût remarqué et approfondi la fréquente sublimation de l'image architecturale en une image zoomorphique ou géomorphique (voir, par exemple, les textes cités aux pp 113, 152, 182 et 205), pour que nous n'eussions plus à souhaiter que quelqu'un fasse l'étude définitive du thème architectural chez Proust.
(JOHN MCCLELLAND)

N. David Keypour. *André Gide: écriture et réversibilité dans 'Les Faux-Monnayeurs'*
Les Presses de l'Université de Montréal / Didier. 261. $19.75

Valérie Raoul. *The French Fictional Journal: Fictional Narcissism / Narcissistic Fiction*
University of Toronto Press. 158. $12.50

Chacun de ces deux ouvrages situe son questionnement dans le cadre d'une étude des structures narratives, se donnant pour objet d'analyse le premier un texte ponctuel, *Les Faux-Monnayeurs* de Gide, le second une forme générique, le journal fictif tel qu'il est exemplifié par la tradition française du 19e et du 20e siècles.

Pour être ponctuel le texte gidien de référence n'en est pas moins fort complexe puisqu'il réunit et fait jouer différents procédés narratifs – monologue, lettre, dialogue, journal – dont la première partie de l'ouvrage de N. David Keypour examine la composante morphologique, procédant à une identification des voix narratives qui s'y manifestent et à une détermination de leurs fonctions et caractéristiques. Ce faisant l'auteur choisit de privilégier dans son approche la spécificité gidienne, s'attachant d'abord à restituer chacun des procédés dans l'intertexte de l'œuvre pour en étudier ensuite la pratique immanente, mais en tant qu'elle se rapporte à un projet d'écriture. 'Il n'est pas vain d'espérer reconnaître l'homme au bout du chemin' (p 16). Dans cette perspective les outils théoriques, empruntés aux travaux narratologiques les plus récents, en particulier à ceux de Genette, sont invoqués comme un savoir qu'il s'agit moins de postuler ou de vérifier que de mettre au service de la lecture textuelle. Cet usage adjuvant de la théorie n'en est pas moins fort habile et contribue sur bien des points à en affiner l'incidence heuristique. Soucieux d'articuler structures discursives et structures thématiques concomitantes, le travail d'analyse procède avec une grande minutie dont il faudrait pouvoir retracer le développement. Retenons simplement quelques propositions majeures.

D'un emploi limité, le monologue romanesque tel qu'il est pratiqué dans *Les Faux-Monnayeurs* serait moins chargé d'exprimer la pensée en gestation, le courant de conscience des modernes, que de réécrire le monologue dramatique des classiques dont il conserve certaines marques lyriques: apostrophe, invocation, emphase. Modalisé par le style indirect libre, il est pris en charge par la voix du narrateur, d'un narrateur ironique et indiscret. 'Par là, l'indiscrétion et ses conséquences deviennent significatives de la manière d'être de l'auteur en littérature' (p 47). Le recours au procédé épistolaire vise la caractérisation par différenciation, en même temps que l'emploi gidien de la lettre tend vers une conversion de la narration romanesque en narration directe. Car si le journal peut être considéré comme la forme écrite d'un monologue, l'échange de lettres se présente comme l'équivalent transcrit d'un dialogue. Ici encore se fait jour la composante théâtrale, de même qu'à l'indiscrétion narrative du monologue se substitue l'indiscrétion entre personnages. Quant au dialogue, il est dans *Les Faux-Monnayeurs* une forme privilégiée du récit. 'C'est que chez Gide l'imagination est essentiellement verbale' (p 70). Sa valeur est d'abord heuristique pour le romancier qui y trouve le moyen de découvrir progressivement la spécificité de ses personnages, instrument de caractérisation donc mais qui médiatise aussi l'ironie. Remarquons que l'analyse s'attache moins ici au fonctionnement du discours ironique qu'à sa thématisation, et que ce qu'elle identifie d'autre part comme étant la fonction métaphorique du dialogue ne donne lieu qu'à un commentaire sur la valeur symbolique de son contenu. Le dialogue enfin est ce lieu du récit où peuvent s'exposer les thèses de la pensée gidienne, mais réparties en points de vue souvent contradictoires dont la coexistence permet d'éviter l'écueil de ces 'exécrables romans à thèses' (*Les Faux-Monnayeurs*, pp 1083-4) et de convertir l'ironie en vouloir interrogatif. Avec le dialogue, le journal demeure le procédé narratif le plus fréquemment exploité. Le journal d'Edouard réunit, dans ses limites propres, dialogues, lettres, monologues et journal, reflétant ainsi, comme par une mise en abyme, la structure du roman en son entier. Outre ses fonctions de datation et de régie, de relais narratif, de support réflexif, il dénonce la fiction en même temps qu'il y participe, 'il fonctionne comme un miroir posé de biais, où se reflètent les personnages qui se trouvent dans le tableau présenté par le narrateur' (p 107). Mais concurremment, ce journal-miroir est réfléchi dans le tableau de ce dernier. Cette première partie s'achève sur l'examen de l'ostensibilité du narrateur dans le récit, de ses corollaires et de sa justification, et met en place une structure à trois termes dont la première instance serait représentée par le personnage-récitant, contribuant à la narration mais sans le savoir, la seconde par le narrateur défini comme une instance fonctionnelle et linguistique (p 111), la troisième par l'auteur implicite conçu en tant que conscience organisatrice et scripturale.

La seconde partie, de caractère synthétique, s'attache à relever les ambiguïtés de la voix narrative et les interférences entre niveaux. 'Il y a transgression si par exemple la participation des personnages à la narration est accompagnée de signes révélateurs de leur complicité dans l'acte narratif; ou si un personnage écrivant semble partager la fonction de l'instance de l'écriture; ou si inversement, l'auteur [implicite] semble approprier à ses fins l'écriture des personnages' (p 147). De ce point de vue, le système narratif des *Faux-Monnayeurs* est éminemment métaleptique et contrevient à chaque instant à la logique des niveaux. En conclusion, l'analyse des structures cède le pas à celle des intentions et se met à l'écoute de l'expérience existentielle de l'homme Gide dans son rapport à l'autre.

L'étude pénétrante et sensible de Keypour constitue une contribution importante aux études gidiennes et si elle s'impose à ce titre à l'attention des spécialistes de l'auteur des *Faux-Monnayeurs*, elle mérite aussi l'intérêt de ceux que préoccupent les problèmes posés par la lecture immanente d'un texte romanesque.

Dans son ouvrage *The French Fictional Journal* Valérie Raoul se propose d'étudier le roman français en forme de journal à partir d'un corpus de textes empruntés aux 19e et 20e siècles. L'argument central de l'étude, que l'on admettra facilement, repose sur l'idée que la spécificité de ce genre romanesque réside essentiellement dans l'assujetissement des conventions du journal à celles du roman, résultant en une interférence de codes. D'où deux niveaux de fonctionnement concomitants: celui du roman ayant l'auteur pour scripteur, celui du journal s'originant dans le discours d'un narrateur.

Cette dualité engendre deux points de vue critiques, l'un de caractère herméneutique qui s'attachera à l'élucidation du pacte de lecture, l'autre d'ordre narratologique qui se donnera pour objet d'analyse le texte dans son fonctionnement immanent. La première partie de l'ouvrage, intitulée 'The Journal and the Novel,' insiste sur la figure du lecteur et sur ses réflexes de lecture tels qu'anticipés et manipulés par l'auteur. Si le journal fictif retient les traits pertinents du journal proprement dit (narration au jour le jour à la première personne et production d'un compte-rendu écrit), il s'en distingue fondamentalement par sa situation extradiégétique, c'est-à-dire par le pacte de lecture qui s'institue entre auteur et lecteur. Le journal fictif ne prétend pas à la vérité et son caractère fictif est d'emblée reconnu par l'instance lectrice dont l'activité de déchiffrement demeure en grande partie programmée par l'instance d'écriture. Car le juste décodage du journal fictif demande que le lecteur reconnaisse dans le texte qu'il compulse et le code du journal et son statut imité. Feinte de l'appareil éditorial, dispositif titrologique et discours préfaciel représentent à cet égard autant de moyens de manipulation et de contrôle auxquels viennent s'ajouter dans le corps du récit les marques qui relèvent de l'ordonnance narrative et de la *dispositio*, motifs récurrents, parallélismes, antithèses, mises en abyme, en somme tout ce qui contribue au maintien de l'intérêt romanesque. La première partie s'achève sur un chapitre qui dresse le portrait de l'intimiste: aptitude à écrire et à bien écrire, isolement conflictuel ou crise de conscience qui provoquent une compulsion d'intelligibilité (*Le Horla, La Nausée*).

La seconde partie de l'ouvrage, 'The Journal in the Novel,' examine les structures intradiégétiques du journal fictif. Le narrateur s'y fragmente selon trois rôles: sujet, objet, destinataire, désignés par le recours à la typologie des cas: nominatif, accusatif, datif. Cette triple division du sujet rendue sensible par divers effets de miroir et de réflection manifeste son statut fondamentalement temporel: le narrateur du journal fictif s'y saisit comme objet au passé, s'assume comme sujet dans le présent de son énonciation et s'adresse à lui-même comme lecteur futur. Le problème de l'identité se négocie dès lors en termes de discontinuité. D'autre part le journal fictif fait prédominer les fonctions métalinguistique et poétique. A l'opposé du monologue intérieur qui oblitère le procès de l'écriture en en masquant le caractère arrangé, le journal fictif met en scène la praxis scripturale en en faisant l'objet d'une thématisation: mimétisme stylistique, conscience de faire de la littérature et référence à ses modèles, et en posant le journal lui-même comme élément de l'intrigue. 'The fictional journal is on the one hand a story disguised as commentary, on the other a commentary on fiction-writing, disguised as a story' (p 68).

La troisième partie établit le modèle constitutionnel du journal fictif pour en éprouver ensuite le fonctionnement à partir d'un exemple archétypal, *Eva ou le journal interrompu* de Jacques Chardonne, et en déterminer enfin le jeu des variantes. Les fonctions nominative, accusative et dative, diversifiées dans le roman, se fixent dans le journal fictif sur la seule personne du narrateur. Celui-ci remplit les divers rôles du schéma actantiel, à l'exception de celui d'adjuvant dont la fonction ablative est assurée par le journal lui-même. Les postes du triangle flexionnel ainsi obtenu sont en rapport d'homologie avec les instances temporelles (voir ci-dessus) qui, à leur tour, correspondent aux modalisations de la voix grammaticale. 'The "voice" category is related to the "writing" aspect of the journal, since this activity records the past self (passive), transforms the narrator self (middle), and produces a text (active) which the future self may read' (p 73). Cette structure triplement triangulaire (cas, temps, voix), de caractère intradiégétique, vient se superposer à la structure extradiégétique – auteur, personnage, lecteur – pour former une figure pyramidale complexe (p 74) qui simule par le jeu de ses éléments géométriques les relations constitutives du journal fictif.

D'une façon générale, le mérite de l'auteur dans cet ouvrage est d'abord de proposer à notre réflexion un objet romanesque dont les caractères génériques ont été jusqu'à maintenant peu étudiés, ensuite de présenter de cet objet une description précise et souvent séduisante qui démontre de sérieuses qualités de synthèse. Mais pourquoi ne pas inclure dans le corpus de référence des textes du 18e siècle qui auraient pu enrichir l'analyse, tels *La Religieuse* dont la 'technique bâtarde,' aux dires de G. May (*Diderot et 'La Religieuse,'* 1954, p 215), est 'celle du journal intime subrepticement greffé sur des mémoires'? On peut estimer d'autre part que la figure du lecteur est un concept méthodologique encore trop peu rigoureux pour servir de pilier à l'analyse. L'objection toutefois dépasse le cadre de l'ouvrage et s'adresse plus généralement à la théorie toujours embryonnaire de la réception. (ROLAND LE HUENEN)

Mark Boulby. *Karl Philipp Moritz: At the Fringe of Genius*
University of Toronto Press 1979. xii, 308. $20.00

It will come as a surprise to English-speaking readers that a list of the '100 Books of World Literature' rather solemnly selected in 1979 by a jury of German critics and published in the weekly *Die Zeit* (Hamburg) included the novel *Anton Reiser* by Karl Philipp Moritz (1756–93). What on earth, baffled anglophones may ask, is the name of Moritz doing among the Dantes and the Dostoevskis, the Virgils and the Voltaires, of 'World Literature'? And yet, even if eyebrows may be raised about his being listed among the illustrious 100, a case can be made (from the German point of view) for the choice, or at least, as Dr Boulby more modestly argues, for Moritz's deserving to be known outside Germany. For only one of his works has been translated into English, his *Journeys of a German in England in 1782*, which enjoyed a vogue in England from 1795 onward, and of which a new English edition was prepared as late as 1965. It was precisely this travelogue, alongside *Anton Reiser* (1785–90), which first drew Goethe's attention to his friend to be. In some ways Moritz's enduring fame within German letters rests on two pillars: on Goethe's friendship and esteem and on *Anton Reiser*. What Boulby attempts to do in his carefully researched and closely reasoned study of Moritz's life and works (and Boulby is remarkably successful in achieving that elusive synthesis of critical approaches – biographical, historical, aesthetic, philosophical, and psychological facets of his topic are nicely fused into a coherent whole) is to add a third reason for our according Moritz the international recognition he deserves: that he was 'ahead of his time, a harbinger of the future' (p xii).

Though firmly rooted in the empiricism of the Enlightenment, Moritz's cast of mind, in part engendered by the cruel misfortunes he had to endure because of his poverty, lowly social status, and physical and mental ill health (Boulby depicts Moritz the man with sympathy and understanding), does indeed point forward to later developments on the literary and intellectual scene. *Anton Reiser* is, as Boulby says, not only a proto-Romantic work, but is more 'modern' than Goethe's *Werther* as a 'systematic psychological case-book' (p 49); the novel's 'social psychology' (p 45) and egalitarian sentiments are of significance as an early critique of social oppression and class rigidity of the period; its hero (so largely autobiographical that Boulby is able to integrate his 50-page discussion of the novel with a description of Moritz's early life) is important in European literature as 'one of the very first characters in a novel who tries to live out his life as if it itself *were* a novel' (p 115). Moritz's originality, his near-genius (even though his intellect was, perhaps, 'second-rate,' p 251), is extraordinarily intriguing; for example, in his treatise *On the Creative Imitation of the Beautiful* (1788) Moritz gave expression to the notion of the autonomous work of art two years before Kant's *Critique of Judgement* appeared; and Moritz 'may be regarded as the initiator of clinical psychological journalism in Germany' (p 137) through his editorship of, and contributions to, his *Magazin zur Erfahrungsseelenkunde* (10 vols, 1783–93).

There is a brief retrospective review in English of two issues (vol 6, 1788) of the *Magazin* in the Supplement to *The German Museum or Monthly Repository of the Literature of Germany, the North and the Continent in General* (London, 1800, vol 1, p 581), which, though not cited by Boulby, expresses quintessentially the peculiar fascination Moritz exerted on his contemporaries. The *Magazin*, the anonymous reviewer of 1800 writes, contains 'highly interesting psychological facts, together with explanatory observations, in which are laid open some of the most hidden recesses of the human mind.' Almost two centuries later Mark Boulby has laid open, critically, sensitively, and drawing on his fund of knowledge of a host of major and minor figures of the German Enlightenment and periods beyond, the recesses of the mind, life, and times of Karl Philipp Moritz, which had hitherto been regrettably hidden from all but a few specialists in the English-speaking world. This monograph is a 'must' for all scholars working in the field of eighteenth- and early nineteenth-century European studies. The publisher is to be congratulated on matching the taut elegance of Boulby's arrangement and style with equally elegant design and printing; the only fault I could find was the omission of two of Boulby's own articles from the 'Select Bibliography,' which in turn leaves at least two footnotes (ch 1, n 15, and ch 3, n 12) dangling and incomplete. (ANTHONY W. RILEY)

Marketa Goetz-Stankiewicz. *The Silenced Theatre: Czech Playwrights without a Stage*
University of Toronto Press 1979. 319. $25.00

N.N. Shneidman. *Soviet Literature in the 1970s: Artistic Diversity and Ideological Conformity*
University of Toronto Press 1979. 128. $15.00

Scholars who study Soviet or East European literature are often faced with a unique kind of problem: political and ideological censorship prevents the official appearance of certain themes, styles, or individual authors, so that the literary and critical works which are published comprise a narrowed field, often excluding many of the issues most relevant for the society. In recent years the possibilities of foreign publication in the original and in translation and of *samizdat* (self-publication through typed manuscripts), even in regularly numbered editions such as Czechoslovakia's *Edice petlice* (Padlock Press), have enabled writers who are blacklisted or forced into emigration to continue their serious artistic endeavours without censorship and to reach both an international audience and their own countrymen. The stature of this 'unofficial' literature is nowhere greater than in Czechoslovakia, where the Soviet invasion of 1968 and the subsequent 'normalization' of politics and culture resulted in the blacklisting of all writers who had lent support to Dubček's 'socialism with a human face' and who refused to recant. This ultimately resulted in the official non-existence of an entire generation of the nation's writers, including the three major novelists Milan Kundera, Ludvík Vaculík, and Josef Škvorecký, as well as virtually all of the important dramatists of the 1960s.

Thus, Marketa Goetz-Stankiewicz's *The Silenced Theatre* is likely to remain for the foreseeable future *the* authoritative work on Czech theatre of the last two decades. A study of this highly creative period would clearly be impossible inside today's 'normalized' Czechoslovakia, and, in fact, the plays of the 1970s have never been officially published or performed in their home country. Even the gathering of the texts themselves was invaluable. In addition, the author has succeeded in smoothly incorporating accurate and concise descriptions of the structure, plot, and *mise en scène* of nearly fifty plays without slowing the book's lively and engaging intellectual pace.

Goetz-Stankiewicz's purpose may be seen as twofold: first, to represent accurately and completely the evolution to date of Czechoslovakia's major contemporary playwrights (Václav Havel, Ivan Klíma, Pavel Kohout, Josef Topol, and Ladislav Smoček) and to discuss as well the most significant plays of a dozen other dramatists; secondly, to place this body of drama in its historical context with respect both to Czech literature and to theatre in the West. The cornerstone for this latter consideration is the literature of the absurd. Thus, in the opening chapters the author discusses the legacy of two great Prague writers born in the same year, Franz Kafka and Jaroslav Hašek (author of *Good Soldier Švejk*), as well as the impact made in Czechoslovakia by such Western absurdists as Ionesco, Beckett, Genet, Pinter, and Albee. This framework allows consideration not only of similarities in style and structure but of interrelated themes: the alienation of the individual, the world's increasing automatism and amorality, the devaluation and destruction of language, and the psychological distortions wrought by power. The principal contrast which emerges between the theatre of the absurd in the West and in Czechoslovakia may be seen, in simplified terms, as follows: in the work of Western absurdists the alienated state of man, the failure of language, and the ascendancy of force as the definer of value tend to be seen as inevitable consequences of man's essential nature, whereas in Czech absurdist plays the organization of society, its coercive powers, and its control and distortion of language are often more clearly comprehensible causes, with the protagonists viewed not only as victims but as accomplices in their own dehumanization. This essential model greatly illuminates discussion of the two major Czech absurdists, Havel and Klíma. While not denying the political significance of these plays (often the only aspect considered by Western critics), Goetz-Stankiewicz argues convincingly that Havel and Klíma have made other contributions, dramatizing how the distortion of language on political and social levels inevitably leads to the destruction of human relationships and of human personality itself.

The framework of 'absurdism' is somewhat less adequate to the diverse works of Kohout and to the rapidly evolving poetic symbolism of Topol.

But in these chapters the author analyses the structures employed by Kohout and Topol on their own terms, as they occur in the individual plays. The concreteness of argument and the constant substantiation with lucid examples are evident here as in the rest of the volume. The courageous playwrights of Czechoslovakia, determined that a national literature shall not perish by political fiat, could only be heartened by the detail, comprehensiveness, lively involvement, and eminent readability of *The Silenced Theatre*.

Although official literature cannot deal with many pressing political and social issues, we should not be ignorant of those writers who are published and read widely in their own country, and whose works form the basis for scholarly literary criticism in their nation's journals and spirited commentary in its press. Some of the better Soviet writers who fall in this category (Chingiz Aitmatov, Sergei Zalygin, Valentin Rasputin, Iurii Trifonov, Vasil' Bykov, and Iurii Bondarev) form the core of N.N. Shneidman's *Soviet Literature in the 1970s*. This monograph is a very valuable contribution, both for the accurate description it gives of the debates within Soviet literary criticism and theory as to the directions which 'socialist realism' ought to take (debates prompted in particular by certain aspects of the works considered), and for its concrete description and analysis of the themes addressed by the above-named writers and the general evolution of their prose. The dominant theme is, in fact, the lack of moral values among Soviet citizens, particularly among the younger generation, the city-dwellers, the technocracy, and many of the representatives of the official state and party apparatus. Other related issues are the growing alienation of man from nature, the negative impact of technological progress on life, and the disintegration of the family and its values. The positive characters in the works frequently come from the older generation and from a rural culture – they are clear representatives of traditional values. These issues illustrate quite dramatically the author's contention that official literature does manage to reflect some of the society's most crucial concerns. Needless to say, the considerable controversy provoked by many of the works discussed – and Shneidman documents this controversy well – has helped broaden the narrow parameters of 'socialist realism,' at least in practice.

Although the focus of Shneidman's analysis is themes rather than structure or style, the author does examine narrative structure in the large, the use of fantasy and folklore, and the introduction of local regional dialects and urban idiom in many of the works. Although enough is said to establish the particular uniqueness and merit, in particular, of the writers Aitmatov, Zalygin, Rasputin, and Trifonov, no specific stylistic examples are given. This well might be the subject of a future volume. (HERBERT EAGLE)

Robert Lecker and Jack David, editors. *The Annotated Bibliography of Canada's Major Authors: Volume One*
ECW Press (York University) 1979. 263. $19.95 cloth, $12.95 paper

Deborah Raths, compiler. *Register of the Frederick Philip Grove Collection*
Department of Archives and Rare Books, University of Manitoba Libraries 1979. 65. $3.00 paper

The flowering of Canadian literature in the last few decades has resulted in a growing need for convenient and reliable bibliographical aids. I am not, of course, advocating more books designed primarily for bibliophiles or bibliomaniacs; I am merely pointing out that serious literary students need to consult all the available works of the writers in whom they are interested, and up to the present this has not been easy in the case of Canadian authors. The locating of manuscript material has been another related problem. But the last few months have seen the appearance of both the first volume in the ECW Press's *Annotated Bibliography of Canada's Major Authors* series and a guide to the rich University of Manitoba holdings of a prominent Canadian novelist. Here is more evidence that Canadian literature is at last being taken seriously, and the two works should be welcomed for that reason alone.

In the case of the ECW bibliography, there is much much more to welcome. First of all, it is the initial publication in what is described as 'an ongoing, multi-volume series.' It contains sections on Margaret Atwood (prose only; her poetry is to be treated in a later volume), Margaret Laurence, Hugh MacLennan, Mordecai Richler, and Gabrielle Roy. Another 45 subjects are scheduled for subsequent treatment, though there are some distinguished names omitted from the list that one hopes will be added eventually. Moreover, the bibliographies are sensibly planned, conveniently cross-referenced, and easy to use. Listings include not only the information one would expect (books, manuscripts, contributions to periodicals, etc) but generously annotated accounts of secondary sources, theses, and selected book reviews. Inevitably, in both the annotations and the selection a subjective element enters, but the compilers succeed in giving a succinct and informative digest of the material (I particularly liked the following: 'A simplistic review which describes *Surfacing* as a woman's book.' What more does the consulting scholar need to know?).

To review a bibliography adequately is a thankless, perhaps impossible task. I could pedantically search for omissions (the only one I noted, with regret, was that John Baxter's article on *The Stone Angel* in the first issue of *The Compass* had somehow slipped through the net), brood upon oddities (why is an article by Robertson Davies on MacLennan listed and annotated twice?), keep an eye skinned for typographical errors (remarkably few, I suspect, for a work of this size and scope), or wonder darkly about the effect on Richler's literary reputation of including all his slickly titled contributions to popular journalism. But no, that kind of review would be inappropriate. Instead, all that is necessary is to congratulate everyone concerned on the launching of a dauntingly ambitious project that promises to become an indispensable tool for Canadian literary studies. When one notes that ECW is planning a complementary series (even larger in scope) making up a vast critical history of Canadian literature under the overall title *Canadian Writers and Their Work*, one can only wonder at this press's energy and confidence (no sign of cutbacks here) and wish it all possible success.

Anyone interested in Frederick Philip Grove will be pleased to hear that the *Register of the Frederick Philip Collection* in the Elizabeth Dafoe Library is now available from the University of Manitoba. Since much of Grove's work is still unpublished, a checklist of this kind is more than usually welcome. Unfortunately, however, it is repetitious, badly written, awkwardly arranged, and carelessly edited. For instance, a chronology of important dates is followed by a biographical sketch that writes up the same information in the empty prose we have come to expect from not-very-promising undergraduates ('Much has been written of this man and much more will be written in the years to come because of the power of his writings, their enduring popularity, and because of his own life and personality').

This book is frustratingly difficult to use because manuscripts of published short stories and articles are listed in one place and the details of their publication in another; one is therefore continually searching to and fro for complete information. Above all, mistakes abound, and many of these are sadly revealing. *Settlers of the Marsh* is *Letters of the Marsh* at one point, while 'The Lean Kine,' The Hillside,' and 'The Green-Eyed Monster' become respectively 'The Lean Five,' 'The Hellside,' and 'The Green-Eyed Mother'! Names are often wrong (Willard B. Holliday is transformed into Willord B. Halliday); a foreword becomes a 'forward' (that unpromising undergraduate again). Incredibly, a list is offered of the stories Desmond Pacey is supposed to have omitted from *Tales from the Margin*, but six out of the seven were in fact included. When so many errors can be discovered before going near the holdings (I could list many more without undertaking a rigorous search), one's confidence in the material that one is not in a position to check is seriously undermined. The *Register* will be consulted by all devoted scholars of Grove, but (to put the matter bluntly) why should they tolerate this kind of incompetence? (W.J. KEITH)

Wilfrid Eggleston. *Literary Friends*
Borealis Press. vi, 134. $19.95 cloth, $12.95 paper

George Woodcock. *The World of Canadian Writing: Critiques and Recollections*
Douglas and McIntyre. ix, 306. $16.95

Directly or indirectly, both these books approach the category of literary memoir, reminding us not only that the period of serious artistic activity and achievement in Canada is now extensive, but also that there is a wealth of oral evidence and testimony about our writers and their lives that will pass into oblivion if not preserved in print. Both Eggleston and Woodcock are prairie-born, but they belong to different generations – almost, one is tempted to say, to different worlds. Eggleston's is the world of Bliss Carman poetry-readings, picnics with Charles G.D. Roberts and family, conversations with the Groves and Duncan Campbell Scott; Woodcock's is a post-war Canada, recalling older figures like Ethel Wilson, Roderick Haig-Brown, and John Glassco but also coming to terms critically with younger writers as diverse as Margaret Atwood, Matt Cohen, and Pat Lowther. Eggleston was essentially an amateur in Canadian letters, his literary activities packed into whatever time was left after a full day's work as journalist or parliamentary reporter; Woodcock is very much the professional man of letters but also, in Grove's phrase, a latter-day pioneer patiently creating a literary milieu in which to be a full-time man of letters in Canada comes within the realm of possibility.

Wilfrid Eggleston has already written his autobiography, and *Literary Friends* is less an account of himself than a memoir of the numerous literary acquaintances he made over the course of a long and active life. It provides fascinating but equivocal evidence for the perilous exercise of comparing past with present. 'Looking back,' he writes, 'I realize that up to my nineteenth birthday [in 1920] my cultural opportunities were much inferior to what might have been enjoyed by any boy in Bonn or Boston or Sheffield a hundred years earlier.' Perhaps, but on the next page he reports how in 1919 he had attended Regina Collegiate, where 'high school students played Chopin on the piano of the school auditorium during the lunch hour.' Today we have a flourishing, officially sanctioned 'Canadian literature' but what are the chances of hearing Chopin at the equivalent of Regina Collegiate now? Later he can refer casually to *Maclean's* as a literary and intellectual attraction of Toronto, whereupon one is tempted to look back to those palmy cultured days with amazement and envy. Then he goes on to describe his early years on the Toronto *Star* where the reporters' room seemed positively cluttered with poets; most of them, admittedly, are forgotten now, but who can believe that any modern-day Canadian newspaper has so many employees seriously and creatively concerned with words?

Eggleston's later chapters are devoted to genial memories of specific literary figures – particularly Lloyd Roberts, Grove, Scott, and the Knisters. He quotes generously from personal letters and from his well-kept files from his days as conscientious journalist. What is most valuable, perhaps, is his capacity to reproduce his own sense of buoyant enthusiasm, evoking the days when a fully-fledged Canadian literature was still a dream and a vision, when the frustrations must have been considerable but the sense of standing on the threshold of a literary renaissance both dizzying and inspiring. At a time when practically every book of quality has to be heavily subsidized and 'Canadian literature' has become a subject for solemn study rather than a joy and a discovery, this warmly human series of reminiscences reproduces the freshness of an early world that we lose contact with at our peril.

Somewhere in the course of my education (if I may reminisce myself for a moment) I remember being told that Coleridge was the last man who could legitimately claim to have read everything. Faced with another book by George Woodcock, one wonders if one should not perhaps think again. His range, even when he confines himself to Canadian material, is staggering. *The World of Canadian Writing*, like its predecessor *Odysseus Ever Returning*, is a gathering of previously published articles and reviews, and it therefore makes no claim either to comprehensiveness of coverage or to consistency of approach. Even so, he writes on fiction, poetry, and criticism as well as offering a number of his own personal 'recollections.' In the introduction Woodcock himself describes the book as 'a mosaic picture of the world of Canadian writing from the idiosyncratic and perhaps eccentric viewpoint of one who has lived and worked at its centre over the past quarter of a century, certainly the most exciting period in the literary culture of Canada.' Woodcock has always been an unabashedly personal writer; he refuses to turn out the faceless, sterilized academic prose that passes for serious 'objective' criticism in too many learned journals. There is always a sense of the man behind the print, but in the reminiscences included here the retrospective mood is especially strong. His accounts of returning to Canada from England in 1949 and of founding *Canadian Literature* in 1959 are not only readable and moving in themselves but essential evidence in the cultural development of a nation. The more traditional memoirs of Ethel Wilson and Roderick Haig-Brown similarly tap the wellsprings of memory, never letting us forget the impact of the human being behind the work, and many of the most impressive moments in the critical essays involve Woodcock's own anecdotes that clarify and sometimes even clinch his argument.

This collection lays a particular emphasis on fiction, and although I find his criticism of novels less pointed and incisive than his treatment of poetry or even non-fiction, there is much shrewd commentary on Margaret Laurence and Morley Callaghan and Hugh Hood. I confess, however, that his discussions of novelists who have not yet appealed to me (Mavis Gallant, Matt Cohen) do not encourage me to think again, though I am persuaded that, despite my suspicion of his subject-matter, I must investigate the work of David Watmough. Significantly, perhaps, the most satisfying discussion of fiction in the book concerns Margaret Atwood, whose 'other self' as a poet enables him to discuss her novels in the terms he has evolved when considering her poetry.

Above all, there are two extraordinarily perceptive essays on Northrop Frye and Marshall McLuhan. His comparison of Frye with Sir James Frazer provides him with an elegant and original structure out of which genuine insight can emerge. As critics, of course, Frye and Woodcock are poles apart. Woodcock categorizes Frye as a 'critical mandarin, who works always by afterthought, considering literature long after it has happened, as a substance already marmoreal.' The full account is clear-sighted and balanced, though Woodcock cannot resist drawing attention to Frye's excursions into his own region: that of the 'public critic.' But his tribute is all the more convincing by reason of its independent stance. The treatment of McLuhan, on the other hand, shows Woodcock at his most virulent. The essay reads rather sadly now (I write within a few weeks of McLuhan's death) yet one cannot help being impressed by the firmness of Woodcock's judgment. It is hard to believe that the essay first appeared in 1971, when the failure of McLuhan's prophetic generalizations was less obvious and the temptation – and pressure – to take him at his own valuation far stronger. I always admire the critic prepared to take his stand when the better part of valour is to defer to the response of the fashionable multitude. Woodcock's integrity – evident in the whole book and, indeed, in his whole career – is nowhere more prominent than here. It is a thorough justification of his present position as doyen of Canadian letters. (W.J. KEITH)

Theatre History in Canada / Histoire du théâtre au Canada
Edited by Ann Saddlemyer and Richard Plant
Vol 1, no. 1 (Spring 1980). 80
2 issues yearly. Subscriptions: $7.00 within Canada, $8.00 outside Canada

Canadian theatre history is a rapidly growing area of research, and about time. There are too many horror stories of important material being destroyed just before scholars could get to it. The establishment of an active, visible group of specialists should help; and the appearance of this journal is just what is needed. Its first issue promises well; it is handsomely produced, and – by the standards of our penny-pinching times – lavishly illustrated. It covers a good range, from the early circus to Rick Salutin's *Les Canadiens*. Despite its bilingual title, the French fact is represented only in the book review section, but perhaps future issues will redress the balance.

David Gardner's affectionate tribute to Dora Mavor Moore makes an appropriate opening article not only because Gardner sets a standard for other contributors by presenting a wealth of material with elegance and economy, but because the lady in question embodied in her own career so much of the theatre she served. She was a hard-working, stubborn pioneer. Though the theatre she worked for was in large measure an import industry, she encouraged Canadian playwriting to a degree that will surprise those who assume that it all began in 1970. She died while Gardner's tribute was in preparation; and it is appropriate that the first issue of this journal should be, in a way, a memorial to her.

For the rest, nineteenth-century material dominates – appropriately, as this is a peculiarly rich period for the theatre historian. The main interest for the non-specialist reader is in the sometimes quirky, sometimes highly revealing primary material, from which the authors quote generously. We read of Claire McDowell's appearance in *Caste* at the age of five months; of a spectacular and 'exact' representation of the death of Captain Cook, followed by 'a procession of the Natives to the MONUMENT OF CAPTAIN COOK With MILITARY HONOURS' (p 17 – not the same natives who killed him, one assumes); and we are treated to the Prize Address composed for the opening of Montreal's Theatre Royal in 1825, a prime candidate for any future edition of *The Stuffed Owl*:

> When golden commerce fraught with honest zeal,
> First over the Atlantic, urged her loaded Reel;
> And winds and waves, at length auspicious bore
> Her proofs of science to this Mountain's shore
> Where nature, lovely in her wildest vest,
> Beamed Emerald bright, within her water's breast ...   (P 34)

Most revealing is the recollection of an American circus performer who toured Canada around the beginning of the nineteenth century: 'The Canadian inhabitants thought our horses were supernatural, that it was impossible horses could dance and keep time to music ... we where [sic] the first equestrians that ever was in Canada, therefore the Canadians where [sic] ignorent [sic] of the science and thought the whole a conjuration' (p 12). The spiritual descendants of that performer, and of his audience, are still with us.   (ALEXANDER LEGGATT)

David Helwig, editor. *Love and Money: The Politics of Culture*
Oberon Press. 187. $15.95 cloth, $7.95 paper

Despite the quality of some individual essays, this collection adds up to a disappointing grab-bag. Nothing better demonstrates this than the inclusion of an excerpt from John Metcalf's latest novel, *General Ludd*.

Funny, trenchant, bang-on the chapter may be, but of what use remains something essentially a satire (and therefore quite properly devoid of the dull virtues of balance and practicality) in a collection of factual pieces? No one picking up the book needs to be told that all is not well with government support of the arts in this country. A collection of essays on the subject ought not only to inform the reader about details of the mess that might have escaped him, but also offer some generally coherent notions of a way out. In fact, an editor of such a collection of mostly new essays might even have attempted to establish links among the pieces, whether by exercising greater control over the choice of essays, 'heavier' editing and revision of the works themselves, or the interleaving of his own commentary throughout the collection.

We do need coherent studies of government arts support, and its failings. The arts agencies suffer the budgetary squeeze endured by every educational and social agency. In addition, Treasury Board concepts of 'accountability' force an increasing bureaucratization of the granting process, while the Department of Communications throws its weight behind a concept of the 'arts industry' as simply another enterprise to be rationalized and turned into a profit-making venture. Especially in the performing arts, the tension remains between support of ever-expanding established companies in national centres and encouragement of groups fulfilling regional needs. Place these and many more difficulties within a nation whose tastes in films, TV, and music are largely shaped by American giants, and the prospects appear bleak indeed. No one could reasonably expect a collection of essays to get at all these problems, but one could expect a unified, coherent attack upon a single issue, such as federal vs provincial jurisdications, national vs regional companies, or a directed focus upon such public institutions as the Canada Council and the CBC. The former organization, by the way, continues to resist both its politicization and the persistent complaints against it from the arts community it helps to nourish. The upshot of it all may be that artists may trash the Council sufficiently before the Applebaum-Hebert Committee to ensure that they trade King Log for the King Stork of the Department of Communications. Such are the ironies of cultural politics in what one of the contributors here calls the 'cultural welfare state.'

Among the essays which will repay reading are those by Michael Macklem, Paul Stuewe, Frank Milligan, and Heather Robertson. Yet their topics – book publishing, censorship, the Canada Council, and the general government support of the arts – indicate how uneasily they nestle together except as components in one of those vast Sociology 101 anthologies on culture or communications or media or the universe. Yet I would still advise anyone interested in the question of public support of the arts – and I cannot imagine a cultivated taxpayer who is not – to dip into this collection, so long as the reader realizes that it is up to him to pick out the choicest bits from the stew. (DENNIS DUFFY)

Tony Wilden. *The Imaginary Canadian*
Pulp Press. 261. $11.95 cloth, $6.95 paper

Recent reviews in these pages have called for a Canadian criticism that transcends the surface analysis of imagery and theme. For critics seeking a cultural viewpoint Wilden's book will be vital even if it is not about Canadian writing. In fact, the book is the first study of the whole system of myth and stereotype that makes up the Canada of popular misconception, the imaginary peaceable kingdom masking the real land of divisive exploitation and deferred nationhood. The book is more than this. It is also a nodal point in the emerging network of communication and cultural studies, in particular what Wilden elsewhere calls 'ecosystemic theory' or 'the critical science of long-range survival.'

Entry into this field is made easy by a distinction between 'imaginary' and 'real' relationships. Wilden develops it from two sources: first, from the French psychoanalyst Jacques Lacan (see Wilden, *The Language of the Self*, 1968) and second, from Gregory Bateson, to whom Wilden dedicated his *System and Structure* (1972, revised 1980). Real relationships are those that make up the deep, long-range, hierarchical picture of 'society-in-nature-in-history.' Imaginary relationships when imposed on the domain of the real for the sake of some short-term and typically exploitative goal tend to flatten any hierarchy of contexts into an either/or surface dilemma. Ecological relations become repressed in consciousness to appear as a mechanistic identity of opposites (self-other, culture-nature, man-woman, Ottawa-Alberta). This view of reification recalls Sartre's concept of the ego as thing-in-itself as well as the Marxian notion of the fetish of commodity. I think it also represents what a popular book of 1980, Hofstadter's *Gödel, Escher, Bach*, calls a 'tangled hierarchy' or 'strange loop' in thinking, for the imaginary is pre-eminently the realm of the category mistake, the error in logic that expresses itself in paradox.

Caught in paradox, the mind oscillates between false choices accepted for the real conditions they distort. Lacan saw the psychological consequence as paranoia about 'the other' and the enlargement of negation (*dubito ergo sum*) to the level of a nervous tic in human response. For Bateson the same double-bind was the precondition for the 'who am I?' of schizophrenia, seen as a reaction to a situation in which either way 'you can't win' (Wilden points out that this expression was first heard in Canada). The imaginary is then the prism through which Canadians define their nationhood, 'as if we dwelt in Notland,' Wilden says, 'where "being Canadian" means *not* being someone else.' The theory therefore explains a national personality disorder that writers have variously called 'paranoid schizophrenia' (Atwood), 'elegiac manic depression' (Lee), 'a petulant and sullen martyrdom' (Symons), and 'that old identity question.' But the theory accounts for the disorder specifically as a communications breakdown resulting from the repressive colonization of consciousness, where myths disfigure while they perpetuate the problems of the real.

For a theorist concerned with the living texture of communication instead of with fatalistically polarized absolutes, 'a victim complex is not a thing we have, it is a relation we are in.' Wilden analyses this state of affairs in chapters on cultural stereotypes in Canada, on law and order, civil rights, resource control, the divide-to-rule strategy of corporations and state, and the tyranny of government power. The discussion is punctuated by 71 quotations drawn from popular culture and officially sanctioned misconception. His argument singles out the source of the problem in an 'imaginary' middle class that never earned its rights through struggle as the middle classes did in Britain, France, and America. In a key chapter nostalgically titled 'The First Canadian Civil War' Wilden demonstrates how the Canadian bourgeoisie through its historians has negated its indigenous traditions of radical democracy in Mackenzie, Papineau, and the battalion that later bore their names.

By embodying this very anti-colonial spirit the work has the qualities of a guerrilla handbook, which is to say that it is obsessive, anecdotal, documented, unbalanced, committed, and rude. This is essentially a crucial essay extended into book-length form by an articulate anger with currents of real sorrow in it, and by an infectious, almost boyish optimism with a delight in tactics. Where does this radical democracy come from? In accordance with guerrilla strategy it keeps its base camp hidden. But if the informing politics of the book are not up front, the general theory of exploitation certainly is. The distinction between the imaginary and the real promises the critic a way of distinguishing between the imaginary and the imaginative in cultural thought and expression. Where miscommunication seems to be a national pastime (and communication theory a salient feature of Canadian intellectual life), Wilden's short-term aim is to crack the code of colonialization in which, as Gunnar Myrdal said, 'ignorance, like knowledge, is purposefully directed.' (SEAN KANE)

K.P. Stich, editor. *The Duncan Campbell Scott Symposium*
University of Ottawa Press. xiv, 157. $6.00 paper

The University of Ottawa's annual symposia on selected Canadian novelists and poets have become an established and useful part of the Canadian critical scene. Each fall the announcement of the author to be examined in the following spring is awaited by Canadianists with emotions somewhat akin to those attendant on the arrival of April in the Ottawa valley for Archibald Lampman. The volumes devolving from the Ottawa symposia are also eagerly awaited. In general they have been worthy if not always central contributions to the criticism of the authors treated; in particular, the Reappraisals series, with volumes on Klein, Pratt, Lampman, Crawford, and now D.C. Scott, has widened our understanding of Canadian poetry of the Confederation and modern periods. This is not the place for a retrospective assessment of the series, though clearly one is becoming due.

The present volume follows what has become under Lorraine McMullen's general editorship, an established format. There is a brief, primarily descriptive introduction (where Professor Stich could perhaps have been a little more ambitious in the direction of reappraisal). There are articles of varying length and quality on Scott's poetry (6), his fiction (2), and various aspects of his life and milieu (4). (Since neither Peter Haworth's illustrated presentation on Scott's treatment of the Indians nor the comments of the panel on Scott's achievement are reproduced, the editor was doubtless right to include three papers that were not read at the symposium.) The volume concludes with a 'Selected Bibliography' of works by and about Scott; compiled by Catherine E. Kelly, who wrote her doctoral thesis on Scott at the University of New Brunswick, the bibliography would have been more useful if it had listed theses such as her own and that of Leon Slonim. Nevertheless Sister Kelly's bibliography is the most complete to date and is no doubt already proving useful to Scott students.

There are three high points in the volume: Gordon Johnston's 'The Significance of Scott's Minor Poems' (because it is evaluative, hard-nosed, and provocative of reappraisal), Robert L. McDougall's 'D.C. Scott: A Trace of Documents and a Touch of Life' (because its sage scholarship whets the appetite for his biography of Scott, without which a full reappraisal is impossible), and Stan Dragland and Martin Ware's ' "Spring on Mattagami": A Reconsideration' (because, though self-indulgently long, it affirms that reappraisal must be contingent, in A.J.M. Smith's words, upon a 'careful examination of every poem, line by line and stanza by stanza'). Also of considerable value are the essays of Sandra Campbell on Scott's relationship with Pelham Edgar and of James Doyle on the poet's relation to American literature. Each of the other essays on Scott's poetry contains points of interest and food for thought, though none tends as clearly towards reappraisal as those already mentioned. John P. Matthews, Kathy Mezei, and Sister Kelly in their different ways offer approaches that are tenable and stimulating, but which move Scott criticism laterally rather than forward. Fred Cogswell's Lowesian journey on the road to Arll is attractively imaginative but, based as it is on 'highly circumstantial' evidence, its central hypothesis remains unconvincing. And with *symboliste* aesthetics, Pre-Raphaelite detail, and *art nouveau* embellishment (that 'plenitude of silver leaves') so central to 'The Piper of Arll,' how pertinent is it to gloss the poem with the works of Alexander Barclay (1475–1552), even granting that he was 'dealt with in nearly all important nineteenth-century reference works on British literature, works that were liable to have been in many manses and college libraries in Canada ...'?

But perhaps the weakest papers in the volume are those concerned with Scott's fiction, an area in which there is a clear need for the evaluative criticism, sage scholarship, close analysis, and true reappraisal which are, happily, present in several essays in *The Duncan Campbell Scott Symposium*. (D.M.R. BENTLEY)

William Christian, editor. *The Idea File of Harold Adams Innis*
University of Toronto Press, xxiv, 288. $20.00 cloth, $7.50 paper

Between 1945 and his death in 1951 Harold Innis maintained a cross-referenced set of index cards containing notes related to his communications studies; and from these cards he prepared a typescript apparently intended for some sort of limited circulation. Here, even more than in his other 'late work,' his pen, like his mind, tended to leap from one highly condensed concept to another without intervening logical connections. For this reason a committee which dealt with Innis's papers after his death concluded that this 'idea file' was impenetrable to the point of being unpublishable. More recently, however, in a foreword to the revised edition of Innis's *Empire and Communications*, Marshall McLuhan contended that Innis's stylistic peculiarities, so far from being a private or specialist language, handed us 'the keys to understanding technologies in their psychic and social operation in any time or place.' Readers of Innis will likely still fall within one of these two camps.

Many entries in the file, however, are easily understandable. For example: '*Readers Digest* accepts no advertising and attacks advertisers – *New Yorker* accepts advertising and ridicules pretensions of advertisers – advertises advertisers by exploiting pretences' (5–108). But other passages, perhaps more representative of the mind of Innis in full flight, need more patience to be puzzled out. 'Rise of mysticism,' he could write,

> with clash of one group of symbols with another, i.e. simplifying scriptures and scholastic philosophy for German nuns led to mysticism. Developed concepts difficult to get into simpler language – Latin abstractions into German or Greek into Latin – philosophy versus law – missionaries teaching hell to Esquimos. Impact of science and scientific thought on humanities produces social sciences or form of mysticism. But also makes for inventions and abstraction. Newton dynamics – American constitution. Darwin's evolution on social sciences. Hardness of scientific thought produces fuzziness at points encroaching on humanities. Limits of education as device to reduce gap between illiterary and abstractions of learned language – emphasized symbols of Middle Ages. (5–87)

Not every reader is likely to agree that the social sciences are a form of mysticism.

This book is admirably introduced by William Christian who, beyond identifying persons referred to by Innis, attempts no exegesis of particular entries. (GRAEME H. PATTERSON)

> Robertson Davies. *The Enthusiasms of Robertson Davies.*
> Edited by Judith Skelton Grant
> McClelland and Stewart 1979. 320. $14.95

The Canadian longing for an urbane and sophisticated spokesman (a longing which finds expression in our reluctant endorsement of Pierre Elliott Trudeau) may be assuaged at least temporarily by the presence of Robertson Davies. The latest collection of his prose, *The Enthusiasms of Robertson Davies*, presents not merely the wit and cleverness which in our fear of provincialism we might find ample, but wit which is also intelligent and thoughtful. Furthermore, surprisingly and reassuringly, the selections of Davies' prose which delight and amuse us here are garnered from articles, reviews, weekly columns contributed over the last forty years mainly to Canadian magazines and newspapers, notably the Peterborough *Examiner*, Toronto *Star*, and *Saturday Night*. Editor Judith Grant has omitted material on Canadian theatre and literature, intending to publish this in a separate volume, and has organized selections from the remaining journalism under the headings of 'Characters,' 'Books,' and 'Robertson Davies.'

Davies' range of subject-matter is wide, his allusions scholarly, his views provocative and decided, his style polished. And yet, if I may indulge in the cliché of applying a critic's judgment of another to himself and echo Davies' words on an obscure biographer, Daniel George: '[He] lacks that air of being too fine for this gross world which is the mannerism of so many men of letters; his taste is sprightly, his humour earthy, his curiosity insatiable. He seems ready to read anything, however unpromising it may appear, and if there is a pearl in a neglected old book, he will find it.'

So, sympathetically and knowledgeably, Davies discusses opera and vaudeville, Father Knox and Madame de Pompadour, G.B. Shaw and Gilbert and Sullivan, Tess of the D'Urbervilles and mehitabel the cat, Ivy Compton-Burnett and Ouida, psychoanalysis and circuses, *The Consolation of Philosophy* and *The History of Underclothes*. In a collection of articles made diverse and eclectic by his fascination with eccentrics and his propensity to 'rummage in the rubbish heaps of literature,' several convictions recur. Emphatically Davies rejects the cult of the common man and the democratic chains of uniformity which, as substitutes for self-knowledge, he sees to be the central weakness of modern civilization.

He is consequently scathing in references to some modern fiction, 'dreary tales of adultery in surburbia, of the despair of illiterates who have never known hope, of pinheads who fear they are incapable of love.' In place of facile pessimism Davies defends true comedy, comedy which is more than mere laughter, which recognizes the farcical lying side by side with the tragic, which 'rejoices in the wild luxuriance of the human spirit.' Discussing Canada, too, he sees a capacity for spiritual adventures, if we would acknowledge a northern, mystical spirit presently concealed under the façade of a Scotch banker. These views are not particularly surprising to readers of Davies' fiction, and often Davies does anticipate the novels, with comments on the value of Jungian psychology, on small-town wartime xenophobia, on a macabre, romantic world unrecognized by the sobersided, on the devil as the unexamined side of life.

Often, as with Max Beerbohm, the subject-matter of the pieces (which includes the apparently trivial) is less enticing than the sparkling manner in which it is discussed; one enjoys the companion as much as the scenery along the way. In place of impersonal anonymity Davies confides his cautious respect for St Bernards, his difficulty grappling with Santayana's major philosophical works, his preference for farce spiced with indecency, his irreverent notion that parts of Thomas Mann deal extensively in hot air. Surprisingly and instructively, in spite of an audience of newspaper readers, he does not condescend nor does he make concessions to Canadian prudery. Unexpectedly too, despite a keen eye for the ridiculous, he occasionally passes up the opportunity for an easy satirical thrust – in discussing third-rate music or the comical pictures of long-gone actors, for instance – suggesting instead the necessity to understand the underlying human aspiration; wit does not become mere defence. Throughout the collection the apt turns of phrase and epigrammatic keenness make quotation irresistible: 'Authors like cats because they are such quiet, lovable, wise creatures, and cats like authors for the same reasons' or 'An author is like a horse pulling a coal-cart down an icy hill; he ought to stop, but when he reflects that it would probably kill him to try, he goes right on, neighing and rolling his eyes.'

One can quibble over aspects of *The Enthusiasms of Robertson Davies*. Didacticism creeps in, in spite of the humour, when for instance Davies contrives a dialogue between 'Myself' and a self-proclaimed 'Great Reader.' Various of his confident proclamations will provoke disagreement. My own eyebrows rise at his repeated insistence on the profound innate gulf between men and women: 'Boys are educable ... Girls, after sixteen or so, are ineducable; they learn, but they are their own teachers, or else they learn from men with whom they are in love.' Furthermore, Davies' conclusions, on the value of communication in marriage for instance, are not always profound. Even in these occasional lapses from originality, however, the freshness and vigour of his language catch the reader's attention. One can only salute this author as he plunges on, neighing and rolling his eyes with enthusiasm. (HELEN HOY)

Robert G. Lawrence and Samuel L. Macey, editors. *Studies in Robertson Davies' Deptford Trilogy*
University of Victoria. 123. $4.25 paper

In February 1977 the *Journal of Canadian Studies* devoted a special issue to Robertson Davies. Of its seven articles much the most important was Gordon Roper's 'A Davies Log' with its pioneering work on biographical data and its lists of Davies' publications and of critical work on Davies. Now Robert G. Lawrence and Samuel L. Macey have drawn together ten articles on the Deptford trilogy. These articles testify to the complexity and resilience of Davies' last three novels and they offer more substantial critical insights than the earlier collection.

Three articles are particularly fine. Macey's examination of Davies' idiom – 'the idiom that relates the modern Western technological Devil to time and clockwork' – produces a sensitive reading of the novels and explains Dunstan's preoccupation with precise dates and Magnus's with clocks and automata. Peter Brigg's exploration of the law in *The Manticore* is thorough and well-written. Though I was surprised that he does not refer to Davies' 'Lawyer as Protagonist: A Star of a Particular Kind' (*The Advocate*, 12:1 [1977], 3–5), I decided that the omission is not serious since he independently grasps the points Davies raised and places them accurately in his own broader analysis of the subject. Patricia Monk's consideration of the archeological data in the Swiss cave incident in *The Manticore* is likewise excellent. She marshalls her evidence for Davies' use of particular sources meticulously and by comparing source with text reveals 'some of the literary strategies by which Davies proceeds.' She observes that, by the time Davies reworks his source material, it becomes 'pseudo-fact – a reasonable analogue of true fact.' Since pseudo-fact is a recurring phenomenon in Davies' plays and novels, Monk here draws attention to a characteristic which would reward further investigation.

That the remaining articles are less good is frustrating since they all contain productive ideas. Two are lists – lists which could have served as the foundation for critical insight. F.L. Radford's reading of the Salterton novels 'as preliminary exercises in the development of certain themes and motifs that are brought to mature expression in the later novels' illuminates neither the early novels nor the later trilogy. Yet, in the context of a critical biography, the continuity in idea and the shift in emphasis Radford reveals would be useful. Lawrence's enumeration of the parallels between Sir John Tresize's tour of Canada and Sir John

Martin-Harvey's tours could profitably have prefaced answers to questions like these: Why did Davies resuscitate this chunk of Canada's theatrical past? Is *World of Wonders* an historical novel? Does the theatre material tug away from the novel's central energies?

Two more articles violate critical principles. Terry Goldie, surveying folklore in *Fifth Business*, does not use available bibliographic aids. Had he discovered Davies' paper 'Ben Jonson and Alchemy' in Roper's 'Log,' for example, he could have simplified part of his argument. It would also have made him see E.J. Holmyard's *Alchemy* as an important source worth more than a cursory glance, and have alerted him to the existence of Lynn Thorndike's *History of Magic and Experimental Science from the Twelfth to the Sixteenth Century*. Radford's second contribution, on Jungian ideas in *Fifth Business*, has no principle for how far it is legitimate to take a myth or a Jungian idea. Nor has Radford decided what he is doing with such data – illuminating Davies' thought processes? demonstrating Jungian and mythic possibilities? His article is unnecessarily long as he introduces a wealth of information with too little regard for its relevance to Davies' carefully structured patterns.

The remaining two critical articles ignore evidence which counters their arguments. David Monaghan, tackling 'the public figure,' for example, feels that Dunstan's and Magnus's malicious behaviour is inconsistent with the wholeness and balance the two characters are supposed to achieve. We may not like it, but Davies himself seems quite comfortable with negative energies in characters who have reached self-knowledge. He has Dr von Haller tell David: 'Your real self may not be a good little boy. It would be very unfortunate if that were so. Your real self may be something very disagreeable and unpleasant.' Also, because Monaghan sees Magnus only in relation to Willard and Sir John Tresize, ignoring the more profound influences of Mrs Constantinescu and of Milady Tresize, he distorts Magnus's development. Patricia Merivale runs into difficulties too. Seeing *Fifth Business* as elegiac romance places the novel in a refreshingly new context, but alas Davies' novel does not entirely fit into the category. Her definition reveals its limitations: 'elegiac romance is a grouping of (chiefly) Anglo-American novels in which the narrator, allegedly telling the story of his much-admired dead friend, turns out in the end to be telling his own story, in terms of his relationship with his hero, and of his transcending, through the very act of narration, the now dead hero's influence.'

Finally, a word about Robertson Davies' contribution to the volume. In it, as well as commenting on the various reactions to the trilogy, he supplies the notebook germ (à la Henry James) for *Fifth Business* and his reasons for having David narrate *The Manticore*. The notes, made 'certainly not later than 1960,' provide a fascinating behind-the-scenes glimpse of his creative process. The revelations concerning *The Manticore* are similarly provocative. Talking to Margaret Penman on 'Sunday Supplement' in October 1975, however, he gave the story another slant:

> One particular critic said of *Fifth Business* that it was very conventional, that I never attempted experiment or anything of that sort. So I thought, all right my fine friend, field this one. So I wrote *The Manticore*, which is all about Boy Staunton, but he isn't the principal character. It's the way he's reflected from his son. And did that fat head see it? No, he did not, predictably.

This does not necessarily conflict with the account of *The Manticore*'s genesis in Lawrence and Macey's collection, but it is a reminder that truth is many-faceted, and that Davies is not the man to diminish its variety. (JUDITH SKELTON GRANT)

Robert Kroetsch. *The Crow Journals*
NeWest Press. 92. $12.95 cloth, $6.95 paper

The novel has been traced, in part at least, to the traditions of memoir, diary, and journal, of Protestant self-scrutiny and, later, Romantic self-indulgence. Modern novelists such as Gide and Huxley adapted the form by incorporating journals into their works, using them to give dramatic intimacy and to offer a running commentary on the composition of their novels. Robert Kroetsch now extends the tradition by publishing a journal kept while he was writing his novel *What the Crow Said*. *The Crow Journals* is an intimate literary diary, a blending of truth and artfulness that portrays the artist in pursuit of the truth of his art.

Kroetsch calls it 'only sort of a book, a not-quite-a-book book,' but its unfinished quality is deliberate and effective. Set between 1973 and 1978, the journal is necessarily orderly and chronological; however, its entries are so short and varied, often impressionistic rather than factual, that the effect is erratic. Moreover, Kroetsch is always in transit. He travels back and forth from Binghamton, New York, to Saskatchewan, to Manhattan, to Alberta, to Ontario, to Vancouver Island. This route continually takes him back to the area in western Canada where he was born and where he has set his novel, the 'new old place' that he must rediscover in both life and literature. It takes him to friends, relatives, students, and colleagues with whom he discusses literary problems. It provides him with ideas and details – bees, crows, flying, clowns, magic, names, an old print shop, tall tales – that readers familiar with *What the Crow Said* will recognize from the novel. This fragmentary style gives the journal the quality of much of Kroetsch's poetry. It is puzzling but provoking. Each fragment indirectly comments on every other one, making the work as a whole grow rich in significance and suggestion. This technique encourages us to look for what Kroetsch calls the 'text beneath the text, an everlasting grope into the shape of that darkness.' Like the author composing his novel, we seek the ordering themes and principles that give coherence to the apparent randomness of his comments.

One organizing agent in *The Crow Journals* is simply the voice of the author. It is inquisitive but hesitant, puzzled by itself but pleased with its own eloquence. Kroetsch deprecates his talent even as he tries to muster it in order to write his novel. In short, he speaks in the voice of a writer fascinated by the nature and power of his artistry. He turns a seemingly haphazard diary into a carefully drawn self-portrait of the artist undertaking the essential task of his life. Because his writing arises from his varied experiences, he must examine his past, roots, loves, and friends to see how they have contributed to his work. Ultimately his concern is the paradoxical relation between his life and his work, that is, between artist and artefact, history and story, truth and fiction. He sums up the relation in a series of paradoxes and oxymorons. The writer must 'learn to be naive'; 'I invent my theory of the uninvention of the world'; 'I am the merest vehicle, the tool, of my novel's ambition'; 'The only way I can write poems / is by not being a poet.' The last example is presented as a poem, as if to deny (or confirm) what it states. There is a certain delight in being contrary in such comments, but they do contribute to a consistent – and fundamentally Romantic – view of the artist and the imaginative truth he expresses in fictions that are themselves distortions of the facts of his life. From his life the writer creates a verbal universe that takes on a life of its own. *The Crow Journals*, therefore, is an account and demonstration, not just of the composition of one novel, but of the craft and inspiration of fiction generally.   (JON KERTZER)

>Maurice Lemire, editor. *Dictionnaire des œuvres littéraires du Québec.*
>I: *Des origines à 1900*; II: *1900 à 1939*
>Fides 1978; 1980. lxvi, 918; xcvi, 1363. $35.00; $45.00

The publication of the first two volumes of the *Dictionnaire des œuvres littéraires du Québec* is a capital event in Canadian letters. This compendium of writings in a wide variety of areas (treating 'œuvres littéraires' broadly and including, particularly in volume I, essays, travel accounts, biographies, works of history and geography, song collections – indeed, individual sheet music – as well as the traditional literary genres) will be a vital source of information for researchers, cultural historians, teachers and students, and just curious readers. Faced with this mass of data, analyses, bibliographies, and comparative chronologies, the reviewer has before him an embarrassment of riches and finds it hard to stop long enough to take stock of the enterprise as a whole, and to devour article after article without end.

Volumes I and II will be followed by a third, covering the period from 1940 to 1959, and a fourth, dealing with publications that appeared between 1960 and 1975. Each of the volumes published to date begins with an introduction by Maurice Lemire of Laval University, which aims at presenting a synthesis of the major socio-cultural developments in Quebec in the period covered. Against this background the evolution of the diverse genres is studied in global fashion. Although volume I covers the entire period up to 1900, the introduction deals, in fact, solely with the nineteenth century, leaving aside the French régime, although works that appeared before the turn of the nineteenth century are of course covered through the individual articles. Each volume contains at the end useful bibliographies of literary works (indicating which ones are covered in individual articles and which carry a biographical note on the author), reference works consulted by the compilers, critical studies, a list of the contributors and the articles they have prepared, another of the abundant illustrations, and finally an index of all names cited therein.

The aim of individual articles is to evaluate the given work according to its importance in the author's corpus or in the literature as a whole, sum up the plot, analyse the work's form and structure, and note its fortunes. At the end of most articles there are notes concerning the various editions, if applicable, and the critical bibliography evoked by the text in question.

Lemire's introductions are generally of a high quality and will be most useful to all those working in the field of French-Canadian letters. Lemire shows in his introductory article to volume I how francophone literature in the last century was almost totally harnessed to the ideology of the traditional élites who became dominant after the defeat of the rebellions of 1837–8: 'La littérature ... servira l'ordre établi et, au lieu de signaler les problèmes, s'ingéniera à les camoufler.' In his introduction to volume II Lemire organizes his entire argument around the conflict between the 'régionalistes' and the 'exotiques,' which he sees as marking decisively the evolution of francophone literature from the turn of the century to the Second World War in its difficult march towards modernism. In the period covered by the second volume, he points out, literary criticism begins to carve out an important place for itself. The church now reaches the height of its power, and nationalist discourse is wedded to 'agriculturisme.'

While Lemire looks with a jaundiced eye at many of the manifestations of clerico-conservative control of cultural institutions, he himself shies away from even mentioning the embracing of corporatism, the anti-Semitism, and the flirtation with fascism on the part of leading francophone ideologues, especially Lionel Groulx, who occupies a large place in the introduction and throughout volume II. This blind-spot is evident, too, in Lemire's article on Groulx's novel *L'Appel de la race*. His panegyric on this problem novel, his glossing over its dominant tone of ethnic determinism and chauvinism, his unqualified praise for its defenders, such as Cardinal Villeneuve and Bruno Lafleur, are regrettable. The same can be said for Lemire's constant use of 'race' and 'racial,' and 'Anglais,' without quotation marks, in an anthropologically or ethnically incorrect way. (Fortunately, some of the contributors, like Lucie Robert and Sylvain Simard, were more conscious of the extreme right-wing current in francophone thought, but their articles touching on it would have been clearer had Lemire taken cognizance of the phenomenon in his introduction. The general editor could have taken a leaf from writers such as Jean-Pierre Gaboury and Denis Monière and the editors of the Laval series 'Histoire et sociologie de la culture,' J.-P. Montminy and Fernand Dumont, in treating Groulx in a more balanced way.)

Lemire ends his introduction to volume II with some exploratory reflections on the state of publishing, book distribution, and journalistic criticism in the forty years covered. Here more questions are asked than answers given, but this is a positive first step towards further research into these areas of the sociology of literature. In his introductions and his numerous articles Lemire also refines somewhat the concept of 'roman de la fidélité,' suggesting a sort of 'pre-classical' period in the nineteenth century before the dominant model of this approach emerged in the twentieth.

It is difficult (and unfair) to select those articles in the *Dictionnaire* which stand out unless one has read every last word in the two volumes. My random sampling nevertheless found Roger Le Moine's treatment of Laure Conan's novels, Lemire's texts on *L'Influence d'un livre* and *La Terre paternelle*, David M. Hayne's especially fine piece on Fréchette's *La Légende d'un peuple* (among his numerous articles on that author), Kenneth Landry's comments on *La Lanterne*, and Gilles Girard's ideological reading of *Le Théâtre de Neptune* particularly interesting in volume I. In volume II Nicole Deschamps on *Maria Chapdelaine*, Gilles Dorion on *La Scouine*, Antoine Sirois on *Trente arpents*, Renée Legris on *Un homme et son péché*, François Ricard on *Menaud maître-draveur*, and the major poetry articles are important contributions.

It was pleasant, too, to find a healthy dose of humour in many of the articles. One that comes to mind is Jean-Pierre Cantin's piece on *Louis Riel à la Rivière-du-Loup*, a true account of an impersonation of the famous Métis leader in 1874, somewhat reminiscent of Gogol's *Revizor* (The Inspector-General), an event marked by special dinners and other honours. Writes Cantin: 'la mystification fut si bien réussie qu'une jeune fille, qui avait connu Riel dans l'Ouest, l'identifia avec enthousiasme. Il faut ajouter qu'elle était aveugle'!

Considering the amount of type required to fill these two imposing volumes, relatively few errors came to my attention. There are some misspellings of titles (*Si les Canadiennes le voulaient*, for example, becoming masculinized, I, 10; or the English translation of Laberge's *La Scouine* becoming *Better Bread* (instead of *Bitter!* II, 998), some confusion in dates and spellings of place names. More serious is the indication at II, 675, following André Vanasse's article on *Marie Calumet*, that there was only one single version of this novel. The truncated 1946 edition, which formed the basis for the Fides reprint of 1973, should have been noted both in the bibliographical notes as well as in Vanasse's article, for the major watering down of anti-clerical and sexually suggestive material in these last two versions surely distorted the original 1904 form of the novel. Also, given my views expressed above on *L'Appel de la race*, I personally found it hard to accept that this work received eight pages in comparison with only five and a half for Nelligan's collected verse, seven and half for *Menaud*, and two for *Marie Calumet*.

However, this latter objection and others that one might raise about the interpretation of this or that work are somewhat petty when confronting the immensely positive task which Lemire and his collaborators have accomplished. In addition to everything else, I should mention that the design of the two volumes is very attractive, in spite of the shift to less glossy stock for volume II, undoubtedly for financial reasons. Considering the high price of hard-cover books these days, the first two volumes of the *Dictionnaire* are surely a first-class bargain. (B.-Z. SHEK)

G.-A. Vachon. *Esthétique pour Patricia*, suivi d'un *Ecrit de Patricia B.*
Les Presses de l'Université de Montréal. 144

André Brochu et Gilles Marcotte. *La Littérature et le reste (livre de lettres)*
Quinze. 185

Délaissant le discours savant et son dispositif habituel de notes et de bibliographies, trois professeurs de l'Université de Montréal nous livrent leurs réflexions sur la littérature.

Georges-André Vachon dans son *Esthétique pour Patricia* nous propose une leçon sur le discours poétique et l'écriture. Nous reconnaîtrons ici des idées familières. Contrairement au langage ordinaire qui a pour fonction d'être traversé puis oublié, le texte poétique opposerait une résistance à l'intelligence. Son étrangeté ou son incongruité, le vide qu'il crée dans les mots, forcerait l'attention et la relecture, consacrant ainsi sa fonction esthétique. Cette fonction, comme on sait, n'est pas exclusive au domaine littéraire, mais est repérable aussi dans les messages publicitaires, les lapsus et les erreurs de traduction.

L'objet esthétique se trouverait donc manifesté par la recontre fortuite ou incongrue d'éléments habituellement disjoints. Voilà rééditée la théorie de l'écart qui, chez Vachon, vient s'articuler sur une métaphysique de l'écriture: 'A vrai, c'est peut-être mal nommer l'espace qui s'étend entre les éléments du poème, que de l'appeler *vide* ... Loin de créer une impression d'absence, il rend présent l'être, comme jamais la vie quotidienne n'a su le faire apparaître' (p 44). Le vide, l'être seront aussi synonymes de réalité, d'inconscient, de vérité, d'origine, ou de moi profond. L'écriture serait la démarche obligée, essentielle de la découverte ou du dévoilement de la présence cachée des choses. L'écriture aurait une fonction heuristique que n'aurait pas, par exemple, le rêve ou la fiction qui s'emploieraient au contraire à nous divertir, à nous dissimuler la réalité ou notre vérité. Les hasards du langage trouveraient leur loi, leur logos dans le sujet qui écrit; celui-ci étant l'autre en moi, l'égo fondamental, transcendantal qui permet d'échapper aux contingences et aux misères du quotidien. Ainsi la révélation de l'être passerait par l'exercice de l'écriture qui remplacerait l'ancienne spéculation philosophique. Le hasard objectif ou la fonction poétique deviendrait la voie royale du *gnoti séauton*.

Si l'écriture dissout le sujet, le fait disparaître, l'anéantit, c'est en tant que moi social ou socialisé, alors qu'elle permet l'émergence d'un nouveau sujet plus authentique, plus réel. Si Vachon propose ainsi de tuer le Père, c'est pour le faire réapparaître ailleurs dans le sujet de l'énonciation. Il faut écrire pour tuer celui qui a partie liée avec la fausse conscience de soi, qui met un obstacle à la création, qui empêche l'avènement du sujet authentique. Il faut se débarrasser du Père, s'en affranchir pour l'engendrer en soi et s'en rendre maître. Telle est la résolution de l'Oedipe littéraire qui devrait s'effectuer à la faveur du nouveau cogito: 'J'écris, donc je suis' (p 137).

Cette leçon est suivie d'un écrit signé par Patricia B. On aurait pu s'attendre ici, de la part d'une jeune fille de 'vingt, vingt et un ans,' à une réplique féministe, à l'expression d'une dissidence, à un dialogue au moins avec ce qui venait d'être dit. Or Patricia B. ne discute pas, elle se contente de reproduire et de prolonger cette réflexion. La reprise du même discours par un autre sujet, n'indiquerait-elle pas l'échec de la leçon du maître qui se voulait une invitation à la libération, à l'affranchissement de toute parole de maîtrise extérieure à soi? Paradoxalement ce qui aurait dû servir d'illustration aux propos du mentor me semble venir ici les contredire, les infirmer.

Dans *La Littérature et le reste* d'André Brochu et Gilles Marcotte, on assiste au contraire au dialogue de deux voix autonomes et irréductibles, qui ont décidé de correspondre pour mettre au clair leurs positions respectives sur la littérature. Il s'agit en fait d'une correspondance destinée d'abord à la publication: c'est dire le jeu et la complicité engagés dans ce match verbal. La forme épistolaire permet aux interlocuteurs de se vider le cœur, d'aborder plusieurs sujets sans se voir obligés de développer ou de conclure. Ainsi bien des sujets restent en suspens. On y parle à bâtons rompus de l'infini, des nouveaux philosophes, des intellectuels québécois, du thomisme, de la psychose ... et bien sûr de critique littéraire.

Chacun annonce ses couleurs. Brochu se montre préoccupé par la phénoménologie et l'existentialisme sartrien. Il énonce un projet que d'aucuns jugeront téméraire. Il voudrait faire correspondre une 'problématique littéraire' avec les 'aspirations culturelles de notre milieu' (p 9). Il dit être à la recherche d'une sorte de cogito national. 'En fait, je rêve, écrit-il, ... d'un livre total, voyez le genre, qui serait une manifestation de ce que j'appellerais la *raison québécoise*' (p 172). La critique littéraire serait le lieu privilégié de cette opération totalisante qui rappelle le rêve de toute philosophie idéaliste.

Marcotte, lui, plus prudent, plus modeste et circonspect, se méfie des philosophies. Considérant l'ambition de Brochu comme prématurée, il se montre plus pragmatique ('positiviste,' dit Brochu), c'est-à-dire plus préoccupé par le faire (forme et performance) du texte que par son dire (idéologie). Lorsqu'il examine un roman il veut porter son attention sur le genre lui-même et sur son rapport avec la société. On reconnaîtra là l'intention développée dans *Le Roman à l'imparfait* (1976).

Malgré ces positions divergentes et les malentendus qui en découlent, qui ne sont pas sans intérêt, les deux critiques tombent d'accord sur un certain nombre de points. Je retiendrai, entre autres, ce diagnostic: la misère de la critique québécoise proviendrait en partie d'un manque du côté des œuvres. Marcotte: 'Notre critique vit en symbiose trop étroite avec la littérature québécoise, qui n'est pas assez riche pour lui offrir les grands défis dont elle aurait besoin pour se développer' (p 149). Pour cette raison Brochu se tourne vers Sartre et *La Nausée*, dont l'analyse et la discussion occupent plus du tiers du volume, et Marcotte (qui se laisse entraîner avec réticence sur ce terrain) préfère argumenter à partir de Balzac et de Lukács.

Les deux critiques, las des limites du corpus national, cherchent ailleurs que dans la littérature québécoise des réponses à leurs questions et à leurs inquiétudes. La belle époque du consensus ou de la complicité entre les créateurs et les intellectuels (universitaires) serait-elle terminée? Le projet utopique du premier et les préoccupations sociologiques du second seraient peut-être une autre façon d'exprimer le désir de retrouver, dans le champ de la théorie, l'unanimité perdue. (JACQUES MICHON)

Archives québécoises de la radio et de la télévision
Vol I: Pierre Pagé, Renée Legris, and Louise Blouin. *Répertoire des œuvres de la littérature radiophonique québécoise, 1930–1970*
Vol II: Renée Legris. *Robert Choquette, romancier et dramaturge de la radio-télévision*
Vol III: Pierre Pagé and Renée Legris. *Répertoire des dramatiques québécoises à la télévision, 1952–1977*
Fides. 1975; 1977; 1977. 826; 287; 252. $22.50; $12.95; $10.00

Pierre Pagé and Renée Legris. *Le Comique et l'humour à la radio québécoise: aperçus historiques et textes choisis, 1930–1970*
Vol I: La Presse 1976; vol II: Fides 1979. 677; 736. Each $14.95

Jean Laflamme and Rémi Tourangeau. *L'Eglise et le théâtre au Québec*
Fides 1979. 356. $13.95

Jean-Cléo Godin and Laurent Mailhot. *Théâtre québécois II: nouveaux auteurs, autres spectacles*
Hurtubise HMH. 248. $9.50

Annette Saint-Pierre. *Le Rideau se lève au Manitoba*
St Boniface: Editions des Plaines. 318. $25.00

Over the past decade the stage arts in French Canada have attracted more, and generally more competent, attention from researchers than in the entire previous history of the craft in this country. The wait seemed a long one between Jean Béraud's still useful *350 ans de théâtre au Canada français* (1958) and the successive, complementary studies of the 1970s: Baudoin Burger's seminal *Activité théâtrale au Québec, 1765–1825* (1974); E.-G. Rinfret's monumental *Théâtre canadien d'expression française: répertoire analytique des origines à nos jours* (4 vols, 1975–8); the rich collection of critical and historical essays and interviews offered by vol 5 of Archives des lettres canadiennes, entitled *Le Théâtre canadien-français* (1976); the chronicles and analyses dealing with the contemporary period: Michel Bélair's *Le Nouveau Théâtre québécois* (1973), Martial Dassylva's *Un théâtre en effervescence* (1975); the thematic studies, such as Jacques Cotnam's *Le Théâtre québécois: instrument de contestation sociale et politique* (1976), Pierre Gobin's *Le Fou et ses doubles: figures de la dramaturgie québécoise* (1975), E.-F. Duval's *Anthologie thématique du théâtre québécois au XIXe siècle* (1978). The wait has been worthwhile. The research and publication – archival, historical, synthetic – continue at high pace, as the eight additional volumes reviewed here clearly testify.

What is perhaps most striking about these recent publications is their reliance upon collaboration: all but two of these eight volumes proceed from partnerships. For sheer dedication, displayed in the quantity and originality of their output, no team compares with that of Pierre Pagé and Renée Legris, whose labours in an area little known and less appreciated, the 'paratheatre' of radio and television, have opened up the most promising new perspectives upon the evolution of theatrical forms in

Québec. Their *Répertoire des œuvres de la littérature radiophonique québécoise, 1930–1970*, the first in a three-volume series entitled Archives québécoises de la radio et de la télévision, appeared in 1975. It represents a true pioneering undertaking, the culmination of more than five years of systematic perusal of newspapers, periodicals, and private papers, often in difficult conditions and in the face of academic reaction ranging from lukewarm approbation to disdainful hostility. Pagé, Legris, Louise Blouin, and their helpers have managed to assemble and classify an astounding collection of original scripts, some 2000 titles, representing well over half a million pages of original material. Incredible as it now seems, the principal disseminator of these spoken texts, Radio-Canada, had preserved scarcely anything before 1955: one had to seek out the authors themselves, the performers of the scripts, their technical assistants, or their families. Despite this, Pagé affirms that the *Répertoire* represents something over 95 per cent of the textual material (practically no recorded materials have survived) actually broadcast in the categories included in its purview: original fictional creations written for radio, excluding all adapted or imported works. Moreover – and the fact bears underlining – the titles listed represent not merely programmes identifiable from programme notes in newspapers and periodicals but the *texts* themselves. This first volume is thus a guide to a potential source of cultural information of incalculable significance.

For the forty years in question the majority of the population of Québec could react on a daily basis to the adventures of a vast range and variety of fictional characters, some briefly delineated (the editors distinguish between *radiothéâtre*, basically a single-unit broadcast, and *radioroman* or serial, some of which continued for twenty years and more), others soon as familiar as one's nearest neighbour. As early as 1937 some 57 per cent of Québec households possessed a radio, a figure that had risen to more than 70 per cent by 1941. For the first time in the history of French Canada a true agent of collective cultural dissemination had appeared, with results upon language and social values that the sociologist, linguist, and historian will henceforth be in a better position to evaluate. As Pagé points out, the corpus he and his collaborators have rendered accessible represented, for the mass of Québécois, the first series of consistent, coherent images of and from their own society. Within a decade the listening public rose from the few thousands an author might reach with a stage play (if that play were inordinately successful) to scores or even hundreds of thousands, and for intrinsically comparable material.

The arrangement of this large volume is a model of clarity. After Pagé's thoughtful introduction, comprising some 65 pages, comes the *Répertoire* itself, alphabetically by author; then a series of useful appendices running through 250 pages: a chronological listing by year showing the constant evolution of the medium from 1931 through 1970; a succession of graphs tracing the life of an individual series in its symbiosis with other, concurrent ones; an alphabetical index of titles of each programme or series; an index of directors; and, finally, a list of scripters, producers, and technical advisers. A beautiful, rational, comprehensive work.

The second volume in this same series, Renée Legris's *Robert Choquette, romancier et dramaturge de la radio-télévision*, illustrates the potential offered by the first volume. Before this monograph, undertaken as a doctoral dissertation, was written, Choquette had generally been classed as an important poet of the second rank, as a marginal novelist, and had been ignored as a playwright. After this study it will be inappropriate to continue that ranking, at least for his prose works.

Although it was as a poet that Choquette first made his mark in the mid-1920s, his *La Pension Leblanc* (1927) bears re-examination, as Legris demonstrates, as the earliest urban novel, appearing well before J.-C. Harvey's *Les Demi-civilisés* (1933) or the better-known works by Roger Lemelin and Gabrielle Roy in the 1940s. A pioneer in radio as well, Choquette quickly grasped the potential of this new medium, writing for it the first dramatic series, *Au coin du feu* (1931–2). He followed this with an uninterrupted sequence of *radioromans* and *radiothéâtres* into the 1950s when, foreseeing that in television lay the future of dramatic talents such as his, he began to compose plays and serials that would continue well into the 1970s. Legris sets out to establish the true corpus of this production, managing to identify and describe some 50,000 pages of materials Choquette has written for Canadian radio and television, as well as the works he had published separately as 'literature.' The delimitation of this corpus represents the first division of Legris's work.

In the second part Legris depicts the overall evolution she has perceived within this material, with particular attention to the social settings (by strong preponderance, Montréal) in which Choquette places his characters. The third and final part of her study explores the themes and characters identifying this huge body of original material, as she carefully delineates Choquette's conception of Québec's society (particularly its urban society) in the years 1925–70. As she shows, this is a partial view, rarely taking account of the working class or the ethnic minorities in the province, but fascinated primarily with the transition from a predominantly rural to a predominantly urban way of life. Her analysis is a sympathetic and solid one: a trifle too sympathetic at times, perhaps, when she rushes in to defend Choquette from the adverse criticism his productions sometimes attracted. She has demonstrated that the task was well worthwhile, and that a new assessment of this author was imperative, one drawing more heavily upon the para- (but not, she eloquently argues, 'infra'-) literature he produced for radio and television. One suspects this is merely the first of several such corrective reappraisals we shall observe in the near future.

The third volume is closer to what one might have expected in a series entitled Archives québécoises de la radio et de la télévision: it is a

Répertoire des dramatiques québécoises à la télévision, 1952–1977, and is meant to be complementary to volume I. This time both Pierre Pagé and Renée Legris appear as editors on the title-page, and their thirty pages of introduction sensitively describe the materials included, portray the main stages in the evolution of televised drama, and specify the problems now encountered by archivists and researchers. As was the case with radio productions, one learns that CBC/Radio-Canada has paid little attention to storage of videotapes and manuscript materials except for specific, internal purposes. What archival materials are available are not generally accessible to the outsider. Consequently, a good deal (too much, perhaps?) of this introduction is prescriptive, setting down what *should* be done about the retention, storage, classification, and access to this admittedly significant portion of Canada's cultural history.

Unlike the first volume, this one lists only the programmes themselves, without cataloguing corresponding manuscript materials. The research has thus led further away from dramatic paraliterature, and the result is a tool that will probably be more useful for social historians than for *littérateurs.* It is divided into three categories: 'Téléthéâtres,' 'Feuilletons,' and 'Dramatiques pour enfants,' each presented alphabetically by name of principal author, but including also the director and full cast, where known. Each section is then followed by a chronological listing, and by graphs illustrating the concurrent production at any given time. Finally comes a series of indexes: a short-listing by author's name, useful when he or she has works listed in more than one category; an index of titles; an index of directors. In all, some 477 productions are inventoried.

By far the best illustration of the wealth of the corpus disinterred by these dauntless researchers (and a better complement to volume I) is the large two-volume publication by Pierre Pagé and Renée Legris, *Le Comique et l'humour à la radio québécoise: aperçus historiques et textes choisis, 1930–1970.* As Pagé points out in his introduction to the first volume, this undertaking was a logical sequel to their *Répertoire de la littérature radiophonique.* It is also ample justification for the funds and the years of research expended. On linguistic, sociological, or literary grounds, this anthology is a treasure-trove of information on the most formative period in the development of modern Québec's collective consciousness. Drawing upon a corpus of some 75,000 manuscript pages, Pagé and Legris have put together a broad, readable 'sampler' of characteristic programming over those forty years (volume I deals with the period 1930–53; volume II continues to 1970). The forms are diverse: from the broad farce of the 15-minute sketches involving Fridolin (Gratien Gélinas), through the gentle, sophisticated humour of *Radio Carabin,* to the sometimes mordant social satire of *Carte blanche.* And how fresh so many of these specimens remain twenty, thirty, forty years after their original broadcast!

The editors have chosen their texts in the light of criteria which they are very careful to justify. They have sought, in the main, the texts of programmes that 'caught on,' that succeeded in creating 'des types comiques québécois, et qui ont ainsi mis en circulation des personnages en lesquels le public s'est reconnu, dans ses travers ou ses manies.' Thus, apart from the irrepressible Fridolin-Gélinas, are resuscitated Max Potvin, Nazaire and Barnabé, Josette and Joson, Jean Narache, the inimitable Miville ... most of them little the worse for wear.

Whether it would have been so recognized *before* their intervention, what Pagé and Legris have here produced becomes literature. In reading these texts it becomes obvious that their roots in folklore and oral tradition are deep and proximate, despite their reliance upon a new technology for their diffusion. This is a mirror in which two full generations of Québécois looked deeply at themselves and came away strengthened by their reflection.

Not the least important aspect of this significant work is the vast source of original material it immediately opens up for the diachronic study of French as spoken in Québec, particularly that linguistic middle ground which the broadcast medium itself doubtless had no small role in creating. Unlike most French-Canadian authors, those who wrote for radio were unconcerned about any non-Québécois audience: their creations use the homespun language appropriate to the actual listening public. The virtuosity they developed in using that language has surely prepared the way for the confident affirmation of the rights of that tongue today. In short, any serious analysis of Canada's French culture, its language, its drama cannot afford, in future, to ignore these two volumes.

Jean Laflamme and Rémi Tourangeau's *L'Eglise et le théâtre au Québec* is another work that should appear on the shelf of any future researcher, teacher, or student of Québec's theatre history. The authors, both attached to the centre for the study of drama at the Université du Québec à Trois-Rivières, deal with the interaction between church and stage in French Canada in the period 1606-1962, that is, from the date of Marc Lescarbot's *Théâtre de Neptune* (hardly, let us note in passing, an incident in the history of Québec's stage!) to the termination of the second Vatican Council, after which a more universalist policy seems to have been adopted by the Catholic Church in Québec. Their presentation is by chronological sequence of action and reaction in three main time periods. The first part encompasses the years preceding the Patriote uprising of 1837-8; the second continues the study to 1896, marking the apogee of the church's social and moral influence in Québec; the third delineates the slow evolution of the church's position in the twentieth century.

Although there is little new information on theatrical activity itself, the authors reveal much that was hitherto unknown regarding the church's reaction to that activity. The authors have carefully examined all available material from church archives, from published and unpublished *mande-*

ments, circulars, and pastoral letters, from correspondence and journals. The resulting synthesis casts rich new light upon incidents and documents already known. For the academic reader in particular the result is nothing less than fascinating. Laflamme and Tourangeau have taken a topic one knew to be important and made the knowledge of it essential to any understanding of the history of theatre in Québec. They chronicle the waxing and waning of the church's opposition to stage drama (imported drama, that is: the authors claim that Catholic authorities almost never opposed indigenous works), while showing at the same time the remarkable consistency of the principles underlying that opposition. The interrelationship is always complex, for it was the same church that had espoused theatrical forms for the pedagogy used in its own schools from the middle of the seventeenth century, which had made use of those forms for broader propagandizing purposes from the late 1850s, which aided and encouraged Fathers Emile Legault, Gustave Lamarche, and Laurent Tremblay in their efforts to establish a native theatrical tradition in the 1930s. As Laflamme and Tourangeau make clear, the opposition was not to theatre as such, but to a certain frivolous, amoral, or 'godless' tradition of the public stage, particularly the stage identified with the Parisian boulevards.

Are the authors justified in perceiving a dissolution of all antagonisms since 1962? Did church authorities really have no role to play in the attempts at suppressing Jean Frigon's *Ti-Jésus, bonjour* (by withdrawal of subsidy from lay sources, in this case) in 1977 or of Denise Boucher's *Les Fées ont soif* in the following year? There are those who would venture to disagree.

Théâtre québécois II: nouveaux auteurs, autres spectacles by Jean-Cléo Godin and Laurent Mailhot represents the latest in this series of *travaux d'équipe* bearing upon Québec drama. Godin and Mailhot, unlike our two previous teams, operate in tandem, each chapter in this collection of critical essays being signed by one of the two, with the sometimes refreshing result of varying evaluations – or, at least, of evaluations differently nuanced – where both touch upon the same theme, the same author, or play. The volume is a sequel to their 1970 collaboration, *Le Théâtre québécois: introduction à dix dramaturges contemporains*, the basis of that first volume having been a university-level course broadcast in 1969–70. *Théâtre québécois II* comprises eleven essay-chapters, divided into two parts, the first entitled 'Fonctions, formes, spectacles,' the second 'Univers dramatiques.' Those divisions reflect the authors' attempt to infuse some sense of order into their perceptions of such a disorderly phenomenon as the Québec stage in the past decade: first, by thematic groupings (chapters on 'théâtre sur théâtre,' where the play itself becomes the subject/object of the author's attention; on plays with a historical theme; on those with contemporary political preoccupations; on the experimental avant garde); then, more traditionally, by chapters devoted to individual authors, particularly those who have made their mark since 1970. Thus we find critical studies of Jean-Claude Germain, Michel Garneau, Jean Barbeau, as well as Michel Tremblay and Robert Gurik. A short general introduction and conclusion supplement these essays, along with a useful bibliography and an index.

It is a lively and rewarding work to read, as was *Théâtre québécois I*, and it is sure to elicit divergent critical reaction. Those who prefer their monographs more fully predigested will experience some degree of disorientation, for Godin and Mailhot display no condescension and little indulgence towards their readers. An eclectic but indispensable volume. Perhaps the authors should consider, at some future date, drawing upon the best from both volumes and providing a single, easier-to-use synthesis? Perhaps, also, they might consider either attenuating the subtle but pervasive cultural imperialism of Québec-based critics, or else exclude that least *québécoise* of French-Canadian writers, Antonine Maillet.

This last remark may serve as thematic introduction to the last work included here, this time from a single toiler in a hitherto practically uncharted domain: Annette Saint-Pierre's *Le Rideau se lève au Manitoba*. Saint-Pierre's work, like that of Pagé and Legris, is a pioneering one, for little had been written previously about theatrical activity in that embattled francophone bastion on the Red River. Her thoughtful, thought-provoking study of the first century of the stage arts in her adoptive province was undertaken as a doctoral dissertation, and that fact is reflected in the attention to scholarly method and detail her text displays. The other, less welcome characteristics of that scholars' apprenticeship, the PH D thesis, have all but disappeared. The scope of her study is sensible, sensibly pursued; the structure is sound and logical. Her conclusions seem unassailable.

With loving care Saint-Pierre traces the evolution of French Manitoban theatre through its first heady years, when the province seemed to germinate with a renewed, expanded Canadian *francophonie*; through the generation of trial and frustrating defeat, as the 1890s witnessed the trends which would culminate in the legal elimination of French as a viable language of instruction in 1916; through the tenacious obstinacy of the generations since then which have clung to language and culture, refusing even now to accept that total defeat, long heralded but ever postponed. That cultural vigour is evidenced here in her carefully documented accounts of productions of indigenous plays, imported plays, adapted plays, staged by a practically unbroken succession of amateur companies since 1870. With little or no help, except for federal subsidies, from outside Manitoba's boundaries, one might add: what more ironic note than her account of the long-awaited visit from Montréal's Théâtre du Nouveau-Monde in 1958, which offered the new play by Québec's up-and-coming playwright, Marcel Dubé, *Le Temps des lilas* ... in English!

Saint-Pierre's study encompasses five areas: first, a history of theatre in the educational institutions, for it was there that the art took root in Manitoba, as it had in Québec; next, an account of stage performances in the little French-speaking parishes, followed by a history of such activity in the growing municipal centres of St Boniface and Winnipeg. She then provides a detailed study of the Cercle Molière, now entering its 56th season and, lastly, a useful analysis of theatre written in Manitoba to the present. A solid conclusion follows (in which the author does not resist the temptation to tell her most avid readers, the Franco-Manitobans, how they should conduct their cultural affairs in future), but the opus is really crowned by the admirable appendix she provides.

This is a listing, in chronological order, by locality, and apparently in complete form, of all known French-language plays and programmes performed between June 1870 and January 1977 – some 1300 productions. What a boon for student and researcher, and perhaps especially for those interested in probing the reasons behind the often remarkable similarity one notices between the fare offered in that semi-exotic, semi-*far-ouest*, and what was being presented at any given time to more 'sophisticated' audiences in Montréal and Québec! Saint-Pierre's warm, detailed reconstruction may perhaps someday be expanded upon. One feels it will never be superseded.

From these eight volumes, viewed in conjunction with the other studies that have appeared since 1970, comes a better understanding of the genetic forces at work over the centuries and an informed appreciation of the immediate roots of current drama in French. But perhaps more striking still is the sophistication of the tools here employed, and the concomitant maturity of the critical approaches displayed. Few critics would now dispute that French-Canadian theatre has come of age: has French-Canadian theatre-criticism reached the age of reason as well? (L.E. DOUCETTE)

Nicole Deschamps, Raymonde Héroux, and Normand Villeneuve. *Le Mythe de Maria Chapdelaine*
Les Presses de l'Université de Montréal. 263. $19.75

Louis Hémon. *Maria Chapdelaine, Récit du Canada français*
Préface by Nicole Deschamps, annotated by Ghislaine Legendre
Boréal Express. 216. $8.75

Gilbert Lévesque. *Louis Hémon, aventurier ou philosophe?*
Fides. 64. $3.00

Louis Hémon. *Maria Chapdelaine.* Illustrated by Clarence Gagnon
Art global / Libre Expression. 206. $70.00

The year 1980 marked the centenary of the birth of Louis Hémon, author of one of the world's biggest best-sellers, *Maria Chapdelaine*, a work that has been translated into nearly twenty languages. Besides the festivities that marked this event in Péribonka, in the Lac Saint-Jean region of the novel's setting, with the participation of the author's daughter Lydia Kathleen, last year also saw the publication of two significant editions of the novel: one, the first based on the original manuscript; the other, a variant of the 1933 deluxe Paris edition with colour illustrations by Clarence Gagnon. There also appeared an important critical study, *Le Mythe de Maria Chapdelaine*, under the guidance of Nicole Deschamps, who had already edited Hémon's letters to his family, and who discovered the original manuscript for the novel in Quimper, Britanny, in 1966, in the family's archives. A number of other publications also appeared in honour of the anniversary.

Le Mythe de Maria Chapdelaine by Nicole Deschamps, Raymonde Héroux, and Normand Villeneuve is clearly a major study, the fruit of meticulous research into the origins and development of the cult centred on Hémon's novel in France and in French Canada. Deschamps, in her preface, notes the plethora of commentaries on *Maria Chapdelaine*, 'divergeant du récit de Hémon, l'occultant, le prolongeant, le modulant, parfois le recréant jusque dans ses données fondamentales,' adding that rarely in contemporary literary history has one seen such an immense *après-texte*. Hémon's novel has inspired lectures, poems, dramatizations, films (the third – and the first one to be made by a Canadian, Denys Arcand – is now in preparation), theses, political slogans, comic strips, and so on. Deschamps and her collaborators make a strong case for their contention that the basic content and texture of *Maria Chapdelaine* have been deformed in order to serve ideological and political causes of the right, and sometimes the extreme right. Villeneuve sums up succinctly this *embrigadement*: 'Maria Chapdelaine n'est donc pas un roman vraiment lu, mais plutôt imaginé, qui finit par devenir conforme aux illusions d'un groupe.' The gist of their critique is that conservative lay and clerical forces in France and in Canada masked the harshness of the portrayal of Hémon's pioneers and the absurdity of their isolated endeavours and hopeless resignation in order to portray these *colonisés* as *colonisateurs*.

In both countries the appearance of Hémon's work during and just after the First World War coincided with a period in which traditional rural societies and values were entering a deep crisis and in which ideologues of the old order sought reassuring models to help stem the tide of urbanization and industrialization. The three individual studies in *Le Mythe de Maria Chapdelaine* analyse the ways in which the novel was utilized in this process.

Deschamps studies minutely the text and context of the publication in 1927 of a speech, entitled 'Maria Chapdelaine, l'épouse et la mère,' by Joseph-Edouard Perrault, minister of colonization in the Taschereau régime. She shows how Maria, 'd'une vierge éplorée, amoureuse déçue et fiancée sans amour,' is transformed into 'une radieuse mère de famille nombreuse,' thus feeding the optimistic myth of the collective destiny of French Canada.

In the second chapter of her study Deschamps examines the changes wrought upon the original manuscript of *Maria Chapdelaine* by a number of editors and publishers in France and Canada, starting with those of the Paris daily *Le Temps*, where the novel first appeared in serial form in 1914. In addition to making useful corrections, these editors took the liberty of putting in quotation marks a large number of *canadianismes, archaïsmes*, and *anglicismes* which Hémon had incorporated naturally into the speech of his characters and into his narration. Deschamps sees this move as the first in a series of alienating acts vis-à-vis Hémon's text. Even more alienating were the changes made by Louvigny de Montigny in the first publication of the novel as a book, by Lefebvre in Montreal, in 1916. 'Paradoxalement,' writes Deschamps, 'l'édition canadienne est celle qui cherche le plus à se conformer au français normatif.' (She might have linked these distancing incursions with those carried out by prominent nineteenth-century Quebec writers like Aubert de Gaspé, who 'folklorized' the speech of their characters by the use of italics.) In time the French Grasset edition of 1921 would become the (deformed) model from which all subsequent editions would take their lead.

Deschamps analyses skilfully the first chapter of the novel, which she calls a microcosm in which the alternating descriptive and meditative modes are brought into play. She also elucidates the dialectical relationship between realism and symbolism in the novel.

Héroux picks up one thread of Deschamps's preface to concentrate on the making of a best-seller in France by Bernard Grasset, with the collaboration of a host of politicians, diplomats, bishops, Academicians, editors and publishers, book-store owners, and their respective inferiors. She also shows how the political and educational élites with whom the Hémon family was linked helped in the process by which Louis Hémon, the unstable wanderer and religious sceptic, emerged as a loyal son of Brittany and the creator of a 'chef-d'œuvre du catholicisme.' France, in addition to facing a crisis in traditional rural society, was also living through the first decades of official secularization following the separation of church and state in 1905, and thus Hémon's novel was recruited to defend a church which perceived itself threatened by the legal changes. Héroux also analyses the critical reception of *Maria Chapdelaine* in France, showing that traditonal critics spoke vaguely of the book's actual content and that few applied rigorous methods in evaluating the work. She traces manifestations of the myth surviving into the 1970s, pointing to biographical errors in a recent television documentary on Hémon produced by the French government network.

In the third section of the book Villeneuve deals with the Quebec context in his study, '*Maria Chapdelaine*, catéchisme de la survivance nationale.' He shows that when the novel first appeared in 1916, there was little favourable critical comment in Canada, yet, little by little, 'la province fut conditionné à marcher au pas de Maria Chapdelaine.' Villeneuve studies the reception of the book in three regions of Quebec: the Saguenay–Lac Saint-Jean area of the novel's action, the Quebec City region, and that of Montreal. The durability of the myth would bring the novel practically unscathed into the 1950s, when André Laurendeau and other intellectuals began to question its value as a model for French-Canadian culture and society. Its main proponents, however, were powerful public figures like Cardinal Rodrigue Villeneuve, Lionel Groulx, and Camille Roy. The myth held sway for so long, especially in the countryside, because it met a real need: 'Il trahit une obsession du réel, un réel souvent perçu comme insaisissable et menaçant.' The myth was the basis of a publicity campaign 'qui cherche à canaliser des besoins et à repousser des angoisses par le moyen d'images sécurisantes.' Although some discordant voices in the 1920s raised serious doubts about the truthfulness of the portrayal of the clergy and the too sombre colours in the text of that 'étranger mélancolique,' Hémon, the principal ideologues soon achieved near unanimity in shaping their interpretations of the work to the moral and ethical needs of the ruling élites. Maria was even 'conscripted' into the fight against women's suffrage and social emancipation for, as wrote Arsène Bessette, French-Canadian ladies, instead of seeking to become lawyers or electors, would be better off following the example of the farm-girl heroine, 'dont le sein de belle fille ne tressaillit que pour les maternités futures'!

Le Mythe de Maria Chapdelaine, then, is an important book, but it is not without its faults. Deschamps, the work's prime mover, said in an interview with *Le Devoir* (18 October 1980): 'Si j'avais à faire l'autocritique de notre ouvrage, je me demanderais si nous ne sommes pas allés un peu loin sous prétexte d'arracher *Maria Chapdelaine* à cet écran qui a été fait par la propagande de droite, en présentant un Louis Hémon qui serait presque un être de gauche.' Indeed, while rightly exposing the deformation of certain key aspects of the novel, Deschamps and her collaborators have attributed to Hémon certain aims which were clearly not his. A striking example is this quotation from Villeneuve: 'De fait, l'écrivain français avait utilisé l'artifice des voix pour faire connaître l'idéologie de la classe dirigeante canadienne-française de cette époque ... De cette manière, Louis Hémon ne contredisait pas ce qu'il avait suggéré auparavant: il avait justement décrit le défricheur canadien comme un être soumis aux mots d'ordre de l'élite et résigné par la suite à se battre contre une nature hostile et étouffante.'

This tack is too simplistic to take account of the text itself and its contradictions, as well as the 'pre-text' of Hémon's journal notations which already show a propensity towards French-Canadian nationalism and the cult of the noble pioneer. Clearly the problem of the eruption of the mystical voices towards the end of the novel is a difficult one, linked as it is to the otherwise dominantly sombre picture of the colonists, the touches of anti-clericalism, the silence of Maria, eloquently stressed by Deschamps, and the instability of Samuel Chapdelaine, perhaps a reflection of Hémon's own unsettled nature. This complex structure, then, needs more probing.

Nicole Deschamps, in her preface to the 'édition intégrale' of *Maria Chapdelaine* published by Boréal Express, again uses some of the same sweeping phrases that I have just criticized. However, she gives us revealing excerpts from the first reader's report which led to the original publication in serial form of *Maria Chapdelaine* in *Le Temps*: 'Chamant récit, écrit d'une langue alerte et facile ... L'auteur décrit avec sympathie la *rude* existence des paysans canadiens, leur *lutte incessante* avec les éléments, le *froid terrible*, la terre *hostile*, la *solitude effrayante* des grands bois ... joies et douleurs, mariages et deuils' (my emphasis). She links, interestingly, Hémon's creative approach to French-Canadian popular speech with that of contemporary writers of Quebec, deploring the frequent quotation marks that *Le Temps* saw fit to employ (inconsistently), and even more the 'corrections' of Louvigny de Montigny for the first publication in book form: 'toué' became 'toi,' 'ouais,' 'oui,' 'icitte' was dropped altogether, and blasphemies were euphemized.

Ghislaine Legendre has provided the reader with notes and variations found in the diverse editions of *Maria Chapdelaine*, as well as a useful index of characters and places in the novel. A careful comparison of these variations with the present text, which is based on the manuscript, shows certain patterns in the subsequent editions. As well as the 'correction' or setting off of *canadianismes*, there is an elimination of repetition (sometimes unfortunate, because of the stylistic nuances desired by Hémon) and a removal of qualifiers or agents. Sometimes there is a complete change in the texture of the writing, as when the word 'vent' replaces 'ennemi' in this extract from the manuscript: 'La maison de bois frissonait du sol à la cheminée et semblait osciller sur sa base, si bien que ses habitants, entendant les mugissements et les clameurs aigües de l'ennemi ... souffraient en vérité de presque toute l'horreur de la tempête.'

However, Deschamps seems to ignore the fact that in some of the subsequent issues there is a reversal of the procedure concerning *canadianismes*. Occasionally 'icitte' replaces 'ici,' 'mon père' becomes 'son père,' and 'ça été' is substituted for 'ça a été,' all these changes making the language truer to Canadian popular usage, even though they are far from uniform. The same problem occurs when pleonastic 'ne' is dropped from the dialogues (but also, wrongly, from the narration). Regrettably, some errors in the page references and a dropping of important semicolons in the 'notes et variantes' lead to some confusion. Nevertheless, this reconstituted original text will be most useful to students and teachers of this much-used novel, restoring to it its original 'feel.'

Gilbert Lévesque's pretentiously titled *Louis Hémon, aventurier ou philosophe?* adds little to our knowledge of the author of *Maria Chapdelaine*. It is in the direct line of the mythification of that work in its selection of quotations from the novel underlining the static nature of traditional French-Canadian society and in its claim that Hémon, a foreigner, was the true discoverer of the French-Canadian 'soul.' Its vague references to Hémon's affair of the heart and to the non-existent 'Madame Louis Hémon' are in the same vein. In addition, there is a great deal of confusion in the use of quotations and end notes, and too many examples of faulty grammar, weak transitions, and a dropping of accents. The most interesting aspect of this booklet is the reproduction of excerpts from correspondence and conversations with Lydia, Hémon's daughter, which seem to contradict some of the statements in her supportive open letter (*Le Devoir*, 29 November 1980) concerning the character of her aunt, Marie, Louis's sister.

Of a different order is the publication of a beautifully bound and printed edition of *Maria Chapdelaine* by Art global / Libre Expression, based on the 1933 Paris text issued by Mornay, with colour illustrations by the late Clarence Gagnon. Although there is no direct statement in the note opposite the title page as to how the text was established, a random scanning shows that some of the popular turns of phrase ('Mon Dou,' 'je vas,' 'icitte') follow the manuscript, although they are usually enclosed in those pernicious quotation marks.

Most interesting here are the more than fifty illustrations by Gagnon. I have tried, by looking at them carefully and noting their insertion into the text, to gauge his reading of Hémon's novel. First, both the cover and title page carry a small illustration showing a desolate autumn sunset scene, characterized by stumps and truncated remnants of a forest fire, as well as sparse fall foliage. There are no human figures present. This choice of a central image underlines the isolation and barrenness of the novel's setting. Another characteristic of the illustrations is that in most the characters of the drama – Maria, her parents, Samuel and Laura, François Paradis, Eutrope Gagnon – are seen from behind, or in scant profile, or with barely defined facial features. It is as if Gagnon had read Nicole Deschamps's judgment that 'les héros de Hémon existent surtout en qualité de symboles,' for the artist seems to have seen the characters as representative, not individual, figures.

The colours used for the dominant winter setting of the Chapdelaine farm are usually sombre, especially for the menacing forest that surrounds it. The often inaccessible church and village of Péribonka, however, are treated in bright pastel colours, even in winter, as are the flashbacks or projections to the village of Saint-Prime or to an imaginary Massachusetts homestead, set in the summer. Sometimes the artist uses a 'montage' technique to contrast these imaginary sites and the alternating 'objective' ones (e.g., from the end of chapter 12 to the first two illustrations of chapter 13). There are also striking illustrations treating the physical labour of both pioneers and loggers, sometimes, too, in close proximity as in the final illustration of chapter 4 and the second one of chapter 5. These, together with scenes of haying, give a feeling of movement and effort through the arching of the bodies.

Maria is not idealized, the artist stressing, as does the text, her robustness and broad frame. In almost all the illustrations she is wearing a coarsely woven greyish dress, sometimes partly covered by a blue apron. However, the single illustration that relates to the mysterious voices shows a vaguely defined couple, the woman resembling Maria in build, in a peaceful flower-decked meadow beside a gentle stream. In the background, beyond the dark wood-covered hills, is a prominent blue-tinted one. The small final signature of an evergreen bough and a cross also endorses the traditional interpretation of the novel.

The publication of this edition and Nicole Deschamps's brief analysis of the illustrations by Suzor-Côté for the original Lefebvre book in *Le Mythe de Maria Chapdelaine* ('les illustrations ... sont des mises entre guillemets de la réalité québécoise ... Personnages, objets, animaux, paysages, la première imagerie inspirée par *Maria Chapdelaine* appartient déjà au *folklore*') point to the need for a careful comparative study of the iconography relating to the novel.

The books reviewed here and the other valuable publications of the centenary year, too, should whet the appetite of Hémon researchers for further probing. (B.-Z. SHEK)

Serge A. Thériault. *La Quête d'équilibre dans l'œuvre romanesque d'Anne Hébert*
Hull: Editions Asticou. 223. $12.00

Serge A. Thériault et René Juéry. *Approches structurales des textes*
Hull: Editions Asticou. 240. $14.00

John D. Erickson et Irène Pagès. *Proust et le texte producteur*
Lawrence, Kansas: L'Esprit créateur. 143

Ces trois ouvrages de prime abord hétérogènes pour ce qui est des œuvres étudiées, témoignent toutefois d'une visée commune, à savoir la volonté d'articuler le texte littéraire par l'entremise de modèles à valeur théorique. La première étude de Serge Thériault sur l'œuvre romanesque d'Anne Hébert se propose d'une part de déterminer et de circonscrire un modèle psychologique et d'autre part vise à faire voir comment la représentation s'organise de manière à faire saisir cet objet. La seconde, *Approches structurales des textes,* reposant sur une problématique du signe linguistique, comprend deux études: l'une d'inspiration sémiotique et l'autre de caractère sémantique. Enfin, le troisième ouvrage collectif, issu d'un colloque tenu à l'Université Guelph en mai 1978, réunit dix communications qui malgré leur diversité présentent l'objectif commun de relire le texte proustien dans l'optique de la modernité.

Alors que les études figurant dans le dernier ouvrage inscrivent à divers degrés l'œuvre proustienne sous le signe du pluriel et de l'intertextuel: le texte comme travail et transformation d'une multiplicité d'autres textes, le texte étoilé dont la lecture et le commentaire tentent de tracer, de structurer les différentes zones du déplacement du sens, de repérer la trame des codes et la traversée de citations, le texte comme fonctionnement, comme opération langagière; les analyses de Thériault et de René Juéry revendiquent par contre un statut d'exemplarité méthodologique et théorique. Leur démarche se veut structurale: 'Science avec patience le supplice est sûr,' et l'analyse des discours narratifs, tout en mettant en place des modèles généraux, demeure soucieuse de rendre compte de l'articulation d'un assez grand nombre de textes particuliers appartenant à divers régimes de discours. En ce sens, les applications, hypothétiquement du moins, pourraient se manifester comme différentes pratiques susceptibles de vérifier, de confirmer ou de rectifier la théorie. Et certes, ces ouvrages ont le mérite indéniable de vouloir répondre à un manque dans le champ d'application de méthodes jusqu'ici peu ou mal fondées. Cependant, dans une optique critique (l'examen du statut des modèles théoriques qui informent la pratique de Thériault et de Juéry), on pourrait faire nôtre, tout en l'infléchissant légèrement, la locution figée: 'il en est de la sémiotique comme des auberges espagnoles ... ; on n'y trouve que ce qu'on y apporte.' Qu'en est-il de l'apport méthodologique et théorique de ces deux ouvrages?

Au début de son travail sur l'œuvre romanesque d'Hébert, Thériault se fixe l'objectif d'étudier le personnage de roman par l'entremise d'un modèle psychologique emprunté à Eugène T. Gendlin qui traite le problème des modifications du changement de la personnalité de l'homme. Mais, comme l'a souligné Roman Jakobson, bien que l'emprunt de méthodes développées dans une discipline puisse ouvrir de vastes perspectives dans une autre discipline, voire même opérer une rectification de la théorie du départ, il faut au préalable définir le plus exactement possible la relation entre les deux domaines afin de déterminer s'il existe des conflits entre ces deux modes d'approche. D'entrée de jeu, Thériault assimile le personnage de roman à la personnalité de vivants et constate que puisque la personnalité (du personnage? de la personne?) n'est pas stable elle peut donc se modifier dans ses contenus. Le concept de contenu lui permet d'enchaîner des notions à valeur opératoire distincte et de poser, par exemple, un rapport de nécessité entre le changement de personnalité chez Gendlin et 'l'entreprise d'investigation narrative présentée par Claude Bremond dans son ouvrage *Logique du récit*' (p 9). En d'autres termes, les changements du contenu de la personnalité sont d'entrée de jeu assimilés sans distinction aucune aux fonctions (contenus?) logiques qui programment le récit. Suit alors un étrange amalgame du 'symbole,' du 'référent,' du 'processus de symbolisation,' de 'l'ordre de la narration,' de 'l'individu,' de 'vectorialisation du réseau des configurations,' de 'la structure actantielle,' de 'personnage' et des 'processus de modification des contenus de la personnalité' (pp 10-11).

Trois remarques s'imposent ici sur la méthodologie qui gouverne et organise cette analyse de l'œuvre romanesque d'Hébert. D'abord, on ne saurait confondre personnage de roman et personnalité. Il s'agit là de deux ordres entièrement et radicalement différents, car seule une théorie du texte et des productions symboliques de type lacanien (qui est aussi évoquée en passant) pourrait hypothétiquement permettre, par l'entremise d'un langage descriptif commun, l'articulation des relations entre les structures formelles d'une œuvre et les propriétés structurales de la situation qui l'a produite. Deuxièmement, les psychologues pour la plupart considèrent les faits de culture comme des symboles et non comme des signes. Les symboles non-conventionnels et non-arbitraires sont décodés comme l'expression des intentions humaines se rapportant au sens, se déployant sur l'arrière-plan de redondances mythiques, etc, et de ce fait les symboles ne peuvent pas se constituer en systèmes sémiotiques car leur signification ne dépend ni de leur fonction ni du lieu qu'ils occupent dans le système. A ce titre, les symboles sont considérés comme des structures situées en dehors du système. (Voir la critique de A.J. Greimas dans *Sémantique structurale*, Paris 1966, pp 55-60). Troisièmement, Thériault confond hiérarchie et série, niveau et processus, et bien qu'il reconnaisse dans sa description deux processus similaires appartenant à deux niveaux différents, il convertit l'un dans l'autre sans élaborer au préalable les médiateurs théoriques nécessaires pour passer d'un niveau à l'autre. En somme, procédant par la voix de l'empirie, il identifie une série et la traduit dans une seconde série appartenant à un autre niveau hiérarchique; et ainsi de suite.

Le deuxième ouvrage, *Approches structurales des textes*, résulte de l'intention pédagogique de deux enseignants de fournir des informations à des lecteurs parfois démunis et découragés devant la complexité des discours théoriques ambiants. Propédeutiques, les études proposées visent à initier les étudiants du secondaire et du premier cycle universitaire à l'analyse structurale. L'originalité indéniable de ce travail d'un grand mérite est de répondre à une lacune et de poser les premiers jalons d'un renouvellement de l'enseignement et de l'apprentissage de la littérature depuis trop longtemps sous la coupe des méthodes empiriques ou esthétiques. En se fixant comme but le maniement de concepts opératoires définissables, non seulement encouragent-ils le développement du goût de la recherche chez l'étudiant, mais encore lui offrent-ils la possibilité de maîtriser la production de son propre discours.

Conscients des nombreux problèmes rencontrés dans l'initiation aux différentes méthodes de l'analyse narrative, les auteurs ont judicieusement divisé leur travail en deux parties d'égale longueur, procédant stratégiquement du plus simple au plus complexe, du plus intuitif au plus construit. Dans un premier temps Thériault présente de façon générale la problématique de l'interprétation textuelle et de l'analyse structurale tout en indiquant une autre voie possible: le psychostructuralisme. Dans un second temps, il passe au fonctionnement syntaxique de l'analyse narrative et propose une systématisation pédagogique avec des exercices faits par lui et quelques étudiants. Enfin, la troisième section traite de la pratique de l'analyse narrative et la quatrième comprend des travaux effectués par des étudiants de premier cycle.

Les analyses sont en général assez bien menées mais un peu rapides, vu l'importance des textes étudiés. Toutefois, on se heurte aux mêmes problèmes rencontrés lors de l'examen de l'ouvrage précédent, à savoir: hiérarchie, série; mélange de niveaux, mise en correlation de Bremond, Greimas et d'autres auteurs. A titre d'exemple, l'utilisation du carré sémiotique au cours des différentes analyses est parfois trop hâtive dans la mesure où son élaboration découle tout simplement de la formalisation de motifs ou de thèmes récurrents, repérés au moment de la lecture. Si l'activité lectrice relève de la nomination, et a donc un fondement empirique, par contre, la formalisation relève de la construction logique. Nommer, uniquement à partir d'une lecture des dernières instances où la signification se manifeste (niveau figuratif du texte), l'instance *ab quo* où la substance sémantique reçoit ses premières articulations en faisant l'économie des parcours génératifs qui articulent le sens, c'est s'interdire à jamais toute possibilité de vérifier les résultats.

A la différence des travaux précédents, le but de Juéry est à la fois plus modeste et plus ambitieux. Plus modeste, car il se propose d'examiner un seul récit; plus ambitieux, puisqu'il *construit* 'un langage artificiel susceptible de rendre compte des articulations du contenu' (p 128), de 'La Robe corail' d'Hébert. Empruntant des modèles actantiels et actoriels à Greimas dont il voudrait vérifier l'efficacité et la généralité, Juéry n'applique pas servilement une méthode mais innove en affinant un appareil méthodologique trop souvent mal compris et mal employé. La brièveté du conte lui permet d'inventorier, de définir et de classer les unités de signification en se servant de procédés tels que la recherche des couples d'opposition, la commutation, etc; et d'obtenir une 'succession d'énoncés ayant un sens susceptible d'une interprétation globale' (p 131).

Refusant la glose, et se plaçant dans l'optique d'une construction logico-sémantique, Juéry découpe le récit en sept séquences correspondant à des unités de signifiés de sorte qu'à chaque inventaire des unités syntagmatiques correspond une formalisation du récit et parfois même du discours. L'inventaire terminé, le texte se manifeste comme une succession d'effets de sens et l'auteur passe au stade suivant de la description, c'est-à-dire, à l'élaboration des modèles fonctionnel et qualificatif narratifs qui organisent le texte. La dernière étape, qui consiste en une exploitation des résultats obtenus au cours de la description, sanctionne la mise en place des ultimes modèles qualificatif et fonctionnel discursifs.

La contribution de Juéry, menée selon de solides bases, est doublement importante; d'une part elle constitue un véritable apport sur les plans théorique et méthodologique, et d'autre part elle nous éclaire sur le fonctionnement du conte hébertien. Les analyses fines et rigoureuses, les interrogations subtiles et percutantes ainsi que les commentaires lucides et pénétrants témoignent d'une grande maîtrise d'un champ important de la sémiotique, et de ce fait, rendent cet ouvrage indispensable à tous ceux qui œuvrent dans le domaine de l'analyse structurale des textes. On regrette cependant un nombre excessif de coquilles qu'une lecture soigneuse des épreuves aurait pu éviter.

Le collectif *Proust et le texte producteur* comprend dix communications d'une longueur et d'un intérêt inégaux, ainsi que de trop brefs extraits des débats prononcés lors du colloque Proust à l'Université Guelph. Puisqu'il n'est pas possible dans les limites d'une recension d'examiner chaque intervention écrite et orale en détail, il s'agit avant tout de situer globalement les différentes démarches plutôt que de se pencher sur les aspects particuliers de chacune. Toutefois, il revient à Jean Milly dans son étude séminale bien que programmatique de mettre en relation les diverses pratiques représentées dans le volume: 'La perspective stylistique, par rapport à la majorité des approches qui ont été faites dans les communications précédentes, consiste essentiellement à prendre comme objet d'étude la manifestation du discours, au niveau superficiel, à relier les formes d'expression à des formes de contenu, à rechercher comment ces formes d'expression et de contenu constituent, chez un écrivain particulier, un système spécifique de contraintes autres que celles du pur code linguistique' (p 49).

Au lu de ce qui précède, si l'on considère le texte proustien comme système de signes, trois voies distinctes semblent s'ouvrir à l'exégèse moderne: celle qui se focalise sur la forme de l'expression et s'évertue à mettre au jour les lois qui gouvernent la production du signifiant; celle qui consiste à élaborer les structures logico-sémantiques de la forme du contenu; et enfin, celle qui tente de représenter le texte par l'entremise de modèles sémiotiques reliant les formes d'expression à des formes du contenu. Selon la perspective critique implicitement ou explicitement adoptée, chacune des études peut se situer et se définir par rapport à une ou à plusieurs de ces options. On remarque cependant que certaines analyses passent d'un plan à l'autre sans se préoccuper de mettre en place les médiateurs théoriques qui pourraient légitimer un tel changement de niveau. Ainsi du travail de E. Marantz qui joue à la fois sur le plan de l'*ethos* des structures et celui de leur fonction de générateurs du *mythos* topologique de *A la recherche du temps perdu*.

Bien que d'excellentes études, notamment la brillante intervention de Serge Doubrovsky d'inspiration lacanienne, ainsi que la non moins sérieuse communication de M. Raimond programmant une analyse structurale des scènes mondaines dans *A la recherche*, s'accommodent de la définition quelque peu restrictive du texte comme système de signes suggérée par les remarques de Milly, d'autres travaux innovateurs, se fondant sur la notion d'*intertextualité*, ébranlent le concept de texte comme système clos obéissant à un seul ordre interne. Se pose dès lors le problème fondamental en sémiotique de la circonscription des limites ou des bornes d'un système de signes. Et c'est avant tout dans l'optique d'une problématisation de la définition structuraliste du système comme ensemble clos qu'il faudrait situer les travaux importants de M. Muller et de Ricardou, car non seulement sommes-nous incités à remettre en question la valeur opératoire de la notion étroite de système, mais encore sommes-nous amenés à repenser le texte comme production et à réévaluer l'activité critique. L'intérêt de cet important volume ne se limite donc pas à la seule œuvre de Proust puisque les études qui y figurent soulèvent les grandes questions théoriques qui traversent le champ critique actuel. (PAUL PERRON)

Louis-Alexandre Bélisle. *Dictionnaire nord-américain de la langue française*
Beauchemin 1979. 1196. $32.50

Léandre Bergeron. *Dictionnaire de la langue québécoise*
VLB. 572. $28.95

Jean-Pierre Pichette. *Le Guide raisonné des jurons*
Quinze. 305. $14.95

Le dictionnaire de Bélisle est une réédition 'revue, augmentée et mise au point' (introduction non paginée) de son *Dictionnaire général de la langue française au Canada*, paru pour la première fois en 1957. Son nouvel intitulé s'expliquerait par le fait qu'il prétend embrasser 'tous les mots usuels de la langue française, telle qu'on la parle, telle qu'on l'écrit et telle qu'on la comprend en Amérique française – tout particulièrement au Québec, en Acadie, dans le reste du Canada et en Nouvelle-Angleterre'; à noter qu'il n'est pas fait mention de la Louisiane. En fait, l'ensemble géolinguistique ainsi délimité est une aire qui a pour foyer le Québec et dont le vocabulaire spécifique est constitué de 'canadianismes' tels qu'ils sont définis par l'Office de la langue française du Québec et inventoriés à partir du *Glossaire du parler français au Canada* (1930) et des compilations personnelles de l'auteur 'recueilles dans les milieux du Québec où ... j'ai eu à exercer mon activité pendant plus d'un demi-siècle.' La seule nouveauté de cette édition est l'apparition de citations pour illustrer l'usage canadien (il y a aussi deux suppléments onomastiques en appendice). La bibliographie liminaire donne la liste des auteurs canadiens cités; sous les lettres *Ba* et *Ma* du dictionnaire (38 pages serrées), neuf auteurs sont cités douze fois (H. Bernard, A. Nantel, Ringuet, R. Girard, Guèvremont, A. Rivard, Cl.-H. Grignon, M. Trudel, A. Laberge). La partie 'français de France,' tout comme la conception de l'ouvrage, continue à être marquée par l'influence de Littré, à qui Bélisle a emprunté la majeure partie de la nomenclature. Aussi la presque totalité des citations françaises, données comme garants de l'usage contemporain (?), proviennent-elles d'auteurs classiques; en revanche, le nombre des citations a été considérablement réduit: dans la partie *M-Mal* (9½ pages), 24 auteurs (dont Boileau, Diderot, Voltaire, La Fontaine, Corneille, Molière, Bossuet, Sévigné, La Bruyère, Rousseau, Pascal, Racine) sont cités 42 fois, contre 103 citations dans l'édition de 1971. L'ouvrage est délibérément normatif et conservateur: 'malgré le nombre croissant de Canadiens qui suivront le bon usage, on prendra du temps, je le crois bien, à empêcher les gens du peuple d'*aller voir les filles*, de *prendre une petite brosse* et d'*avoir du fonne* à l'occasion'; 'tous nos efforts doivent viser à effectuer une transposition graduelle du *populaire* à l'*universel*, de la langue paysanne à la langue de culture, du français de conversation, donc familier et populaire, à la langue littéraire' (introduction).

Si le choix des citations françaises rend parfois suspect le caractère contemporain de l'usage consigné dans le dictionnaire, le statut linguistique des entrées est souvent ambigu et le choix de catégorie d'usage quelquefois discutable. Selon l'introduction, les trois types de canadianismes – 'canadianismes littéraires, ou de bon aloi,' 'canadianismes familiers ou folkoriques,' 'mots à proscrire du style soutenu' – sont signalés respectivement par les signes ©, ✤ et ⊗, alors que les sens et emplois non précédés d'un signe particulier relèveraient du français de France contemporain employé ou compris en Amérique française. En fait, la notion de 'compréhension' ouvre la porte à des mots qui ne s'emploient pas de ce côté-ci de l'Atlantique: *gosse* 'jeune enfant,' *pelote de neige*, *bachot*, *poser un lapin*. Au lieu que *maîtrise* 'grade universitaire' n'est présenté que comme mot canadien, on donne pour *baccalauréat* un usage canadien et un usage français, lequel est défini en termes qui le distinguent mal de la réalité canadienne (on dit simplement 'premier grade universitaire'). En revanche, *bachelor*, *bar laitier* ('canadianisme familier ou folklorique' dans l'édition de 1971), *mashé* ('canadianisme à proscrire' en 1971) et *maringouin*, donnés comme français, sont typiquement canadiens. Il y a d'autres mots qui relèvent du français international mais que Bélisle qualifie de canadiens: ainsi *magnétoscope* et *magnétoscopique* (promus de la catégorie 'canadianismes familiers ou folkloriques' (!) à celle de 'canadianismes de bon aloi'), *majorette*, *maîtresse* 'institutrice' et *baiser* 'duper, tromper; faire l'amour.' Les trois quarts de l'article *fourrer* concernent l'usage français, alors que la partie canadienne ne donne que les sens de 'duper; mettre, jeter; dépasser'; il faut chercher le sémantisme de ce mot s.v. *fourreur* 'fornicateur.' Le mot *back-stop* est incorrectement classé comme 'mot à proscrire,' car il n'a pas d'équivalent 'soutenu,' du moins Bélisle n'en donne pas. La règle générale de l'articulation des articles veut que tout ce qui précède les signes ©, ✤ et ⊗ soit du français de France et que tout ce qui les suit soit du français canadien. Or quand une expression située au milieu de la partie 'français de France' est considérée dans la nouvelle édition comme un canadianisme, sans qu'elle change de place, le système est faussé: ainsi *maison garnie* (*maison*, ligne 11), *être son maître* (*maître*, ligne 5).

Au chapitre des lacunes, on pourra regretter l'absence de *banque* au sens figuré, très développé au Canada (*banque du sang, de mots, de données, de terminologie*), ainsi que celle de *logiciel* et de *matériel* au profit de *software* et de *hardware*. Les définitions manquent parfois de rigueur: *tourne-disque* 'reproducteur phonographique qui porte en France le nom de *pick-up*' (*tourne-disque* est le mot courant en France); *magnétophone* 'appareil qui enregistre sur un ruban magnétique les sons, la voix et même les émissions de télévision en noir et en couleurs' (la télévision est l'affaire du magnétoscope).

Si la nomenclature comporte des additions dans l'ensemble elle a été sensiblement réduite. Pour les lettres *Ba*, *Ma* et *Ta*, le nombre de vedettes est comme suit: *Ba* 686 (42 ajoutées, 134 supprimées par rapport à l'édition de 1971), *Ma* 1114 (+57, −157), *Ta* 433 (+8, −55). La plupart des vedettes supprimées sont des mots rares, vieux ou vieillis: *babel*, *babillement*, *baccarat*, *bacchanal*, *bacchique*, *bacchius*, *bacha*, *bachelette*, *bachoteur*, etc. Les additions relèvent en général de la langue contemporaine: *bachelor*, *bachotage*, *bactériologique*, *badge*, *bain-marie*, *balconnet*, *balkaniser*, *banaliser*, etc. Pour *Ba*, on compte également l'addition de 68 sens ou emplois, contre 363 suppressions. Sous la même lettre, environ 150 définitions et exemples ont été modifiés, le plus souvent pour devenir plus brefs. Les citations (v. *supra*) et les illustrations sont également moins nombreuses. L'ensemble du texte est ainsi beaucoup plus court: 1103 pages contre 1390 pour l'édition de 1971. La typographie de la nouvelle édition est améliorée, mais elle reste très pauvre; ceci, joint à l'articulation linéaire des articles (absence presque totale de subordination), fait qu'un long article comme *prendre* ou *venir* est presque inconsultable.

Si le dictionnaire de Bélisle se réclame de la lexicographie académique, l'ouvrage de Bergeron se veut délibérément contestataire. Avant de l'ouvrir, il faut enlever une bande publicitaire qui porte l'avertissement 'Interdit aux moins de dix-huit ans, aux professeurs de français, aux linguistes et aux annonceurs de Radio-Canada!' – on connaît le sort des interdits. Il s'agit d'un parti pris à la fois pratique et idéologique. Pratique, d'une part parce que le livre remplit une lacune et répond à un besoin – il n'y avait pas de recueil complet des mots spécifiquement québécois (Bergeron puise son lexique dans tous les recueils existants ainsi que dans ses carnets personnels); d'autre part parce qu'il laisse pour une étape ultérieure l'inclusion du vocabulaire commun au français du Québec et au français de France, vocabulaire que l'auteur invite son lecteur à chercher dans des dictionnaires comme *Le Petit Robert*. Idéologique, puisque Bergeron s'adresse directement à ses concitoyens québécois sans se référer aux normes culturo-lexicographiques héritées de la France. En conséquence, les définitions sont rédigées en français québécois et il y a une absence quasi totale d'indications normatives; mots techniques, vieillis, nouveaux, rares, courants, polis et vulgaires se côtoient sans discrimination. Comme dit l'auteur dans sa préface, 'c'est le friforolle'!

Tout en acceptant la position adoptée par Bergeron, on peut formuler un certain nombre de critiques à l'égard de son ouvrage. Le titre, 'Dictionnaire de la langue québécoise,' est inexact, puisqu'il s'agit des particularismes lexicaux du parler québécois. D'autre part, certains de ces mots s'emploient aussi bien en France qu'au Québec: *bacon*, *badge*, *bain* 'baignoire,' *stérilet*, *pot de chambre*, *jeans*, *jet* 'avion à réaction.' La nomenclature est forcément lacunaire; l'auteur invite ses lecteurs à l'aider à la compléter – une collègue, originaire de Trois-Rivières, propose *balafe* 'gifle' et *cochon* 'bille qu'on vise au jeu de billes.' La transcription des entrées, tantôt graphique ou étymologique, tantôt phonétique, semble parfois arbitraire: alors que *poéson* 'poison,' *abadenner* 'abandonner' ou *pofte-ouite* 'puffed wheat' ont droit à la nomenclature, *naouère* (donné comme prononciation de *nowhere*) ou *floche* (prononciation de *flush*) en sont exclus. Les nombreux items de l'article *faire* sont donnés dans le désordre complet. Une énigme: le mot *geneviève* (n.f.), défini 'galcopside.' Dans le contexte où le place son auteur, le dictionnaire permettra aux Québécois de se reconnaître et il leur expliquera, ainsi qu'aux non-Québécois, le sens des mots qu'ils ne connaissent pas. Le dictionnaire général du français du Québec, qu'il soit descriptif ou normatif, paraîtra un jour.

Il est significatif que les études-recueils les plus importants consacrés aux 'gros mots' utilisés en français portent, pour le domaine français, sur les injures (Robert Edouard, *Dictionnaire des injures*, Tchou 1967), et, pour le domaine québécois, sur les jurons (Pichette). Le livre d'Edouard était destiné 'aux gens sains et bien élevés, soucieux d'enrichir leur culture – et leur vocabulaire – de locutions propres à les aider à se tirer de situations parfois fort déplaisantes' (p 15); l'intention de Pichette est de 'rendre le lecteur davantage conscient [de l'ampleur du phénomène du juron au Canada français et plus particulièrement au Québec] et ensuite de donner un aperçu du gigantisme de cette manie nationale par la description et l'étude de ses diverses catégories de témoignages' (p 143). Ethnologue au Centre d'études sur la langue, les arts et traditions populaires de l'Université Laval, Pichette exploite une documentation très riche pour étudier, dans la première partie de son ouvrage, différents aspects lexicaux – terminologie, formation, dérivation, classification – des jurons (il laisse au linguiste le soin de pousser plus loin ses analyses) et plus spécialement la littérature orale: l'anecdote, la légende, les histoires, jeux, devinettes, concours de sacres, chansons et formules. *Jurer, jureur* et *juron* sont situés par rapport à leurs synonymes et parasynonymes, tels que *sacrer, sacreur, sacre, jurement, blasphème, blasphémer, patois, serment, injure*, etc. Dans une deuxième partie, l'histoire du juron est soigneusement tracée, en France, en Nouvelle-France et au Canada, depuis le Moyen Age jusqu'au présent, à travers les ordonnances et lois et les peines encourues (allant de la mort à l'amende, en passant par la langue percée), les témoignages et mandements. Dans les 133 pages du dictionnaire qui complète l'ouvrage sont répertoriés les quelque 1800 jurons réunis par Pichette à partir d'enquêtes menées à travers le Québec dans les milieux essentiellement estudiantins, et secondairement en puisant dans des sources écrites: glossaires, romans, contes, récits, études, etc. Chaque article présente un juron avec sa graphie, sa prononciation et son étymologie, ainsi que sa provenance: région(s) où il a été relevé et/ou source(s) écrite(s); est donnée éventuellement la mention de son utilisation en France d'après les dictionnaires français. Le lecteur peut se faire une idée assez exacte de la diffusion des jurons en se reportant à un tableau (pp 20–4) qui indique pour 340 termes les régions (neuf québécoises et une acadienne) où chacun a été relevé. Cet ouvrage érudit rendra de grands services aux historiens de la langue et de la société du Canada français.

Quelques remarques de détail. Les références bibliographiques contenues dans les articles du dictionnaire pourraient être allégées par la suppression de la mention des intitulés (ex: '1974, Charest, LLDSEBQ' > '1974, Charest'). En tant que juron, *viarge* est la forme non marquée et *vierge* la forme marquée; c'est la première qui serait plus logiquement donnée en vedette. *Bull-shit* est présenté comme étant une traduction de *merde de bœuf*; c'est sûrement le contraire. Parmi les jurons répertoriés par Bergeron, il y a plusieurs qui manquent à Pichette: citons *abîmations* (terminologie), *fuck* et *saints fumiers*. Une collègue de Trois-Rivières connaît *hostie mal toastée*. (TERENCE RUSSON WOOLDRIDGE)

Dennis Reid. *Notre patrie le Canada: Mémoires sur les aspirations nationales des principaux paysagistes de Montréal et de Toronto 1860–1890* (also published in English as *Our Own Country Canada, Being an Account of the National Aspirations of the Principal Landscape Artists in Montreal and Toronto 1860–1890*) Galerie nationale du Canada / Musées nationaux du Canada 1979. 454. $29.95

L'ouvrage riche, complexe et polysémique reflète les années de recherche que Dennis Reid, alors conservateur de l'art canadien de la période post-confédérale à la Galerie nationale du Canada, a consacré au sujet. L'historien a eu le courage de porter son attention sur un sujet identifié et jugé comme primordial par les historiens d'art au Canada depuis près de trente ans. Ses études antérieures sur Morrice et le Groupe des Sept commandaient en quelque sorte qu'il remonte le courant historique de façon à entreprendre cette étude qui porte sur un des problèmes centraux du développement de l'art dans notre pays. La période concernée (1860–90) est celle même où le paysage d'observation connaît un grand intérêt à travers le monde occidental.

Plus le sujet est important, plus il est vierge, plus il prête à des découvertes valables et Reid a eu la main particulièrement heureuse. Alors que des personnalités artistiques aussi notables que William Notman, John A. Fraser ou Lucius O'Brien nous étaient encore relativement peu connus, Reid révèle, au sujet de ceux-ci et d'artistes qui eurent un rayonnement moindre, des informations biographiques et une introduction à leur œuvre qui ouvrent de nombreuses perspectives d'études. L'interrelation des multiples biographies et des événements sociopolitiques est recréée de façon magistrale. La vie culturelle canadienne de la période étudiée revit à travers l'examen des activités des sociétés artistiques, du rôle des commanditaires et des projets multiples et ambitieux. Les milieux de travail, la dynamique des rapports personnels ou institutionnels sont présentés de façon à élucider leur impact sur la création visuelle. L'apport essentiel du livre me paraît être ce portrait de la vie artistique du milieu anglophone étudiée sous le prisme de l'activité des artistes paysagistes.

L'approche historique fait une percée importante dans la périodicisation de l'art canadien en ce qu'elle impose une lecture de l'histoire artistique qui ne soit pas une copie de l'événementiel politique. Reid hésite cependant à inscrire en majuscule sur la couverture 1858 et 1886 comme dates limites de la période étudiée. Pourtant les deux dates que constituent l'ouverture du studio du photographe William Notman à Montréal et l'année du voyage de Fraser et O'Brien dans les Rocheuses sont bien celles qui encadrent sa synthèse.

Le récit est strictement chronologique. Reid, en ce qu'il est conscient que cette forme narrative n'assure pas pour autant à ce déroulement linéaire une plus grande objectivité, prévient le lecteur qu'il ne dira pas 'toute' *la* vérité. Puisqu'il ne s'agit que d'aspects de vérités, comment celles-ci sont-elles abordées? Le titre, même s'il se camoufle derrière une citation, situe l'ouvrage dans un projet politique que la Galerie nationale en tant qu'institution fédérale se doit de refléter. Le plan du texte cependant se conforme au sous-titre en ce que le développement des deux villes est traité de façon parallèle, chacune semblant trouver son dynamisme dans une réaction aux activités de l'autre. Reid démontre que les projets de ces artistes et de leur milieu ne furent pas d'envergure nationale mais bien métropolitaine et régionale. La conquête du marché, les projets personnels, les rivalités individuelles qui certes ne facilitent pas l'interprétation, furent les pivots de ce développement et paraissent faussés lorsqu'ils sont reportés dans une structure politique. Même si certains artistes furent très proches des détenteurs du pouvoir politique et économique, surent-ils incarner les aspirations de la classe dirigeante? Alors que le besoin de propagande anime les mécènes industriels, les comportements des gouverneurs généraux apparaissent basés sur des considérations d'ordre esthétique certes, mais surtout mondain et professionnel plutôt que national.

L'auteur cautionne la théorie selon laquelle l'écart entre les milieux artistiques francophones et anglophones tel qu'il s'est manifesté à ce moment est dû à la non reconnaissance de la part du groupe culturel britannique de l'héritage historique français. Cette brève interprétation tient trop peu compte des cultures fondamentalement différentes et des mouvements d'idées contradictoires. Le Canada français de 1860 vit replié dans sa version d'un univers ultramontain que l'utopie économico-politico-géographique du Canada anglais ne peut remplacer.

Dans son style et sa forme l'ouvrage, principalement parce qu'il n'admet pas les notes, est lourd, encore plus dans la traduction française, parfois incompréhensible. Ce parti pris surcharge le texte de détails (adresse des artistes, nombre d'enfants, localisation des œuvres, etc) et de références au sources premières, ce qui ajoute au ton descriptif. Ce texte témoigne de l'état de la recherche en histoire de l'art au Canada en ce que les historiens travaillant de façon isolée et utilisant une méthodologie traditionnelle doivent encore explorer les aspects premiers des questions qu'ils traitent (inventaire, catalogue et chronologie). Les interprétations récentes de l'histoire, les connaissances dans les sciences humaines et sociales, les questionnements de l'histoire de l'art ne sont que rarement intégrés. Ici par exemple, l'examen de la réception critique n'est jamais confronté aux idées développées dans la littérature contemporaine ou la philosophie telle qu'enseignée à Toronto au même moment.

Comme le suggère G. Stephen Vickers dans son avant-propos, l'ouvrage s'ouvre sur plusieurs problématiques, parmi les plus importantes celle des analyses stylistiques qui sont ici esquissées au plan technique et formel. Une iconographie et une iconologie des lieux dépeints seraient à tracer. Les espaces représentés réussirent-ils à nourrir les attentes d'un imaginaire collectif en train de se constituer? La question des rapports avec la photographie est maintenant mieux documentée mais il faudrait aller au-delà de l'identification des sources et des mises en page, communes avec la peinture, pour pénétrer des aspects concernant la conception et la perception de l'espace en rapport avec le rôle de la couleur, par exemple. Les échanges (voyages, expositions) avec les Etats-Unis qui sont illustrés à plusieurs reprises dans le texte de Reid méritent que l'on pousse plus avant l'étude de ces réseaux.

Parce qu'il perpétue le 'mythe' du paysage canadien, sans analyser les fondements de cet à-priori et sans proposer l'examen des différentes conceptions du paysage, le livre de Reid achoppe dans sa démonstration. En ce qu'elle soulève de nombreuses questions et parce qu'elle fournira les prochaines décennies en informations, cette publication est appelée à jouer un rôle primordial. (LAURIER LACROIX)

George A. Proctor. *Canadian Music of the Twentieth Century*
University of Toronto Press. xxvi, 297. $27.50

In 1947 the CBC issued a *Catalogue of Canadian Composers* in which there were 238 names. In 1952, when it was revised and enlarged by Helmut Kallmann to include composers from colonial times to the date of issue, the catalogue contained the astonishing total of 356 names of composers, of whom about 80 per cent had been born after 1880 and were living in 1950. Even allowing for the fact that the list included almost anyone who ever set pen to music paper, two things are obvious from the catalogue: the first is the sheer number of people who showed some interest in writing music and who had somehow managed to set it before a public; the second is how overwhelmingly has musical composition in Canada been an activity of the twentieth century. Very few people in that CBC catologue, however, would have thought of themselves first as composers as opposed to being, say, teachers or organists who composed; and very little of the music they wrote had much scope or substance, being mostly songs and ballads, anthems or piano pieces. Around 1950 both the self-image and the musical range of our composers changed.

In 1951 the Canadian League of Composers was formed, and in 1959 the first office of the Canadian Music Centre opened in Toronto. When *Contemporary Canadian Composers*, a biographical dictionary edited by John Beckwith and Keith MacMillan, appeared in 1975 it listed 144 composers. The number was much smaller than was the case with the earlier CBC catalogue, but almost all the composers in the 1975 dictionary were alive and flourishing and, most importantly, they were all serious composers, men and women with reputations for craft and originality, composers whose work would not be out of place in any contemporary concert hall.

Although the existence of composers in Canada is now a recognized fact and their work is studied and performed, the general level of awareness of their activity remains lamentably low even among musicians. One of the reasons for this is the lack of expert writing about music in Canada. Our newspapers treat music shabbily and there is no magazine or journal in the country that gives music the slightest serious attention, least of all new music. Our composers need critics, chroniclers, and propagandists to help develop an informed and receptive society for their music. Now for the first time we have in George Proctor's book an authoritative survey of musical composition in Canada.

The relatively sparse activity up to mid-century and the concentration of composers and music in the past three decades pose a problem of presentation of material for an author who seeks to treat the subject comprehensively from 1900 to the present. Proctor has organized his book in seven chapters, more or less by decades except for the separate treatment of the centennial year, 1967. Each chapter is subdivided into genres – piano music, songs, choral, orchestral, chamber, and organ music. This allows clear reference to hundreds of works in an orderly fashion, but regrettably it clouds any view of the continuity of stylistic development either in the general nature of composition in Canada or in individual composers. What we learn about the piano works of a composer in 1950, for example, is isolated from comments about his chamber music in 1960. A great deal of repetition of critical statements occurs in a presentation which is episodic and discontinuous.

Despite his obvious devotion to his subject and his inspection of many scores over many years, the author seems not entirely free of the shadow of Canadian Insecurity. No one could guess that any composer in Canada sounds distinctive; everyone sounds like someone else or betrays the influence of some famous composer on the international scene. This referential treatment of Canadians may be reasonable to a degree in the attempt to convey a sense of a work, particularly to an audience outside Canada with no opportunity to hear the music or study a score, but it is overworked. It is inevitably unfair to those composers who sound like themselves – and we have many – and it reinforces the notion that the best we can manage is music that is derivative. In some cases the insistence on having an external reference entirely misrepresents a work.

Reservations about the organization of the material and the treatment of the repertoire notwithstanding, Proctor's *Canadian Music of the Twentieth Century* is one of the most important books so far published on music in Canada. It contains an extraordinary amount of information accurately and clearly set out in a handsomely bound and printed volume designed by Antje Linger at the University of Toronto Press. There are extremely useful lists of publishers and recording companies with full addresses, chapter lists of representative repertoire, a brief chronology of music, history, and the arts from 1900 to 1979, a selective but none the less extensive bibliography, and a thorough index. We must hope that the Press will promote Proctor's book vigorously here and abroad and that it will long remain on the list of current publications.   (CARL MOREY)

A.H. de Trémaudin. *Histoire de la Nation métisse dans l'Ouest-canadien*
Les Editions des Plaines 1979. 450

Mary V. Jordan. *De ta soeur, Sara Riel*
Les Editions des Plaines. 182

The reappearance of Auguste-Henri de Trémaudin's massive and partisan history of the Métis and the translation of Mary Jordan's edition of Sara Riel's letters to her more famous brother do not add much to the sum of human knowledge. They do indicate something of the trend of Canadian public opinion since 1936 when the late M. de Trémaudin's work was completed and published by his friends in le comité historique de l'Union nationale métisse.

When de Trémaudin's work first appeared, it was still controversial to offer an almost wholly uncritical portrayal of the Métis and their best known leader. Among those who still believed that Louis Riel had been prevented from handing the Red River over to the Americans, it was news to discover that he, rather than the Wolseley expedition, had preserved the North West for Canada.

Almost two generations after de Trémaudin's death in California, the pendulum has swung very far. It is now almost obligatory to refer to Riel as the founder of Manitoba and a monument to his memory decorates the grounds of the provincial legislature. At Regina, scene of his ultimate humiliation and execution, a superhuman statue makes belated amends. Awkward and inconvenient as he undoubtedly was in life, Louis Riel in death becomes an all-purpose symbol to be wielded in countless contradictory causes.

To be fair, the influence of de Trémaudin's book has been infinitely less in achieving a redefinition of Riel and the Métis than the work of George Stanley. *The Birth of Western Canada*, Stanley's Oxford thesis, appeared in the same year as *Histoire de la Nation métisse*. Because it was a work of literary flair, unprecedented scholarship, and, above all, because it was in English, George Stanley's book forced a revision of thought in precisely that part of the Canadian community where most changing had to occur. For de Trémaudin's French-speaking readership, long inured to a historiography of saintly heroes and *orangiste* villains, no fresh thinking was required.

Reprinting de Trémaudin's book in a facsimile edition may recall the devoted contribution of its author and his committee and it undoubtedly provides contemporary Franco-Manitobans with a gratifying self-image. The publishers may also have reckoned, like many of their contemporaries, that virtually anything on Riel, however bad or outdated, will sell. They have backed that commercial judgment by translating most of Mary Jordan's 1974 book, *To Louis from your sister who loves you, Sara Riel*. Understandably, the French originals of the letters, published in the earlier volume, have been left out of this edition. In slovenly fashion neither the author nor her publisher has bothered to explain the provenance of the new book. The impression is left that translation was largely the work of the author herself with the collaboration of Rossel Vien.

Mary Jordan brings to Sara and her older brother some of the uncritical sympathy she lavished on her 1975 biography of Bob Russell, her former employer and the hero of the Winnipeg General Strike. She claims that Sara Riel gave herself to the religious life almost as a substitute when Louis Riel quit the Seminary in Montreal and abandoned his religious vocation. The letters reveal a little of convent life in St Boniface, the difficulties of Sara's journey to the mission station of Ile à la Crosse in northern Saskatchewan, and the hardships of a remote mission station. It was there, after a life marked by poor health and perhaps few accomplishments, that Sara died in 1883.

Sara's letters to her brother are neither eloquent nor revealing, beyond confirming the deep affection that Louis could draw from his long-suffering family. The periods of insanity and religious apostasy appear to have been discreetly ignored. The pain of realizing that her beloved brother had married without even bothering to inform his sister is swallowed with dutiful good wishes to his new 'companion.'

The conventional *bondieuserie* of Jordan's book, like the uncritical hero-worship of de Trémaudin, may now represent a fading baseline in the historiography of Riel and the Métis. Thomas Flanagan's examination of Riel's religious and political thought, one of the finest recent works on Riel and the Northwest and one of the few to explore new ground, has given us tools to examine central aspects of the Métis leader's life which authors like Jordan and Trémaudin might well have found embarrassing. Doug Owram's study of Canadian expansionism in the West breaks the link which the late W.L. Morton had sought to establish between Riel and the tradition of western protest. Since history is always interpreted through the prism of our own time, the age of Islamic revolutions and ayatollahs has reminded us that rebels may as easily be reactionary as progressive.

There were two sets of rebels in the West in 1870. One of them, with close links to Ontario and a weak presence on the spot, saw their goal as the creation of a fundamentally British nation extending from coast to coast. The other, with far more tenuous links to Quebec, sought to preserve their society largely as it was. The Manitoba Act of 1870 was very largely a triumph for the conservative solution and Riel expected to find his livelihood in the one trade left to a man who would not be a farmer, a lawyer, or a priest, that of professional politician. If he had fulfilled his ambition, he might have emerged as a durable, respected political figure or he might have shared the fate of his Manitoba contemporaries and been tarred by corruption, compromise, and failure.

Instead, a single fatal decision denied him amnesty and a political career, drove him to exile, insanity, and the tragic mismanagement of 1885. To achieve respect for his shaky provisional government, he had authorized the killing of Thomas Scott. 'We must make Ottawa respect us,' Riel explained. It was not unlike the real reason the Macdonald government would condemn Riel himself to die in 1885: Canadian authority over the West could no longer be challenged by rebellion. Progress and expansion could not be halted again.

It is both the challenge and the frustration of history that each generation writes its own version. The disinterring of de Trémaudin's book, complete with misprints and marginal errors, is a reminder of how far we have changed and of how the past continues to change.

(DESMOND MORTON)

Yvan Lamonde. *La Philosophie et son enseignement au Québec (1665–1920)*
Hurtubise HMH. 312.

Until recently Canadian historiography has been primarily concerned with military, constitutional, political, economic, and social history with little attention to the intellectual aspects of culture. But a change has been occurring; and nowhere has the interest been greater than in Québec. In the last twenty years of ferment the philosophy formerly taught in Québec has come to be treated as an ideology used to sustain a church-state nexus collaborating with 'foreign' economic powers to oppress the Québécois nation. This view has become almost an article of faith amongst the new élites.

Yvan Lamonde has written a copiously documented study of 'quand, par qui, pour qui, comment et pourquoi' certain doctrines were promulgated and inculcated. His first chapter, covering 1665–1759, deals with the teaching of philosophy in New France by the Collège des Jésuites de Québec. The second, on the period 1770–1835, concerns the formation of the first colleges, the reorganization of the teaching of philosophy, and the first Québecois 'manuel' by Jérôme Demers. The third, the 'plaque-tournante' of his analysis, explains the evolution (1835–79) from a period of confusion, through the search for a 'Catholic' philosophy, to the circumstances of and reasons for the restoration of Thomism with the encyclical *Aeterni patris*. The last chapter takes us up to 1920, explains the way in which pedagogy in college philosophy was structured and made uniform, and outlines the social changes that justified the publication of a second Québécois 'manuel' by Stanislas-Alfred Lortie.

What is significant is that Lamonde's account is detailed, circumstantial, based on extensive archival research, and, whenever possible, quantitative. We are provided with various charts, graphs, lists of teachers showing where they taught and were taught, and a substantial bibliography. This enables us to argue theories on a better factual basis than heretofore and for this we are in his debt. What is Lamonde's own theoretical framework?

He takes as his general setting the importation of traditional European philosophies into the New World and their modification and dissemination in the new social setting with its special demands: Québec is but one intellectual colony among the others of North and South America. (The British philosopher C.D. Broad once said that all good ideas, when they die, go to America and are revived as the latest inventions of the local professors.) He treats philosophical discourse as an ideological discourse, but without entering into nuanced sectarian debates about the nature of ideologies. It is fair to say (see p 242) that Lamonde's work is intended to corroborate and support the thesis of Pierre Thibault's *Savoir et pouvoir*. Lamonde provides detailed evidence at the level of local élite culture, 'une culture scolaire, livresque, rhétoricienne.' He correlates the teaching of philosophy, both its matter and its manner, with the changing fortunes of the Church – 'l'Église souffrante, militante et triomphante' – whose power varied with its resources, which were in turn affected by the political and economic climate of Quebec. Lamonde presents a convincing case.

It would be unfortunate, however, if the general thesis obscured such diversity of thought as has existed in Québec and thus reinforced the stereotype of a monolithic mentality. Lamonde does in fact consider the development of philosophy outside the colleges and the dissemination of radical thought among the bourgeoisie of the liberal professions in the nineteenth century. But there is still work to be done. There is not a single reference to philosophy at McGill, that Québec institution which tolerated, barely, the philosopher John Clark Murray, a defender of women and workers. And one awaits with interest a book as admirable as Lamonde's on the period 1920–80.

Lamonde's work should be of interest to philosophers as well as historians. Just as the philosophy of science has been radically changed in the last two decades by a new fusion with the history of science, so too other aspects of philosophy could be changed by a new relation with a kind of sociology of philosophy. Lamonde's work is of the same genre as Kuklick's *The Rise of American Philosophy* (1860–1930). The hypothesis is that the institutionalization of a discipline affects both its matter and its manner, and that to treat these as platonic entities affected only by their internal logic is a mistake. What is needed is evidence, such as Lamonde has provided, to confirm the hypothesis. (J.T. STEVENSON)

Ernest Joós, editor. *Scolastique: certitude et recherche. En Hommage à Louis-Marie Régis*
Bellarmin. 211. $12.00

It is pleasing to welcome this volume of essays in honour of one of the most distinguished contemporary Canadian philosophers. Professor Régis's thought has always been grounded in a profound study of Aristotle and St Thomas Aquinas, and his contributions to Aristotelian and Thomistic scholarship are well known. But, as the editor of this volume, Ernest Joós, points out, Régis has above all been a follower of the spirit of these great philosophers of the past and has been particularly concerned to take the point of departure for his own philosophy from the cultural and philosophical preoccupations of our own times. Also in the spirit of Aquinas and Aristotle, however, he is no historical relativist and has looked to modern preoccupations in order to make a critical examination of their presuppositions. This critical examination tends to raise fundamental metaphysical questions that have not always been welcome to all modern philosophers. The scholastic method, as it were, of Régis does not, though, conclude with the dogmatic pronouncement of metaphysical doctrine against which all modern thought is found wanting. His emphasis is on the comprehension and understanding of modern positions that can result from a continuing critical comparison of metaphysical presuppositions. This methodological point of view is implied in the contrast between, indeed delicate balancing of, *certitude et recherche*, as indicated in the title of this collection of essays.

As the editor remarks, the contributions to the volume are written in much the same spirit as that which characterizes Régis's own work. The title, taken from the contribution of Father Marie-Dominique Chenu OP not only describes the life and work of Régis, but 'il exprime également l'esprit des autres contributions par ce qu'elles ont en commun, la certitude, c'est-à-dire une métaphysique, mais qui est en même temps recherche, car elle revérifie constamment ses présupposés et ses réponses à la lumière des nouvelles découvertes.' These contributors are certainly not members of some rigidly defined school, nor is there a dogmatic metaphysical position running through the book. Rather they, like the philosopher they honour, are concerned to compare modern positions with those of philosophers of the past. The length and scope of the book are modest, but it contains much good scholarship and much good critical metaphysics.

The volume begins with the short piece which contributes to its title, 'Foi: certitude et recherche' by Chenu. Here the tension between *certitude* and *recherche* is considered in an explicitly theological context. This is followed by a contribution from Étienne Gilson. Because of the state of his health when this volume was being planned (indeed he died some time before its appearance) Gilson was unable to contribute a new essay, but he authorized the republication of his appendix to *Being and Some Philosophers*, 'On Some Difficulties of Interpretation,' in which he replied to critical comments that had been made by Régis. The other contributions to the volume are 'Logique et épistémologie du signe chez Aristote et chez les Stoïciens' by Dominique Dubarle, 'Ce qui est (τὸ ὄν) se dit en plusieurs sens' by Louis-Bertrand Geiger, ' "Diversificata in diversis" – Aquinas, In 1 Sent., Prol. 1, 2' by Joseph Owens, 'Être et connaître: l'irréductibilité de l'aristotélisme au platonisme' by Venant Cauchy, 'Maurice Merleau-Ponty: de l' "*intentio intellectus*" à l' "*intentio rei*," ou de la phénoménologie à la métaphysique' by Ernest Joós, and 'Pour une démystification de la "mort-de-Dieu" nietzschéenne' by Charles Murin. Joós follows these essays with what he calls 'Post-scriptum: la nouvelle scolastique de Louis-Marie Régis,' in which he provides a critical appreciation of Régis's point of view and philosophical methodology as it is expressed in his most recent work. The postscript is not quite the end, however. Next we have 'Louis-Marie Régis. O.P.: Quelques dates et faits marquants de sa vie' by Albert-M. Landry. This includes both biographical notes and a comprehensive, chronologically ordered bibliography of Régis's publications. Finally, the editor reprints a letter of appreciation to Louis-Marie Régis from Henri-Irénée Marrou, written at the time (1949) of Régis's contribution to the series *Conférences Albert-le-Grand*, sponsored by the Institut d'études médiévales in Montreal, where Régis was then director and Marrou visiting professor. It is an eloquent and warmly human tribute to Régis and provides a fitting conclusion for the book.

As the titles of the individual essays indicate, many of them are about problems in ancient and medieval philosophy, which is particularly appropriate for this volume. Again, as is obvious from the titles, there are essays primarily devoted to aspects of the thought of Nietzsche and Merleau-Ponty, who for better or worse are not usually regarded as central figures by contemporary English-speaking philosophers. Although the contributors to this volume do not and could not represent the full range of interests of contemporary French-speaking philosophers, it will be interesting for English-speaking scholars to note the sorts of comparisons made in many of the more historical essays. One sees little sign of Wittgenstein and Russell, let alone Ryle, Strawson, Quine, Chomsky, or Kripke; rather there are comparisons with Hegel, Heidegger, Foucault, etc. Thus, a reading of this collection might also make a contribution to bicultural philosophic understanding. It is in many ways an interesting book and a worthy tribute to Father Régis. (JOHN A. TRENTMAN)

Georges Hélal. *La Philosophie comme panphysique: la philosophie des sciences de A.N. Whitehead*
Bellarmin 1979. 270. $11.95

This is a well-organized, carefully documented exposition and criticism of A.N. Whitehead's philosophy of nature (or alternatively his philosophy of science). Professor Hélal is concerned to discuss not only the structure of Whitehead's thought but also its intent. In introducing critical material the author reminds us that Whitehead himself, for example, in the preface of *The Principles of Natural Knowledge*, admits numerous defects.

Effective introductory and concluding sections add greatly to the value of this book. Each chapter is set out with useful subheadings and a perceptive summary conclusion. The book provides a serviceable bibliography and an adequate index. There is a tendency to quote rather extensively. This involves, on occasion, repetition, which can, perhaps, be justified on the basis of clarification and emphasis.

Hélal contends that Whitehead's philosophy, in general, can be understood in terms of three fundamental principles (or characteristics of thought). These are: 1 / Emphasis on (tendency to) empiricism; 2 / concern for the achievement of a unified intellectual grasp of the world; and 3 / emphasis on subjectivity. He is well aware of Whitehead's contention, in his 'philosophy of science' period, that nature is closed to mind – in the sense that mental activities are not to be considered as part of, or contributory to, the phenomena of nature. Thus the subjectivity principle is not directly or decisively involved in Whitehead's philosophy of nature. However, in considering epistemological problems and in his discussion of the 'bifurcation of nature,' there is reference to the importance of mental activity (subjectivity). Indeed, implicit in Whitehead's position is the assumption that, even if nature is an objective fact, it is known by a mental (subjectivistic) process. In any case, in Whitehead's metaphysics (from *Science and the Modern World*, through *Process and Reality* and *Adventures of Ideas*, and subsequently) one is confronted by a thoroughly subjectivistic approach to the universe, indeed to the world of nature (as well as by a strong empirical emphasis and a vigorous concern to achieve a unified world view through carefully honed intellectually effective categories). All this Hélal states in his introduction and elsewhere throughout the book.

However, despite considerable background discussion, the main concern of this book, as its title indicates, is with Whitehead's philosophy of science (philosophy of nature). Having pointed out why, in his opinion, Whitehead was interested in such issues, Hélal provides an informed discussion of Whitehead's treatment of them. It is relevant to note that the most extensive of his five chapters (in his 248 pages of text), namely chapters 3 and 4, deal with 'L'unité intelligible du donné empirique: les données de la nature' (60 pages) and 'L'unité intelligible du donné empirique: l'abstraction extensive' (84 pages). Specifically the treatment of events and objects is thorough. His discussion of extensive abstraction, and the application of this concept (technique) to mathematical and scientific problems, is very extensive. Indeed it might be objected that, on occasion, he allows himself to be 'lured away' into excessive discussion of some very technical details of Whitehead's philosophy of science, thus endangering the balance of his book (consider, for example, his extensive comments on the concept of 'rect'). Worthy of special favourable note is his incisive discussion of the 'bifurcation of nature' theme in chapter 5.

In general, Hélal is competent and sagacious in his use of the history of science and of philosophy. He has benefited from contemporary Whitehead studies. This book will repay careful attention. (A.H. JOHNSON)

Donald Evans. *Faith, Authenticity, and Morality*
University of Toronto Press. xiii, 298. $25.00

There's something for every student of religion in this book. Evans has collected five essays originally published between 1971 and 1977 in various journals and anthologies ranging from *Religious Studies* to the *American Journal of Jurisprudence* to *Faith and the Contemporary Epistemologies*, and has added some new material as well in an introduction, a concluding chapter, and in introductory remarks and postscripts to each of the five essays.

The topics range widely. There is material on religious language which extends and provides wholesale revision to the angle of approach of Evans's *The Logic of Self-Involvement*. There is a chapter each on an interpretive exposition of Ian Ramsey's theory of transcendence, on Sam Keen's ethics of being, and on Gregory Baum's theory of liberation and faith. In these three chapters Evans's focus is on constructing a theology from a theory of human nature. Following the chapter on Baum Evans critically examines Paul Ramsey's defence of exceptionless moral rules, conceding that there are 'virtually exceptionless moral rules' but arguing that their foundation must be on a theory of love which is more open and creative than the fidelity-love of Paul Ramsey's therefore unhealthily narrow account. This is followed by an explanatory presentation of the new creed authorized by the United Church of Canada for use in congregational worship. Evans speaks with double authority here, having been a member of the committee which drafted the creed. However, his account is not limited to exposition. Evans also provides a postscript to the chapter in which he makes an about-face on four views expressed in the body of the chapter, including the notion that appeal to the authority of tradition and scripture is the main basis for accepting an 'onlook' such as 'I look on people as brothers and sisters for whom Christ died.' Instead, Evans argues in his revised view that the proper justification of an 'onlook' is given in the degree to which the onlook facilitates discernments of the divine and the degree to which it contributes to human fulfillment. The book closes with a discussion of the shifts in viewpoint which Evans has had since *The Logic of Self-Involvement*. His central argument here is an attempt to articulate what must be counted – despite the wide array of subject-matter – as the central thread of the book: that a cosmic stance or basic attitude towards the world, for example, trust, commits one to a belief in God.

Since the latter argument articulates the core position of the book not only in the sense that it serves as the linking theme of the chapters – having had the ground prepared for it in the first chapter, having been brought out into the open in the three chapters on theological anthropology, having been tacitly re-introduced in the postscript to the chapter on the creed, and having been given stage centre in the ultimate chapter – but more importantly in the sense that without the soundness of this position the subject-matter of the debates will appear foundationless, I shall attempt, however briefly, to comment on it here.

There are two aspects to the argument. One is the argument itself which states 1 / that having an attitude of basic trust is a necessary condition of human fulfilment, and 2 / that basic trust entails belief in God. The other is a metatheory of language and attitude which infuses the argument.

According to the metatheory there are two theories of language use. The *objectivist* holds that 'meaning is best expressed in language which can be correctly understood in a neutral, impersonal way, and truth is best understood by a disinterested, detached observer' (p 22). According to the *existentialist*, however, 'a specific kind of self-involvement is a prerequisite for understanding what is being said and for discovering the truth' (p 22). Martin Buber, for example, is an existentialist because he held that one cannot understand I-Thou relations without having experienced I-Thou attitudes. Evans goes on to make one or two other explanatory remarks concerning this distinction which are not likely to make the distinction any more rigorous than the Buber example. But he does, in a footnote, refer his reader to his 'Faith and Belief' (*Religious Studies*, 10 [1974]) for 'an extensive discussion' of existential versus non-existential beliefs. In 'Faith and Belief' Evans defines an existential belief as one which can't be understood by one who doesn't have certain deep and authentic commitments, attitudes, and life-experiences.

I find the language here unhelpful, for it suggests that only existentialist beliefs cannot be understood without the having of profound attitudes. ('A non-existential belief is one which has no such conditions for understanding,' p 250, here.) All in all, Evans has not given us the wherewithal to distinguish between the following:

1 An existentialist is one who holds that the use of self-involved language is crucial to getting at the truth about the cosmos and the human place in it.
2 An existentialist is one who holds beliefs which can't be understood unless one has had one of a more or less fixed set of experiences including prominently an experience of facing resolutely the meaningless absurdity of the cosmos, experiencing I-Thou attitudes, and experiences of profound exaltation, awe, and wonder.
3 An existentialist is one who holds beliefs which can't be understood unless one has experienced basic, profound, and non-universally experienced attitudes underlying the belief.

It is not at all clear that these are mutually reinforcing senses. Senses 2 and 3 would produce very different lists of existentialists, and since 1 defines a meta-existentialist, the cogency of whose position is dependent on the cogency of either 2 or 3, the two interpretations of it would also produce different lists of existentialists. For example, the Buddhist whose beliefs concerning desire as the cause of suffering stem from an attitude of thoroughgoing detachment would be an existentialist in sense 3. But he would have a belief whose underlying attitude is the very opposite of the type of involvement characteristic of the paradigms of sense 2.

Perhaps the most disturbing aspect of this section of the argument is that it ignores the common truth that the cynic is as much involved in his superiority as the timid is involved in his deference. Similarly, the emotional 'observer' is as much involved in his neutrality as the emotional participant is involved in his community, and the judge can have as much at stake in guarding his unprejudiced neutrality as the defendant can have in establishing his innocence. We are all participants in our stances and attitudes, and so it is difficult to see how the existentialist can be defined in terms of his self-involvement. To make this point in the way most relevant to the theory of religion, the links from neutrality to non-attachment, to contemplation, to joyous union are stronger than Evans's distinction allows for.

In the last analysis, then, the burden of the argument falls on the two notions that basic trust is a constituent of human fulfilment and that basic trust entails belief in God. Of these two notions, the first is treated in detail in Evans's *Struggle and Fulfilment*. It is the second which receives articulation here.

Evans holds that every attitude entails the belief that the focus of the attitude exists. He concedes that some emotions are relatively focusless, for example, joy and elation. Evans denies, however, that basic trust or thankfulness for one's existence is similarly focusless. If one feels gratitude towards the cosmos for one's existence, for example, then one is committed to the belief in a focus appropriate to the feeling of gratitude, and that belief will be tantamount to a belief in Providence.

There are really two claims involved in this. The first concerns the separability of feelings and beliefs. The second is about the sort of focus appropriate to emotions like cosmic gratitude. On what is apparently a reference to the question of separability, Evans simply states 'that the feeling of cosmic thankfulness is "like the feeling of thankfulness minus the belief that someone has done us a good turn" ... is not an intelligible notion' (p 254). He goes on immediately to state that 'any attitude – and any feeling which includes an attitude – implies a belief that the focus of the attitude exists.' The latter statement is true, but does not justify the first – since the character of the focus is what is at stake in the first statement but only the existence of some focus is what is established in the second statement. So, despite the door-opening remark on the separability question, Evans relies exclusively on his discussion of the sort of focus appropriate to attitudes like cosmic gratitude and basic trust.

Gratitude is traditionally analysed by theorists of the emotions as a feeling of benefit with the attribution of responsibility for receiving the benefit to some focus outside of the self. Three elements in the feeling of gratitude, then, are the joy of the benefit, the consciousness that one is not oneself responsible for the benefit, and the attribution of responsibility to some focus outside of the self. If one were to grant for the sake of argument that having the feeling comprising those three elements entails belief in the existence of a focus who is a responsible agent, it would follow that one who has that feeling towards the cosmos would be committed to a belief in something tantamount to Providence. But what about having the feeling which comprises only the first two of those three elements? I'm not sure that such a feeling is full-fledged gratitude, but I wouldn't be the slightest bit surprised to find someone saying 'I feel gratitude towards the cosmos for my existence, but I don't see that that feeling entails belief in a providential cosmic agent,' and mean thereby that in the gratitude he feels there is so little of the third element mentioned above that the belief in the existence of an agent responsible for his benefit does not follow. Indeed, he might go on to describe his feeling of gratitude as comprising a feeling of joy of benefit, consciousness of not being responsible for the benefit, and a belief that no such responsible agent exists. Of course we can be linguistically hard-nosed and refuse to allow him to call his feeling 'gratitude.' But that wouldn't help show that having a basic attitude of cosmic *gratitude manquée* entails a belief in the existence of a responsible agent doing good work in the cosmos at large, nor that the difference between full-fledged cosmic gratitude and cosmic *gratitude manquée* is so significant as to warrant his conclusion in a meaningful way.

And the same argument holds for basic trust. Indeed, Evans agrees that basic trust *simpliciter* does not entail belief in a God: the focus of basic trust might be nature, for example. So Evans only purports to show that one can decide that one's prelinguistic experience of basic trust is most appropriately articulated in such a way that it entails a providential focus (and decide to behave in an appropriate way, for example, worship). One can also decide that one's prelinguistic experience of basic trust is most appropriately articulated in such a way that it entails no providential focus. Evans avers in the chapter on Keen that if one holds the cosmic reality to be trustworthy in the sense that it can be relied on for the security and meaning and integrity of human life, one has a cosmic conviction 'which is very close to traditional religious belief in divine Providence' (p 93). Close, perhaps. But isn't an important distinguishing feature whether or not one attributes responsible agency to the cosmic focus for the achievability of meaning in one's life?

So one can only be in wholehearted agreement with Evans when he states in the last paragraph of the book: 'Some people who are professed theists are dominated by distrust at a pre-linguistic level, and others who are professed atheists are profoundly trustful at that level' (p 263). And I trust that there will be further installments on the 'neo-Kantian anthropological-logical argument' to augment what we have so far received.

Substantive debates aside, though, the book is stimulating throughout and moves masterfully through its topics. Every serious student of religion will find much food for thought in it. I have some quibbles with the structure of the book, however. Too frequently one reads through a chapter to find Evans having changed his mind in the postscript to the chapter or in the last chapter of the book, and keeping track of all the positions can be trying.   (LEONARD ANGEL)

Les Etudes sociales

CÉLINE SAINT-PIERRE

Deux anthropologues québécois, Sylvie Vincent et Bernard Arcand, viennent de publier un livre important aux éditions Hurtubise HMH intitulé *L'Image de l'Amérindien dans les manuels scolaires du Québec*, (collection Cahiers du Québec, 334, $13.95). Au Québec plusieurs travaux ont, depuis quelques années, mis en relief l'image de la femme et celle du Canadien français dans les manuels d'enseignement à l'école primaire et secondaire et la recherche de Vincent et Arcand vient compléter l'analyse de l'idéologie qui se dégage des manuels scolaires lorsqu'il s'agit de décrire les minorités. L'étude que les auteurs ont menée leur permet de démontrer que la seule place octroyée aux autochtones dans les manuels, est celle qu'ils occupent dans leurs relations avec les Blancs. Ils y sont marginalisés et les caractéristiques qui leur sont attribuées sont totalement négatives, ce qui a comme fonction de justifier la façon dont les Blancs les considèrent, les exploitent et les dépossèdent. Si l'un des buts de l'étude est de dégager l'image spécifique de l'Amérindien que tracent les manuels scolaires, il en est un autre tout aussi important qui consiste à vérifier 'si l'image véhiculée par les manuels scolaires risque d'inculquer aux enfants des préjugés envers les Amérindiens et dans quelle mesure cette image toute faite est négative, ce qui risquerait de préparer ces enfants au racisme et à la discrimination.'

L'étude porte sur l'ensemble des manuels scolaires approuvés par le Ministère de l'éducation du Québec et susceptibles de parler des Amérindiens ou des Inuits, soit 105 manuels. En ce qui concerne la méthode de traitement des données, les auteurs ont rejeté l'analyse statistique et l'analyse linguistique pour des raisons qu'ils nous expliquent dans leur introduction; ils s'en remettent à une analyse de contenu du discours qui tente d'en dégager son véritable sens par une mise à jour 'de l'ensemble des relations liant chacun de ses divers éléments.' Cette méthode inspirée de l'anthropologie structurale et de certaines études récentes en sémiologie exige que soit faite une place importante à l'intuition des analystes. Les cinq premiers chapitres du livre ont été structurés sur la base de thèmes construits à partir des caractéristiques générales qui se retrouvent dans les manuels d'histoire à propos des Amérindiens; ainsi ceux-ci se révèlent hostiles, généreux, maniables et autonomes. Les quatre chapitres suivants traitent de la position de ces mêmes manuels sur la culture, le primitivisme, le génocide et la question des droits territoriaux. Dans leur recherche, les auteurs ont constaté l'extrême pauvreté des informations concernant les Inuits et les Métis comparativement aux Amérindiens et pour ces raisons ils ont décidé de leur consacrer deux chapitres en particulier, les autres chapitres traitant de ces derniers.

Etant donnée la méthode choisie, cela explique pourquoi les auteurs ont dû inclure dans leur analyse une bonne partie de leur matériel, ce qui a eu comme conséquence d'allonger considérablement le texte et d'en faire un livre passablement long. C'est aussi ce qui fait sa richesse, car elle permet aux lecteurs de faire la vérification des conclusions formulées par les auteurs. Ce pourrait être aussi un outil précieux pour les enseignants qui ont à utiliser ces manuels et qui pourront dès lors enrichir leur enseignement et enrayer ainsi l'efficacité du discours produit par ces manuels sur la réalité amérindienne auprès de nos enfants. Ce livre est très riche par le matériel qu'il analyse, très important par les questions qu'il explore et très inquiétant par les conclusions qui s'en dégagent.

Toujours aux éditions Hurtubise HMH, paraît dans la collection des Cahiers du Québec, un livre de Jacques Rivet intitulé *Grammaire du journal politique* (350, $18.95). Tout comme le livre dont nous venons de parler, celui-ci a aussi comme objet de décoder, de décrypter à travers l'analyse de d'autres textes, soit, dans le cas présent, des textes de presse, le contenu et les orientations politiques qui les marquent. De moins en moins, comme l'auteur tentera de le démontrer, l'écriture journalistique n'est laissée au hasard de l'inspiration, laquelle fait place à des mécanismes standardisés qui s'érigent en un système d'écriture plutôt rigoureux. Il y a des règles d'écriture que se doivent de connaître les journalistes s'ils veulent survivre dans l'équipe de rédaction d'un journal. Selon l'auteur, 'l'activité de presse invente au jour le jour une écriture grammaticale qui lui est spécifique.' Le texte de presse est un langage qui met en action la parole du journaliste, ses sources et souvent ses lecteurs. Ce qui me semble fort original dans l'étude que fait Jacques Rivet c'est de montrer comment un journal, s'il est un instrument de persuasion, fonctionne aussi au niveau de son argumentation comme producteur d'indices qui guident les journalistes dans l'exercice de leur métier. Si l'écriture de presse est presque toujours une 'réécriture' à partir d'un traitement d'informations déjà organisées par des agences de presse, le journaliste doit donc dorénavant travailler à partir de textes déjà construits et il se doit de leur poser toutes les questions. Il doit recourir pour ce faire aux techniques documentaires de traitement de l'information. Là-dessus les écoles de journalisme ont élaboré et enseigné des techniques d'écriture qui se constituent en véritables règles syntaxiques du langage du journal. C'est donc à la construction de cette grammaire journalistique que s'est attaqué l'auteur à travers une analyse quotidienne de deux journaux politiques: *Le Devoir* et *Le Jour* durant la période allant de 1er janvier au 1er novembre 1974. Le matériel sur lequel porte l'étude est composé des titres et des *leads* des articles contenus dans ces deux journaux pendant cette période, l'objectif de l'auteur étant de faire un inventaire des faits d'écriture et de saisir les formes de l'expression politique de la presse quotidienne. Il s'agit donc de dégager des contenus de presse le rôle politique d'une publication. Tout le contenu du journal a été prélevé aux fins de cette recherche à l'exception de l'information sportive, boursière, artistique et de l'information internationale qui n'impliquait pas le Québec et le Canada. L'auteur nous explique la méthode qu'il a suivie pour compiler ce matériel, méthode que nous sommes à même de voir à l'œuvre tout au long des chapitres qui composent ce livre. A l'aide de cette méthode, l'auteur analyse les éditoriaux et les éditorialistes, puis l'écriture de presse et la déontologie du journal et du journaliste, le journal producteur d'un message global, la matière politique du journal et enfin le journal comme acte politique; il propose dans un chapitre final une définition du contrôle politique exercé dans et par l'écriture journalistique. Ce livre est fort impressionnant de par la méthode qu'il propose pour produire le questionnement du rôle politique des journaux et du journal comme acteur politique. L'auteur rend accessible aux lecteurs les outils qui lui ont permis de procéder à son travail d'enquête et d'analyse et c'est là un de ses points forts. Le peu de recherches réalisées au Québec sur le sujet fait de ce livre une étape importante dans la connaissance de la structure et du rôle politique des journaux que nous lisons chaque jour.

Depuis une quinzaine d'années, on a vu se multiplier les campagnes de sensibilisation pour la sauvegarde et la conservation du patrimoine québécois. Parallèlement, l'archéologie a connu au Québec une expansion importante et c'est pour faire état de cette discipline que René Lévesque (archéologue et professeur à l'Université Laval) a préparé et publié un livre intitulé *Initiation à l'archéologie* chez Leméac (385, $19.95). Son but étant de démocratiser l'accessibilité à cette science, le livre en est un de vulgarisation et il pourra ainsi permettre à des amateurs sérieux de systématiser leurs connaissances acquises par la voie de l'expérience. Le texte est construit comme un manuel d'enseignement. Chaque chapitre est précédé d'un plan de l'exposé, illustré de photos et de dessins, et il se termine par un questionnaire détaillé sur la matière du chapitre qui vient d'être présentée. Une bonne bibliographie ainsi qu'un lexique de l'ensemble des termes spécialisés qui forment le vocabulaire de l'archéologue sont présentés en annexes du livre. Lévesque pose dans son étude la question des origines de l'homme d'Amérique et décrit les diverses phases de l'évolution de cet *Homo quebequensis*: Paléo-Indiens, Archaïques, Sylvicoles, Esquimoïdes. Les deux derniers chapitres portent sur la méthode à suivre pour procéder à l'inventaire des sites et à leur fouille. Dans ce livre, l'auteur a su transmettre le fruit de son expérience et il a su la traduire dans un cheminement fort bien conçu pédagogiquement.

Je me dois de souligner la réédition d'un livre fort important sur le mouvement ouvrier québécois. Il s'agit d'un ensemble de textes écrits par divers auteurs et réunis par le sociologue Fernand Harvey, sous le titre *Le Mouvement ouvrier au Québec* (Boréal Express, 330, $12.95). La première édition portait un titre un peu différent, *Aspects historiques du mouvement ouvrier au Québec*, et elle est maintenant épuisée. Les textes rassemblés dans la seconde édition sont fort différents dans l'ensemble de ceux inclus dans le première. Pour construire son livre, l'auteur a utilisé une approche thématique plutôt que chronologique tout en se préoccupant cependant de choisir des textes qui couvrent différentes périodes du 19e et du 20e siècles. Le livre s'ouvre sur un texte de Harvey dans lequel il fait état de la recherche sur le mouvement ouvrier au Québec. Pour lui, trois facteurs principaux expliquent l'émergence depuis une quinzaine d'années des études sur l'histoire des travailleurs: 'l'évolution historique du Québec moderne, l'essor de l'histoire sociale et la conjoncture des années 1970.' Deux chapitres portent chacun sur l'analyse de deux grèves importantes qui ont marqué l'histoire du mouvement ouvrier au Québec, soit la grève des charretiers de Montréal en 1864 et la grève de l'amiante en 1949. L'influence américaine sur la constitution et les orientations du syndicalisme au Québec est abordée dans deux chapitres dont l'un porte sur les Chevaliers du travail et leur implantation au Québec, et l'autre sur Samuel Gompers et les travailleurs québécois de 1900 à 1914. Sur cette même période, nous retrouvons un article de Jacques Rouillard sur l'action politique ouvrière au début du 20e siècle. Deux autres chapitres posent le problème du développement historique du mouvement ouvrier: il s'agit de l'étude de Jacques Dofny et Paul Bernard sur 'L'Évolution historique du syndicalisme au Québec' et celle d'Hélène David sur 'L'Étude des rapports de classe au Québec de 1945 à 1967.' Un article de Louis-Marie Tremblay analyse 'L'Influence extragène en matière de direction syndicale,' alors que le livre se clôt par un texte de Jean Boivin sur 'Les Règles du jeu et rapport de force dans les secteurs public et para-public québécois.' C'est un livre bourré d'informations; il présente en même temps une série d'analyses sur les orientations et la pratique du mouvement ouvrier, analyses qui ne sont pas toutes convergentes dans leur approche et leur diagnostic, ce qui ajoute à l'intérêt du livre.

Toujours dans le cadre de l'histoire du mouvement ouvrier, paraît chez Leméac, une monographie écrite par Raymond Boily sur *Les Irlandais et le canal Lachine* (270, $13.95). Cette étude porte plus particulièrement sur la grève de 1843 à laquelle des historiens accordent une grande importance pour la compréhension de cette période de constitution du mouvement ouvrier. Son objectif est donc de rendre compte des événements qui se sont déroulés en 1843 sur les chantiers de Beauharnois et de Lachine. Il faut rappeler qu'à cette époque, 3,000 ouvriers travaillaient à la construction des canaux de navigation afin d'aménager les eaux du Saint-Laurent et les rendre navigables. La plupart de ces ouvriers sont

Irlandais, catholiques et protestants, et une minorité est composée d'autochtones. En plus d'être divisés entre eux, ces travailleurs illettrés, déracinés, inorganisés, seront l'objet d'une exploitation très forte de la part de leurs employeurs. Vers 1842, une prise de conscience se développe chez les travailleurs et ils formulent des revendications qui les mèneront à des affrontements avec leurs employeurs, affrontements qui se transformeront en émeutes sanglantes en juin 1843. Ce sont sur ces événements plus particuliers que l'auteur fait porter son étude composée de trois parties: '1) le déroulement chronologique des événements; 2) les témoignages recueillis par les commissaires chargés d'enquêter sur les émeutes du mois de juin 1843; 3) le rapport des enquêteurs.' Sa recherche est très fouillée et présente beaucoup de données brutes. Des extraits de documents sont reproduits ainsi que des desseins illustrant certains faits et situations rattachés à ces événements. Ce livre tire sa valeur surtout de l'énorme travail accompli par l'auteur pour colliger les archives et mettre en relief les documents les plus significatifs. Cette façon de présenter le matériel sur lequel il s'appuie pour reconstituer l'histoire de la grève de 1843, permet en même temps aux lecteurs de voir de plus près l'état de la condition ouvrière de cette époque et le jeu des rapports de classe. Il est à souhaiter que des monographies comme celle-ci se multiplient car elles permettent de découvrir les dessous d'une histoire, celle des travailleurs, et d'une période, le 19e siècle, encore malheureusement beaucoup trop méconnues encore aujourd'hui.

Dans une période où la question centrale qui se pose au Québec est celle de son identité nationale et de sa place dans la société canadienne, André Patry, politicologue bien connu, publie chez Leméac un livre intitulé *Le Québec dans le monde* (167, $8.95). Sa question principale l'amène à étudier l'évolution des relations internationales du Québec, à situer les intervenants qui ont tenté de modifier l'image du Québec sur la scène politique ou diplomatique et à évaluer les résultats de leurs efforts. L'auteur, cependant, ne veut pas dans ce livre faire une histoire des relations internationales du Québec. Il veut surtout rendre compte des faits dont il a été témoin au cours des quatre dernières décennies. Dans un premier chapitre, l'auteur rappelle un certain nombre d'événements qui ont fait de la ville de Québec une ville internationale; il cite à titre d'exemple des événements survenus entre 1943 et 1945 tels le séjour des Habsbourg, les conférences au sommet entre le président Roosevelt et le premier ministre Winston Churchill, la Conférence des Nations-Unies et l'affaire des trésors polonais. Puis dans le chapitre suivant, il aborde l'attitude des Québécois face aux affaires internationales. Depuis l'Union, les journaux relatent les grands événements qui marquent l'histoire de l'Europe. Puis, peu à peu, à la faveur de l'isolement des Québécois vis-à-vis de l'Europe pendant la Deuxième Guerre, ceux-ci se tournent vers l'Amérique latine et vers Haïti. Après la Deuxième Guerre, les relations du Québec avec l'Europe vont reprendre, notamment avec la France, et elles iront en s'accentuant surtout après 1960.

La majeure partie du livre est consacrée à l'analyse de la période de 1960 à 1979. Dans cette partie, l'auteur relate les principaux événements qui marquent la politique en matière de relations internationales des gouvernements québécois qui se succèdent. Il raconte avec maints détails la forme prise par les relations que le Québec va entretenir avec les pays d'Europe de l'Ouest et plus particulièrement avec la France, l'Angleterre et l'Italie. Il y fait état aussi des efforts que le Québec va déployer pour se faire reconnaître auprès des organismes internationaux tels l'UNESCO. Le livre se termine sur la période qui a débuté avec l'élection du Parti québécois en 1976; celui-ci va tenter, comme on le sait, de faire reconnaître le Québec sur le plan international comme s'il s'agissait d'un état pleinement souverain. Dans l'ensemble, ce livre trouve son intérêt dans le sujet qu'il aborde et dans le fait qu'il se présente comme l'une des premières historiographies traitant des relations internationales du Québec depuis la Seconde Guerre mondiale.

Les enseignants en cette année 1980 n'ont pas été laissés pour compte par les diverses maisons d'éditions. En effet, plusieurs anthologies regroupant des textes inédits, des articles, des chapitres de livres déjà publiés ailleurs sont parues. A titre d'exemple, je donnerai celle qu'a publiée Boréal Express, *Le Québec en textes* (566, $18.50) et dont les auteurs – c'est-à-dire dans le cas présent, ceux à qui revient le mérite d'avoir rassemblés et colligés les différents textes qui composent le livre – sont Gérard Boismenu, Laurent Mailhot et Jacques Rouillard. Il a été conçu plus particulièrement pour répondre aux besoins d'un programme d'enseignement dispensé à la Faculté des arts et des sciences de l'Université de Montréal, le programme de 'mineur en Etudes québécoises.' Cependant il répondra, j'en suis sûre, à des besoins de d'autres programmes. Les auteurs écrivent que 'ce recueil de textes a été conçu pour offrir une vue générale des rapports sociaux dans toutes les sphères d'activité au Québec depuis la deuxième guerre mondiale.' Ceux qui ont mis en forme cette anthologie nous disent qu'ils ont puisé dans des textes de tout genre pour retenir 'des extraits d'analyse, de récits, de créations artistiques et de contributions diverses, dont les auteurs sont presque tous du Québec.' Les textes sont distribués selon deux périodes: celle de 1940–60 et celle de 1960–80, et c'est à travers eux que l'histoire du Québec est reconstituée. Chaque texte reproduit est précédé d'un court paragraphe dans lequel est résumé l'idée majeure ou l'objectif poursuivi par les auteurs choisis. Ce résumé trop court s'avère d'autant plus nécessaire que, dans la grande majorité des cas, les textes reproduits ne le sont pas complètement mais sous forme d'extraits seulement. Si l'on arrive à saisir assez bien les principes qui ont guidé les auteurs de l'anthologie dans le choix des textes du recueil, on réussit moins bien à comprendre sur quoi ils se sont fondés pour découper les extraits des textes retenus. C'est là, à mon avis, la faiblesse d'un outil si riche en documents de toutes sortes. Il est difficile de saisir la portée de textes ainsi amputés d'une bonne partie de leur contenu, difficile de les expliquer à des étudiants ou à des non-familiers puisque, très souvent, les questions de départ qui ont servi à les produire n'y sont pas intégrées, pas plus que les conclusions. Les lecteurs risquent souvent de faire fausse route dans leur réflexion s'ils se limitent à la lecture de ces seuls extraits. C'est pourquoi, pour trouver toute son efficacité, ce livre ne peut pas, à mon avis, être utilisé indépendamment, isolément, d'une démarche d'ensemble sur l'histoire du Québec. Cette démarche peut se faire dans un cours mais aussi par le biais d'un recours à d'autres sources permettant de recréer le contexte global de ces quatre décennies.

Religion

EMERO STIEGMAN

Certain topics in religion can command our attention only when those who write about them have established their credentials. What has long been ardently discussed tends to become the banner or the target of complacent partisans and, to the same extent, both the boredom of the disengaged and the despair of that faith which seeks understanding and respects information. Papal power is such a topic. With appropriate suspicion we ask why the writer is interested in the subject. Have not both Roman Catholic descriptive accounts and opposing versions been routine exercises in denominational apologetics? Jean-Guy Vaillancourt, a Université de Montréal sociologist, is in an unusually strong position to draw a new quality of attention to his subject, *Papal Power: A Study of Vatican Control over Lay Catholic Elites* (University of California Press, xiv, 361, $16.95).

Vaillancourt, after three years as a student of sociology in Rome, obtained in 1966 over a hundred interviews with Catholic lay leaders in France. The following year, in order to study the composition of the delegates to the Third World Congress for the Lay Apostolate to be held in Rome, he developed a questionnaire. This was tested at the April 1967 Congress of the National Council of Catholic Men in Pittsburgh, refined, and translated from the English and French originals with the help of German and Spanish sociologists into these other two official languages of the World Congress later held in Rome. In 1972, as a journalist for Radio-Canada, the author accompanied Pope Paul vi during his trip around the world. With this kind of preparation he began a study, not only of relevant materials available in libraries, but also and especially of documentary materials obtained from two Vatican agencies, the Permanent Committee for International Congresses of the Lay Apostolate and the Council on the Laity. This unusually extensive work matured finally under his PH D dissertation mentors at the University of California in Berkeley. One may presume that Vaillancourt has something to say.

Dismiss all fears of the rewritten doctoral treatise! *Papal Power* is the composition of an experienced journalist. The data is organized into a smooth narrative, simple definitions are attentively supplied, and the documentation is judicious. Think, instead, of the chastening influence of a doctoral-dissertation committee supervising so complex an undertaking as the analysis of Vatican control over the Catholic laity.

The analysis of papal power cannot be grounded exclusively in theology, says Vaillancourt, or in the personality traits of the principal agents in any generation. What is needed is a 'mixture of historical, empirical, and theoretical perspectives,' with an emphasis on cultural and institutional factors, including political and socioeconomic aspects (p 281). Concretely, this means that the study of papal power must undertake, first, to retrace the history both of the papacy and of a lay movement; secondly, to gather data on contemporary Vatican-laity relationships; and thirdly, to offer a cultural and institutional analysis both of the contemporary papacy and of that part of the laity under consideration. The author, accordingly, divides his work into three parts.

Vaillancourt's brief history of Christianity is not seminary fare. He is guided by scholars who, in tracing ecclesiastical evolution, place great weight upon the political and economic factors as they condition the development of institutions – for example, Troeltsch, Weber, Kautsky, Wauch, and Falconi. His end is in his beginning. Yet for each of his views one could find a school of eminent Roman Catholic New Testament scholars and historical theologians in simple agreement. His historical conclusion:

> As the Roman Empire in the West faded from the scene, the Pope became a sort of religious counterpart image of the former emperor ... relegating the lower clergy and the laity to secondary positions ... And as the laity started to build a strong movement that threatened to gain some independence vis-à-vis papal authority, the Vatican used co-optation and condemnation as means of control. (Pp 58–9)

Equally important to the author is the direction of papal control over the laity. He contends that lay Catholic organizations have been viewed by the Vatican 'as extensions of clerical and hierarchical influence in secular society, to be used in the political arena whenever it was advantageous' (p 59). In a separate chapter the author finds examples of this generalization in the first two World Congresses of the Lay Apostolate and in the laity's participation in the Second Vatican Council. He reads these as Vatican attempts to centralize the lay movement the better to remove its control from local bishops.

In the second part of his work Vaillancourt gathers information on present-day power relationships between the Vatican and lay Catholic élites, an expression he uses to designate lay people who as organizational heads are chosen by the Vatican to be representatives. He reviews the issues and events of the Third World Congress for the Lay Apostolate held in 1967, two years after the close of Vatican II. While the first Synod of Bishops, assembled also in Rome and at the same time, was showing itself to function as merely a consultative body to the Vatican, the lay congress openly challenged several of the more conservative ideas of the Pope. The main objectives of the lay delegates were a kind of democratization of the church and a socially engaged and ecumenical Christianity. They requested that an elected body represent them in Rome, and caused a stir by publishing a resolution that the technical means of birth control be left to the consciences of spouses. How the Vatican acted to control this unforeseen outburst is, in precise detail, the heart of Vaillancourt's study. It fell to Cardinal Maurice Roy of Quebec, president of the Ecclesiastical Commission of the Congress, and a prelate of certain liberal credentials, to exercise the heavy restraining hand. 'Most delegates,' says the author, 'were shocked by what they considered to be not only paternalistic clericalism but downright manipulation on the part of the hierarchy' (p 115). The Synod of Bishops addressed a letter of admonition to the laity, and Pope Paul VI expressed his displeasure over the congress. Since then there has been no proposal for a fourth congress.

Who were these 3,000 delegates who so embarrassed the Vatican? They had been considered a tame group of 'official laymen,' well observed before selection, and not expected to challenge the *status quo*. The author's questionnaire distributed at the congress made possible the discovery of several correlates of religious ideology, such as age, religious behaviour, and political ideology. One sample only: 'Sacramentally and ritually active and biblically ignorant laymen,' it was found, 'are more inclined to be ... anti-Communist, favourable to clericalism, Christian institutions, and the Vatican bureaucracy, and closed to religious change ... [and] lay participation and power' (p 164). Though 'sacramentally active,' many delegates were of a moderately liberal political persuasion and had become freer and more critical of church authorities during the pontificate of John XXIII and during the Vatican II years. Besides, thinks Vaillancourt, 'co-optation is not a one-way street' (pp 167–8), and even 'in a token granting of autonomy and participation there will always be some element of the real thing' (p 169).

In the final third of his work the author's analysis of papal power works explicitly from a theoretical neo-Marxist perspective. He demonstrates, I would say, that in operating from an independent Vatican City the papacy has not enjoyed the political and economic autonomy hoped for in such an arrangement, but has suffered grave pressures from Italian politics. These pressures condition its control of the worldwide laity. A careful survey of the pontificate of Paul VI (1963-78) reveals this pope to be not at all the progressive thinker he was once reputed to be. The author's insistence here borders on tedium. Very enlightening is the claim that near-traumatic Vatican reactions to the social and political disturbances of the late sixties account in significant part for the closing of the windows opened by John XXIII. Introducing an exploration of Vatican finances, Vaillancourt assesses Paul's reign as one that went a long way 'to maintain the sacred alliance of church, state, and capital in Italy' (p 245). In the concluding chapter the author works out a new typology of the means of control, making his requisite contribution to social science jargon – perhaps to remind us of what we have escaped in the original dissertation. He traces the evolution of these means as the Vatican has used them through changing times. Attempting an explanation of the phenomena he has described, Vaillancourt writes: 'If the Vatican did not pursue the *aggiornamento* launched by John XXIII, it was because it could not do so without negating and destroying itself' (p 282). Today the Vatican and the local bishops, he thinks, have lost their strong control over the lay movement; they will probably not regain it. 'It is not authority as such which is rejected, but authority exercised as domination rather than as service and love' (p 294).

Vaillancourt's study of papal power is a strikingly informative and persuasive performance in academic sociology and it can make an immense contribution to church reform. The author believes that certain subtle control mechanisms are characteristic of all religious institutions. It is possible to harbour serious doubts about the universal effectiveness of his neo-Marxist perspective and at the same time to perceive with him links between institutional politics and economics and hierarchical control. Besides, his description of power stratagems may be appreciated from other perspectives. As broad as his approach is, I would have found solace time and again in more explicit openings for theological consideration. There are a few allusions to superior religious options omitted in the Vatican conduct of affairs – love rather than domination, or prophecy rather than diplomacy – and the author professes to view the Church 'primarily (*but not only*) as a bureaucratic organization' (p 12); yet some accounts are strained in the search for an explanation that may minimize the obvious religious one. The reason for the unforeseen rebellion of the delegates to the 1967 congress for the laity was multiple, of course; and the liberating work of Vatican II is mentioned, but barely mentioned. This theological share of the explanation would seem to be larger than the author acknowledges. The maintenance of papal power can be accounted for as an instance of institutional self-preservation. But, after centuries of theological defence of their position, are not the popes and the men of the Roman Curia believers in their own case? Marx may need the assistance of some New Testament exegetes here (weak ones) and some curial canonists (strong ones). To the discerning reader, none of this will detract seriously from the work. For all his esteem of his predecessors in the field, Vaillancourt has written the most penetrating book on the Vatican currently available.

Whether it be the Vatican or a minor ecclesiastical institution, every organizational element in the church of the present era tends to be validated in so far as it is a service to that which *is* the church. Rémi Parent, of the Université de Montréal, in *Communion et pluralité dans l'église: pour une pratique de l'unité ecclésiale* (Fides, 262), declares that the church is a dynamic unity among many ecclesial bodies. This volume is number 24 in the series Héritage et projet, which proposes to offer writings both of rigorously precise research and of substantial but readily accessible theology. Fides publishers would do well to include Parent in both categories. His study of the church breaks new ground on a theme of classic difficulty – the conception of the unity of the church in the face of denominationalism and of tensions upon orthodoxy within denominations; and it does so, primarily, without appeal to any radically revisionist history or to recondite currents of philosophy. His disciplined theological manner is uncommonly close to the common-sense critique of the non-professional.

The author calls attention to the lack of love in much talk about the church today. There are two reasons for this, in his view. First, the church generally inhabits the imagination as an exterior reality, something above or to one side of human existence. It seems difficult to think of the church, or to live it, as that which takes part in all that one is and does. Secondly, the church is conceived as static. Ecclesiology has fastened upon one idea too exclusively, the church as definitive accomplishment in Christ. When this is translated as permanance, one views the church as existing in history but not subject to the laws of the historical order. How, then, will people be able to speak of the church in the way they speak of themselves? The gap is too wide, keeping apart the image of the church and the concrete ways according to which believers and communities perceive themselves as historical.

Parent sees the church in the perspective of its unity. To think of this unity, he says, as a communion perfectly accomplished is incorrect. He wishes to make two points. First, the unity of the church is a complex reality. That the church is a mystical communion must, of course, be affirmed as one of its essential dimensions. But, there is another essential element almost massively neglected – pluralism. (By pluralism, *pluralité*, Parent implies no connotations derivative of a liberal social ideology, only the condition of being plural.) The thesis of *Communion et pluralité dans l'église* is that pluralism and communion are, one to the other, conditions of possibility. Pluralism is not an adventitious tragedy in church history; it is an essential condition of unity, since without it the communion in which believers are bonded in the church is not historically possible. To conceive of church unity properly one must not exclude that pluralism which inevitably results when human beings remain true to their historical experiences. (Though Parent's study is not dominantly historical, he would be able to cite the historians' symposium, *The Shaping of Christianity in the Second and Third Centuries*, reviewed below, as a corroborative companion volume.) The second point is that in giving value to pluralism one is led to consider the unity of the church as a practice; one has always to undertake it.

Organizational aspects are not part of the inquiry. Parent addresses the mystery of the church and considers its spiritual structure to be part of that. Institutional reforms which are not guided by a vision of essential structure, he thinks, are futile. They pretend that organization is an object rather than a service.

There are a great many exceedingly rich particulars. The author's discussion of a distinction in Hans Küng's ecclesiology is one of these. Küng asserts that one must see both the essence of the church and its historical face. While accepting this as the valuable highlighting of a neglected polarity, Parent insists that it be made more concrete. What exists concretely is a church in its unity where many Christians and many communities in their pluralism gather so that their coming together may bear witness to the saving unity, or communion, which they receive in Christ. Reflecting further on the 'historical face,' he notes that communion which has ruled out pluralism has tended too much to uniformity; pluralism which has neglected communion has produced division; but a unity perceived as both pluralism and communion issues in the practice of unity as an imperative.

In an extended discussion of how certain exalted conceptions of the church are a denial of our human condition where death rules, Parent reflects upon what he considers unresolved problems of the priesthood among Roman Catholics. Does the church here determine to live in two separate worlds – a heaven of consecrated priests who are super-Christians established in Christ's communion and an earth of the simple faithful who gather to be admitted to a communion which priests control? The author's difficulty is with the conception of the priesthood as a spiritual 'power,' making those who minister 'mediators' between God and humanity.

Communion et pluralité dans l'église will and should provoke discussion. Parent ventures as a theologian with admirable simplicity into areas of ecclesiology littered with dead reputations. For his new thoughts he does not rely upon new data or powerful new allies. His theology is grounded in severe dialectics – a relentless though humanely rounded examination of rejected alternatives – and, above all, in a remarkably sensitive reading of his own religious experience. Theology, he remarks (p 92), never entirely precedes experience. People of faith will revel in the paradox that the insights of systematic ecumenists such as Hans Küng are given their necessary speculative precision and integration in Rémi Parent's spirituality.

A spirituality similarly attuned to earthly realities is found in Jean-Luc Hétu's *Croissance humaine et instinct spirituel: une réflexion sur la croissance humaine à partir de la psychologie existentialiste et de la tradition judéo-chrétienne* (Leméac, 209, $9.95 paper). Hétu, who teaches the psychology of religion at the Université de Montréal, concludes after many years as a psychologist that the close affinities he has perceived between existential psychology and the Judeo-Christian tradition amount to a confirmed hypothesis. He begins by reviewing A. Maslow's study of peak experiences, where an interior religiousness can be contrasted with merely institutional forms. In the preaching of Jesus, says Hétu, we shall find the equivalent of 'peakers' and 'non-peakers' – in the parables of the pearl and of the treasure in the field, in the condemnation of the 'non-peaker' Pharisees. In St Paul these types are represented by the spiritual man and the unspiritual man (e.g., in 1 Cor 2:10–15). The author makes clear that, though psychology should not be understood as diminishing the mystery of God, it can diminish the area of self-delusion and superstition.

The principal theoretical claim of *Croissance humaine* has to do with spiritual instinct. While respecting the gratuity of divine grace, which might be thought inconsistent with the notion of instinct, Hétu insists that a spiritual instinct suggests a continuous function even in the ordinary processes of decision making. Existential psychology attests to such a function and makes possible the delineation of a phenomenology of Christian life. Affirming a spiritual instinct, Hétu can elicit human confidence. He writes: 'L'être humain possède en lui tout ce dont il a besoin pour s'orienter dans son existence d'une façon féconde' (p 191).

The confidence of Christian writers, he thinks, has too frequently derived from a rationalist bias. On the contrary, Jesus underlines our human ambiguities, exhorting us now to have peace and now to put ourselves in question, but always to respect the cyclical movements within the self – 'à laisser la vie émerger à son rythme à elle' (p 112). It is a rationalist fear of the spiritual instinct that Maslow refers to when he speaks of the recoiling from new possibilities as the Jonas complex.

The insights of other existential psychologists are compared to the anthropology and the natural law ethics of Aquinas. The author is impressed by many points of contact, especially in the developmental psychology of Rogers, Erikson, Piaget, Kohlberg, Lowen, and again Maslow. A concluding chapter refutes the accusation of those who associate the human potential movement with a privatizing ethic, one unresponsive to the biblical demand for social justice. Examining Maslow's traits of the socially engaged personality, Hétu observes that considerable maturity is required. Some people's need for a protected growth phase should be respected. Existential psychology does not propose a privatizing middle-class morality.

The author is correct in foreseeing this objection. Others have written about an ultimacy of the self in humanistic psychology and have perceived it to be an alternative to biblical religion. More sensitivity to the issue would have strengthened *Croissance humaine*. In this generation of social drop-outs are Hétu's psychologists a solution or part of the problem? The author wants to identify Christian growth with human growth and feels that the language of those who chart personality development can be appropriated for this purpose. Christian apologetics must take this direction, and it seems an unkind cut to suggest that Christian apologetics is forever in danger of subverting Christianity. I am on Hétu's side in the conviction that the danger must be faced. In his preface Jacques Grand'Maison quips that the author is not afraid to consort with pagans. The evidence of a little fear, actually, would entice me to follow Hétu with more confidence. Two examples only. First, in his study of existential psychology, what he offers as a theological criterion of evaluation is the Judeo-Christian tradition. Whatever Jewish people may feel about allowing Jesus to speak for such a tradition, some Christian theologians will question whether the Jesus of *Croissance humaine* is sufficiently the Christ. He is a teacher, but his death and resurrection are not central to the revelation of what it means to be human. Then there is the question whether the gift of grace can be called a spiritual instinct. Recognizing the theological problem, the author opts for the functional character of instinct (p 56) and brackets the question of origin. It is ironic that this up-to-date attempt at moral practicality lands precisely on what Augustine and, later, the Reformers criticized in some monastic asceticism: it neglects explicit awareness of the gift character of our moral power. A diminished sense of the divine love which empowers the Christian is not a loss merely in the order of theoretical refinements.

But I suspect Hétu has identified a Judeo-Christian audience to whom he offers a needed message. He succeeds admirably in saying that biblical faith enjoins upon its devotees a religious growth which moves, not away from human nature, but within it. The morality that issues from biblical faith has human authenticity.

Donald Evans of the University of Toronto's Department of Philosophy, in *Faith, Authenticity, and Morality* (University of Toronto Press, xiii, 298, $25.00), studies the conjunction of three areas – 'the language and experience of religious faith, the personal and political attitudes which constitute authentic human existence, and the fundamental framework for moral decisions' (p 3). He concludes that certain basic attitudes are the common core of faith, authenticity, and morality. The exposition of this tenet, however convincing and significant, is overwhelmed by a pervasive element of intellectual autobiography. It is a matter of considerable interest when a distinguished author argues his way out of positions for which he has been a spokesman. In this work Evans, the philosopher in the tradition of linguistic analysis, insists that philosophical reflection must be an attempt to articulate prelinguistic experience; and Evans, the ethicist who has evolved a language to express the ethical centrality of a kind of covenant-fidelity, protests that, 'quite apart from the specific convenantal revelation to which the scriptures bear witness' (p 195), human nature itself claims the love which grounds ethical behaviour. Through these and less radical shifts he is enabled to perceive the common core, as he calls it, of the three areas which until now he has had to consider separately. There is special meaning in the change of position; but the attempt to treat each issue in its erstwhile separateness and simultaneously to gather each into an argument does not succeed.

A problem in *Faith, Authenticity, and Morality*, more significant than this loss of focus, is one that may lie more in the bias of academics than in the general reader. Evans claims he is working in three branches of philosophy; but, in the training of most scholars today, he is working in three matching branches of theology as well and resolutely ignoring the difference. This fact does not argue the writer wrong, but it may account for certain unnecessary confusions in the reader. In fact, it may be the reason that many, to their own loss, will not read him, and that some others will fail to recognize the merit of his work.

Before Evans is summoned to the bar by philosophers or theologians, it can be hoped that both will ask whether they have anything to oppose him with that escapes proof by definition. The conviction that philosophy and theology have a common subject-matter and should be equated as competing historical, rational belief systems has been held by some eminent thinkers – for example, Troeltsch, Royce, H.R. Niebuhr, and Berdyaev. I have, myself, been uncomfortable (after the counsel of Aquinas) with that view; but I must concede that human authenticity, as the centre of the author's three-part problem, would seem to commend it. In fact, while highly recommending *Faith, Authenticity, and Morality*, I find myself amused at the fantasy of the methodological purists' annoyance. Does not the author fail to notice how his mentor, Ian Ramsey, continuously 'confuses' the idea-deduction of God with the experience-gift of faith? *Real* philosophers and *real* theologians may look with either embarrassment or condescension upon Evans the linguistic analyst blooded in the rediscovery that experience might be the subject-matter of philosophy; but as they read him they may themselves discover that exclusivist Philosophers of Religion and exclusivist Fundamental Theologians are not yet the full beneficiaries of that discovery. Nevertheless, had Evans acknowledged the problem, he might have helped, clarifying what the *idea* of God in his first two chapters had to do with the *faith* of his title.

The author develops his work as a series of reflections upon the writings of Ian Ramsey, Sam Keen, Gregory Baum, and Paul Ramsey. We shall omit detailed exposition of content and refer readers to the review of Evans by a philosopher earlier in this volume (see pp 211–15). Near the end, annoyingly late, Evans draws together his several themes and sets about addressing the question implicit in his title. Working through a concrete study of the liturgical creed authorized by the United Church of Canada, he offers 'an outline sketch for a whole philosophy of faith and morality' (p 7). Studying the creed is a genial idea for bringing concreteness to the discussion; and discovering the simple beauty of the creed itself will be a windfall for anyone who does not know of it. Evans insists that faith and morality be authentically human. Authenticity is assured by receptivity, the central element in pervasive trust, which is an 'attitude-virtue' (p 245) – that is, both a religious attitude and a moral virtue. Receptivity *allows* God to act. There are eight attitude-virtues, corresponding roughly to 'the eight stances advocated by Erik Erikson for each of the successive eight crises in human life.' Faith and morality have a 'common origin in the divine activity which is at work in the receptive person.' They have, besides, the same constituents, 'the set of attitude-virtues which are constituents of human fulfilment' (p 245).

What is most attractive about the author's conception of morality is that it seems to avoid the decapitation of the specifically Christian conscience from the body of rational ethics – in the same manner that his conception of faith has avoided a separation from human experience. This achievement of integration is made possible by his several intellectual conversions and by the admittedly problematic approach he takes to the study of the philosophy of religion.

With this work Evans emerges as a thinker whose critical awareness of intellectual bias is of a superior order. He has advanced his understanding, and ours, of how academics may regress from making distinctions to establishing separateness. Separateness is then taken to justify disciplinary exclusion. Although it is possible that Evans will not be unanimously thanked, he has written a systematic work of great merit, as well as an intriguing, if somewhat tortuous, personal history.

A radically changed perception of history can be the most stimulating of subjects. At McMaster University a five-year research project begun in 1976, involving the collaboration of eminent scholars from several countries, has focused upon a pattern of development in both Judaism and Christianity in the second and third centuries. This pattern is described as the process of achieving normative self-definition. The first of the three volumes which have been planned to record three major symposia has been published under the editorship of E.P. Sanders as *Jewish and Christian Self-Definition*, volume 1: *The Shaping of Christianity in the Second and Third Centuries* (Fortress Press, xviii, 314, $15.95). Dominant themes are the growth of Christianity from sect to church, the social setting of Christians, the way they appeared to outsiders, and above all why the church rejected gnosticism. 'It is now as much the dogma of scholarship as its opposite used to be,' remarks one contributor, that 'orthodoxy is not the presupposition of the early church but the result of a process of growth and development' (G. Macrae, p 127). That is a desirably succinct way of formulating the radically changed perception of history I have referred to. This part of the McMaster project sets out to discover factors in the process – an ambitious study of the interplay of event and meaning, of the kind which every generation needs to perform.

The significance of early church developments has always figured prominently in the justification of later Christian groups as they diverged from one another. The selection of a credible panel for the present discussion, then, is crucial to the possibility of fostering a dialogue that could win the attention of a pluralistic audience. In point of fact, the selection is admirable.

Recognizing that by the third century both the Christians and their pagan contemporaries acknowledged the Christian group to be a sharply defined 'foreign body,' R.A. Markus sets out to find the social determinants of this consciousness. 'There is an insistent family-likeness about early Christian communities and many of the classic examples of the sect-type,' he says (p 2). Christians formed 'a cliquish subculture' (p 3). While socially close, they tolerated among themselves many theological options. Markus explores the hypothesis that the emergence of a sharpened theological self-definition can be seen in two stages. The first is the confrontation with gnosticism. The second is the rise to prominence of early Catholicism. With social acceptance a tendency formed towards an always narrower orthodoxy as the principle of religious identity. Among the several doctrinal mind-sets justified in the New Testament, one alone became established. All others came to be ruled out as heretical. Eusebius's history, with its evolution from orthodoxy to heresy, caps a movement to compose a new past for the church, one congenial to the Constantinian era. The sectarian social pattern of the early church was exchanged, in the great church, for a sectarian intellectual pattern – 'an inability to preserve the ecumenicity of diverse traditions' (p 15). Contributing to this effect were such conservative forces as the increasing menace of social breakdown in the empire and the growing elaboration of ecclesiastical structures.

Add to this article Robert M. Grant's fine delineation of the social setting of second-century Christians, and the broad canvas of the symposium is firmly in place. Grant is most impressed by 'the general coincidence between the life-styles and attitudes of non-Christians and Christians alike' (p 29). William R. Schoedel contributes a view of the social requirements which the church known to Ignatius of Antioch made of its members. Despite Grant's 'coincidence,' Schoedel finds that these congregations drew firm boundaries between the church and the world, made comprehensible basically in terms of Christ's passion. He sees Ignatius's 'uncomfortably passionate desire for martyrdom' (p 55) as typical of the church which Ignatius addressed, and admits to some puzzlement over it.

Normative self-definition proceeded at a faster pace in Rome than it did in the East. The tensions between Rome and Constantinople which erupted into schism in the Middle Ages can be traced in the earliest time of the church as an East-West struggle involving Antioch and Rome, 'The Two Sees of Peter.' Under this title Jaroslav Pelikan, with his usual clarity and urbanity, studies the problem. He finds that even the classic issues of division, the Trinity and Rome's authority, may be traced to these times. Reviewing the outcome of several disputes, he remarks: 'By the end of the second century ... Rome had evidently acquired the ability to draw a sharp line between heterodoxy and orthodoxy and to identify its own position with the latter – or the latter with its own position' (p 70). In an afterthought, Pelikan offers the kind of reflection which welcomes attention to the present-day point of view on his research which only the sure-footed historian is comfortable in revealing. He notes that in Irenaeus various alternative theories of normative self-definition became components of a single, though composite, theory – 'apostolic scripture interpreted in accordance with apostolic tradition by those who stood in apostolic succession' (p 73). The eventual schism between East and West and later the Reformation were dissolutions of that composite theory. Christian history even to this day, Pelikan thinks, reflects the differences observed in the pace of normative self-definition during the second and third centuries.

In these early centuries the rejection of gnosticism held Christianity close to its Jewish parent and thereby made it possible for Christians to receive a good deal from the Hellenic philosophy of their millieu. 'The Self-Definition of Christianity in Relation to Later Platonism' is considered by Dalhousie University's A. Hilary Armstrong. The subject is vast, and much instruction comes of listening to Armstrong catalogue all the alluring topics he plans not to treat. The most important thing to say about the studied relationship is that the Hellenic philosophers were present to educated early Christians of a philosophical bent 'as independent witnesses to a variety of other possible ways of thinking about God, man and the world, which are always available to Christians who wish to ... redefine their faith' (p 99).

How the Greeks and the Romans saw the Christians is discussed by Robert L. Wilken. Three characteristics of the Christian movement emerge in this perspective: '(1) A philosophical school whose teacher and founder was Jesus; (2) a religious association whose cult-hero was Christ; (3) an apostate Jewish sect' (p 123).

George W. Macrae studies gnosticism and, mainly from New Testament evidence, suggests that the church rejected it for three reasons: 1 / Gnostic language and speculation opened on to the danger of libertinism; 2 / gnostics denied that the God of Jesus was the God of creation; and 3 / gnosticism was a denigration of the flesh and a denial of the humanity of Jesus. On the same subject Jacques E. Ménard examines two texts recently collated for the Nag Hammadi Project of Laval University and concludes that true Gnosis is 'a mystical theology of the identification of God with the Self' (p 149). For Birger A. Pearson it is plausible to conclude that gnosticism originated among 'Jewish intellectuals eager to redefine their own religious self-understanding' (p 159). Irenaeus's refutation of the gnostics is examined by Gérard Vallée of McMaster University. While not minimizing theological arguments, Vallée calls attention to the non-theological bias in Irenaeus which reacted vigorously to the threat against apostolic authority in the church.

Apostolicity, as Gerd Lüdemann insists, was so important an element of the church's self-concept that, with a possibly erroneous appeal to history, the Christians of Pella made a determined claim on it. To be rooted in history was so necessary in the ancient world, says Raoul Mortley, that Clement of Alexandria claimed Moses as that Christian forebear from whom Plato himself had borrowed. The symposium finishes with a strong piece on Origen by Mount Allison University's P.M. O'Cleirigh. 'By presenting Christianity as wisdom in terms of contemporary philosophical culture,' he says, 'Origen to a greater degree than his predecessors broadened one of the bases of Christian self-definition' (p 216).

To pretend that these essays do not require a fund of cultivated interest in late antiquity and in Christian beginnings would be less than honest. But I would be tempted to that pretension out of a desire to lure the general reader into a project so well executed as to be quite accessible to those who might miss the dates of Eusebius and Irenaeus and Origen by a few centuries. The McMaster Project is scholarly work that is fresh, confident, vigorously purposeful, and therefore not forbidding. *The Shaping of Christianity in the Second and Third Centuries* reflects the work of an authentic conference, a group-learning experience. Having attended the conference, I can attest to that. Were I to wish for more, it would be that this dimension appeared with greater strength, that the traces of constructive disagreement were more visible. The character of the early church can be so germinal a discovery, so *normative* (just once more) for the present, that a reader is correct in asking that no scholar's best effort remain untested. The editorial hand of Sanders is firm and deft. He has won from his panel a common language with which he builds a book rather than collates symposium papers. Conferences, even such real ones, are not transposed into print beyond this; it's just not done. Pity. With notes, an extensive bibliography, and multiple indices, this original research project offers the conveniences of a well-crafted manual. It draws a picture of post-apostolic Christianity as seen from the twentieth century.

Most Western theological movements in the twentieth century have attempted to address a new condition of society, perceived differently in the different areas which have spawned them. Theologians have tried to understand Christian faith in the context of their own nations. But 'theology in anglophone Canada is perhaps the least contextual of all Christian theology in the contemporary world,' says Douglas Hall in *The Canada Crisis: A Christian Perspective* (Anglican Book Centre, 123, $5.95 paper). Canadians have been the last to view their society as sharing the critical state affecting all Western peoples. Hall, who teaches religious studies at McGill, offers a systematic reflection on what the Task Force on Canadian Unity (1979) describes as a crisis, not of development, but of existence itself. He pleads with Christians to have care for the nation, insisting that such Christian care is different from the ideology of nationalism. His theology centres upon hope – not that facile secular optimism dressed in religious language, but the hope in Christ's redemption which grows out of the despair of all else. The awareness of crisis, then, is the hopeful beginning of a capacity for despair. Entering into the night of our crisis we may yet become a nation, for 'nations do not simply happen because of orders in council or meetings in Charlottetown' (p 46). Ancient Israel became a nation when it faced the Red Sea and the impossibility of a future.

Hall develops the theme of hope by contrasting it with *sin*, acknowledging that anyone who wants to communicate through this most abused of words must redeem it from both religious superficiality and secular mockery. Sin in our era takes the form of the loss of meaning, the condition of despair. Unless Christianity can talk to our despair, it cannot be *gospel* to us. The anglophone Canadian form of despair, hidden and immersed in forgetfulness, is different from the more open European form. Theologies of hope have impressed us little, brimming over as we are with official hope. With this record of successful repression and evasion, we would do well at this point in our experience to be 'more conscious of the negating dimensions of our corporate life than of the positive, cohesive side' (p 76). One instinctively mistrusts those in the majority who make liberal Christian proposals for 'reconciliation' between English and French

Canada. Such proposals are common among those who do not suffer exposure to the deep manifestations of alienation between the two solitudes. Only after the acknowledgment of sin can one 'hope against hope' (Romans 4).

There are intimations of hope in Canadian society. The author suggests to those who look covetously south of the border that there are potential advantages to living in a winter land, where nature and history have posed obstacles to the full acceptance of the modern vision. Among signs of hope he dwells upon the emergence in French Canada of 'a people whose "remembering" has at last articulated itself in an astonishing mood of hope' (p 82). Anglophone Canadians consistently misconstrue the phenomenon as an obsolescent and destructive nationalism, says Hall. 'It is just this that prevents what is hope for Québec from becoming hope for Canada' (p 83).

The last two chapters of the book present the author's understanding of the church and its role in tendering hope to the nation. He is eloquent in describing the servant church, called to be midwife to that mother in labour which is humanity. Part of the possibility for eloquence, however, is the single-mindedness with which all other models of the church are so reduced as to eliminate the intellectual complexity which would interfere with the midwife image. The lyricism is costly. Hall does better with the church as self-critical, always under reform. A church freed of ethnic, economic, and class interests and identities can become a community of dialogue – for example, for Anglo-Canada and French Canada. It can establish solidarity with the oppressed. It can become a steward of nature.

The Canada Crisis is written with a passion that exemplifies the care for the nation that the author solicits from his readers. Hall continually and effectively appeals to Canada's literary artists as witnesses to his social critique. In an excellent foreword Gregory Baum remarks that the book may signal the emergence of 'a new spirituality of empowerment.' We do not have in *The Canada Crisis* a new contribution to political theology of the kind that addresses the hard questions routinely put to this mode of Christian thought. Those who wonder why little more should be asked of new social structures than that they replace old defective ones, or why all striving for social newness should be pronounced God's action, may not find their answer here. But objectivist solutions to all radically theoretical questions are not the first order of necessity in this book. Douglas Hall will move many to care about the renewal of Canada by providing them with a new clarity of Christian motivation. There is impressive originality in that.

New clarity is brought to another subject by fifteen of thirty-four papers prepared for Acadia University's international symposium 'Baptists in Canada 1760–1980,' edited by Jarold K. Zeman in *Baptists in Canada: Search for Identity Amidst Diversity* (G.R. Welch, x, 282, $8.50). In October 1979, for the first time in this century, all major Baptist groups in Canada met to interpret selected aspects of the Canadian Baptist tradition. This volume records the highly informative, and at times surprising, results. Part I, on influences and identity, emphasizes the role of the British Baptist and British Free Church antecedents as distinguished from the continental Reformation tradition which shaped the Baptists of the United States. Canadian Baptist beginnings date back to the pre-Loyalist settlers in the Maritimes. With the coming of the Scottish Baptists early in the nineteenth century large-scale British influence was reinforced. Gradually accommodation was made with mainline Protestantism. In Quebec an indigenous Baptist movement took hold at the time of the Papineau rebellion, profiting from Roman Catholic anti-clerical sentiment accentuated by the Francophone hierarchy's support of the British cause. Generally, the Baptist evangelizing efforts among immigrants have been uniquely successful. In the 1961 census Baptists, as compared to other mainline Protestant denominations and Roman Catholics, showed the highest proportion of members who were of origins other than British, French, or Indian-Eskimo. Various groups of German-speaking Baptist immigrants eventually formed the North American Baptist General Conference in Ontario and the Canadian West. These many streams of tradition are all recognizably Baptist in the preservation of characteristic beliefs and ideas. Nevertheless, says Samuel J. Mikolaski, 'Baptists have been so consistently identified with Protestantism in Canada that their distinctive ecclesiology and views on discipleship have been blurred' (p 14).

Part II of *Baptists in Canada* deals with public life and social responsibility. It is worth noting that a third of this volume concerns itself with subject-matter that many other Christians do not associate with Baptists. A review of the record shows that a good many Baptist leaders and editors pursued 'social gospel' ideals in the generation before the First World War. Baptist ministers were active in Social Credit and the CCF. Yet, in an essay as admirable for its scholarship as for its avoidance of complacence, Paul R. Dekar vigorously delineates the failures of Baptists in responding to significant human rights issues.

In the final section, on theological trends and conflicts, the controversy between T.T. Shields and L.H. Marshall at McMaster University, issuing in the 1927 split of the denomination, is examined in articles by Clark H. Pinnock and Leslie K. Tarr. As an alternative to the more usual account, both writers present the thesis that a better understanding of the issue can be achieved by inquiring whether a modernist theology was indeed being taught at McMaster, as Shields so truculently declared, rather than centring attention upon Shields's regrettable truculence. What is intriguing about the hypothesis is what lifts the question itself above concern with an inert past: is it liberal evasiveness rather than fundamentalist abrasiveness that destroys communication among Christians? Other topics treated are styles of Baptist leadership, the struggle for unity, and patterns of belief among Baptist ministers. This is as authoritative a contemporary sourcebook as one may hope to find on the Baptists of Canada. It succeeds in avoiding the double peril of triumphalism to the right and a luxurious self-deprecation to the left. *Baptists in Canada* is the perceptive kind of report that builds the future.

Contributors

FICTION
Helen Hoy, Department of English, University of Lethbridge
R.P. Bilan, Department of English, Queen's University

ROMANS
Paul-André Bourque, Département des littératures, Université Laval

POETRY
Sandra Djwa, Department of English, Simon Fraser University

POÉSIE
Caroline Bayard, Department of Romance Languages, McMaster University

DRAMA
Ronald Huebert, Department of English, Dalhousie University

THÉÂTRE
Gilles Girard, Département des littératures, Université Laval

TRANSLATIONS
John J. O'Connor, Department of English and St Michael's College, University of Toronto

HUMANITIES
Leonard Angel, Department of Philosophy, University of British Columbia

John H. Astington, Department of English and Erindale College, University of Toronto
D.M.R. Bentley, Department of English, University of Western Ontario
David Blewett, Department of English, McMaster University
Timothy Brownlow, Department of English, St Mary's University
Brian Corman, Department of English and Erindale College, University of Toronto
Eric Domville, Department of English and New College, University of Toronto
L.E. Doucette, Division of Humanities, Scarborough College, University of Toronto
Dennis Duffy, Department of English and Innis College, University of Toronto
Geoffrey Durrant, Department of English, University of British Columbia
Herbert Eagle, Department of Slavic Languages and Literatures, University of Michigan
Ila Goody, Department of English and Innis College, University of Toronto
Judith Skelton Grant, Department of English, University of Guelph
John Henderson, King's College, Cambridge
Richard Hoffpauir, Department of English, University of Alberta

Helen Hoy, Department of English, University of Lethbridge

David Jackel, Department of English, University of Alberta

A.H. Johnson, Professor Emeritus, Department of Philosophy, University of Western Ontario

Sean Kane, Department of English, Trent University

W.J. Keith, Department of English and University College, University of Toronto

Jon Kertzer, Department of English, University of Calgary

David N. Klausner, Centre for Medieval Studies, University of Toronto

Martin Kreiswirth, Department of English, University of Toronto

Laurier Lacroix, Department of Art History, Concordia University

Alexander Leggatt, Department of English and University College, University of Toronto

Roland Le Huenen, Department of French and Victoria College, University of Toronto

Stephen K. Levine, Department of Social Science, York University

Elaine Limbrick, Department of French Language and Literature, University of Victoria

John McClelland, Department of French and Victoria College, University of Toronto

Robert McRae, Professor Emeritus, Department of Philosophy, University of Toronto

Anne McWhir, Department of English, University of Calgary

Jacques Michon, Département d'études françaises, Université de Sherbrooke

Margaret Moran, Bertrand Russell Editorial Project, McMaster University

Carl Morey, Faculty of Music, University of Toronto

Desmond Morton, Department of History, University of Toronto

James E. Neufeld, Department of English, Trent University

W.J.B. Owen, Department of English, McMaster University

Graeme H. Patterson, Department of History, University of Toronto

Paul Perron, Department of French and Victoria College, University of Toronto

Richard Rastall, Department of Music, University of Leeds

Anthony W. Riley, Department of German Language and Literature, Queen's University

John M. Robson, Department of English and Victoria College, University of Toronto

Malcolm Ross, Department of English, Dalhousie University

W. David Shaw, Department of English and Victoria College, University of Toronto

B.-Z. Shek, Department of French and University College, University of Toronto

Michael J. Sidnell, Department of English and Trinity College, University of Toronto

J. Percy Smith, Professor Emeritus, Department of Drama, University of Guelph

J.T. Stevenson, Department of Philosophy, University of Toronto

John A. Trentman, Department of Philosophy, McGill University

William Whitla, Departments of English and Humanities, York University

Terence Wooldridge, Department of French, University of Toronto

LES ÉTUDES SOCIALES
Céline Saint-Pierre, Département de sociologie, Université du Québec à Montréal

RELIGION
Emero Stiegman, Department of Religious Studies, Saint Mary's University

Index to Books Reviewed

Allen, Robert *Hawryliw Process* 7
Arcand, Bernard. *See* Vincent, Sylvie
Archambault, Gilles *The Umbrella Pines*, trans David Lobdell 88
Arnason, David *March Burning* 32
Audet, Noël *Quand la voile faseille* 25

Baker, Jeffrey *Time and Mind in Wordsworth's Poetry* 123
Beaulieu, Victor-Lévy *A Québécois Dream*, trans Ray Chamberlain 78
Beausoleil, Claude *Au milieu du corps l'attraction s'insinue* 46
Bélisle, Louis-Alexandre *Dictionnaire nord-américain de la langue française* 195
Bergeron, Léandre *Dictionnaire de la langue québécoise* 198
Bersianik, Louky *Maternative* 52
Bevis, Richard *The Laughing Tradition* 112
Bilan, R.P. *The Literary Criticism of F.R. Leavis* 137
bissett, bill *Beyond Even Faithful Legends* 39
Blais, Marie-Claire *Le Sourd dans la ville* 21
Blissett, William, ed *Editing Illustrated Books* 100
Blouin, Louise. *See* Pagé, Pierre
Boily, Raymond *Les Irlandais et le canal Lachine* 219
Boismenu, Gérard, Laurent Mailhot et Jacques Rouillard *Le Québec en textes* 221
Boisvert, Yves *Simulacre dictatoriel* 54
Bongie, Laurence L. *See* Condillac, Etienne Bonnet de
Boulby, Mark *Karl Philipp Moritz* 150
Bourlier, Kay *Marcel Proust et l'architecture* 145
Bowering, George *Particular Accidents* 39
Bowering, Marilyn *Sleeping with Lambs* 33
Brady, Carolee *Winter Lily* 4
Brochmann, Elizabeth *What's the Matter Girl?* 4

Brochu, André, et Gilles Marcotte *La Littérature et le reste* 175
Brossard, Nicole *Amantes* 43; *Daydream Mechanics*, trans Larry Shouldice 91; *Le Sens apparent* 43; *Les Stratégies du réel / The Story So Far 6* 77
Brown, Alan. *See* Roy, Gabrielle
Burke, Martyn *Laughing War* 4
Byrnes, Terence *Wintering Over* 2

Callaghan, Barry. *See* Marteau, Robert
Caron, Louis *The Draft Dodger*, trans David Toby Homel 83
Carrier, Roch *La Céleste Bicyclette* 72
Chamberland, Paul *Terre souveraine* 50
Chamberlin, Ray. *See* Beaulieu, Victor-Lévy
Charlebois, Gaëtan *Aléola* 59
Charlebois, Jean *Plaine lune et corps fou* 46
Charlton, Brian *Angel & the Bear* 6
Christian, William. *See* Innis, Harold Adams
Clements, Patricia, and Juliet Grindle, eds *The Poetry of Thomas Hardy* 126
Clifford, Wayne *An Ache in the Ear* 38
Cogswell, Fred *A Long Apprenticeship* 29
Coleridge, Samuel Taylor *Marginalia 1*, ed George Whalley 119
Condillac, Etienne Bonnot de *Les Monades*, ed Laurence L. Bongie 143
Côté, Lili *Ellipse en mémoire* 50
Czarnecki, Mark. *See* Major, André

Daigle, Jean *Le Mal à l'âme* 71
Davey, Frank *The Arches* 39
David, Jack. *See* Lecker, Robert
Davies, Robertson *The Enthusiasms of Robertson Davies*, ed Judith Skelton Grant 166
de Bellefeuille, Normand *Dans la conversation et la diction des monstres* 45
Delisle, Jeanne-Mance *Un reel ben beau, ben triste* 73
Déry, Francine *Un train bulgare* 45

Desautels, Denise *La Promeneuse et l'oiseau* 46
Deschamps, Nicole *Le Mythe de Maria Chapdelaine* 185
des Marchais, Gilles *Demain d'hier l'antan* 50
Desruisseaux, Pierre *Ici la parole jusqu'à mes yeux* 53
de Trémaudin, A.H. *Histoire de la Nation métisse dans l'Ouest canadien* 204
Dor, Georges *Poèmes et chansons* 47
Doyle, Charles, ed *William Carlos Williams* 140
Dudek, Louis *Cross-Section* 39
Dutka, JoAnna *Music in the English Mystery Plays* 105

Eggleston, Wilfrid *Literary Friends* 157
Ellipse (nos 23–4) 78
Ellis, David. *See* Marteau, Robert
Epps, Bernard *Pilgarlic the Death* 4
Erickson, John D., et Irène Pagès *Proust et le texte producteur* 194
Etudes Littéraires (no 13:3) 74
Evans, Donald *Faith, Authenticity, and Morality* 211, 229

Felx, Jocelyne *Les Feuillets embryonnaires* 53
Fennario, David *Balconville* 59
Filion, Jean-Paul *Cap Tourmente* 25
Finch, Robert *Variations and Theme* 34
Fox, Gail *In Search of Living Things* 33
Freiberg, Stanley *Nightmare Tales* 2
French, David *Jitters* 62
Frye, Northrop *Creation and Recreation* 95

Geddes, Gary *Conrad's Later Novels* 132
Gélinas, Gratien *Les Fridolinades, 1945 et 1946* 68; *Tit-Coq* 68
Godin, Jean-Cléo, et Laurent Mailhot *Théâtre québécois II* 74, 182
Goetz-Stankiewicz, Marketa *The Silenced Theatre* 153
Gom, Leona *Land of the Peace* 32
Gose, Elliott B. *The Transformation Process in Joyce's Ulysses* 133
Graham, Victor E., and W. McAllister Johnson *The Royal Tour of France by Charles IX and Catherine de' Medici* 141
Grant, Judith Skelton. *See* Davies, Robertson
Gray, J.M. *Thro' the Vision of the Night* 125

Grindle, Juliet. *See* Clements, Patricia
Grosskurth, Phyllis *Havelock Ellis: A Biography* 129
Gustafson, Ralph *Landscape with Rain* 38; *The Vivid Air* 3

Hall, Douglas *The Canada Crisis* 235
Harvey, Fernand *Le Mouvement ouvrier au Québec* 219
Hébert, Anne *Anne Hébert: Poems*, trans A. Poulin, Jr 89; *Héloïse* 22
Hébert, François *Le Rendez-vous* 26
Hébert, Marie-Francine *Cé tellement 'cute' des enfants* 73
Hélal, Georges *La Philosophie comme panphysique* 210
Helwig, David, ed *Love and Money* 160
Hémon, Louis *Maria Chapdelaine* 189; *Maria Chapdelaine, Récit du Canada français* 188
Hétu, Jean-Luc *Croissance humaine et instinct spirituel* 228
Hibbard, George, ed *Bartholmew Fair* 107
Hine, Daryl *Selected Poems* 36
Homel, David Toby. *See* Caron, Louis
Hood, Hugh *None Genuine Without This Signature* 11

Innis, Harold Adams *The Idea File of Harold Adams Innis*, ed William Christian 165

Jackson, J.R. de J. *Poetry of the Romantic Period* 114
Jacques, Maurice *Les Voix closes* 51
Jasmin, Claude *Le Veau dort* 72
Jeu (nos 15, 16) 73
Un jeu d'enfants 73
Johnson, W. McAllister. *See* Graham, Victor E.
Joós, Ernest, ed *Scolastique: certitude et recherche* 208
Jordan, Mary V. *De ta sœur, Sara Riel* 205
Juéry, René. *See* Thériault, Serge A.

Keith, W.J. *The Poetry of Nature* 123
Keypour, N. David *André Gide* 146
Kleiman, Ed *The Immortals* 2
Krissdottir, Morine *John Cowper Powys and the Magical Quest* 136
Kroetsch, Robert *The Crow Journals* 170
Kudelka, Jan *Circus Gothic* 55
Kushner, Donn *The Witnesses and Other Stories* 2

La Bossière, Camille *Joseph Conrad and the Science of Unknowing* 131
Laflamme, Jean, et Rémi Tourangeau *L'Eglise et le théâtre au Québec* 181
Lamonde, Yvan *La Philosophie et son enseignement au Québec (1665–1920)* 206
Lancashire, Anne, ed *The Second Maiden's Tragedy* 107
Langevin, Gilbert *Le Fou solidaire* 47
Lapointe, Gatien *Arbre-Radar* 48
Lapointe, Paul-Marie *Ecritures* 52
Lawrence, Robert G., and Samuel L. Macey, eds *Studies in Robertson Davies' Deptford Trilogy* 168
Layton, Irving *Love Poems* 38
Lebeau, Suzanne, et Georgette Rondeau *Une lune entre deux maisons* 73
Le Blanc, Huguette *Bernadette Dupuis ou la Mort apprivoisée* 24
Lecker, Robert, and Jack David, eds *The Annotated Bibliography of Canada's Major Authors: Volume One* 155
Legris, Renée *Robert Choquette, romancier et dramaturge de la radio-télévision* 179; see also Pagé, Pierre
Lemire, Maurice, ed *Dictionnaire des œuvres littéraires du Québec*. I: *Des origines à 1900*; II: *1900 à 1939* 171
Lévesque, Gilbert *Louis Hémon, aventurier ou philosophe?* 189
Lévesque, René *Initiation à l'archéologie* 218
Lobdell, David. See Archambault, Gilles; Rajic, Négovan; Thériault, Marie-José
Lochhead, Douglas *High Marsh Road* 28

McCaffery, Steve *Intimate Distortions* 38
McCracken, Kathleen *Into Celebration* 33
Macey, Samuel L. See Lawrence, Robert G.
MacKinnon, Stuart *Mazinaw* 30
McLachlan, Ian *Helen in Exile* 15
MacLennan, Hugh *Voices in Time* 18
Mailhot, Laurent, et Doris-Michel Montpetit, éds *Monologues québécois 1890–1980* 69; see also Boismenu, Gérard; Godin, Jean-Cléo
Major, André *Inspector Therrien*, trans Mark Czarnecki 84
Marcotte, Gilles. See Brochu, André
Marlatt, Daphne *Net Work* 39
Marshall, Tom *The Elements* 35
Marteau, Robert *Atlante*, trans Barry Callaghan 81; *Pentecost*, trans David Ellis 81; *Salamander*, trans Anne Winters 79; *Treatise on White and Tincture*, trans Barry Callaghan 80
Meloche, Suzanne *Aurores fulminantes* 45
Merrett, Robert James *Daniel Defoe's Moral and Rhetorical Ideas* 110
Miron, Gaston *The Agonized Life*, trans Marc Plourde 90; 'Femme sans fin,' *Possibles* (printemps 1980) 49
Monette, Madeleine *Le Double suspect* 24
Monette, Pierre *Ajustements qu'il faut* 44
Montpetit, Doris-Michel. See Mailhot, Laurent
Musgrave, Susan *The Charcoal Burners* 5

Namian, Alexandre *Mon pays éventré* 51
Naubert, Yvette *Tales of Solitude*, trans Margaret Rose 76
Nepveu, Pierre *Couleur chair* 48
nicol, b.p. *As Elected* 39

Ouellette, Fernand *La Mort vive* 24
Outram, Richard *Promise of Light* 33

Pagé, Pierre, et Renée Legris *Le Comique et l'humour à la radio québécoise*, 2 vols 180; Pagé et Legris *Répertoire des dramatiques québécoises à la télévision, 1952–1977* 179; Pagé, Legris et Louise Blouin *Répertoire des œuvres de la littérature radiophonique québécoise, 1930–1970* 177
Pagès, Irène. See Erickson, John D.
Parent, Rémi *Communion et pluralité dans l'église* 226
Patry, André *Le Québec dans le monde* 220
Pichette, Jean-Pierre *Le Guide raisonné des jurons* 199
Plourde, Marc. See Miron, Gaston
Poulin, A., Jr. See Hébert, Anne
Poupart, Jean-Marie *Le Champion de cinq heures moins dix* 26
Pozier, Bernard *Tête de lecture* 54
Proctor, George A. *Canadian Music of the Twentieth Century* 202
Puhvel, Martin *Beowulf and Celtic Tradition* 103

Quinn, Kenneth *Texts and Contexts* 97

Rajan, Tilottama *Dark Interpreter* 117
Rajic, Négovan *The Mole Men*, trans David Lobdell 86

Raoul, Valérie *The French Fictional Journal* 148
Raths, Deborah, comp *Register of the Frederick Philip Grove Collection* 156
Reid, Dennis *Notre patrie le Canada* 200
Richler, Mordecai *Joshua Then and Now* 16
Ripley, John *Julius Caesar on Stage in England and America* 106
Ritter, Erika *Automatic Pilot* 55
Rivet, Jacques *Grammaire du journal politique* 217
Rondeau, Georgette. See Lebeau, Suzanne
Rooke, Leon *Cry Evil* 9; *Fat Woman* 10
Rose, Margaret. See Naubert, Yvette
Ross, Veronica *Goodbye Summer* 2
Rouillard, Jacques. See Boismenu, Gérard
Roy, André *Le Petit Supplément aux passions* 44
Roy, Gabrielle *The Tin Flute*, trans Alan Brown 92
Roy, Louise, et Louis Saia *Une amie d'enfance* 72
Royer, Jean *Femme souveraine* 47
Rule, Jane *Contract with the World* 15
Ryan, Oscar *Soon To Be Born* 4

Saia, Louis. See Roy, Louise
Saint-Pierre, Annette *Le Rideau se lève au Manitoba* 183
Sanders, E.P., ed *Jewish and Christian Self-Definition* 232
Sapergia, Barbara *Dirt Hills Mirage* 33
Scobie, Stephen *McAlmon's Chinese Opera* 37
Shneidman, N.N. *Soviet Literature in the 1970s* 154
Shouldice, Larry. See Brossard, Nicole
Solway, David *Mephistopheles and the Astronaut* 36
Souster, Raymond *Collected Poems*, vol 1 39
Stich, K.P., ed *The Duncan Campbell Scott Symposium* 163

Theatre History in Canada 159
Théoret, France *Nécessairement putain* 44
Thériault, Marie-José *The Ceremony*, trans David Lobdell 87
Thériault, Serge A. *La Quête d'équilibre dans l'œuvre romanesque d'Anne Hébert* 191; et

René Juéry *Approches structurales des textes* 192
Thomas, W.K. *The Fizz Inside* 99
Tourangeau, Rémi. See Laflamme, Jean
Tremblay, Michel *L'Impromptu d'Outremont* 701; *Thérèse et Pierrette à l'école des Saints-Anges* 27
Turner, Gordon *No Country for White Men* 30

Vachon, G.-A. *Esthétique pour Patricia* 174
Vaillancourt, Jean-Guy *Papal Power* 222
Vanier, Denis *Les Œuvres poétiques complètes* 52
van Schendel, Michel *De l'œil et de l'écoute* 48
La Vie à trois étages 73
Villemaire, Yolande *La Vie en prose* 23, 44
Villeneuve, Jocelyne *La Saison des papillons* 51
Vincent, Sylvie, et Bernard Arcand *L'Image de l'Amérindien dans les manuels scolaires du Québec* 216
Virgo, Seán *White Lies and Other Fictions* 3

Wah, Fred *Loki is Buried at Smoky Creek* 39
Walker, George F. *Gossip* 61; *Rumours of Our Death* 61
Walmsley, Tom *Something Red* 62
Watson, Sheila *Four Stories* 9
Wayman, Tom *A Planet Mostly Sea* 37
Weinzweig, Helen *Basic Black With Pearls* 13
Whalley, George. See Coleridge, Samuel Taylor
Wiebe, Rudy *The Mad Trapper* 14
Wilden, Tony *The Imaginary Canadian* 162
Winters, Anne. See Marteau, Robert
Wisenthal, J.L., ed *Shaw and Ibsen* 128
Woodcock, George *The World of Canadian Writing* 157
Wright, Richard *First Things* 12
Wynand, Derk *One Cook, Once Dreaming* 6
Wynne-Jones, Tim *Odd's End* 4

Zeman, Jarold K., ed *Baptists in Canada* 236
Zieroth, Dale *Mid-River* 30